VALUES EDUCATION FOR CITIZENS IN THE NEW CENTURY

Values Education for Citizens in the New Century

Edited by

Roger H. M. Cheng,
John C. K. Lee and Leslie N. K. Lo

The Chinese University Press

Hong Kong Institute of Educational Research

Values Education for Citizens in the New Century
Edited by Roger H. M. Cheng, John C. K. Lee and
Leslie N. K. Lo

ISBN 962–996–153–9

THE CHINESE UNIVERSITY PRESS
The Chinese University of Hong Kong
SHA TIN, N.T., HONG KONG
Fax: +852 2603 6692
+852 2603 7355
E-mail: cup@cuhk.edu.hk
Web-site: www.chineseupress.com

HONG KONG INSTITUTE OF EDUCATIONAL RESEARCH
The Chinese University of Hong Kong
SHA TIN, N.T., HONG KONG
Fax: +852 2603 6850
E-mail: hkier@cuhk.edu.hk
Web-site: www.fed.cuhk.edu.hk/~hkier

Printed in Hong Kong

Contents

Notes on Contributors vii

Chapter 1. Values Education for Citizens in the New Century: Meaning, Desirability and Practice 1
Roger H. M. Cheng, John C. K. Lee and Leslie N. K. Lo

Part I. Theoretical Explorations Underlying Values Education for Citizens

Chapter 2. Values Education and Citizenship Education in Modern Society 39
Torsten Husén

Chapter 3. Valuation, Evaluation, and Value Education — On Acquiring the Ability to Value: A Philosophical Perspective 49
May Mei-lin Ng

Chapter 4. Knowledge of the Value of Knowledge and Values Education: A Redundancy? 67
Maria Andrelita Cenzon

Chapter 5. Quality Assurance, Language Policy, and Civic Participation: A Paradoxical Argument on the Educational Values of Hong Kong 85
Ronald W. Y. Tang

Part II. Varieties of Values Education for Citizens

Chapter 6. The Development of Values Through the School Curriculum 107
Monica J. Taylor

Chapter 7. Preservation of Wilderness: The Need to Go Beyond Intrinsic Values and Rights? 133
Wing-po Lam and John C. K. Lee

Chapter 8. Education That Is Religious Education 151
Peter T. M. Ng

Chapter 9. Teaching Compassionate Social Studies 165
Matthew Hirshberg

Chapter 10. Does Citizenship Education Make Moral Education Redundant? 197
Mark Halstead

Chapter 11. Science Is Not Values-Free — Neither in Research, nor in School 217
Jean-Luc Patry

Part III. Issues in Values Education for Citizens

Chapter 12. The IEA Civic Education Study: Ideal Communities of Practice and Realities of Political Experience Among 14-Year-Olds in 28 Countries 235
Judith Torney-Purta

Chapter 13. Citizenship in Transition and Its Implications to Citizenship Education: The Case of Hong Kong 251
Wing-kwong Tsang

Chapter 14. Representation of Citizenship in the Junior Secondary School Curriculum: The Cases of Hong Kong and Macau 287
Kwan-choi Tse

Chapter 15. Values Education in Thailand: Preparation for Globalization 319
Kriengsak Chareonwongsak

Chapter 16. Girls' Status as Learner-Citizens: Issues for Values Education and Citizenship Education 347
Victoria Foster

Chapter 17. Understanding Professional Communities: Positive Teacher Professional Development Outcomes in Values and Citizenship Education 365
Libby Tudball

Notes on Contributors

Maria Andrelita Cenzon is Assistant Professor in the Department of Philosophy at The University of Asia and the Pacific, the Philippines.

Kriengsak Chareonwongsak is a member of the Executive Board of Democrat Party, Thailand.

Roger H. M. Cheng is Professional Consultant in the Department of Educational Administration and Policy at The Chinese University of Hong Kong.

Victoria Foster is Associate Professor and Honorary Fellow in the School of Anthropology, Geography and Environmental Sciences at the University of Melbourne.

Mark Halstead is Professor of Education and Head of the Department of Community and International Education at the University of Huddersfield. He is the author (with Mark Pike) of *Citizenship and Moral Education* (Routledge, 2006).

Matthew Hirshberg was a member of the Political Science Faculty at University of Canterbury, New Zealand, from 1990 to 2005. He is currently a journalist in New York.

Torsten Husén is Professor Emeritus in International and Comparative Education of Institute of International Education at Stockholm University, Sweden.

Wing-po Lam is School Development Officer of Centre for University and School Partnership, The Chinese University of Hong Kong.

John C. K. Lee is Dean of Education and Professor in the Department of Curriculum and Instruction at The Chinese University of Hong Kong.

Leslie N. K. Lo is Chair Professor of Educational Administration and Policy and Director of Hong Kong Institute of Educational Research at The Chinese University of Hong Kong.

May Mei-lin Ng is Assistant Professor in the Faculty of Education at The University of Macau.

Peter T. M. Ng is Professor in the Department of Cultural and Religious Studies at The Chinese University of Hong Kong.

Jean-Luc Patry is Professor of Education and working at the Department of Education and Sociology at the University of Salzburg, Austria.

Ronald W. Y. Tang is Teaching Fellow in the Department of Educational Policy and Administration at The Hong Kong Institute of Education.

Monica J. Taylor is Editor of *Journal of Moral Education* and a Research Associate at Institute of Education, University of London. She has been Principal Research Fellow at National Foundation for Educational Research in England & Wales, President of the Association for Moral Education — the first from outside North America, and a founder member and first Chair of the Values Education Council of the United Kingdom.

Judith Torney-Purta is Professor of Human Development and Affiliate Professor of Public Affairs at University of Maryland, College Park, United States.

Wing-kwong Tsang is Professor in the Department of Educational Administration and Policy at The Chinese University of Hong Kong.

Kwan-choi Tse is Associate Professor in the Department of Educational Administration and Policy at The Chinese University of Hong Kong.

Libby Tudball is a lecturer and teacher in the Faculty of Education at Monash University in Melbourne, Australia.

CHAPTER 1

Values Education for Citizens in the New Century: Meaning, Desirability and Practice

Roger H. M. Cheng, John C. K. Lee and Leslie N. K. Lo

Abstract

The chapter begins by exploring three questions on values education for citizens in the new century: meaning, desirability and practice. What does values education mean? Why is values education desirable? How is values education to be practiced? It is argued that the sort of education for citizenship in the new century should be values education which, on the one hand, can provide citizens rich and valuable sources for their identity formation in drawing on their embeddedness (e.g. traditions constituted by relations and belongings) while, on the other hand, can nurture values to be embodied in citizens, if necessary, helping the migration (e.g. learning, working and living cross boundaries) they are increasingly likely to make in some forms in the new century. Along such line of thinking, the chapter further draws on and introduces the following 16 chapters in the book. They are grouped into three parts, which respectively touch upon theoretical exploration, varieties and issues in values education for citizens. These contributions from different countries of the world reveal a rich diversity on the meaning, desirability and practice of values education across cultures and regions. But is there any underlying unity? How could commonality (e.g. commonly shared values) and diversity (e.g. multiculturalism) be balanced in values education? The chapter concludes by suggesting a "Cone Model" for the quest for unity in diversity.

Educating Values in Citizens and Identity Formation

"Who am I?" How could and would values education help citizens to answer this question of identity by themselves? Would this line of thinking suggest ways to reflect upon values education for citizens in the new century, and chapters in this book? However, in order to make the fullest meaning out of such line of thinking and this book as well, one may further wonder: What does this question mean and why is it worth answering? Wisdom may be tapped from the communitarian critics of liberal individualism (Crittenden, 1992), for instance, Charles Taylor (1989), once the Chichele Professor of Social and Political Theory at the University of Oxford, wrote:

> "Who am I?" But this can't necessarily be answered by giving name and genealogy. What does answer this question for us is an understanding of what is of crucial importance to us. To know who I am is a species of knowing where I stand. My identity is defined by the commitments and identifications which provide the frame or horizon within which I can try to determine from case to case what is good, or valuable, or what ought to be done, or what I endorse or oppose. In other words, it is horizon within which I am capable of taking a stand. (p. 27)

Following such line of thinking, the new century in the modern world poses an urgency for educating values in citizens in the making of their identities — in opening their horizon, knowing where they stand, and defining their commitments and identifications — so that they can become autonomous citizens who, with sufficient self-understanding, can exercise their self-determination on value issues. In short, values education provides sources for citizens to form their identities, thereby answering "who am I?".

However, the question "who am I?" is contextual, that is, partly defined by its involved temporal and spatial features. For instance, taking the very act of writing this introduction as its context, the answer is that we are editors for this book of 17 chapters constituted by 19 contributors, leaving aside the other unnamed supporters. Nevertheless, such a way of answering is somehow ungrammatical as the question is in the singular form while the grammatical subject of the answer is plural. Such mismatch is symptomatic, according to the method of "grammatical investigation" of Ludwig Wittgenstein (1967), which actually helps unearth the underlying line of thinking. When asked "Are you the editor of this book?", I can answer "yes, I am" but I need to qualify by saying that "yes, but I am one among the three editors" as our shared identity is constituted by a common good: to provide the best editorial service to all chapter contributors and numerous prospective readers as well. Behind the scene of shared values, the three editors (Cheng, Lee and Lo) have their own personal identities, constituted by different formative backgrounds with diverse values. The formation of each of us has been embedded in different contexts and has embodied different sets of values. Each editor is autonomous but all of us are constitutive of the book project. Thus, each of us has one's own sets of desires to be satisfied and (personal) qualities to be actualized even within our joint venture of editing this book.

The identity quest leads to the theme of unity in diversity, which may be exemplified as follows. By disciplinary training, our diverse scholarly backgrounds in philosophy, comparative politics and geography converge on the concern of values education for citizenship. Besides, we are historically related to this concern in diverse ways. For example, Lo was a co-editor of a book (published in 1996) to which this book may be perceived as a sequel. In introducing the book, Lo and Man (1996) has a chapter titled "Nurturing the Moral Citizens of the Future" that has successfully traced the history of ideas back to Plato's *Republic* of the West and to the Confucian idea of the "superior man" (*junzi*) of the Chinese tradition unto the present predicament in preparing moral citizens for the future. Following this historical continuity, the concern in mind would be on how the education of values, including moral and civic values, could prepare citizens for the new century. As part of our selves, each of us is related to different others and belongs as a member to different groups or communities. For example, Cheng received his postgraduate training predominantly in the British-and-European tradition and has been a member of the Philosophy of Education Society of Great Britain. Thus, he finds himself inclined, or a little bit biased in his tendency, to agree with, for example, how Halstead and Taylor (1996) frame the principles and practices of values education across the globe as follows:

> One of the main differences between the American and the British approaches to values education is that the former, in the absence of organized traditions of religious or social authority in public institutions, places a stronger emphasis on democratic education, both in terms of teaching the child about how society works and in terms of preparation for citizenship through active participation in school life. Values education in British schools, as in much of Europe, is affected by closer involvement with religion: a third of British schools are denominational institutions, religious education still a compulsory part of the basic curriculum in all schools.... (p. 10)

In response even to the same quotation in the above, Lee may think along the line of curriculum practice in relation to the school-university partnership and change for school development as Lee (2002) has recently been involved in many related projects in Hong Kong. Besides, principles and practice of values education in the local context in Hong Kong as a Chinese society would be more in quest, since missing in the above quote.

The above line of thinking has already exemplified that, philosophically, the idea of identity can be analyzed as meaning three kinds: personal identity, relational identity and communal (or collective) identity. If each citizen possesses identities of these three sorts and an identity is partly constituted by values, then re-conceiving values education for citizenship in terms of identity formation should be able to provide a fruitful way of reading from the following chapters. As a human being is born to care about oneself, it is natural to begin with personal identity first. What does it mean? In short, the personal identity means that the person remains the same person (identical) over time (and space). For example, am I still the same person if I lose most of my memory of my past and have most of my bodily parts replaced by machines (like a cyborg)? This has been much discussed in the philosophical literature (e.g. Parfit, 1984). It is not irrelevant here as newly emerged "Communitarian" philosophers like MacIntyre (1985) and Taylor (1989) have challenged such idea of personal identity by reviving the narrative dimension of the idea of identity, thereby re-asserting the importance of relations and belongings. I am a person who has my past, my present and my future — these three moments being connected into a life story in which I live.

The narrative approach to identity and the self provides narrative unity (Ricoeur, 1991) which connects personal identity with relational identity and communal identity. To know me is *de facto* to know my life story in which those individuals (e.g. my relatives) who are related to me and those communities (e.g. The Chinese University of Hong Kong) to which I belong as a member are also known. It follows that to ignore the place of my significant others and my attached communities in my life is *de jure* unjust to my identity. In understanding my relational identity, my significant others and how they are closely related to me are bound to be comprehended. Relations with my parents, relatives, peers, friends, colleagues, etc. could be constitutive of my identity, of who I am, more than I can comprehend. Furthermore, voluntarily or not, consciously or not, each of us have been members (or ex-members) of some communities. In facing the sometimes unfriendly question "Who are you?" by local residents when arriving in a new "home," many immigrants find themselves returning to their original ethnical identity — that is, aboriginality. Thus, to emit the utterance "I am Chinese" would mean different things in different contexts, for example, in Hong Kong, in the Chinese Mainland or London's China Town. To put this into a semiotic point (Austin, 1971; Chandler, 2002): the same utterance in different contexts could be a different speech act: struggling with one's cultural identity, clarifying one's ethnic identity, asserting one's national identity, and so forth. It is hoped that the above clarification on identity suffices as philosophical preparation to throw a new light on values education for citizens in the new century.

Following the above line of thinking, then what sort of education for citizenship would be the most desirable? To put the answer in a short form: it should be values education which, on the one hand, can provide citizens rich and valuable sources for their identity formation in drawing on their embeddedness (e.g. traditions constituted by relations and belongings) while, on the other hand, can nurture values to be embodied in citizens, if necessary, helping the migration they are increasingly likely to make in some forms in the new century (e.g. learning, working and living across boundaries). Then, what is the form of values education that future citizens most need in the new century? This chapter will structure such quest for the desirable form of educating values for citizens in the new century along the three questions: what, why and how, leading to a synopsis of the tripartite chapters, and ending with a conclusion. The remaining part of this chapter will be divided into seven sections as follows:

(1) Conceptual clarification of meaning: What does values education mean?
(2) Contextual characterization for desirability: Why is values education desirable?
(3) Concrete wisdom for practice: How is values education to be practised?
(4) Theoretical exploration underlying values education for citizens
(5) Varieties of values education for citizens
(6) Issues in values education for citizens
(7) Concluding the quest for unity in diversity

Conceptual Clarification of Meaning: What Does Values Education Mean?

What does values education mean? The idea of values education sounds like a new currency, the status of which is analogous to the status of the Euro for the recently formed European Union (formerly European Community), a currency which acquires its identity from within a community of varieties. As Halstead and Taylor (1996) trace the emergence of values education:

> The term *values education* has a much shorter history in England and Wales than it has in North America, or even in Scotland. Nevertheless, a recent directory of research and resources in values education in the UK lists 113 entries, made up of research projects, organizations, publications and other initiatives (Taylor, 1994).... [I]ts purpose being "the promotion and development of values in the context in education as a lifelong process, to help individuals develop as responsible and caring persons and lives participating members of a pluralist society". (p. 8)

Thus, values education serves as an umbrella term to cover various forms of teaching values in education: civic education, moral education, sex education, aesthetic education, religious education and health education, just to name a few. This list is very different from the list of subjects in the school curriculum: language, mathematics, science, music, history, geography, that most schools have endorsed for their curricular arrangements. Such contrast may be sharpened by looking into the recent curriculum reform in Hong Kong. In *Learning to Learn*, the Curriculum Development Council (2001) has made explicit "a tripodic curricular philosophy," framing the school curriculum in terms of three pillars: knowledge and concepts, competencies and skills, and values and attitudes. Knowledge and concepts to be learned will be structured in terms of eight Key Learning Areas (KLA): Chinese language education, English language education, mathematics education, science education, technology education, art education, physical education, and (the most controversial) personal, social and humanities education. Within each KLA, learning outcomes include not just competencies and skills, but also values and attitudes. While competencies and skills are relatively measurable or amenable to assessment of some forms, values and attitudes are advocated as expected learning outcomes of schooling but their forms of evaluation are still unclear in the curriculum documents. This finds an echo in Chapter 9 by Hirshberg in advocating teaching social science from a compassionate perspective, in supplementing the "capability" perspective. Thus, citizens are educated to become not just capable, but also compassionate.

However, capability and compassion could have a mismatch as it seems to be the case in Hong Kong during the transition period around 1997. In analyzing the predicament of the transition of Hong Kong from a British colony to the Special Administrative Region of China, under the institutional arrangement based on the idea of "One Country, Two Systems," Cheng (1996) makes use of two distinctions in forming the following matrix about caring citizens:

Caring citizens	Being egoistic	Being altruistic
Bad sense/ form of	Selfish egoism: Maximizing one's interests even at the expense of others (even harming others)	Sacrificing altruism: Maximizing collective interests even at the expense of individual interests (even harming oneself and others)
Good sense/ form of	Self-centred egoism: Caring about oneself without doing harm to others (but also without care about others)	Reciprocal altruism: Caring about oneself and others together in terms of mutual beneficiality (or common good)

It may be natural for a country to have these four types of citizens, but values education should aim at nurturing citizens to become "reciprocal altruists." However, adding capability to the situation, the worst scenario would be if citizenry were entirely composed by the "capable egoists" and the "incapable altruists." This seems to have happened in Hong Kong: domination of the former before 1997 and emergence of the latter after 1997. The analysis is as follows: While living in a British colony influenced heavily by the modern individualist and liberal culture of the West, Hong Kong people tended to be egoistic, in the strong sense of being selfish in maximizing one's desire-satisfaction even at the expense of others, and in the weak sense of being egocentric (self-centred), caring only about oneself (with no care about others, or public affairs). Thus, before 1997, while the minds of the Hong Kong residents were trained to become smart, competent workers in making the capitalistic economy prosperous, their hearts of civic concern are not cultivated to become caring citizens, thereby helping the colony to be kept relatively stable. While changing into a Chinese Special Administrative Region influenced by the modern collectivist and authoritarian culture of China, Hong Kong people tended to become altruistic, in the good sense of being caring about others by contributing to the needs, but also in the bad sense of over-sacrificing oneself (and other individuals) for the sake of the so-called collective good. The fact of 1997 acted like an alarm in changing political apathy to a division between democratic allegiance and national loyalty. In Chapter 13, Tsang has shared the findings on two cohorts of voters right after the 1995 and 1998 Legislative Council geographical-constituency elections. The philosophical and sociological studies support each other, while giving strong force to teach social science or personal, social and humanities education from both capability and compassionate perspectives.

The two aforementioned lists, that is, of varieties of values education and of school subjects or KLAs, also epitomize a dichotomy between the subjective and the objective in the modern age. While knowledge is objective and thereby teachable in schools, values are too subjective to be taught in school. Such a dualistic stance in the last century may have been too pervasive as to preclude a proper place for values in school education. Perhaps it is time in the new century to go beyond such a division by seeing them as a sort of division of labour instead of unsurpassingly divided domains. Ridiculing the predicament in terms of "a redundancy argument" through raising the intellectually challenging question "Why is knowledge valuable?", Cenzon in Chapter 4 tries to undermine such dualism in disclosing the subjective value and the objective value of knowing. For example, historical knowledge is objectively valuable in its being accurate historical records and subjectively valuable in the attempt to interpret and understand these accounts. This is equally applicable to scientific knowledge, she continues. Thus, as her argument implies, the list of school subjects or KLAs is bound to be subsumed under the education of values in citizens via knowing science, history and other subjects or areas of learning. But how are the subjective and the objective to be unified?

As argued in Cheng (2000b), the subjective and the objective find unity in the dialogue on desiring the desirable. That paper tackles three basic questions on values education: Should values be taught? Why? And how? The argument firstly undermines the sceptical exclusion of values from education since that only neutral, objective things, for example, knowledge, should be taught is *de facto* one form of values education. Though sharing the ontology about values as being subjective (desire-independent), subjectivists argue contrarily for that schools should empower students to have the autonomy to deal with value conflicts, hence educating their desires as constructing one's own hierarchy of desires — leading to the liberal values pedagogy — thin but too weak. That not all desires are desirable calls for the objectivist alternative which claims that values are objectively there, embedded in traditions as being desirable, to be transmitted to next generations and deserved as their objects of desires — inclining towards the conservative values pedagogy — thick but too strong. Furthermore, insights are then drawn from hermeneutics, for example, "strong evaluation" of Taylor (1989), and a "3D" framework on values education is generated based on the "3Ds" and conceived at two levels: (1) methodologically, values are disclosed in the emerging dialogue between the valuing subjects (autonomous desiring agents) and the valued objects (embodying the principles of desirability); (2) pedagogically, values educators and values educands are having a dialogue over their values (and their value judgments). Thus, values education is conceived as a three-dimensional dialogue on desiring the desirable (3Ds) by (1) values educands as desiring subjects; (2) valued objects as the desirable and (3) values educators as agencies for the latter but of equal status with the former. Re-captulating the above line of thinking into the perspective of educating values in citizens for their identity formation, citizens are helped by the custodians of cultural traditions from which sources are drawn on to form their identities, including personal, relational and communal forms of identities, in desiring the valued objects.

Contextual Characterization for Desirability: Why Is Values Education Desirable?

Why is values education desirable? The two preceding sections should have already provided a partial answer, which however needs further characterization by looking into the context: What makes the new century new? However, such contextual characterization may at least be a mixture of the global, the national and the local. It would be over-simplistic to expect the world to be a global village in the 21st century in contrast to the 20th century as a nationalistic era. If "warfare" (e.g., two world wars) is one of the main causes for immigration of ethnic groups from one nation to another, then "welfare" may be another new cause for citizens of one nation to migrate to other nations. As more citizens migrate across the globe more frequently in more innovative forms in the new century of emerging changes, the identity quest discussed above acquires new significance. Though it may be too bold to claim that, in the 21st century, the idea of citizen would no longer be confined to national identity as in the past centuries, at least it is worth deliberating that education for citizenship should be re-conceptualized from the perspective of identity formation, thereby going beyond the horizon of the national, in facing the global changes. William (2001), a renowned scholar from the domain of geography education, has helped to provide a significant clarification of the identity perspective for citizenship education in the new century:

> It is commonplace to consider citizenship narrowly within the context of the nation state: citizenship is commonly conceptualized as the identity of an individual bounded by national frontiers. However, it is extremely important to acknowledge that nation states, as human artifacts have a remarkably short history. Their frontiers change as result of alliances, wars and agreements. Changes are made to their names often at times of major ideological and constitutional shifts. Further, the internal authority and power of nation states are being weakened as a consequence of new international trade relationships, ecological trends and the modernisation of telecommunications. These changes are important not only because they alter definitions of citizenship but also because they provide the background against which curriculum changes occur. (p. 31)

The significance of citizens being educated with values cuts across the three contexts: the global, the national and the local. For example, as Husén depicts in Chapter 2, people migrate between religions as well as countries in the changing world. Values education is in need to cope with the global changes. More and more people are born in one country, grown up in another, educated somewhere else and then work in yet another place; then they may have children repeating the same pattern but in different places. Even within the same country, that is, within the national boundary, especially big nations such as China, the United States or the United Kingdom, people migrate across boundaries, regional or cultural. This is especially phenomenal in Asian-Pacific region where citizens migrate across cities. Values vary across regions. Thus, citizens would need values in coping with crossing regions. It is not difficult to imagine the life of, for example, an American citizen, who works as an expatriate in a city, for example, Hong Kong, delivers more income from the global financial market, pays taxes to the local government and his original nation (in this case, the United States), enjoys entertainment from the French cultural industries, married a Chinese wife from the Chinese Mainland (resides in Hong Kong), has two sons studying at the English Schools Foundations schools, spends most of his holidays in Asian countries. How would he answer the identity question "Who am I"? The space of the life of a migrating citizen is ever changing — moving backward and forward, migrating from one culture to another. Thus, the identity of a migrating citizen is fluidic. Even returning to the first culture after the second, one will find oneself a stranger like living in a third culture. This is particularly phenomenal for children of migrating parents (e.g. missionaries, military personnel, global entrepreneurs, and perhaps international scholars as well) and hence the study on "third culture kids" (Pollock & Reken, 1999) becomes interestingly inspiring for the new century.

The relationship between identity formation and citizenship education is much clearer in some regions. For example, Tang in Chapter 5 has provided a critical diagnosis on language policy discourse colonial Hong Kong in relation to the post-colonial educational reform in the name of quality. In questioning the narrow-mindedness on the educational values of language while going beyond the underlying technico-instrumental conception, the author leads us to the quality of language as constitutive of the formation of one's self, life history and identity. Thus, language learning could be important in helping citizens to articulate their entitled voices, thereby to speak for themselves, in the public. Globally, the IEA civic education study shared by Torney-Purta in Chapter 12 on the political experience among 14-year-olds in 28 countries also reveals that learning in civic-related areas is related to the formation of identities, linking experiences in families with experiences with friends in and out of school. It also indicates that the learning of citizenship values cannot be limited to rote learning, but rather involving meaningful learning of civic concepts, active involvement in communities of practices, and concern for students' identities. For instance, there should be more attention paid to gender inequality affecting girls as learner-citizens, as Foster in Chapter 16 alerts us.

That the significance of citizens being educated with values cuts across the three contexts, that is, the global, the national and the local, is nowhere more prominent than the case of Hong Kong under "One Country, Two Systems" after 1997. As pointed out in Morris et al. (2000) on civic identity to be nurtured through education in Hong Kong:

> The government's desire to develop a distinctive identity by pursuing a de-conlonising reform agenda has been constrained by the need to promote an image of stability and continuity and by the legacies inherited from the period of British colonialism.... In terms of civic identity, the handover has seen a shift from the state denying the existence of a local culture and identity towards its more actively promoting a totalising conception of self-identity based upon a national cultural and moral agenda. (p. 260)

Thus, the government of Hong Kong wants to retain the city as an international city (in Asia), in which citizens could be nurtured with a national identity that has been absent for the majority of Hong Kong residents. The British legacy becomes one among the many multicultural sources, alongside with, for example, the American influence, in making Hong Kong international. However, Hong Kong people regard themselves as having a strong local identity as "Hongkongers," with their voice articulated in Cantonese, the local dialect. The debate on the medium of instruction, English, Putunghua or Cantonese is indicative of the struggle on the identity quest moving from the local, via the national to the global (taking English as the international language). However, to what extent would one prefer to identify oneself as a "world citizen" (Heater, 1990), that is, going beyond the national, would be an issue to be deliberated by oneself.

Concrete Wisdom for Practice: How Is Values Education to be Practised?

How is values education to be practised? If values could find a natural way to be caught or learned by citizens, then the formal way of educating values in school may not be necessary. If values are found to be so diverse and pluralistic, sometimes full of indeterminancy, then the formal way of educating values in school would seem to be undesirable, as too imposing. Although the sites for values education could include homes, schools and communities, many of the authors in this book would assert the importance of its implementation in schooling. Thus, issues for its practice will include: the development of values through school curriculum (e.g. in Chapter 6), curricular division of labour (e.g. in Chapter 10), instructional materials (e.g. in Chapter 14), pedagogy (e.g. in Chapters 7 and 9), teacher training and professionalism (e.g. in Chapter 17), and so forth. But could school teachers do the job well as values educators? To make more explicit the job required of school teachers — the practitioners — we may re-formulate the question of practice as: How are values to be embodied in our citizens by school teachers as values educators? For school teachers to concretize the educational process of embodying values in their students, there are conditions to meet. Here we discuss two: the identification with shared values (i.e. knowledge of and commitment to the shared values underlying education), and the identity as values educators (i.e. practical wisdom or practical knowledge of educating values).

Let us tackle the condition of identification of and with shared values. Could there be an absence of shared values underlying education entreprise? Hardly. But what should be the commonly shared values among educators? As Lo (1999) observes, the simultaneous pursuit of excellence and equity in educational development has tested the wisdom of educators and policy-makers since the advent of mass schooling. However, the balance of quality and equality in schooling is dependent on the articulation of commonly shared values within the community and the initiation of appropriate political and social actions. Lo cites the recent educational reforms of Hong Kong and the Chinese Mainland as two examples, both of which have eschewed the slogan of "quality education" in recent years. However unclear about the meaning of this advocated idea, efforts to improve the quality of schooling have not been accompanied by measures to safeguard equity. Illuminated by some major issues like stratification, quality improvement and relevance, he then argues that the elistist approach of old can hardly satisfy the requirement of a new information age characterizing the new century. Because of a new set of developmental requirements in the information age, both societies have to dig deep into their own pools of talents and provide opportunities for all children and youths to develop their potentiality to the fullest. In this endeavor, the major function of schooling to nurture talents for development becomes more obvious than ever before. The advent of the information age, therefore, demands a convergence of excellence and equity in education. Within these stories, it is obvious that implementation of educational policies, aimed to facilitate such converged pursuance, has frequently caused confusion among teachers and school administrators who are charged with the responsibilities of improving school education for children of today, citizens of tomorrow. For them to pursue values education with a clear mind and vision, it is necessary for them to be able to identify the shared values underlying education, with which they identify for preparing the citizens of tomorrow.

Knowing the shared values underlying education and committing oneself to these values by no means guarantee one's practical knowledge of educating values to children. In daily terms, willingness does not guarantee capability. As clarified in Cheng (1999), teachers full of theoretical knowledge (on content of learning) and technical knowledge (on instructional procedures) are still in need of practical knowledge to teach well. Such need is especially keen in the practice of values education since educational practice is value-laden. In philosophical terms dating back to Aristotle while explicated by Wilfred Carr (1995), educational practice is a *praxis*:

> Thus, practice can never be understood as a form of technical expertise designed to achieve some externally related end. Nor can these ends be specified in advance of engaging in a practice. Indeed, *praxis* is different from *poiesis* precisely because discernment of the "good" which constitutes its end is inseparable from a discernment of its mode of expression. 'Practice' is thus what we would call morally informed or morally committed action. Within the

Aristotelian tradition all ethical and political activities were regarded as forms of practice. And so too, of course, was education. (p. 68)

Cheng (2000a) further delineates this line of thinking in arguing that a teacher needs to know the values involved (including his or her own) among which some are the ends of his or her own action as a way of realization by his or her agency embodied with certain qualities in virtue of which he or she enacts the identity as a teacher and to know how to solve problems that emerged in such action. Adapting such argument to the practice of values education, a teacher teaching values need to have self-understanding of his or her own values, awareness of values involved in educating values, authenticity to one's personal qualities and hence one's limitation, capacity for diversity of values, flexibility for handling value problems, ability to show the relevance of values, and sensibility to connect values to what student most concerned with, and so forth. Such a demanding list of conditions may explain why school teachers prefer teaching knowledge and skills to teaching values. However, the new century poses an imperative on citizens whose education is bound to have values nurtured. It is hoped that this book can help with such endeavor.

The above is a thematic introduction focusing on conceptualization, contextualization and concretization of values education in understanding the meaning, desirability and practice of educating values in citizens as identity formation in the new century of migration, changes and globalization. The following is a synoptic introduction of the tripartite chapters. The first part is concerned with the underlying theoretical exploration on problems concerned, thereby providing the unity for values education in clarifying its meaning. Then the second and the third parts address two forms of diversity in the unity. The second part is concerned with the diverse varieties of values education, predominantly but not exclusively in a school context, thereby characterizing the desirability of values education, while providing hints for its practice. The third part is concerned with diverse issues surrounding educating values for citizenship globally, nationally and locally, plus gender issue on learners-citizens and training of civics teachers. The conclusion suggests a model for accommodating the unity in diversity (in terms of varieties and issues).

Theoretical Exploration Underlying Values Education for Citizens

In chapter 2, Husén, a world acclaimed and experienced educationist, opens up the horizon behind our discussion of values education by aptly describing the global predicament of the new century in which values education for citizens in a local context needs to find its own way by thinking through some fundamental questions. In our era of globalisation, value pluralism often comes into conflict with moral universalism. Postmodernism with its relativism has added to the seriousness of that conflict. We are faced with that problem in trying to establish an ethos of tolerance which is often preached in international assemblies. When it comes to education we have to realize that shared values are in most cases related to shared cultures in which these values are embedded. We also have to realize that ethnic pluralism in a given society is enhanced by migration between religions and countries. Education in modern changing and pluralistic societies as compared to traditional and more static societies is faced with three fundamental problems related to the goals and values in the systems:

(1) What common values are behind the goals and guidelines for teaching?
(2) How can a more pluralistic approach be achieved with regard to, for instance, civics without ending up in complete relativism?
(3) How can the basic values taught in school be compatible with the ones taught at home?

In short, the overriding problem for educators behind the ones mentioned above is how to combine cultural and social pluralism with certain basic and more universal values that constitute international understanding and tolerance as addressed in, for instance, the UN Declaration of Human Rights.

However inspiring, these theoretical explorations at general level still leaves unclear the internal structure of the axiological acts involved in values education, thereby demanding structural exploration via some sorts of philosophical analysis. Mei-lin Ng in Chapter 3 provides an exploratory attempt to clarify the details, by finding common divisions cutting across varieties of values education. Values Education, in a broad sense, is comprised of the teaching of values as they are involved in issues of various realms, which encompasses Moral Education, Aesthetic Education, Civic Education, Spiritual Education, etc. In contrast, Value Education is proposed to be an education that bypasses the question of diversity in values and focuses mainly on the cultivation of the general ability of valuing. This chapter offers a philosophical analysis of value judgment, seeing the act of valuing as a two-level mental acitivity: non-reflective identification of values as valuation (or valuating) and deliberative judgment of values as evaluation (or evaluating). We criticize the emotivist doctrine of value judgment as unable to get away with the Humean reason/passion dichotomy. We seek to expound a more fruitful understanding of emotion — a conception of emotion that does not preclude reasonableness. With such understanding, we try to show the possibility and necessity of educating our emotions so as to enrich our capacity of valuation and enhance our ability of evaluation. In conclusion, we put forward the thesis that a viable form of Value Education should be one grounded in the Education of Emotion.

While it is important to recognize the place of affection and cognition in values education, it is equally important to relate axiology (theory of values) with epistemology (theory of knowledge). Cenzon in Chapter 4 is courageous in dealing with the circular relationship between valuing and knowing, if not redundancy. Contemporary educational experience shows that knowledge transmission and acquisition are influenced by some underlying theory of knowledge (epistemology) which has somehow been preferred according to a criteria extrinsic to the value of knowledge itself, such as economic utility, personal satisfaction, professional relevance, and so forth (Degenhardt, 1982). Furthermore, the transmission and acquisition of subject knowledge, inclusive of values, are driven by the educator's and learner's *ethos*. This points to two things: On the one hand, knowledge is acquired or applied for a specific value or good (objective value). On the other hand, that value of knowledge is perceived by a person-subject (subjective value). The chapter explores these dimensions in knowledge itself and in scientific and historical knowledge in particular, for their relevance to 21st century citizens. The objective value of science lies in the rigour of its methodology and the process of inter-subjective discourse. Its subjective value is found in the *ethos* of the scientist, the pre-scientific motivations and reasons for which he engages in scientific activity. The objective value of history is seen in accurate gathering of historical records. Its subjective value is found in the historian's attempt to interpret and understand these accounts. Both objective and subjective values of scientific and historical thinking can be made relevant to values education, in particular to citizenship values. It is the aim of the chapter to suggest that any attempt to *educate in values* can beneficially include the education in the *knowledge of the values of knowledge(s)*. The latter expression is an intended redundancy because valuing knowledge (axiology) is dependent on an epistemology (knowing what and how to value knowledge). This idea is discussed attentively for the areas of science and history. Cenzon claims that scientific and historical knowledge, both in their objective and subjective dimensions, have epistemic values that are relevant to education in citizenship. She also maintains that it is not possible to posit a radical dichotomy between objective and subjective dimensions of value and knowledge, knowledge and values, knowing and valuing as acts of the person. Knowing is a value understood as a good. Valuing is a form of knowing. The chapter reiterates the idea that knowledge is required by valuing since the latter occurs with an assumption that an epistemic merit exists in a particular knowledge that is desirable. But precisely because there is no necessary loss of cognition in this process, valuing becomes itself a form of knowing where cognition meshes with volition and affectivity. The simultaneity of the three components of cognition, volition, and affectivity makes valuing integrative. This also implies that valuing requires, in addition to cognition, an experience of a good as desired by the will and the emotions. In this light, the chapter also affirms that valuing cannot be oversimplified to any of three components. Thus, apart from the epistemic aspect, valuing includes anthropological and ethical roots.

Part I ends, if not concludes, with a reflection on local discourse in Hong Kong, a public discourse couched in terms like quality and value-addedness, which however has a relevance to civic participation and the making of identity. Quality and value-addedness are two of the most popular terms that have ever been heard in the current educational reform of Hong Kong, as Tang in Chapter 5 believes that there is no exception in other parts of the world. What makes Hong Kong one of the unique cases is the close connection between the language policy discourse and conception of quality and value, which has clearly been reflected by the community's involvement in the course of its development especially in the past few years. To argue against the current discourse, which has mainly focused on economic rationalism, a more holistic view with the educational value of language with respect to one's civic duty in light of dialogic constructivism will be suggested. It proposes that the quality of language as a resource has to have something to do with the formation of one's self and life history, the identification of a community where one's identity is appropriated, and the proliferation of a potential dialogic environment where creativity emerges in contrast to the current notion of a technical mentality of language use which leads to a closure of meaning making in our language policy. And it is towards such quality, which is based on the kind of value where identity, community, and the potential of a hermeneutic situation play fair that enhances the understanding this chapter is driving.

Though written by different writers, all four chapters in Part I are concerned with clarifying the meaning of values education by providing a theoretical unity. To relate this to the conceptual clarification pursued in the second section, we may return to the contrast of the two lists, that is, of values education and of subjects or Key Learning Areas. It is a contrast between the epistemological (knowing) and the axiological (valuating), as explicated by Cenzon in Chapter 4. The list of school subjects or KLAs is structured and classified on epistemological grounds, that is, some variants from the thesis of forms of knowledge as advocated by curricular philosophers like Paul Hirst (1965). The list of moral education, sex education, religious education, and so forth, is based on the axiological footing, and hence the listed items could be conceived as varieties under values education as their umbrella term, as Mei-lin Ng in Chapter 3 suggests. Thus, varieties of values education are clustered into and discussed in Part II. But what would be the unity in which these varieties constitute a diversity? Ng has done a good service in delineating two common features of these varieties of values education, all of which are aimed at nurturing the general ability of valuing in making value judgements. This finds echoes from John Dewey's *Theory of Valuation* (1939). Firstly, judging in the domain of values involves "non-reflective identification of values as valuation (or valuating)." Secondly, values-judging involves deliberative judgment of values as evaluation (or evaluating). More importantly, both acts are educable. If such two-level analysis is sound, it shows the possibility and necessity of educating our emotions so as to enrich our capacity of valuation and enhance our ability of evaluation. The implications of such theoretical unity for values education for citizens are obvious. Citizens sufficiently nurtured at both levels would become capacious persons who can draw on rich sources for their identity formation from their cultural embeddedness even through affective channels (e.g. feelings involved in the appreciation of stories), and critical evaluators ranging from "weak evaluation" to "strong evaluation" as Taylor (1985, 1989) suggests (see Cheng, 2000b).

Varieties of Values Education for Citizens

Values Education and Values Across the Curriculum

Values education, according to Taylor, author of Chapter 6, is a relatively new umbrella term for a range of common curriculum experiences ranging from spiritual, moral, social and cultural education, personal and social education, religious education, multicultural/antiracist education, cross-curricular themes especially citizenship, environment and health, pastoral care, school ethos, extra-curricular activities, wider community links, collective worship/assembly to the life of the school as a learning community. Despite the wide range of curriculum experiences associated with values education, values education tends to be delivered in the formal curriculum through programmes of moral or religious education and mainstream instruction in civics and social studies. In the mid-80s, an extensive study on values education in the elementary school curriculum in about 90 (Cha, Wong, & Meyer, 1988) countries showed that:

- Whilst the emphasis on moral education showed no signs of declining, less time tended to be given it than was devoted to religious instruction. There were also negative correlations between the two.
- Civics had declined sharply and social studies had increased dramatically in the most recent period (1975–1985).

In the case of England, values education takes place mostly in collective worship and Religious Education (RE). In secondary schools, values education tends to be implemented in separately time-tabled Personal and Social Education (PSE) (Taylor, 2000). In England, citizenship has become a statutory entitlement as a foundation subject in the secondary school. However, as Taylor argues in Chapter 6, "a statutory focus on citizenship will make it more problematic for schools to accommodate RE (Religious Education) and collective worship.... And it is not clear how other important values such as the spiritual, environmental, cultural and aesthetic will be addressed through the school curriculum ... those of us ... are unlikely to be satisfied with a moral education apparently limited to moral responsibility within citizenship" (p. 117). In Hong Kong, the Curriculum Development Council (2001) recommended moral and civic education as one of the four key tasks in future curriculum development and further suggested that value-oriented studies in the school curriculum, including religious education, sex education, health education, environmental education, media education and other themes (such as affective education, life education) can become components of moral and civic education. On the other hand, Pring (1986) argues that different subjects might explore "whether and how they contribute to the development of the more general values and to an "evaluative" appreciation of the more specific issues and contexts" (p. 194). Tomlinson and Quinton (1986) further assert that:

> Children do spend a good deal of time in schools with teachers being taught particular subjects; that such subjects have many value-related aspects; that

> there are varying degrees of concern by various parties for effective values education; that there may be unintended effects of implicit processes as well as intended effects of explicitly directed activities. (p. 2)

These subjects may include seemingly values-free subject areas such as mathematics and science (Aspin, 2000). In sum, there have been diverse trends ranging from using citizenship (or civics) as a core subject, moral and religious education as major vehicles, adopting cross-curricular themes (such as environmental, health and sex education) and mainstream subjects (such as social studies or personal and social education) for values education through the school curriculum to values education across the curriculum. These varying trends in different places suggest that there should be continuous discussion how best values education should be delivered in the school curriculum.

Emerging Issues in Values Education in the School Curriculum

In developing values education in the school curriculum, there have been questions about the extent to which a school reflects the values and structure of society. Given the complexity of the value domain and the diversity of societal contexts, there are calls for values education for a pluralist society. According to Down (2000), pluralism can be briefly understood in three aspects, namely democratic pluralism, social pluralism and epistemological pluralism. Democratic pluralism refers to "power-sharing and the recognition of different, but equally important, interest groups" (p. 236). Social pluralism refers to the possession of core values in individual groups and certain shared values across groups. Epistemological pluralism refers to the "recognition that different groups may have different traditions and claims to knowledge" (p. 237). These strands of pluralism may imply that the school curriculum should be broadened to take into account other societies, other cultures and other religions. In addition, there should be a balance between claims to universal methodology and knowledge in areas such as science and claims to knowledge influenced by different cultures (and values) (Down, 2000). The chapters in Part II tend to throw light on values education related to epistemological pluralism. From a liberal perspective, McLaughlin (1995) discusses the concepts of "public" and "private" values. Based on his ideas, learners and citizens should be encouraged to develop a commitment to "public" values which are free of significantly controversial assumptions and judgments and at the same time be encouraged to explore, reflect on the diversity of values in the private sphere and make their own choices on these "private values." Some moral ideas, however, may be linked up with religious belief and so sometimes interpretation of moral values may be different from a religious and educational point of view. As Haydon (2000) succinctly points out:

> … for many liberal and secular thinkers the only question of moral relevance about anything is "does it do any harm?", whereas some religious thinkers feel that question largely misses the point. (p. 6)

On the other hand, there have been pleas for overcoming the possible drawback of cultural pluralism, knowledge fragmentation, moral atomization and indifference as well as searching for a vision and purpose of values education for the school curriculum (Cairns, 2000). It seems that values educators face the dilemma between helping learners to see certain important common values for human life and to respect differences in the diversity and complexity of values (and its interpretations). After reading these chapters, readers may think about:

- What core, common or "public" values should values education address through the school curriculum? How might values education become more pluralistic (existence of different varieties of values education) and integrative?
- How can the school curriculum facilitate learners in cultivating a good balance of "public" and "private" values? How can values educators help learners to understand, and make their autonomous choices on, different ethical viewpoints?

Part II contains six chapters focusing on the discussion of varieties of values education in the school curriculum. They cover the overview of values education, citizenship education, religious education, environmental education, and values education through social studies and science education.

In Chapter 6, Taylor portrays a landscape for understanding the varieties of values education. She draws examples from evolving policy, practice and research in England to depict some of the social and educational confusions and tensions surrounding values education and suggests ways through which the development of values can be enhanced in the school curriculum. With regard to confusions, she highlights the distinction between nurturing of values and values development through the school curriculum. The former may be related to a faith dimension and a pastoral aspect of the Christian tradition whilst the latter may be associated with the growth towards maturity, which normally occurs as an outcome of values learning experiences in school.

With respect to tensions, Taylor discusses three levels at which tensions occur, namely government policy, school policy and practice, and teacher experience. At the government level, tensions are concerned with goals (development of social and moral values, character and/or key skills and individual achievement), means (age and phase for values education), and visions (international, national and local perspectives). At the school level, a school faces tensions related to: principles and policies such as the relationship between religious education and other aspects of values education, whose values, what values and values in the educational process; implementation and practices including delivery structures, curriculum content, and pedagogic strategies. At the teacher level, tensions exist in issues such as the personal and the private related to the professional and the public, handling sensitive issues, as well as the gap between the formal and informal curriculum. Lastly, Taylor suggests characteristics for effective valuing and values learning in school.

Echoing the forthcoming introduction of citizenship as a separate subject in the curriculum in England, Halstead in Chapter 10 explores the relationship of citizenship education to moral education. He first differentiates two conceptions of citizenship education, namely education *about* citizenship and education *for* citizenship. The former refers to a cognitive orientation, primarily extending children's knowledge and understanding of political ideas, institutions and issues. The latter highlights a broader approach, which encompasses not only political literacy but also moral and social responsibility and community involvement. It also aims to produce both informed and committed citizens. Halstead in turn discusses three models of citizenship education. The first model is education about citizenship, which is basically a value-free approach. The second and third models are education for citizenship and they are value-laden approaches. The second model is education for good citizenship, which includes the assumptions that schools should reflect society's current values and that the role of schools is to socialize pupils into these values. He argues that this model is liable to some shortcomings such as "not be balanced by an openness to competing conceptions of the true and the good or an emphasis on tolerance, respect, democratic debate, personal autonomy and human dignity." (p. 205) The third model is education for active citizenship, which is concerned with preparing children for active participation in the political, civil and social life of the community.

Halstead further argues against merging citizenship with moral education in the light of the third model of citizenship education. Firstly, the model for active citizenship presupposes a liberal framework of values, which is not essential for an understanding of morality in a liberal democracy. It may have the drawback of undermining the social, moral and cultural life of minorities and undervaluing difference. Secondly, the private/public distinction inherent in the model is blurred. This highlights the imperative of a moral critique of citizenship. Thirdly, understanding of and commitment to the law as implied in this model is inadequate for addressing questions of morality. Finally, the linking between citizenship and moral education may not pay full attention to the insights of postmodern critics and visionaries.

In response to the scope of values education, Peter T. M. Ng in Chapter 8 re-evaluates the role and value of religious education. The author first pinpoints the situation that the problem of education today is the misplacement of "life" and the neglect of learners' spirits in education. He then refers to the English experience that religious education has shifted from "Bible-centred" to "Life-centred" approaches and also Michael Grimmett's dual phenomenological and existential approaches of enabling pupils to "learning about religions" and "learning from religions about themselves" respectively. He critically examines the problem of knowledge in schooling and curriculum and concludes that on the one hand the differentiation of knowledge into subjects and disciplines has resulted in learners' reception of disconnected ideas and knowledge about life and wisdom of life have been mis-positioning on the other. In view of this shortcoming, he suggests an integrative religious and life education and illustrates examples from Taiwan and Hong Kong. In the case of Hong Kong, an attempt should be made to help teachers of Religious Education from schools of different religious traditions to work together to search for spiritual qualities in human life.

In the case of environmental education as a variety of values education, Lam and Lee in Chapter 7 use an example of protecting the wilderness in Hong Kong to discuss the issues of which values and whose values. This is done through examining the diversity of value positions for justifying environmental conservation and ethical positions reflected in selected publications of green organizations. The authors discuss various ethical positions including intrinsic values and beauty in Nature, animal rights and instrumental values of Nature to help save the wilderness. They argue that anthropocentrism has often been blamed for the degradation of the environment as the human-centred value system excludes the wilderness for moral consideration. In fact, instrumental value and intrinsic value approaches can be complementary to each other. A pragmatic way for promoting environmental education may be justifying the preservation of the wilderness from a human-centred perspective through making the intrinsic values explicit.

Whilst the previous chapters focus on broad areas of values education such as citizenship, religious and environmental education, the last two chapters in Part II highlight values education in connection with subject areas or disciplines such as science and social studies. In Chapter 11, Jean-Luc argues that science is not values-free and that there is a need to distinguish science as activity (doing research) and science as system of statements. The former, according to the author, is necessarily values-laden whilst the latter may or may not be value-free, depending on whether the system of statements can contain descriptive or normative statements. With regard to science as activity particularly related to empirical research, one must further differentiate two levels (researcher's decisions and theory on which decisions are based) and steps in a research process: research questions, researcher's interest and paradigm, procedure, conclusion and application. The results of the author's analysis concludes that almost all decisions within two levels are based on personal values or values laden except where design and application of the optimal procedure given the principles as well as application of the principles of drawing conclusions are independent of personal values. In science as system of statements, values statements are acceptable so long as they are labeled and justified according to the principles of ethics.

Jean-Luc further suggests that science teaching is also values-laden and then applies Kohlberg's approach in science teaching with a focus on how learners argue in favor or against particular values such as stopping a nuclear plant. The approach contains 10 prototypical steps in teaching both values and subject matters:

(1) introducing dilemma;
(2) making first decision;
(3) putting forth first arguments (dilemma discussion);
(4) exchanging experience and missing information;
(5) looking for evidence;
(6) exchanging information;
(7) putting forth second arguments (dilemma discussion);
(8) synthesizing information;

(9) exchanging experience and missing information again through synthesizing information (i.e. repeating step (4) through step (8) if necessary); and

(10) making generalization.

In Chapter 9, Hirshberg explores and advocates the teaching of social studies from a compassionate perspective for achieving citizenship education goals. He first identifies six types of goals of citizenship education within the political, economic and social realms and two levels, namely collective and individual. Then two values upon which citizenship education goals are based are suggested: capability and compassion. The author argues that capability and compassion goals must be balanced, the latter of which contain political inclusiveness, human rights, distributive justice, social harmony, community, political tolerance, critical thinking, generosity, cooperativeness, empathy and altruism. He further asserts that broad compassion can be promoted through global education. In addition, the potential conflict between globalism and patriotism and such conflict being possibly reconciled through "moderate patriotism" are highlighted. Lastly, he refers to the established social science approach to inquiry, which tends to adopt a dispassionate, removed, amoral and impersonal perspective and reinforces the importance of teaching compassionate social studies which includes thirteen elements: honoring human differences, role taking, engaging discussions, critical thinking, multiple perspectives, compassionate modeling, opportunities for altruism, cooperative learning, global education, rejection of the disciplines, participant's perspective, ethics and values, and emotional expression.

The lines of explorations pursued by these six chapters in Part II cut across each other like a spider web, showing how diverse varieties of values education are related as a whole. Though complex, their interlocking themes help establish ways of showing the desirability of an individual variety of values education on its own while addressing some aspects of the practice of that particular variety. Among the themes, the tension between common values and pluralistic values is prominent, posing a further enquiry that is taken up in the ending conclusion.

Issues in Values Education for Citizens

While Part I provides philosophically-informed theoretical explorations into the global and local contexts of values education for citizens in the new century and Part II offers a cross-curricular diagnosis on varieties of values education, Part III looks into details of citizenship formation at different societies as well as diverse issues involved in values education for citizens. The first three chapters share details of studies on citizenship education, with one mainly on 28 countries and two focused on Hong Kong. The last three chapters respectively discuss three diverse issues: a national preparation for globalization in Thailand, girls' status as learner-citizens and professional development of civic teachers, both in Australia.

In Chapter 12, Torney-Purta begins by discussing a model of learning in civic education based on Phase 1 of the IEA Study and on the theory of Etienne Wenger. The IEA model has the individual at its centre influenced by family, school and peers, as well as by the discourse in society regarding political, economic, educational and religious values. Wenger's theory points to learning as it is related to experience in constructing meaning individually and with others. Central in this theory is the role of practice of civic skills and values in a community. Further, learning in civic-related areas is related to the formation of identities, linking experiences in families with experiences with friends and at school. The last part of the chapter reports findings from Phase 2 of the IEA Civic Education Study, in which a test and survey was administered to 90,000 students sampled from the grade in which the majority of 14-year-olds are found in 28 countries. Some results from Hong Kong (SAR) are reported and placed the perspective of results from the other participating countries.

Citizenship is usually in transition, as explicated by Tsang in Chapter 13 in the case of Hong Kong. In response to the 1997 transition, Hong Kong Government published two *Guidelines on Civic Education in Schools* in 1984 and 1997 respectively. They signify the belated intent and effort of the retreating colonial government in inculcating political consciousness and citizenship into the future citizens of the HKSAR. In this chapter, Tsang tries to assess the effect of these *Guidelines*, especially the 1984 version, by comparing the political attitudes and opinions of two cohorts of citizens who were at schools before and after the implementation of these *Guidelines*. It was intended to see whether there are significant differences in political attitudes and opinions between these two cohorts. The study is based on data generated from two electoral studies conducted right after the 1995 and 1998 Legislative Council geographical-constituency elections. The study reveals, first of all, that strong senses of political skepticism, helplessness and distrustfulness permeate Hong Kong citizens in general. At the same time they hold a strong faith in democracy and have a strong sense of citizenship. They hold a clear dissenting view against most of the policy stances adopted by the Hong Kong and Chinese Government. Hong Kong citizens also expect their representatives to be in line with their dissenting stances. However, Hong Kong citizens in general expect their representatives not to be too confrontational toward the governmental authorities and even expect them to be accepted by the Beijing authority. Furthermore, in the comparison between the Guideline cohort and the pre-Guideline cohort, it reveals that the young citizens in Hong Kong, that is the Guideline cohort, are politically more distrustful and dissenting than their elderly fellow citizens. Furthermore, they feel less helpless and skeptical in politics. In other words, they feel themselves more efficacious politically than their elderly counterparts.

In Chapter 14, Tse turns to the representation of citizenship in the junior secondary school curriculum in the cases of Hong Kong and Macau. Citizenship education has aroused much public concern in Hong Kong and Macau since the mid-1980s. Informed by the theoretical discussion of citizenship education, this chapter analyses the representation of citizenship in the recent school curriculum in both places. It first gives a brief account of the continuity and change of citizenship education in Hong Kong and Macau in the post-World War II period. Then it contrasts and compares the recent curriculum concerning citizenship education in these places. Finally, it further discusses the implications of these results for future citizenship education programmes in these places. As revealed in recent citizenship education syllabuses at junior secondary levels, both places have defined citizenship education in the broadest sense, and have treated it as a mixture of moral, political and lifeskills education. They juxtapose both nationalistic and democratic education. Also, both pro-establishment and participatory elements are found; and citizenship education in both places stresses international contexts by including elements of global citizenship and/or multi-culturalism. In terms of pedagogy, a more progressive vision of citizenship education is witnessed in both syllabuses. As for evaluation, both syllabuses stress not only cognitive but also affective achievements and behavioral performances. However, Macau's syllabus has a smaller and less adequate coverage of national community, international community, and citizenship than its Hong Kong's counterpart. Also, the dominant orientation of Macau's syllabus was more prone to the mode of "citizenship transmission" mainly concerned with developing moral virtues of good citizens and promoting supportive and accommodating relationships with society, rather than a more reflective and critical approach to citizenship education. However, given that these new syllabuses in Hong Kong and Macau are only offered to a handful of schools, their impact on students remains negligible.

In Chapter 15, Chareonwongsak shares how Thailand prepares itself for globalization. In the push for globalization, especially in developing countries, national development planners have paid insufficient attention to one area, namely, values development. Many countries, including Thailand, have failed to establish clear policy and strategies for the development of the values necessary for success in globalization. To have an ongoing programme of developing human resources, the education system is the best channel for inculcating the appropriate values in students and general citizens alike. This paper argues that values education (VE) must become the cornerstone of all education in Thailand. That is, VE must become compulsory for every student at all levels, thereby securing Thailand's future as a nation. The first section of this chapter defines the phrase "values education" in light of traditional and current literature. Rokeach's system of classifying values is used as the foundation for proposing changes to Thailand's values education system. Then, the author gives a brief history of values education in Thailand from a socio-political/cultural perspective. The section outlining Thailand's current VE programmes includes an analysis of its most relevant problems. The next section outlines the effects of globalization on VE in Thailand. In the future, Thai VE will be required to meet the following needs: (1) to produce personnel who can meet the demands of the new labour market; (2) to create a higher awareness of other cultures and values; (3) to bring balanced development between knowledge and values; (4) to become more contemporary; (5) to combat the dissemination of improper foreign values and (6) to select and teach positive Thai values. The fourth section of this chapter delineates necessary changes in Thailand's VE system. Changes include: (1) deciding which values are preferred; (2) encoding these values within a curriculum; (3) developing a methodology for values teaching; (4) developing VE teachers; (5) developing an evaluation system, and (6) distributing the responsibility for developing values to various institutions within society. Finally, the author recommends various changes in policy including: (1) creating a strong policy that would ensure the nurturing of preferred values in students; and (2) engaging in VE research.

In Chapter 16, Foster examines the newly emerging relationship between two contemporary international trends in education. The first trend is that in most western countries, girls are now achieving statistically slightly better average school-leaving results than boys, in an apparent move towards sexual equality, in turn occasioning a hostile populist "backlash" against this success. A recent international collection argues that education in the 21st century will be a "dangerous terrain" for women. The second trend is the revival of interest in participatory democratic theory which is reflected in the strong current focus on civics and citizenship education in education systems. Despite this second trend, however, gender issues are currently receiving little attention in discussions of citizenship education, as Professor David Hicks pointed out in his Keynote Address, "Praxis of the Heart," at the 1999 UNESCO-ACEID Conference in Bangkok. The chapter then presents recent research which further develops the theoretical arguments put forward in Foster's "Feminist Theory and the Construction of Citizenship Education in the Modern State" (collected in Kennedy, 1997). The chapter argues that in the present international climate, it is impossible for girls to be equal with boys as learner-citizens. Girls remain adjuncts to the learner-citizen as male, a problem which is not addressed in current models of citizenship education. The two trends under discussion are contradictory, positioning girls in a dialectic of desire and threat in their quests for citizenship. The implication for questions of moral education and values education is drawn out, and comparative material from Australia, Scandinavia and Holland is discussed.

In Chapter 17, Libby shares positive teacher professional development outcomes in Values and Citizenship Education in Australia. As we enter the new millennium, Civics and Citizenship Education (CCE) is high on the formal education agenda in Australia. CCE is defined as one of the core "Common and Agreed Goals for Schooling in Australia in the 21st Century," and values education is implicit in these goals. Classroom teachers also argue that values and CCE are core work for schools, so their students may be empowered to be active, thinking and responsible citizens in the local, national and international contexts. The Australian government is currently funding a range of programmes nationwide, including the development of teacher and student resources and the provision of teacher professional development, with the goal of improving the quality and quantity of CCE in schools. This chapter firstly explores how the concepts of "quality" values and CCE are being interpreted and developed by policy makers and Victorian teachers, and why CCE is being promoted. Case studies are discussed of schools which can be defined as exemplary "professional communities," where positive outcomes have been achieved in the improvement of teacher and student learning in values and CCE. Research has shown that in schools where professional community is strong, teacher learning is a regular feature. It then analyses the range of factors leading to the operation of professional communities, along with the implications of these findings for the development of effective professional development models which will in turn lead to improved student learning in CCE in the future.

These six chapters in Part III share two common features. Firstly, the diverse issues addressed are deeply embedded in their respective context, which provides aspects of showing how values education is desirable in that particular context, be it global, national or local, or a mixture. Secondly, solutions of the issues demand practical deliberation and action in a highly concrete manner. Thus, these chapters are very informative of their respective contexts and practices since they are based on particulars. However, the diversity involved may be so diverse to lose sight of their underlying unity. It is to such theme that the ending conclusion returns.

Concluding the Quest for Unity in Diversity

In most chapters in this book, the site for values education that we have been discussing occurs in "common schools," in which "uncommon identities" of students are however demanding and deserving careful attention as argued by Feinberg (1998). Like it or not, the new century has an inclination towards multi-culturalism as a new context for values education for citizenship. In *Common Schools, Uncommon Identities: National Unity and Cultural Difference*, Feinberg (1998) argues:

> Historically schools were justified as critical in bringing different peoples together to participate in a common and shared identity, one in which every person was recognizable to every other person as a citizen of the same nation. Today the emphasis appears to have shifted, and what was once taken as an important role of the schools — advancing a single common identity — is sometimes viewed as advancing the interests of the dominant group over those who are different and powerless. Yet if the historical mission of the common school is now of certain value, the question remains. How should children from different cultural backgrounds be treated by the public schools, and what, if any, identity work is appropriate for public education? Hence the title of the book might best be read as a question: Given our new understanding of the value of cultural differences, is there any role for a common school, and if there is, then what is it? (p. 3)

In the new century, the tension between commonality and plurality comes to the surface in such a way that values education in practice needs to find a way through. For the theoretical underpinning of values education, many chapters in Part I has provided rich discussions. In particular, Husén of Chapter 2 has helped us by depicting the new context defined by the tension between universalism and pluralism: Education in modern changing and pluralistic societies as compared to traditional and more static societies is faced with three fundamental problems related to the goals and values in the systems. Firstly, what common values are behind the goals and guidelines for teaching? Secondly, how can a more pluralistic approach be achieved with regard to, for instance, civics without ending up in complete relativism? Thirdly, how can the basic values taught in school be compatible with the ones taught at home?

These two lines of thinking, together with the whole book, converge on the search for a framework for values education which can accommodate diversity within unity of some sort. On the diversity side, why are differences desirable, if inevitable? While Haydon (2000) reminds us to understand the diversity of diversity, Lee (2002) tries to establish a case for valuing differences. On the unity side, could we cultivate commonly shared values in our citizens? If no common value is to be shared by citizens, would citizens cease to be citizens and community cease to have its solidarity?

A "Cone Model" of "cones with diverse tips and common base" borrowed from Cheng (2000b) may be suggestive:

Figure 1.1: The "Cone Model" — Plurality of Values as the Diverse Tips (Values Embedded or Embodied in Different People); Commonly Shared Values as the Unifying Base

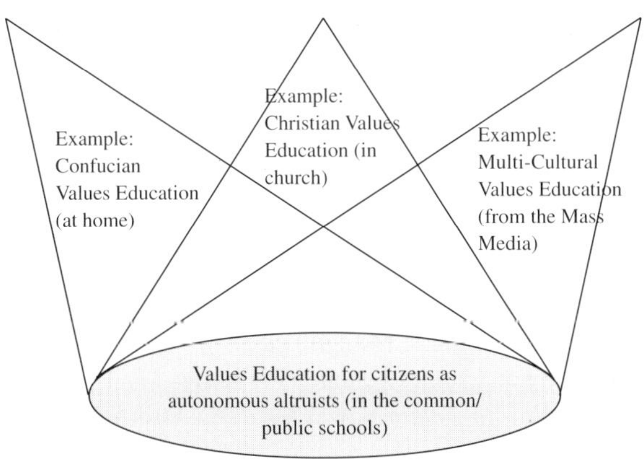

The basic idea behind such "Cone Model" is that it is the values educand, that is, the citizen, who lies at the centre of absorbing sources through multiple forms or sites of values education. Just to reflect narratively on one's formation of values system, one is influenced by one's family, schools, and communities. Some values are substantive and others may be procedural. Some values are thick and others may be thin. Some sites are heavily loaded in cultural traditions and others may be culturally broad. Some sources are unitary and others may be multiple. Returning to the question "Who am I?" in the beginning of this chapter, if the answer takes the form of a storied life, then the narrative would reveal the concrete embodiment of values of all sorts in citizens being taught or caught from multiple sources (e.g. Confucian, Christian and multi-cultural traditions, etc.). Thus, the common schools, or the public schools, which are delegated the task of nurturing citizens for the local, the national and the global, cannot but educate values both of convergence into commonality (e.g. autonomy and altruism) and of divergence into plurality. In other words, the school needs to educate students commonly shared values in a particular context while preparing values of diversity for citizens to live with their identities in the changing world.

Acknowledgement

The first drafts of all chapters (except chapter 1) in this book were presented to the International Conference on Values Education and Citizenship Education in the New Century, 9–11 June 2000, at the Chinese University of Hong Kong. The contributors have been kind and patient to have their revised manuscripts included into this book, the editorial process of which has been lengthier than expected. The editors would like to express their thanks to the collective effort of all contributors in sharing their scholarship on values education with our readers.

References

Aristotle (1976). *Nicomanchean Ethics*. (J. A. K. Thomson, Trans.). Middlesex, UK: Penguin Books.

Aspin, D. (2000). A clarification of some key terms in values discussions. In M. Leicester, C. Modgil, & S. Modgil (Eds.), *Moral education and pluralism* (Education, Culture and Values Volume IV) (pp. 16–31). London: Falmer Press.

Austin, J. L. (1971). *How to do things with words*. Oxford, UK: Oxford University Press.

Cairns, J. (2000). Morals, ethics and citizenship in contemporary teaching. In R. Gardner, J. Cairns, & D. Lawton (Eds.), *Education for values: Morals, ethics and citizenship in contemporary teaching* (pp. 6–23). London: Kogan Page.

Carr, W. (1995). *For education: Towards critical educational inquiry*. Buckingham, UK: Open University Press.

Cha, Y.-K., Wong, S.-Y., & Meyer, J. W. (1988). Values education in the curriculum: Some comparative empirical data. In W. K. Cummings, S. Gopinathan, & Y. Tomoda (Eds.), *The revival of values education in Asia and the West* (pp. 11–28). Oxford, UK: Pergamon Press.

Chandler, D. (2002). *Semiotics: The basic*. London: Routledge.

Clandinin, D. J., & Connelly, F. M. (2000). *Narrative inquiry: Experience and story in qualitative research*. San Fransisco: Jossey-Bass Publishers.

Cheng, H. M. R. (1996, October). *Hong Kong education under the view of "quality-based" education: hearts (attitudes—virtues) and powers (abilities—excellences) in educated persons in becoming quality persons for personal and social well-being*. Paper presented at the Conference on the Vision of Hong Kong organized by the Division of Theology et al., The Chinese University of Hong Kong, 9–10 October, Hong Kong.

Cheng, H. M. R. (1999). Education requiring contextualized epistemology: Restructuring knowledge-based education into quality-based education in contexts. *Education Journal*, *26*(2) & *27*(1), 135–158.

Cheng, H. M. R. (2000a, April). *The threefold knowledge of teachers as educational practitioners: Knowledge of the goods (ends), self-knowledge and problem-solving knowledge*. Paper included into the Proceedings of the Philosophy of Education Society of Great Britain Annual Conference 2000, April 2000.

Cheng, H. M. R. (2000b, June). *Dialogue on desiring the desirable: 3D framework for values education beyond subjectivism and objectivism*. Paper presented at the International Conference on Values Education and Citizenship Education, organized by the Hong Kong Institute of Educational Research et al., The Chinese University of Hong Kong, 9–11 June 2000, Hong Kong.

Crittenden, J. (1992). *Beyond individualism: Reconstituting the liberal self*. Oxford, UK: Oxford University Press.

Curriculum Development Council. (2001). *Learning to learn: The way forward in curriculum development*. Hong Kong: Curriculum Development Council.

Dewey, J. (1939). *Theory of valuation*. Chicago: University of Chicago Press.

Down, B. (2000). Design and technology education for a pluralist society. In M. Leicester, C. Modgil, & S. Modgil (Eds.), *Classroom issues: Practice, pedagogy and curriculum (Education, Culture and Values Volume III)* (pp. 236–247). London: Falmer Press.

Education Commission. (2000). *Reform Proposals for the Education System in Hong Kong*. Hong Kong: Education Commission.

Feinberg, W. (1998). *Common schools/uncommon identities: National identity and cultural difference*. New Haven: Yale University Press.

Halstead, J. M., & Taylor, M. J. (1996). Values and values education in schools. In J. M. Halstead & M. J. Taylor (Eds.), *Values in education and education in values* (pp. 3–14). London: Falmer Press.

Hargreaves, A., & Lo, L. N. K. (2000). The paradoxical profession: Teaching at the turn of the century. *Prospects*, *30*(2), pp. 167–180.

Haydon, G. (2000). Understanding the diversity of diversity. In M. Leicester, C. Modgil, & S. Modgil (Eds.), *Institutional issues: Pupils, schools and teacher education: vol. 2. Education, culture and values* (pp. 3–10). London: Falmer Press.

Heater, D. (1990). *Citizenship: The civic ideal in world history, politics and education*. London: Longman.

Hirst, P. H. (1965). Liberal education and the nature of knowledge. In P. H. Hirst, *Knowledge and the curriculum* (pp. 30–53). London: RKP.

Ho, H. H. (1995). Fuzzy identity and identity without essentialistic commitment. *The Humanities Bulletin*, *4*, 13–19.

Lee, J. C. K. (2002). Valuing differences: Implementation strategies of environmental values education in school. In J. C. K. Lee (Ed.), *Curriculum, teaching and school reforms: Educational development in the new century* (pp. 149–163) [in Chinese]. Hong Kong: The Chinese University Press.

Liu, S.-H. (1995). Identity as philosophical problem: A Neo-Confucian experience. *The Humanities Bulletin*, *4*, 23–37.

Lo, L. N. K., & Man S. W. (1996). Introduction: Nurturing the moral citizens of the future. In L. N. K. Lo & S. W. Man (Eds.), *Research and endeavours in moral and civic education* (pp. ix–xxix). Hong Kong: Hong Kong Institute of Educational Research, The Chinese University of Hong Kong.

Lo, L. N. K. (1999). Quality and equality in the educational development of Hong Kong and the Chinese mainland. *Educational Research Journal*, *14*(1), 13–48.

MacIntyre, A. (1985). *After virtue: A study in moral theory* (2nd ed.). London: Duckworth.

McLaughlin, T. H. (1995). Public values, private values and educational responsibility. In E. Pybus & T. H. McLaughlin (Eds.), *Values, education and responsibility*. St. Andrews, Scotland: University of St. Andrews Centre for Philosophy and Public Affairs.

Morris, P. et al. (2000). Education, civic participation and identity: Continuity and change in Hong Kong. *Cambridge Journal of Education*, *30*(2), 243–262.

Parfit, D. (1984). *Reason and person*. Oxford, UK: Clarendon Press.

Pollock, D. C., & Reken, R. V. (1999). *Third culture kids: The experience of growing up among worlds*. London: Intercutural.

Pring, R. (1986). Aims, problems and curriculum contexts. In P. Tomlinson &

M. Quinton (Eds.), *Values across the curriculum* (pp. 181–194). London: Falmer Press.

Ricoeur, P. (1991). Narrative unity. In D. Wood (Ed.), *On Paul Ricoeur* (pp. 188–199). London: Routldge.

Taylor, C. (1985). What is human agency? In C. Taylor (Ed.), *Human agency and language: Philosophical papers 1* (pp. 15–44). Cambridge, UK: Cambridge University Press.

Taylor, C. (1989). *Sources of the self: The making of the modern identity*. Cambridge, UK: Cambridge University Press.

Taylor, M. J. (1994). *Values education in the UK: A directory of research and resources*. Slough, UK: National Foundation for Educational Research for Gordon Cook Foundation.

Taylor, M. J. (2000). Values education: Issues and challenges in policy and practice. In M. Leicester, C. Modgil, & S. Modgil (Eds.), *Institutional issues: Pupils, schools and teacher education: vol. 2. Education, culture and values* (pp. 151–165). London: Falmer Press.

Tomlinson, P., & Quinton, M. (Eds.) (1986). *Values across the curriculum*. London: Falmer Press.

Wittgenstein, L. (1967). *Philosophical investigations* (3rd ed.). (G.E.M. Anscombe, Trans.). Oxford: Blackwell.

PART I

Theoretical Explorations Underlying Values Education for Citizens

CHAPTER 2

Values Education and Citizenship Education in Modern Society

Torsten Husén

Abstract

In our era of globalisation value pluralism often comes into conflict with moral universalism. Postmodernism with its relativism has added to the seriousness of that conflict. We are faced with that problem in trying to establish an ethos of tolerance which is often preached in international assemblies. When it comes to education we have to realize that shared values are in most cases related to shared cultures in which these values are embedded. We also have to realize that ethnic pluralism in a given society is enhanced by migration between religions and countries.

Education in modern changing and pluralistic as compared to traditional and more static societies is faced with three fundamental problems related to the goals and values in the systems:

What common values are behind the goals and guidelines for teaching?

How can a more pluralistic approach be achieved with regard to, for instance, civics without ending up in complete relativism?

How can the basic values taught in school be compatible with the ones taught at home?

The overriding problem for educators behind also the ones mentioned above is how to combine cultural and social pluralism with certain basic and more universal values that constitute international understanding and tolerance as confined in, for instance, the UN Declaration of Human Rights?

Keynote to the Conference on Values Education and Citizenship Education, 2004, at the CUHK. References are supplemented by the editors of this book.

In discussing the role of values in education we cannot avoid the confrontation between value pluralism and moral universalism as codified, for instance, in the United Nations Declaration of Human Rights. We no longer enjoy the benefits of a static society in which young people are educated mainly within the framework of the family and socialized to the values handed down from one generation to the next. The role of the school, if it exists, is to strengthen the socialization process. Values are, which in the past, were transferred from one generation to the next will have to be explicated and inculcated in an increasing culturally mixed population. With the present trend towards massive migration to seek work or to escape persecution and discrimination, the mass media, not least television, is transgressing national and cultural frontiers and cultural boundaries. Audiences are exposed to other lifestyles and opinions.

In the current wave of postmodernity there is no shortage of values pluralism, not to mention value relativists. This movement has been defined using the brief vernacular formula "anything goes".

Nevertheless, among this often confusing particularism we cannot avoid the question of whether or not we should throw away the Kantian universalism with its categorical imperative. Among the seemingly endless preaching about multiculturalism and tolerance we must face the hard question as to whether the liberal values expressed in democratic constitutions, the rule of law, and, human rights and dignity as solemnly expressed in the UN Declaration of Human Rights, should be looked at just as one option or alternative among many. It can be stated with some confidence, that value pluralism and moral universalism are, not logically exclusive. Society is perhaps at a loss how it will be able to combine them in a kind of ethos of tolerance. It would be presumptuous to try to dictate how this combination could be achieved. Competing values cannot be measured by one unitary standard.

So, how do we transform the insight of value pluralism into a plea for the value of plurality. Needless to say, the common core not only of solemn international conventions, like the one I have already referred to, is that plurality of values is accepted. However we all also solemnly declare our adherence to a universal morality that defends certain human rights and human dignity.

It is far from me, to try to spell out the philosophical intricacies of this combination. It can be explained by a kind of pragmatist ethics according to which there are certain universal features or structures of human action that cut across cultural and national boundaries. It seems to me that this pragmatist ethics, which is found among intellectuals all over the world, maintains in its critique of Kant's categorical imperative that this could be subjected to a universalization test, but not serve as an instrument to find out what actions would be adequate in the first place.

I would also like to posit that in the value systems behind the constitutions and laws of democratic societies we find rules, which can be regarded as translation of universal moral rules into political institutions.

Without any claim to have solved the basic problems other than proclaiming certain of these I am referring to the problem of universalism contra relativism as a background to what I am going to say about the role of values particularly in formal education and the curricula set up for it.

(1) I have been struck by the fact that in many countries where the thorough overhauls of the entire system of formal education has been discussed, the debate has often focused on *means* and not *goals* derived from certain basic values. The setting of goals has been done in terms of targets, for instance what standards have to be achieved, often with international comparisons. Two examples can illustrate this. In the early 1990s, when US President George Bush brought the governors of the 50 states together to set national goals for school education, these goals were, largely set in terms of standards. For instance, by the year 2000, the US students would, by international standards, be top in mathematics and science. Since then, the Third International Study of Mathematics and Science (TIMSS) has been published and we know that that target has not yet been reached. When it comes to schooling even major reforms cannot, within the passage of a mere decade, work wonders. The overriding issue in American school education since the report "A Nation At Risk", published in 1983, has been the competitive standing of American education. What looms large in the underlying rationale for this stance is the implications of competitive standing, is its effect on the world market and for the national GNP. The second example is from my home country, Sweden. Over decades we have had an intensive debate about whether or not school marks should be given, and if they should be given, when and – above all – how. Technical consideration of the means has dominated the debate, whereas the aims and the values embodied in these aims have seldom been discussed.

(2) Before looking more closely at goals and values in school education today, it may be useful to take a historical look at the issue. How have national systems of public education emerged and what role were these systems expected to play and what goals were set for them?

It is also be in order, in this connection, to discuss the role of *shared values* in public education as related to the shared culture embodying these values and how they provide a *common frame of reference* with regard to social and, sometimes, religiously anchored norms.

The problem can be phrased this way: To what extent is a core of shared values, which constitute a common frame of reference, a necessary prerequisite for a consistent education that permeates the instruction in a country's classrooms? If one wishes to widen the issue one can also ask : To what extent is a certain consistency between home and school to be sought, given the fact that disciplinary problems in the school, as shown in empirical studies, are related to value and norm discrepancies between home and school?

(3) Issues of shared values and inconsistencies between various education agents tend to become increasingly acute in modern societies, due to urbanization, migration, and international communication, which tend to bring together people of various backgrounds and expose them to values other than the ones they met during their upbringing.

School curricula in modern societies, particularly in the Western hemisphere, if they specify the teaching of any values at all, aim at promoting of modern pluralistic democratic vlaues often embodied in documents on basic human rights. Pluralism in terms of the right to hold another opinion and of tolerance and respect for other people's values is pronounced. However in the debate about pluralism, it is often underlined that this is more easily said than done. How far should tolerance be stretched vis-à-vis those who say that they are in favor of using violence and terror in promoting their political and /or socio-ethical goals?

In Sweden, for centuries until the late1900s, with a Lutheran state church, religious instruction in the schools was *in Christendom* (of the Lutheran Church brand) until school reforms starting in the middle of the 20th century. Even though other religions were also given some attention, religious instruction had a clear-cut goal in instilling certain religious values in all students. The 1962 major school reform called for the subject called "religion" to be taught in the elementary school along with history and social studies and the instruction is explicitly about Christendom as one of the many religious. Although according to the curricular guidelines teachers are not prohibited from expressing their own values, the overriding principle is pluralism. This has in some cases led to parents belonging to certain religious groups inside or outside the state church, claiming the right to set up private schools where their children are taught according to the religious values of the home.

The United States of America was populated predominantly by so-called WASPS, until the late 19th century, so they were the dominant class. From then on it started receiving an increasing number of immigrants from other parts of Europe. It was faced with the problem of establishing a common frame of reference of values, political and social if not always religious, in the new country, earlier than any other nation, with the exception of Australia. The task of achieving this was assigned to the American public common school, which since the late 19th century has been regarded as a cornerstone not only for American democracy but for American national identity as well. The ceremony with the Pledge of Allegiance was only one of the means used to forge the national identity. This process was, of course, facilitated by the fact that most immigrants who came to America in order to escape poverty, oppression and other social ills, regarded it as the land of promise. In the United States of today most of the immigrants are economic migrants from Latin America. In addition, there is a significant number from Asia, who have come as refugees. At the same time the U.S. has experienced the problem of a massive internal migration of Black people from the Southern states into the cities of the North, over the last few decades.

(4) In the name of pluralism and multiculturalism a movement towards emphasizing ethnic diversity began to gather momentum in the U.S. in the 1960s. One expression of this was the Federal legislation on bilingual education which provided instruction in their mother tongue for children who came from non-English-speaking homes. In states such as Florida and California, this meant instruction in both Spanish and English. In some school districts with an overwhelming majority of immigrants the language of instruction is entirely the mother tongue.

Thus, in contrast to the received philosophy that English should be learned as rapidly and effectively as possible and concomitantly that the mother tongue should be forgotten there were proponents of a *multicultural* approach in school education that not only affected the language of instruction but the content of the curriculum as well. The problem not only of multiculturalism, but also of bilingualism in school education has been challenged by various authors.

In Europe elementary schooling was made universal and compulsory by national legislation during the latter part of the 19th century. It was in most cases part of modern nation-building and an attempt to establish a uniform language in which the entire population was literate. It was also, in non-Catholic countries, a way for the state church to indoctrinate the students. But school education in Europe was class divisive. The elementary school was not a common one for all the citizens. The upper class sent their children to private schools, which prepared students for "public" (fee paying) secondary schools with traditions dating back to the Medieval Ages (grammar schools, lycées, gymnasia) which traditionally educated the elite for leadership. In the United States even though the secondary school was under local governance and drew its enrollment from a local catchment area, it was on the whole a comprehensive institution in terms of bringing children from all walks of life under the same roof and as time went by, it increased its course offerings to cover all kinds of practical competencies. In Europe secondary schools were by tradition entirely academic recruiting a small social and intellectual elite. The enrollment was socially very selective.

(5) The problem now facing Eastern European countries who are, or are intending, to become members of the European Union, is to what extent their – still national – curricula should, or could, be "harmonized" not only with respect to the syllabus in certain subject areas but with regard to goals as well. Given the common trade and labour market there are, of course, certain practical reasons for harmonizing the syllabuses in certain respects in order to make competencies attained in various countries more interchangeable. But what about the goals and the values embedded in these?

(6) Since the 1960s with the rapid growth of the economies in European countries, such as the Federal Republic of Germany and Sweden, and the need for labor, in particular in manufacturing industry and in unqualified service occupations, there has been a massive migration of labor from the Mediterranean area into Western and Northern Europe, a migration which has had an important impact on the educational systems of these countries. To give two examples: In West Berlin by the mid-1980s every fourth child born was of Turkish descent. In Sweden which until 1960 had very few school entrants who had not Swedish as their mother tongue, less than two decades later found that some 10–12 per cent of school entrants came from homes with a wide range of mother tongues other than Swedish.

(7) After World War I President Woodrow Wilson said that the collapse of the Ottoman and Austro-Hungarian Empires and the freedom gained by a large number of ethnic minorities would bring about political stabilization in post-war Europe. But there were others who expressed fear that the opposite would occur. In the Balkans, a new state, Yugoslavia, a geographical conglomerate of states such as Slovenia, Croatia and Serbia, but artificial from the point of view of ethnicity and religion, was created. The new Soviet

Union also became a conglomerate of a large number of ethnic and disparate language groups. Both countries were kept internally together by iron-hard totalitarian governments. But when the regimes collapsed ethnicity and historically rooted tensions erupted. At present, Europe is faced with the paradox of having on the one hand an ongoing integration of trade and labor markets as well as increased communication and migration between regions and countries, but one the other hand a new wave of ethnic claims — by one ethnic group after the other for political independence and self-determination.

(8) A similar tendency can be observed among peoples with different ethnic and language background living in other countries, in most cases as immigrant workers. In Germany they were for a long time conceived, and even defined, as "guest workers"(*Gastarbeiter*), in a similar way to Switzerland which has, for years, had a high proportion of workers migrating back and forth from Mediterranean area. However, in other countries, such as Sweden, legislation was passed that gave immigrant children the right to be instructed in their mother tongue for a certain number of class periods per week. At the same time legislative regulations have given the parents the right to a minimum number of hours of instruction in the tongue of the host country, during paid working time.

(9) In my view education in modern pluralistic societies, (nations) as compared to traditional societies are faced with *three fundamental questions* which are at the core of a debate about goals and values in school education:

1. *What common values*, if any, can constitute guidelines for teaching in the schools of modern society? Are there any universally valid, if not always accepted, values to which teachers can adhere? What kind of common core of such values can be identified? This question addresses what is basically a philosophical issue.

2. In nations, such as the United States of America but, more recently, several European nations as well, with a pluralistic approach with regard to the teaching of civics (social studies), how **can pluralism be achieved without** ending up in value relativism or confusion or both?

3. To what extent can what is taught in school, related to basic values, complement or *be compatible with the values taught at home*? There has been a strong "progressive" movement in modern pedagogy that the school should not only provide certain practical basic competencies, such as the "three Rs", but should also shoulder the role of "fostering" in a broader sense by instilling the basic values of a democratic society, such as cooperative and altruistic attitudes and tolerance. The home has, in a recent

publication from the Educational Testing Service (ETS), been called "America's Smallest School" (Princeton 1993). Can the school completely take over the role of upbringing *in loco parentis*, in spite of the fact that children are there for only some ten per cent of their time?

Conclusions

I do not pretend to have final answers to the questions raised. The reason for raising them is simply to indicate what the consequences for school education are in the wake of increased globalisation and multicultural personal contacts between various cultures and nations. The conflict between postmodern relativism and universalism has been intensified by these changes.

In 1967, I was involved both as an organizer and a few months later as a participant in an international conference to which President Lyndon Johnson, himself a former high school teacher, had invited some 150 educators from around the world. The theme of the meeting explicated in the background document prepared by the first Director of the International Institute for Educational Planning in Paris, Philip Coombs, was *World Crisis in Education* (1967). The main crisis was derived from the strong imbalance between supply and demand of formal education, particularly in the less developed countries. But there was also another imbalance, the one between curricula and the needs of the students. Driving this was, not surprisingly, the rapid changes taking place in the economies concerned.

The main problem that educators, not least school educators, will have to face during the century we have just entered is, as I have already hinted, how to combine cultural, social and, linguistic pluralism with the universalism which is the corner stone of international understanding, tolerance, and acceptance of people who live their lives otherwise than you and I do. We are also entering an era when equality and justice are becoming increasingly basic values. I hope that this conference will contribute at least preliminary answers to the questions I have raised.

I decline to try to indicate any roads to reforms, in the field we are going to deal with for the next couple of days. Suffice to say that there are no universal paradigms for conducting educational reforms. There are, however, a few universal rules. One of them is taking time. School and the content of its activities cannot be changed overnight. It is a slow moving institution lagging behind changes that take place in the socio-economic context at large.

References

Barton, P. & Coley, R. (1992). *America's smallest school: The family*. ETS Policy Information Report. Princeton, NJ: Educational Testing Service.

Beaton, A. E. et al. (1996). *Mathematics achievement in the middle school years: IEA's Third International Mathematics and Science Study* (TIMSS). Chestnut Hill, MA: TIMSS International Study Center, Boston College.

Coleman, J. S., & Husén, T. (1985). *Becoming adult in a changing society*. Paris: Organisation for Economic Co-operation and Development.

Coombs, P. (1967). *The world educational crisis: A systems analysis*. Assisted by the IIEP staff. Paris : International Institute for Educational Planning.

Gardner, D. P. et al. (1983). *A nation at risk: The imperative for educational reform*. A report to the Nation and the Secretary of Education. Washington, DC: The National Commission on Excellence in Education, United States Department of Education.

Husén, T. (1979). *The school in question: A comparative study of the school and its future in Western society*. Oxford, UK: Oxford University Press.

Husén, T. (1983). *An incurable academic: Memoirs of a professor*. (Tom Geddes, trans.). Oxford, UK: Pergamon.

Husén, T. (1986). *The learning society revisited: Essays*. Oxford, UK: Pergamon.

Husén, T. (1990). *Education and the global concern*. Oxford, UK: Pergamon.

Husén, T. (1994). The idea of the university: changing roles, current crisis and future challenges. In T. Husén (Ed.). *The role of the university: A global perspective*. Tokyo: Academic Division, United Nations University.

Husén, T. (1997). An agenda for the education of west world citizens. *Prospects*, *27* (2).

Husén, T. (2001). *Recurrent education and lifelong learning: Reflections of an old educational researcher*. Hong Kong: Hong Kong Institute of Education Research, The Chinese University of Hong Kong.

Husén, T., & Opper, S. (Eds.). (1983). *Multicultural and multilingual education in immigrant countries*. Proceedings of an international symposium held at the Wenner-Gren Center, Stockholm, August 2 and 3, 1982. Oxford, UK: Pergamon, 1983.

Husen, T., & Postlethwaite, T. N. (Eds.). (1985). *The international encyclopedia of education: Research and studies*. Oxford, UK: Pergamon.

Husén, T., & Postlethwaite, T. N. (Eds.). (1989). *The international encyclopedia of education: Research and studies. Supplementary volumes*. Oxford, UK: Pergamon.

Husén, T., & Postlethwaite, T. N. (Eds.). (1994). *The international encyclopedia of education*. 2nd ed. Oxford, UK: Pergamon.

Husén, T., Tuijnman, A., & Halls, W. D. (Eds.). (1992). *Schooling in modern European society: A report of the Academia Europaea*. Oxford, UK: Pergamon Press.

Tjeldvoll, A. (2000). *Torsten Husén: Conversations in comparative education*. Bloomington, IN: Phi Delta Kappa Educational Foundation.

United Nations. (1968). *Universal declaration of human rights*. New York: United Nations.

CHAPTER 3

Valuation, Evaluation, and Value Education — On Acquiring the Ability to Value: A Philosophical Perspective

May Mei-lin Ng

Abstract

Values Education, in a broad sense, is comprised of the teaching of values as they are involved in issues of various realms, which encompasses moral education, aesthetic education, civic education, spiritual education, and so forth. In contrast, value education is proposed to be an education that puts aside for the time being the question of diversity in values and focuses mainly on the cultivation of the general ability of valuing. In this paper, we offer a philosophical analysis of value judgment, seeing the act of valuing as a two-level mental acitivity: non-reflective identification of values as valuation (or valuating) and deliberative judgment of values as evaluation (or evaluating). We criticize the emotivist doctrine of value judgment as unable to get away with the Humean reason/passion dichotomy. We seek to expound a more fruitful understanding of emotion—a conception of emotion that does not preclude reasonableness. With such understanding, we try to show the possibility and necessity of educating our emotion so as to enrich our capacity of valuation and enhance our ability of evaluation. In conclusion, we put forward the thesis that a viable form of value education should be one grounded in education of emotion.

Introduction

Values education, in a broad sense, is comprised of the teaching of values[1] as they are involved in issues in various realms, which encompasses moral education, aesthetic education, civic education, spiritual education, and so forth. Though inescapably fuzzy, the classification points to key aspects of human concern such as morality, beauty and divinity. The experiential content as well as the criteria of judgment varies accordingly with emphases put on different concerns.

In contrast, values education is proposed to be an education that puts aside the question of diversity in values and focuses mainly on the cultivation of the general ability of valuing. It is assumed that amid the different kinds of value judgment we make in life, there exists an underlying ability that characterizes this spectrum of mental activities, namely, the ability to value. We believe that in promoting values education (of any kind), the acquisition of the ability to value should be put at the top of our aims. Since we are now in a pluralistic age devoted to diversity and tolerance of differences, it is no longer acceptable just to pass down the values of our cultural tradition. More importantly, we are obliged to empower the young to judge between diverging values, to adopt some and to develop others on their own, enabling them to live peacefully with people of widely different attitudes. In order to achieve this, it is essential for them to be brought up to become capable and reliable "valuers." In this sense, "Values Education" is understood not as a particular values education programme, but as a signpost to an education of value.

In the following sections, we start from a critique of emotivism as a mistaken thesis on the nature of value judgment and seek to analyse the act of valuing as a two-level mental activity: non-reflexive acceptance of values as valuation (or valuating) and deliberative judgment of values as evaluation (or evaluating). On both levels, we believe that emotion plays a central role. The purpose of our analysis is two-fold: on the one hand, it proposes to break the cultural "spell" of emotivism; on the other hand, it points to the possibility of a theory of value which accounts for the objectivity of value and the reasonableness of value judgment — both of which need to be accounted for before values education can be understood in the fullest and clearest sense. We are going to examine the close relationship between emotion and value, and see how it can be understood beyond the Humean conception of the mind. With such understanding, we try to show that it is both possible and necessary to educate our emotion in order to enrich our capacity, and enhance our ability, of evaluation.

Emotivism and Value Judgment

The general position held by the so-called emotivists[2] can be summarized in the following sentence by MacIntyre (1985):

> Emotivism is the doctrine that all evaluative judgments and more specifically all moral judgments are *nothing but* expressions of preference, expressions of attitude or feeling, insofar as they are moral or evaluative in character. (p. 12)

Thus, value judgments are reduced to psychological operations which are non-rational in nature, and disagreements on values are destined to be unsettlable: there exists no observable qualitative difference between values, but only discrepancies between expressed attitudes (Ayer, 1946/1990, p. 104; Stevenson, 1944, pp. 4–5). Therefore, a particular attitude can never be derived from a factual belief, even though there is a possibility for the factual belief to cause a change in attitude — this is what Stevenson means — by "justifying" an evaluative conclusion (Stevenson, 1963, p. 86). For Ayer, who renders value judgments as cognitively meaningless (Ayer, 1946/1990, chap. 6), there is only a difference in tone between saying "I dislike premarital sex" and "premarital sex is wrong."

Our distrust in such a philosophical doctrine is based on many reasons, some of which we state briefly here. First, in regarding the psychological causation between a factual belief and an attitude as the way to justify a value judgment, Stevenson has misread the reason-giving force as a kind of psychological conditioning processes. Instead, the force of a reason comes from its ruling: a reason typically offers us a norm (or a standard), if established, for accepting or rejecting a claim. It assumes freedom in action — to accept or to reject — that goes beyond accustomed or conditioned psychological responses, and an agreement, hidden or not, on the authority of the rule. Therefore, justifications of value judgment should not be put merely in *de facto* terms: even when we think that a simple fact is enough as a justifying reason, we still need to refer to the reasonableness of the norm, not the fact alone to establish our claim.[3]

Second, the emotivists have assumed a peculiar demarcation of fact/value which, according to Putnam (1981), suggests that "fact and value are totally disjoint realms, that the dichotomy 'statement of fact *or* value judgment' is an absolute one." (p. 127). Such a stance involves on the one hand a linguistic misconception and on the other a mistaken ontological commitment. Emotivists have commonly confused the difference between the meaning and the use of an expression. As Putnam (1981) puts it:

> [O]ne of the many distinctions which have got ten confused together under the general heading 'fact value distinction' is the distinction between using a linguistic expression to describe and using that linguistic expression to praise

> or blame. But this distinction is not a distinction which can be drawn on the basis of vocabulary. (p. 138)

A typical description of a fact, for example, "It is raining," can be used as an excuse for not going out with a friend, or an imperative telling a child not to go out. Similarly, evaluative vocabularies, for example, "lazy," "kind," "courageous," and so forth, can be used in non-evaluative ways, for example, "I bet her kindness will sooner or later bring her to bankruptcy." Emotivists seem to have relied too simple-mindedly on the meaning of some evaluative terms in order to distinguish evaluative uses (emotive meaning) from descriptive uses (cognitive meaning) of our language. Underlying this distinction, there exists a sharp and easily demarcated contrast between facts and values: "Facts" consist of perspective-free and value-free representations of the world, they are objective and mind-independent existence (cf. Taylor, 1989, pp. 22–23; Putnam, 1981, p. 128; Nagel, 1986, p. 7); "values," in contrast, are clusters of un-rational[4] personal avowals expressing only particular emotional states contingently related to factual beliefs. Such naturalistic ontology has discarded values as pseudo-existence and thus has dismissed disagreements on values as rationally irreconcilable. However, as Putnam points out, "the [fact-value] distinction is at the very least hopelessly fuzzy because factual statements themselves, and the practices of scientific inquiry upon which we rely to decide what is and what is not a fact, presuppose values" (Putnam, 1981, p. 128). If we recognize that a transparent self is impossible not only in value judgments but also in factual judgments, we may be able to see that the supposed disparity between facts and values and the discriminations that follow, namely, objective versus subjective, rational versus un-rational, and cognition versus emotion, should all be dropped.[5]

A related point against seeing a value judgment as defined in terms of its emotive meaning is indicated by Wiggins (1987):

> [T]he whole idea of an emotive meaning reckoned separately from cognitive content does insufficient justice to our feeling that divergence of attitude *must itself be founded in something*, and reflect on *a prior or coeval disagreement in something not itself reducible without residue* to emotive attitude. (p. 186; my italics)

Following the emotivist doctrine, the choice between, say, counting people passing by one's door and running an orphanage as the aim of one's life involves no substantial comparison between values, only that the one is more approved than the other. Thus, the value element of a judgment should be understood as reducible to an emotion, other than this, there cannot be any substantial talk about value. Perhaps this is the problem. For instance, when we say "Tom is a good person, he shows compassion to everybody," compassion is the immediate virtue (personal quality) that we refer to Tom when we express our appreciation towards him. Should compassion be further broken down to acts of "helping" and our approval of them, or still further, acts constituting "helping" and our approval ...? Such reductive analysis seems to have missed the point of the original speech — that Tom has in himself some quality that is worth a praise.

Often, when we approve an action or an object, we believe that there is some quality of worthiness (or value) inherent in that particular action or object that is referred to. What is more, in our explicit value vocabularies (terms used frequently in value judgments), there exist comparable levels of qualitative differences like "good/better/best" and also substantial qualitative differences like "generous versus mean." The meanings of these value contents, being rich in depicting qualitative differences, would be lost if a value judgment has got to be analyzed in the emotivist's way.

With the above arguments stated, we may agree, as many philosophers do, that emotivism is vulnerable as a philosophical doctrine (e.g., MacIntyre, 1985, p. 13; Putnam, 1981, p. 127). So why are we so compelled to try and get away with it? It is because even though emotivism is not powerful in its theoretical standing, it is powerful as a cultural force. As MacIntyre (1985) puts it:

> [T]o a large degree people now think, talk and act as if emotivism were true, no matter what their avowed theoretical standpoint may be. Emotivism has become embodied in our culture.... [I]f this is so we ought presumably to discover that a wide variety of our concepts and modes of behavior — and not only our explicitly moral debates and judgments presuppose the truth of emotivism, if not at the level of self-conscious theorizing, at least in everyday practice. (p. 22)

Such cultural embodiment is often manifested in daily conversations, like "I do what I want, how dare you interfere in my decision!" or "Values are subjective, we'd better hold back our comments." It seems as if value judgments, owing to their relationship with our emotions, are private psychological happenings that would fall short of any discussions or objective identification.

In the field of education, the emotivist atmosphere lingers. As Aspin (1999) illustrates, talks about values education are often rebuffed by the blunt question "Whose values?":

> By this question ... people are endeavouring to demonstrate that values are individual, subjective, irreconcilably different, and in no way congruent, such that, on any matter of policy or practice, absolute differences of view are the norm and that therefore the only way of resolving differences in such matters is to have recourse to power of some kind. (p. 132)

Undesirable as the consequence may appear, the phenomenon points to a belief not uncommon among educators: In principle or in practice, differences in values cannot be resolved but deserted. Why? Since "values are individual, subjective, irreconcilably different, and in no way congruent," any one value can be claimed to be as good as any other. In short, values are relative to individuals. The result, in its best phrasing, is a knowledge-centred curriculum and a value-neutral classroom. Even for those advocates of values education, such skepticism on values has made an impact, bringing about the two dominant approaches in values education — the relativistic values clarifications approach and the formalistic cognitive-developmental approach[6] — both regard values as too personal to be the foundation of values education and both avoid substantial value claims in order to remain rationally justifiable and universally applicable.

It seems that if the emotivist culture prevails, there would not be much room for values education to progress, theoretically as well as practically speaking. Therefore, it is necessary for educators to go away from such emotivist mode of thinking. In the following, we try to put forward an alternative philosophical account of valuing that may escape the emotivist trap and its shortcomings.

Valuation and Evaluation

No matter how much we distrust emotivism (as an account of the nature of value judgment), we must admit that the emotivists have come to recognize that value judgments cannot be reduced to statements of fact, that in voicing out a value judgment we are at the same time taking sides. This shows the irreducible subjectivity expressed in a value judgment — our attitude is disclosed by it — no matter whether we are aware of it or not. The problem, however, is that in putting forward a distinction of cognitive and emotive meaning (as the persuasive psychological force), the emotivists have, following Hume's steps (cf. Hume, 1888/1978, p. 415), reified the dichotomy of Reason and Emotion in a radical way: Our emotions cannot but be justified by factual beliefs which can ultimately be proved in the scientific way; for cognition, in the positivistic sense, is the sovereign of Reason. To them, deducing this element from value judgments will leave only pure subjectivity (i.e., arbitrariness) in view.

This might well not be true. As Putnam (1981) states, "Today we tend to be too realistic about physics and too subjectivistic about ethics, and these are connected tendencies" (p. 143). The advances in science seem to have handicapped not only our conception of rationality, but also our self-understanding. Paying awful respect to science, we tend to discard other ways of knowing as not objective enough (and so unreliable) — in our concern for the judgmental power of our emotion — and have in this way impoverished the meaning of "knowing" to a large extent. On the contrary, we believe that "emotions are primitive judgments of value"[7] (Kerner, 1982, p. 52). In the following, we shall expound our position with the help of Kerner's philosophical arguments.

In saying that emotions entail value judgments, we first need to distinguish between emotion as feeling and emotion as attitude: a feeling is lived through, an attitude avowed; a feeling can be intense or moderate, but an attitude can but be resolute or unsure; we may indulge in a feeling, but be committed to an attitude. Attitudes and feelings belong to two different levels of mental act: one coined by Kerner as "ideificating," and the other "judging" (Kerner, 1982, pp. 52–53). Ideificating refers to rather involuntary acts of our consciousness, as when one is absorbed in the imagery of a poetry, or when an idea flashes across one's mind. As we pay attention to, or are aware of, an object of consciousness, we are ideificating. Judging, in contrast, involves claims reflectively laid on certain states of affairs, which imply ontological commitments — as factual judgments point to physical existence, value judgments point to the existence of values.

According to the above explication, we may distinguish "feeling" and "emotion" in the following way:

> In the non-judgmental sense of emotion, an experience — the feeling of an emotion — is merely consummated or lived through … [E]motion, in contrast to a mere feeling, … it seeks to grasp objective value. As such, as emotion constitutes an assessment or appraisal, and it entails that its objects or content really possesses a certain objective value. (Kerner, 1970, p. 183)

> Sentiments and attitudes … are not contents of our consciousness, although they themselves possess contents or objects. Feelings of emotion…, on the other hand, themselves constitute such contents. (Kerner, 1970, p. 184)

While a feeling, as ideification, provides the content for our attitude to perform as a value judgment, an attitude gives an appraisal, through our feelings, to a state of affairs. For example, when we are indignant, we feel outraged because we believe that someone has done something unjust or ungrateful to others. We may at times feel sad about the victims, feel annoyed about the situation, or feel angry of the doer. These feelings all contribute to forming our indignant attitude towards the state of affairs. Besides, we believe that we are justified in upholding such an emotion because something of disvalue has happened, I can tell from the discernment of my emotion, just like I can distinguish between a blue ball and a green one with my eyes. Emotionality is our bestowed ability to grasp the meaning and the actuality of values.

Hence, we may state that:

(1) on the ideification level, we experience the richness and vividness of values from various kinds of feelings — we feel contented with achievements, we feel miserable about mishaps, we feel excited about good news, we feel disappointed with dishonest friends — these experiences we have been living through in our daily lives inform us of the content of values, they teach us how to "valuate," that is, to ascribe values to possible objects of consciousness and to identify their substance;

(2) on the judgment level, our attitude is interpretative of our feelings, and as such it lays value claims to certain states of affairs; in short, we "evaluate," that is, to assess if certain values are actualized in an action or present in a situation.

Our feelings let us savor the quality of values so that in evaluations we know how to attribute them to certain states of affairs; the richer our feelings are, the more discriminative our discernment could become. In this way, our sensitivity contributes to our capacity in valuating. For instance, the sorrow for the death of a dear friend could be discriminated from the unhappiness at the loss of a favourite book. The first designates the value of friendship and the latter designates, perhaps, the value of artifacts. Our attitudes, on the other hand, give rather definite meanings to our feelings so that they can be sustained and deepened. Reflection and the will also help with shaping and upholding our attitudes.[8] Unlike feelings, the avowal of an attitude is a more autonomous act: Even though we cannot nullify our feelings, we can revise our attitude. This is why it is possible for our emotion to hold claims of reason and appropriateness. We can, and more importantly, we should, be responsible for our own emotions.

Up till now, two lines of doubt can be expected: First, it seems true that we are often confused or even misled by our emotions, how is it possible for them to perform a reliable discernment of values? Second, as everyone has his own emotional buildup, are we going to say that values are relative to individuals and there can be no agreement between them except through psychological persuasion and coercion?

Both of these questions need to be addressed if we want to argue against the view that having an emotion is nothing more than being possessed by an emotional impulse. Thus far we have pointed out that emotions can actually speak to situations and require appropriateness. We will now further our argument and elaborate on the claim that we may share an emotion (attitude) reasonably, instead of just following the herd. Let us first take a closer look at the two questions. Underlying the first question is a distrust in our emotionality due to instances of unstable feelings. But it is not reasonable to discard all feelings as uncontrollable impulses when just a few of them, perhaps owing to their links to our natural instincts, are drives falling short of reasoning. What is more, even instinctual feelings are often "programmed" into protective mechanisms and serve as the basic reference of our more cultivated values. For example, fear arises when we sense the coming of a danger. Very often, we are not able to discard the feeling, but we can choose how to handle it — to flee or to fight. Without fear we cannot fully understand either the significance of danger or the value of courage and equanimity.

Sometimes we are perplexed by our feelings and do not know how to react and what to do. In these moments, feelings are often informative rather than misleading for in many of these cases, the situation we face is really complicated and difficult to handle because of the clashes or tensions between different values we deem vital. We cannot come to any responsible resolution without paying substantial attention to our feelings and learning from them the value discordance we encounter. Besides, if we can illustrate how emotions can be appropriate and reasonable, the first query can be set aside; for in an analogous way, we would certainly not doubt the reasoning power of our rationality even though there exist moments when we use ill-supported reasons. As we elaborate on the reasonableness of emotion, we will be able to give an answer to the second doubt by showing how an agreement makes it possible for our attitudes to be reached without coercion.

Emotional discernment can be understood comparatively with the way our sense perception works, in the way Kerner (1970) puts it:

> Sense perceptions are related to external reality, and in expressing them we claim certain states of affairs to be actual. If a certain state of affairs is not actual, we have made a mistake in our sense perception. Our passions, on the other hand, do not reveal external reality. They reveal values. In putting our passions into words, we claim certain states of affairs to be desirable or undesirable, good or bad. If a certain state of affairs does not really possess a certain value, again, we have made a mistake. (p. 181)

As one may mistakenly identify someone else across the road as one's father, one may misjudge a value. So at times we find ourselves mad at an innocent friend without reason, or become fearful without cause. These incidents illustrate that we can "go wrong" with our attitudes because the values we supposed to be there may turn out to be based on mistakes. Thus, if we are not mistaken in paying attention to our attitude, we are able to tell if a value is present in a certain state of affairs. For example, if in expressing our sympathy to a friend we refer to his failure in an important examination (a disvalue) and it turned out that this friend had actually passed the examination, then our sympathy would be, let's say, misplaced. Nonetheless, such a misplacement of judgment does not negate the appropriateness of our sympathy towards failure — this is important because we must make it clear that the misplacement of our value judgment would not disqualify the valuation involved as inappropriate. This is similar to mistakenly taking a mannequin to be a real person. We certainly will not distrust our vision due to such an erred incidence, so why adopt such an attitude with our sympathetic discernment. Therefore, we may say, as perception may constitute our factual judgment, emotion may constitute our value judgment.

We may conclude from the above that:

(1) on the level of valuation, there are degrees of appropriateness with regard to the ascribed value-object. In fact, much of our vocabulary of emotion entails specific values, such as remorse, envy, sympathy, pride, shame, etc. It possesses definite depiction of the objects of appraisal;

(2) on the level of evaluation, the validity of the judgment inherent in the emotions depends on whether the value claims involved are trustworthy or not.

But how can the value claims be trustworthy? For Kerner, apart from the evidential quality present in the evaluated state of affairs, there are requirements upon ourselves: we need to be competent valuers. For a value judgment to be valid, Kerner (1966) writes:

> I must first show that the object of my approval possesses certain characteristics and therefore meets certain standards; second, I must show that certain things hold true of myself by virtue of which I am in a good position to issue the endorsement, that is, that I possess the appropriate competence and have exercised a due amount of care and acumen. (p. 206)

The first condition can be fulfilled *prima facie* by the presence of a certain quality in a particular value-object. If there is disagreement on whether the quality is present, the defender should elaborate on the existing characteristics that are attributed to the value. If there is disagreement on the worthiness of the quality, however, further elaboration should be carried out on the standard (or system of standards) from which the value is justified and through which it obtains richer meaning. For example, members of the Chinese community may tell just from an act (or even a gesture) that one has (or has not) filial respect (孝順) for the parent, which may not be as apparent to a Westerner. If queried, it may be explained by referring to the Chinese espousal of filial piety (孝道) which implies both juniors' respect towards seniors (敬) and seniors' nurturing kindness (慈) towards juniors. These values have been developed from a long tradition of close family ties in the Chinese community and are deeply felt and recognized by its members. They have become the standards upon which we rely to make value judgments. If we investigate still further, we would be able to see the cultural significance of interpersonal relationships (人倫) to the Chinese community (apart from their social functions), which offers an even fuller picture of how and why an obedient action is approved in a Chinese family.

If we say the first condition discussed above represents a requirement of objectivity of valuing, the second one may be considered as a requirement of subjectivity of valuing. For it is concerned not with the criteria of values, but with the authority of the valuer instead. As a competent perceiver must have good eye-sight, a great sense of depth, and so forth, a capable valuer has got to be sensitive, delicate, open-minded, or experienced, and so forth, in order to be able to discern values from our feelings and attitudes, which sometimes are very subtle and intricate. In short, one has got to be "in a good position to issue the endorsement." To get back to the example above, being members of the Chinese community gives (partial) weight to our appraisal of an obedient action. Further confidence can be gained if, for instance, we can show that we have been attentive to the features of the action, or we can tell how a filial act is discriminated from, say, one of loyalty or compliance, as well as using our past experience.

How can we acquire these personal qualities? We believe that experience plays an important role in our learning to become qualified valuers who are capable of feeling and judging.[9] As Dunn (1993) elaborates, from an Aristotelian perspective, it is only through experience that our discernment power got enriched and refined:

> It is, we might say, the insightfulness — or, using Aristotle's own metaphor, "the eye" — of a particular type of experience, and the insights it achieves are turned back into experience, which is in this way constantly reconstructed or enriched. And the more experience is reconstructed in this way, the more sensitive and insightful phronesis [i.e., practical wisdom] becomes[.] (p. 293)

This may be illustrated by our own experience — until we *grow* older (more experienced) — and thus become more apt at distinguishing the precious from the worthless, we don't understand how unwise we had been in making past decisions. Such power to discern has come to us and is constantly reconstructing through our participation and observation in our cultural environment, which is the seedbed for cultivating our emotion.

In light of this, we may be able to see how it is impossible for the values to have been "invented" out of nothing but our isolated subjectivity, as is often implied by value subjectivism (including emotivism). As Ricoeur (1974) insightfully reminds us:

> [W]e are always already preceded by evaluations beginning from which even our doubt and our contestation become possible. We can perhaps 'transvaluate' values, but we can never create them beginning from zero. The passage through tradition has no other justification than this antecedence of the ethical world with regard to every ethical subject. (p. 268)

In the realm of values, perhaps, the reality is constituted by our cultural world, where different attitudes have been, and still are, undergoing processes of convergence and divergence This constituted and yet constituting world is essential in providing a ground for our body of "intersubjectively validated knowledge of values" (cf. Marietta, 1997, p. 27) to take shape and develop.

Of course, disagreements in attitudes arise from time to time. Yet this fact does not prove that emotions are arbitrary and values irreconcilable. We must understand that an agreement cannot be thoughtlessly given nor guaranteed, it can only be reached in conversations or other forms of exchange and interaction. Regulated by the requirements of objectivity and subjectivity of value, it seems possible that an agreement can be reached without recourse to sophisticated psychological tactics or mightiness in political power:

> In convincing you I was not just bringing to bear psychological pressure designed to change your feelings through causal influence, I was asking you to reconsider. I allowed you to look at the matter in a different light, to get your proper bearings. (Kerner, 1970, p. 184)

When we try to convince others to revise their attitude, we ask them to reconsider. A reconsideration of an attitude espoused involves not only a change in our feelings, which offer only the content of our judgment, it is an attempt to revise one's vision — sometimes as clearer, sometimes as wiser, and sometimes as more comprehensive — in the light of alternative points of view. This is done primarily through enriching and broadening our feelings and deepening our attitudes so that we can understand and so accommodate diverging attitudes in an empathetic way. It is, of course, true that not all disagreements in attitude can be resolved. Sometimes they are dissolved (because of our agreement in other attitudes), other times they are just tolerated. All of these ways-out are possible only because we are bestowed with emotionality — the ability to feel and to hold on to some attitudes while deserting others, which needs to be cultivated on the way to maturity.

Emotion and Value Education

We may now be willing to acknowledge that many of our emotions imply an understanding of the value of a state of affairs, or of its significance, or of how it matters to us. In Taylor's words (1985), it is the way we gain access to values in the world:

> [I]f a feeling is our mode of access, the feelings are import-attributing. They incorporate a certain understanding of our predicament, and of the imports it bears. Thus we can feel entitled to say on the strength of certain feelings, or inferences from what we sense through certain feelings, that we know that X is right, or good, or worthy, or valuable; and this even when other feelings and reactions fail to concur, or even have an opposing purport! 'I know that X but I feel that Y' does not oppose knowing to feeling, but rather reflects our conviction that what we sense through certain feelings is valid or adequate, while it devalues others as shallow, blind, distorting or perverse. (p. 63)

An emotion can be ill-founded, only when there is a possibility for it not to be ill-founded. In order to acquire the ability to discriminate between these two conditions and to understand the message the emotions try to convey to us, cultivation of emotion is indispensable. As Kerner (1970) states, "Cognitive advance in ethics would ... have to depend not on the refinement of an impersonal discipline or method but on the education of our passions" (p. 192). To give it a broader meaning: Cognitive advance in values in different cultural realms would depend on the education of our emotionality. For it is through our emotions that we can gain access to values: the richer our feelings become, the wider range of values we can understand; the deeper and wider our attitudes reach, the more profound our value judgments can be.

Therefore, if we believe that more effort should be applied to develop values education, it seems as important to develop value education, which, with its core at education of emotion, aims at enhancing our ability to value — on both valuation and evaluation levels. Such educational efforts seem even more urgent, if we consider how intellectualism and instrumentalism have joined forces in shaping today's educational trends,[10] in a way that weakens rather than strengthens both our capacity to feel and our ability to judge.

After our brief exposition on the relationship between value judgment and emotion, we propose that an experiential approach of value education (that puts emphasis on developing the judgmental power of value of our youth) should be undertaken by values educators, since one cannot but live through one's own feelings. As Marietta (1997) suggests:

> Experience can teach us much about values. Personal experience helps us check the fittingness of our values with the actualities of life. A rich intersubjectivity allows us to learn from our contemporaries, and a knowledge of other cultures and of people's lives in the past gives us perspective on our values. (p. 26)

This suggests that value education can be carried out in three dimensions: personal and social, as well as culturo-historical. In each dimension, aspects of subjectivity and objectivity (founded in established intersubjectivity) should both be taken care of. We should broaden learners' perspectives by expanding their experience in these three dimensions so that they can "experiment" with their judgmental power of values through attempts in valuating and evaluating. In so doing, they can come to grip not only with their feelings, but also with their attitudes towards different cultures and their values. This is crucial to their value cultivation and character formation.

One may challenge any claim that the three dimensions of value education are already taken care of by the existing curriculum's inclusion of subjects such as Ethics, Social Studies, History, and so forth, so efforts at defending such a position seems superfluous. The contrary, however, seems to be true. On the one hand, the presence of certain subjects does not automatically serve the purpose of what is called for in value education — the cultivation of emotion as the way to become a qualified valuer. There are criteria beyond the existing curriculum that are crucial for assessing the achievements of value education, such as how empathetic the students have become, how well they handle the value decisions in their lives, how their self-understanding has advanced, and so forth. All of these are barely taken care of by the existing subjects fitted to the exam-oriented curriculum. On the other hand, the curriculum offers only a framework to work in, not a vision to work with. What should concern us more is the orientation towards the teaching and learning of the subjects as reflected by the curriculum. The curriculum can become the major obstacle to, instead of the platform for value education, if it is designed merely to categorize the students. Unfortunately, this seems to be what is now happening in our education system.

We therefore deem it necessary to urge for a new experiential approach to value education focusing on: (1) cultivation of emotion; (2) understanding of and later reflection on the cherished cultural values in various areas; (3) mastery of the use of our evaluative language. First, through cultivation of emotion, we aim at fostering the potential judgmental power of the learners so that they learn to love the lovable and admire the admirable. This is done through giving the learners chances to feel and to become aware of their emotions, enhancing their sensitivity and responsiveness, letting them acquire the various virtues of a responsible host of emotions, and so forth, so that they can open their hearts to values without fear and disorientation. Secondly, through immersion into our (as well as others') cultural values, we can offer an intelligible environment for the learners to "wander around" in the world of values, such as cultural achievements, historical moments of significance, traditional customs and rites, and so forth, through which the learners can have a way to appreciate the values of their culture. Since, as mentioned before, the cultural environment is the ground from which we can develop our own values. Apart from that, the teachers themselves would become a key educational medium; for they can demonstrate to the learners how values can be actualized by particular persons — they are the immediate persons who set examples to the learners — whether good or bad, by interacting and conversing with them. These experiences are often crucial to how the learners form and reform their own values. Thirdly, through mastering an evaluative language, the learners can acquire a medium of expression and reflection that enables them to come to grips with their feelings and attitudes. Ultimately the learners should be encouraged to explore and create their own personalized language of appraisal, which also performs as an indicator of autonomy in value judgment.

Though they are sketchy, we have thus far pinpointed the three aims that offer us a clue to the ways the learners can be educated to become capable valuers. They point to the direction in which values education should progress — if *how* to become a qualified valuer is taken to be the central concern of any form of values education.

A final statement. In opening our discussion on value judgment and putting forward a concept of value education, it is hoped that we have done more than just offer a justification for an alternative way of undertaking values education. The impact of such debate can be more far-reaching if the discussion kindles our own reflection, as valuers ourselves, upon the values of education: Why does education matter to us? What significance does schooling have with respect to our whole life? If we search for the answers, we will be engaged at the same time in an exercise of our judgmental power of value (that reveals our attitude towards education) and looking at a subtle yet often neglected question concerned with human well-being (which is well worth contemplating).

References

Aspin, D. N. (1999). The nature of values and their place and promotion in schemes of values education. *Educational Philosophy and Theory*, *31*(2), 123–143.

Ayer, A. J. (1990). *Language, truth, and logic*. London: Penguin. (Original work published 1946)

Dunn, J. (1993). Back to the rough ground: "Phronesis" and "Techne" in modern philosophy and in Aristotle. London: Notre Dame.

Fowler, J. W. (1992). Character, conscience, and the education of the public. In F. C. Power & D. K. Lapsley (Eds.), *The challenge of pluralism: Education, politics, and values*. Notre Dame, IL.: University of Notre Dame Press.

Hume, D. (1978). *A treatise of human nature* (L. A. Selby-Bigge & P. H. Nidditch, Eds.). Oxford, UK: Clarendon Press. (Original work published 1888)

Kerner, G. C. (1962). Approvals, reasons and moral argument. *Mind*, *71*(284), 474–486.

Kerner, G. C. (1966). *The revolution in ethical theory*. Oxford, UK: Oxford University Press.

Kerner, G. C. (1970). Passions and the cognitive foundation of ethics. *Philosophy and Phenomenological Research, 31*(2), 177–192.
Kerner, G. C. (1982). Emotions are judgments of value. *Topoi, 1*, 52–56.
MacIntyre, A. (1985). *After virtue: A study in moral theory*. London: Duckworth.
Marietta, D. E., Jr. (1997). The concept of objective value. In J. G. Hart & L. Embree (Eds.), *Phenomenology of Values and Valuing*. Dordrecht, the Netherlands: Kluwer Academic Publishers.
Nagel, T. (1986). *The view from nowhere*. Oxford, UK: Oxford University Press.
Putnam, H. (1981). *Reason, truth and history*. Cambridge, UK: Cambridge University Press.
Ricoeur, P. (1974). *Political and social essay* (D. Stewart & J. Bien, Eds.). Athens, Greece: Ohio University Press.
Stevenson, C. L. (1944). *Ethics and language*. New Haven, CT: Yale University Press.
Stevenson, C. L. (1963). *Facts and values*. New Haven, CT: Yale University Press.
Taylor, C. (1985). *Human agency and language: Philosophical Papers 1*. Cambridge, UK: Cambridge University Press.
Wiggins, D. (1987). *Needs, values, truth: Essays in the philosophy of value*. Oxford, UK: Basil Blackwell.

Notes

1. Two statements need to be explained, one concerning "teaching" of values and the other "values." "Teaching" here is understood in the broadest sense, referring to the educational activities in which learners learn and grow. The teacher does not necessarily perform as a coach or instructor, but inevitably becomes the model from which the learners learn. In order to keep the discussion in focus, it is assumed that when talking about "values" we exclude instrumental values and functional values, which are extrinsic kinds of value, that is, their value rests on their efficacy in bringing about the end or purpose circumscribed.
2. Examples are Ayer (1946/1990) and Stevenson (1944).
3. Such as the fact that "there was a traffic jam caused by an accident" can be an excuse for my being late only when the traffic jam was caused by an unexpected accident but not a daily happening; for otherwise I should have taken it into consideration. Unpredictable occurrences, in similar situations, establish a norm for excused lateness.
4. I have chosen to use "un" instead of "non" nor "ir" here as the negative prefix; for while "irrational" is too strong (it seems to imply insanity) in meaning, "non-rational" would be too weak (it may include what is meant by "trans-rational").
5. It does not follow that all demarcations must be dropped. Instead, the meaning of the demarcations should be modified under a new conceptual framework that is fair to the complicated relationship between "fact" and "value."

6. See Fowler, 1992, p. 231.
7. "Primitive" in the senses that our judgmental power of value originates from our emotionality and that our emotions are in need of cultivation in order to form mature judgments.
8. We reject the departmentalized view of the mind dividing it into separate faculties. Instead, we believe that we should adopt a more integrated view of the mind as an agent acting with its bestowed abilities in a coordinated way.
9. Detailed discussions on this point can be found in Dunn (1993, Chap. 9).
10. We only need to look at the dark sides of professionalism and globalization to see the capitalist shadow shed on education.

CHAPTER 4

Knowledge of the Value of Knowledge and Values Education: A Redundancy?

Maria Andrelita Cenzon

Abstract

Contemporary educational experience shows that knowledge transmission and acquisition are influenced by some underlying theory of knowledge (epistemology) which has somehow been preferred according to criteria extrinsic to the value of knowledge itself, such as economic utility, personal satisfaction, and professional relevance, and so forth (Degenhardt, 1982). Furthermore, the transmission and acquisition of subject knowledge, inclusive of values, is driven by the educator's and learner's ethos. This points to two things: On the one hand, knowledge is acquired or applied for a specific value or good (objective value). On the other hand, that value of knowledge is perceived by a person-subject (subjective value). The paper explores these dimensions in knowledge itself and in scientific and historical knowledge in particular, for their relevance to 21st century citizens. The objective value of science lies in the rigor of its methodology and the process of inter-subjective discourse. Its subjective value is found in the ethos of the scientist, the pre-scientific motivations and reasons for which he engages in scientific activity. The objective value of history is seen in accurate gathering of historical records. Its subjective value is found in the historian's attempt to interpret and understand these accounts. Both objective and subjective values of scientific and historical thinking can be made relevant to values education, in particular to citizenship values. It is the aim of the paper to suggest that any attempt to educate in values can beneficially include the education in the knowledge of the values of knowledge(s). The latter expression is an intended redundancy because valuing knowledge (axiology) is dependent on an epistemology (knowing what and how to value knowledge). This idea is discussed attentively for the areas of science and history. The paper claims that scientific and historical knowledge, both in their objective and subjective dimensions, have epistemic values that are relevant to education in citizenship. It also maintains that it is not possible to posit a radical dichotomy between objective and subjective dimensions of value and knowledge, knowledge and values, knowing and valuing as acts of the person. Knowing is a value understood as a good. Valuing is a form of knowing. The paper reiterates the idea that knowledge is required by valuing since the latter occurs with an assumption that an epistemic merit exists in a particular knowledge that is desirable. But precisely because there is no necessary loss of cognition in this process, valuing becomes itself a form of knowing where cognition meshes with volition and affectivity. The simultaneity of the three components of cognition, volition, and affectivity makes valuing integrative. This also implies that valuing requires, in addition to cognition, an experience of a good as desired by the will and the emotions. In this light, the paper also holds that valuing cannot be oversimplified to any of three components. Thus, apart from the epistemic aspect, valuing includes anthropological and ethical roots.

What is education for? Businessmen expect graduates to be productive and be citizens of integrity in the presence of dishonesty. Governments expect competent and ethical scientists to prevent future bio-chemical terrorism and curb unethical cyber practices. Society wants citizens to know their national heritage and history for them to appreciate its present state of affairs and its future direction. These all show a common expectation: education is an important locus where knowledge and values are learned, acquired, and initially used by citizens (students). We cannot dissociate, therefore, education from two distinguishable but inter-dependent concepts: knowledge and values.

The 21st century prides itself on being rich in knowledge but it is also confounded with societal ills rooted in selfish individualism that results in the absence of ethical and civic values, such as solidarity and compassion for the marginalized (defenseless unborn, the terminally ill, the unemployed). Where is the connection supposed to exist between knowledge and value? We need to review the value that knowledge has so that it contributes to citizenship, not only through a course on values or citizenship education, but also through the existing traditional disciplinary courses in a curriculum.

In this chapter, I intend to propose from a philosophical perspective the idea that, if we want to educate students in values, it is helpful to have some general knowledge about the knowledge of the value of knowledge. I am actually extending the scope of education in values to include education in the knowledge of the value of knowledge(s). Education in values calls for specific values like citizenship, friendship, and compassion, and so forth. It can extend to educating citizens in the value of what it is to know in general, and specifically, what is of value in scientific and historical thinking.

The expression "knowledge of the value of knowledge(s)" is a deliberate repetition because to value knowledge requires that we first need to know, at least generally, about how to value knowledge and how to choose what we value. There is no difficulty in making a distinction between valuating and evaluating by assigning a more cognitive dimension to evaluation while admitting non-cognitive influences to valuation (Ng, 2000). In any case, it seems to me that valuing (axiology) continues to depend on some knowing (epistemology). Conversely, axiology perfects and completes epistemology because volition and affectivity mesh with cognition. Valuing becomes a form of knowing because it does not renounce its epistemic dimension (knowing what, knowing how). Valuing even attaches an element of commitment to cognition. As a result, one not only knows and values but is also convinced. The meshing of cognitive with non-cognitive elements in valuing helps us overcome a rigid objectivity-subjectivity dichotomy. This dichotomy could shape a citizenry that values one knowledge above all else and neglects others.

The knowledge of the value of knowledge(s) for citizenship is relevant because such knowledge informs citizens' choices on public issues. Take the case of state legislation that changes according to the way citizens perceive the value foreign scientists contribute to their country's technological agenda or their threat to nationalistic ideals. In this example, the valuation of these issues tacitly depend on the citizens' cognition and valuation of science's and history's bearing on them.

I will divide this paper into four sections. In "Values and Its Dimensions," I will briefly consider the concept of value and briefly consider its dimensions. These preliminary insights prepare the ground for the discussion of the values of science and history found in the sections "Scientific Knowledge" and "Historical Knowledge" respectively. Other ways of pursuing civic values education through daily practices or other areas like the arts are interesting but go beyond our aim. This paper is limited to science and history for two obvious reasons. First, the progressive breakthroughs in science and technology are a reality that both society collectively and citizens individually can ill afford to ignore if that society wants to survive in the

21st century. Second, the future development of any society and its citizens depends on present conditions, which in turn have been built upon its history. Citizenship requires consideration of present societal conditions in relation to the past and the future. The section "Knowledge, Value of Knowledge(s), Valuing: An Integration" brings to a close the idea that educating in values merits the inclusion of education in valuing scientific and historical knowledge because by understanding the workings of scientific and historical thinking, citizens may have more illuminating epistemic criteria and more powerful non-cognitive elements upon which their valuing judgments and civic-oriented commitments can be based. Without renouncing its cognitive requirements, valuing includes volitional and affective aspects, thereby making it possible to consider valuing a form of knowledge that is not only intellectual but also experientially satisfying. Because of this, valuing in general and valuing knowledge in particular can be taken as an ethical act. It derives from cognition of a good, it is motivated by the desirability of a good, it is accompanied and perfected by the joy of pursuing a good.

Value and Its Dimensions

We speak of a value when we refer to some good quality in some thing which a person recognizes. As good, it is desirable (Aquinas, I, q. 5, a.1,c). That in which good inheres is said to have value or is a value (Alvira, Clavell, & Melendo, 1982/1991). For instance, to say that "citizenship is desirable" means that we recognize it as a good. We thus say, "Citizenship has a value." To say "citizenship is a value" is to say that it has an objective good quality which can be explained by pointing out those recommendable qualities (Hare, 1975). The noun-form "value" here refers to an objective dimension because it is, at least to some extent, independent of a person's judgment such that even when this person may not judge it so, others may. Objective value exists as long as that in which it adheres, exists. To speak of the value of something presupposes that it exists. Existence or reality, in this light, appears to be a root value without which no ulterior one can be predicated. As Stein (1917/1989) puts it, "the reality of a value is itself a value" (p. 102). We do not think of the value "citizenship" without thinking of citizens. Scientists cannot value a discovery without a discovery. Historians and citizens cannot value globalization and its impact to citizenship without understanding past and existing historical realities.

Broadly extending the Scholastic and Husserlian senses of intentionality (Runes, 1976), we always make a concurrent reference to a person-knower when we know something. To affirm the existence of an objective value of something is to disclose a person who recognizes it as a value. Without this recognition, thinking and speaking about the very concept of value is unintelligible and meaningless. When we value, we are making judgments that involve value, non-value, or value-free concepts. In other words, before we can value something as valuable or invaluable, we assume a notion of value. The entire valuing activity is engaged in by the person, a conscious subject, who is not an object-thing. This subjective dimension of value refers to the fact that the act of valuing is done by a subject person. It does not mean subjectivism as commonly understood: prejudiced, arbitrary, aprioristic, irrational or blind emotional judgment. The valuing act connotes an intellectual activity because it is judgment about a value. Valuing citizenship requires knowledge and involves a judgment about the value of citizenship.

Valuing is making a specific judgment about what is good and desirable. In such judgment, we perceive a value as the combination of "good" plus a "reason" for why we think it is good. We pair "good" with a "reason" such as convenience, necessity, usefulness, efficiency, practicality, truth or objectivity. In any given pair, we recognize two things: what is good about something as a matter of information and what is good about it for our life. To know what good it has as information is to know its objective value. This theoretical knowledge of value is associated with the Greek *theorein*, *episteme* or science. Hence, I know about citizenship through civic courses. But to know its relevance is to recognize the value citizenship has in relation to my subjectivity as a person within the historical context, that is, as a citizen. This is practical knowledge, prudence or practical wisdom associated with the Greek *phronesis* (Choza, 1988). The value of citizenship is not practical — at least not directly — in the utilitarian sense of *techne*, that is, knowledge that produces machines.

In contrast to *techne*, *phronesis* is concerned with ethical action and by extension with citizenship because citizenship has an ethical dimension (Daggers, 1997). *Phronesis* is concerned with what is to be done here and now. Therefore, it has to do with practical deliberation in the "area of the contingent" (Garcia-Alonso, 1977, p. 202). It orients us towards an *ethos* for our personal and public life. It directs how we should act as good citizens according to our knowledge of the value of citizenship. In short, we apply *phronesis* to political and civic activities when we make value judgments that are prudential-ethical in character.

Prudential valuing is completed by *dike*, a Greek term that refers to a willful readiness to apply *phronesis* to social, political and civic life (Choza,

1988). While *phronesis* is a matter of reason, *dike* is a matter of the will (willingness, desire to act accordingly). We need both virtues to cultivate what is ethical and civic in ourselves.

The inseparableness of prudential valuing and the willingness to act accordingly makes *phronesis*, more than technical knowledge, uniquely important for ethical deliberation and value judgment (Mansukhani, 1999). This is so because ethical and civic value judgments converge in one concept: good. We know good (citizenship), we value good (citizenship), and we try to act accordingly (good citizens). Prudential valuing requires ethical knowledge and virtue simultaneously because it is cognitive and volitional. It is never separated from the experience in which it is exercised and the person (Carr, 1995). Prudential-ethical value judgment, therefore, is needed for citizenship because it tells us when, how, and to what extent within the historical context we are to be compassionate, help the underprivileged, order our emotions in such a way that our personal interests are balanced with the pursuit of the common good.

While technical knowledge is provided for in the curricula, this is not always the case for education in *phronesis* (prudence) and *dike* (justice). Such absence is due to a disinterest in ethics and civics for their being useless knowledge in the utilitarian sense, lack of space in the curriculum, or ignorance about the value of other kinds of knowledge that can be made relevant to the value of citizenship. But prudential value judgment tells us that we need to know what there is to value about a particular kind of knowledge if we are educators whose main business is knowledge and value transmission. We obviously cannot value a knowledge we know nothing or little about and much less, know its value in relation to citizenship.

Certainly, the subjective dimension (valuing as verb) presupposes the objective dimension (value as noun). If the former were present without the latter, the former would substitute for the latter. Then, we have subjectivism. To say, "I value science and history for its relevance to citizenship" without knowing what there is about scientific and historical thinking that makes them important to civic education is not convincing. As educators, we transmit values based on criteria and knowledge. We do not persuade or indoctrinate based on feelings alone nor primarily. In short, we need to value "value(s)" objectively to strike an effective connection between values and any knowledge form. My knowledge of the value of science and history influence the choices and decisions as to how I, as a citizen, should vote for or against reforms in relation to an ecological program or the creation of a nuclear plant as a hegemonic strategy of a foreign power.

Scientific Knowledge

Experimental science has been long considered the paradigm of objective knowledge. Objectivity is a good and a reason for science's value. To say that "science is good because it consists of objective knowledge" is already a value judgment. The redundancy is intended to show that this value judgment is not value-free itself. The presence of a good (objective value) that is judged by a person (subjective value) suggests that scientific objectivity cannot be values-free, absolutely speaking. This implies admitting an analogical concept of objectivity (Agazzi, 1979). That is to say, objectivity is said of science in a manner different from, but not necessarily opposed to historical science for instance (Adey & Shayer, 1997). It should be possible to speak of varying levels of objectivity as well (Provençal, 1987). And since objectivity, though not identifiable necessarily with truth, is at least an attempt to approach truth (Hamlyn, 1972), we must be open to an analogical concept of truth. It is therefore possible to seek truth in the different types of knowledges.

Many agree that objectivity in science means inter-subjectivity or public discourse (e.g. Artigas, 1989; Fartos-Martinez, 1979; Provençal, 1987). If public discourse is valued, all its processes should be valued too. Such processes are the common understanding of theoretical formulations and their usage as well as the repeatability of experimental methods (Handal, Lauvas, & Lycke, 1990).

There is also a subjective dimension in terms of private reference to intuition and art which, though in themselves, non-scientific, do contribute to the creativity of the scientist (Artigas, 1989). We find an added subjective value in a scientific theory because it might not only be true but it may also be valued as beautiful. Nevertheless, where we find the subjective dimension clearly revealed is in the motivation that drives a scientist to engage in scientific activity and in the goals for applying scientific results. If I decide to clone myself and were asked why I value this application of science, my expertise in genetics would not explain my decision. My knowledge of genetics is valuable as "know-what" and "know-how" to proceed successfully with the cloning technology. It is insufficient to justify my choice, to explain why I should want to clone myself in the first place. In short, a discriminatory line exists. Scientific knowledge tells me that I can clone, that I can teach others to do the same, that I can do this for a civic agenda of producing better cloned citizens. It does not, however, tell me nor can it tell me whether to clone is ethically correct or not. It cannot give me the criteria to judge whether cloning should be the civic way for a society to produce better citizens.

The reasons for engaging in science and the goals for applying it do not come from science itself. They are in fact pre-scientific. Without them, no scientific activity would ever take place and no possible application would be decided. The fact that pre-scientific reasons exist and influence a scientist is an important consideration in science and values education because it is implicitly or explicitly assumed. What is there in science to be researched, taught, applied, or used is dependent on relevancy. But relevancy indicates pre-scientific reasons why such research, information, application or usage are, ultimately speaking, important and valuable to people, scientists and citizens alike. These reasons form part of the scientist's ethos.

Relevancy has to do with what people consider and value as "good" for human and social life. Take the case of the scientists in the Nazi concentration camps who engaged in human experimentation in the name of scientific progress and for ideological purposes. Consider the current overt practice in an Asian country where resident doctors perform unnecessary medical procedures for the exclusive sake of training. A valuation of a good derived from the actions of these scientists and doctors certainly determines the use of their objective knowledge. That valuation can be rationalized for the sake of justifying action.

A good life as valued by scientists can be glimpsed only in a limited sense. Good life means a life of physical, psychological and mental well-being. It is a life where disease is curbed or where technological resources are available for comfort. If we accept that scientific knowledge promises such a life, would science create a society where citizens show solidarity, compassion, fairness and equity? Not necessarily. The conditional feature of the answer lies in the understanding of the value of science as knowledge. Science cannot tell us to create a good civic life, or create a good civic life on its own account.

The knowledge of the value of science's objectivity and its instrumental role in civic life is not derived from science itself. The recognition of the value of human existence and citizenship as far greater than the instrumental value of science is a knowledge and a value judgment that cannot originate from science either. Such recognition comes from a philosophical stance because valuing presupposes a way of viewing life, people, society, and knowledge itself.

Certainly, scientific thinking introduces citizens to generally considered intellectual virtues (Cooper, 1994) as well as the values that are inherent in serious scientific activity: endurance in exploring, rigor in truth-finding, evidence-seeking, patience and perseverance to repeat experiments until the results are satisfactory. It also teaches citizens to understand what it takes to rationally accept a theory based on evidence, given the technology and conceptual frames available at a certain historical moment, the possibility of error (Artigas, 1989), the need for verification, the avoidance of guess work, and the recognition of the difficulties of past and current theoretical frames and therefore of their limitations to explain certain phenomena (Sklar, 2000). Science teaches us the value of team work, a sense of trust (Hamlyn, 1972) and indebtedness to the past. Scientists have to rely and depend on each other since they need to narrow down the range of alternatives for their own researches (Ikuenobe, 1998). These are all added values to science's objectivity.

In this respect, the rigor of scientific thinking instructs scientists and citizens in the virtue of humility because ordinarily scientific truth is acquired painstakingly. There is much more that the physical world has still to reveal of itself. Scientific thinking presupposes an ordered universe, not a chaotic one. It also presupposes that there are explanations for order and for chaos (if present). Ultimately, science seeks to understand this order. Education for citizenship can learn from science the value of seeking for order even if it may not be the kind of neat order sought in scientific laws. Just as environmentalists have learned to respect physical nature and its laws, citizens could similarly understand that there too is a human ecology that can only be sustained if civic values are learned and practiced. That ecology requires the balance of private good and the common good.

Science teaches us that we cannot learn all lessons from it (Maxwell, 1994). Among these are certain lessons that are nonetheless needed for citizenship, such as the value of the indeterminacy of human agency in history and the value of ethical requirements for scientific and civic conduct. These values shall have to be learned from history and ethics respectively.

Historical Knowledge

As another form of knowledge, history is objectively valuable because it obviously provides us with historical information about the past. Such information is "good" regardless of any appreciative mind. Knowledge of the complexities of historical spadework, the instruments and technologies used by historians to plow through documents, artifacts, and other signs of past lived experiences are an addition to history's objective value.

More and more, history uses science to advance in its own discoveries, and to the extent that technology is available, historians gain in rigor and objectivity in the processes of historical work. The media shows science at the service of history when historians attempt to reconstruct ancient civilizations with technological resources. A large number of citizens obtain historical knowledge far more easily through the media although they need to select credible sources. The thoroughly documented program aired in 2000 by the British Broadcasting Corporation on the "People's (20th) Century" is an example. One happy result for citizens is their perception of history as a field that likewise aspires for rigor and objectivity in its own investigations.

Certainly, history has a subjective value in a greater sense than empirical science. This is due to its hermeneutical feature. Historians try not only to gather accurate facts, genuine documents, or credible witnesses to historical events. They have to interpret them according to a historical theory that they think fits the facts best. Historians are obliged to deal with a wider context than science because they have to simultaneously deal with several contexts to understand and interpret given historical situations, events, collective and individual life histories. In doing this, they too, become dependent on past interpretations or current renderings of those contexts (Stone Wiske, 1998).

The effort of historical thinking that combines the objective and subjective values is already by itself a value greater than each of these dimensions taken separately. Moreover, historical thinking, unlike science, has to deal with an element of greater indeterminacy which is human agency. This indeterminacy is intrinsic to it because the agents of history are people whose decisions at best, can only be more or less intelligently guessed but never pre-determined or predicted.

Historical thinking introduces us not only to the past but to its understanding, both of which, we as busy citizens, would not have the time, leisure or interest to pursue. In understanding the past, historical thinking presents unique and concrete realities — not hypothesis or fiction — sometimes shown in their crudest and naked forms. History does not hide painful and even tragic realities from its citizens. Historical thinking teaches citizens of any nation that such lived realities are too complex to account for completely (Phenix, 1964). Take for instance the events of the Holocaust and the recent Kosovo crisis. History, likewise, presents citizens with realities that arise from contradictory and paradoxical contexts. The fall of the Berlin Wall meant the restoration of freedom for Eastern Berliners, increased the economic problems of the West Berliners, and brought the world's attention to a racist attitude towards Turkish workers in Germany. Historical events converge in unknown contemporary ways that the historian is not always able to fully fathom and for which no future direction is clearly envisaged. This is the case in the present Israeli-Palestinian crisis.

We tend to pride ourselves on the 20th century economic and scientific progress. Yet, we embarrass ourselves with its two World Wars and many regional wars, genocides and human rights violations despite the loudest clamor for respect of human dignity ever made in the history of mankind. The popular argument for the importance of history used to be its claim that "history teaches us lessons". We could stretch that by saying that "history also teaches us that we do not always learn its lessons". If history could successfully teach values of citizenship, perhaps we would be less fearful of future wars. It is interesting to note that scientific errors are not usually repeated because no scientist would repeat them. For this reason, science can be valued for its cumulative progress. Galileo built upon Copernicus, Einstein built upon Newton, Microsoft built on MacIntosh, and so forth. This certain neatness is denied history because of its indeterminacy. Collective history requires at least the sum total of individual biographies who have their unique attitudes, values, and free actions. Personal existence cannot be thingified, made static. Personal historical existence unsurprisingly becomes problematic (Polo, 1997). Collective history has its "ups" and "downs". Unless reflection is done and changes made, individual attitudes, values, and mental frames over time, create certain collective ways of life that reflect poverty in values, including citizenship.

In some Western societies where for many years, couples have systematically limited their number of children, the value of generosity in life giving is not transmitted. It is an unknown, un-experienced value. Their history eventually shows social problems that are rooted in selfish individualism. Should we be surprised that their citizens show no compassion for the aged and the lonely? Likewise, if a society has suppressed the basic freedom of its citizens to work in private enterprise like the countries dominated by the former Soviet Union, should we be surprised to find its citizens de-motivated and apathetic to work and indifferent to public life?

There are those who fear the subordination of the value of historical knowledge for political or social ends, and by extension, for education in citizenship. The reason for such fear lies in a perceived undermining of the "deep historical understanding when it forces teachers and students alike to lose sight of the meticulous process by which understanding of the past is established and revised by historians, no matter how difficult and morally problematic the past may be" (Boix-Mansilla, 2000). There should be no difficulty on this point if we understand the objective value of history as earlier discussed. The epistemological value of historical knowledge includes the historical facts and the interpretation of such, as well as the workings of historical research. Like any form of knowledge, we cannot separate the historical knowledge (product) from the cognitive processes historical inquiry requires. Indeed, "knowledge is defined in part by the way we get there" (Zagzebski, 1996, p. 272).

Historical thinking, like scientific thinking, includes both product and process. Those from postmodernist quarters prefer to think that the past should be treated in its own terms without reference to contemporary values. It is certainly legitimate to avoid anachronism, "presentism," and simplistic accounts of history. However, it is not possible to dissociate the past from the present and the present from the future because history itself is essentially constituted by these dimensions of time (Southgate, 1996). People themselves make judgments of value and act within temporality. Therefore, education in values, including values of citizenship should embrace the values of historical thinking advantageously. History provides citizens an awareness that they are a link in a chain between past and future citizens. This should give present citizens a sense of being heirs and transmitters of the values of citizenship. This link is not only understood cognitively. It can also be grasped more powerfully through empathy. As being essentially concerned with people, historical understanding requires something more than the application of reason" (Southgate, 1996, p. 119). We need empathy to understand people of the past, their values of citizenship or otherwise, their emotions. This emotion, like all emotions, is not entirely sentient. Stein (1917/1989) remarks:

> The structure of all feelings requires theoretical acts. When I am joyful over a good deed, this is how the deed's goodness or its positive value faces me. But I must know about the deed in order to be joyful over it — knowledge is fundamental to joy. (p. 101)

Our emotions are always pervaded by intellectuality (Saint Simon, 1992). Those who defend the plausibility of teaching romantic understanding (e.g. Egan, 1997) can support the idea that historical accounts which portray real emotions teach us the value of learning how to empathize with past citizens' dramas.

Citizens not only receive from the past but, more importantly, are made accountable to future citizens. "Memory is creative. We come to be what we can recognize as the self and man is not an agent in history until he has acquired this intimate history" (Dagger, 1997, p. 164). Historicity calls for certain virtues that relate to temporality such as patience (Innerarity, 1994). Solidarity is another, which responds directly to present problems of poverty. This social ill includes the lack of material possessions as well as the deprivation of love, care, and the basic rights that stem from human dignity. We exercise solidarity towards our own contemporaries by actual care giving but we also do this for future citizens by responsibly creating a present culture of solidarity, compassion, fairness, and justice. We owe this civic duty to them. Solidarity and therefore accountability to future citizens is an exercise of the virtue of justice and piety (Polo, 1997).

Some common grounds between citizenship and history can be glimpsed in the following ways: both require an integrating dimension for their understanding. History is in itself integrative since it must make sense of historical facts to reach historical understanding. The historian must imagine the past and seek coherence. Citizenship as a value and virtue on the other hand is "not reducible to specifiable acts or act dispositions" (Zagzebski, 1996, p. 19). In fact, the literature about citizenship presents apparently heterogenous civic traits, virtues, and behavior, ranging from critical thinking to fairness. Besides, citizens do not dissociate their other roles, as parents or employers, for example. They rather integrate them (Daggers, 1997).

History and citizenship also both connect with the ethical and the personal. Questions such as, "What happened in the past?", "What could have happened if ...?", "What should have been ...?" are raised by historians and citizens in an attempt to understand historical events and current public issues. Both ask ethical questions in relation to the past such as, "Who is responsible?", "Was it right or wrong?". These questions include complex value-and citizenship-related questions about peace, war, and the marginalization of individuals, groups and even entire nations. Their answers clearly cannot be oversimplified. Precisely due to historical complexity, Gardner (1999) suggests that misconceptions about historical events be cognitively corrected through the disciplined approach to history. The same solution is suggested for misconceptions in science. Broudy (1988), earlier, had given a similar proposal: "Since schools cannot hope to anticipate the social, economic and political factors that shape or distort the patterns of life, the best the school can do is to validate its choice of exemplar by scholarship" (p. 21).

We can therefore glean, in historical thinking, that a rigid dichotomy of objectivist and subjectivist axiologies cannot be held. Acts of historical thinking are highly selective of their sources. These evaluative acts are also acts of valuing in so far as judgments about historical facts are made and recognized as good. They are acts of valuing too because the historian interprets those facts as not only verifiable but good. Inevitably, ethical judgments are made because the civic virtues of historical men and women are presented as good and valuable.

Knowledge, Value of Knowledge(s), Valuing: An Integration

In the previous sections, I have suggested that at least a general understanding of the nature and levels of objectivity/subjectivity found in scientific and historical knowledge is an epistemic value itself. This means that it is knowledge that enables people to value (verb-form) a field for what epistemic merits it has and to appreciate its relevance to values, in particular citizenship. To understand epistemic merits and complementariness is an intellectual habit that is good and valuable.

Valuing knowledge and intellectual habits, inclusive of *phronesis*, involves a judgment that is on the one hand based on cognitive criteria. Knowledge and intellectual habits are valued for their own epistemic sake. This does not preclude valuing them for an ethos of utility, personal satisfaction, or civic relevancy. An ethos cannot be divorced entirely from one's epistemic stance whereby, on the one hand, one's intellectual pursuit could be said to refer to knowledge/facts (objective and neutral, value-free, impersonal), and on the other hand, one's very engagement in and application of science or history, having to do with ethos, could be said to refer to value (subjective, not neutral, personal). While knowledge and values are distinguishable, there is a certain circularity in their inter-dependence.

Knowledge is good and therefore a value. Valuing is a way of knowing that combines cognition with volition and affectivity. Valuing in its verb form involves a judgment about value and therefore is cognitive. Being cognitive, it has to do with knowing. The discussion on objective values shows that values can be cognitively learned. Specifically, the objective epistemic values of science and history can be learned. Therefore, it should be possible to teach these fields in a way that connects their own epistemic values with other values like citizenship. This approach can be made in addition to, but not in place of, values or citizenship courses.

It is also true that knowledge of value, while retaining its cognitive component, is knowledge of a good. Good is characterized by its relation to an appetency or desirableness that involves a volitional (wanting the good) and affective (liking the good) aspect. Certainly, we can conceptually distinguish the components of cognition, volition and affection. But, in the act of valuing, these components all combine beautifully in way that gives valuing an integral feature. The intimate convergence of cognition, volition and affection makes the dichotomy between objectivity and subjectivity impossible to maintain in an absolute way.

Valuing involves knowing what, how, and to what extent we are to value here and now (*phronesis*). It also simultaneously involves a willingness to value (*dike*) so that we actually perform a valuing act. When we do so, we freely engage our entire self. This further implies that the act of valuing engages a pleasant feeling. Hence, valuing is experienced as a positive feeling whereas devaluing is experienced as a negative feeling. Behind the statement "I value historical knowledge" or "I value fairness" is a pleasant experience of what it takes "to know" history or fairness as objective value or in relation to one's life. The words "to know" no longer refer to a purely intellectual act. It has become a convergence of knowledge (cognition), intention (willfulness), and an affection of pleasantness in a single valuing act. Valuing, like knowing and feeling, becomes a personal and intimate act. Valuing therefore is an intelligent and free act. It cannot be forced. No person can experience the act of valuing for us in the same way as no person can think or will for us. While the objective and more cognitive component of valuing can be learned through courses, its volitional and affective components cannot be learned in this same way. The latter are learned through real experiences of valuing. This entails exposing oneself and others to concrete experiences of the good, inclusive of civic goods. Such experiences range from a satisfying experience of how a history teacher connects historical thinking with citizenship in class through a happy experience of keeping the old and the lonely company, to a good experience of trusting friends or trustworthy public officials.

The apparent circularity of valuing knowledge as dependent on knowing what to value about knowledge on the one hand, and the adaptation of criteria other than knowledge itself to value something in knowledge on the other shows that, at least from a philosophical perspective, at major stages of knowledge acquisition and development in education or research activities, the educator, learner, scientist or historian is always driven, explicitly or tacitly, by an ethos. Such an ethos is never an isolated intellectual affair. As ethos — even when it is a case of pursuing and advancing theoretical science and historical spade work — it is valued. Concomitantly, the valuing agents engage themselves with volition and affectivity, not simply as scientists or historians but as a persons and citizens. Wojtyla (1955/1993) argues against Scheler's emotionalism, that the person is the source of valuing in ethical valuation. This can support the idea that valuing has an integrating feature because it involves knowing what to value (valuing as knowledge) and valuing what is known (valuing as ethos). But the latter in turn requires the engagement of volition and affection, desire and feeling, thus, theory and experience, objectivity and subjectivity, information and purpose, personal and altruistic interests, individual and social relevancy, professional and familial prioritizations all converge in valuing.

The multi-dimensional relations, sketched in this chapter, between knowledge, values, citizenship, and education suggest to us that, at least from a philosophical perspective, valuing must revisit its anthropological and ethical roots. If Wojtyla is right in saying that the person is the source of valuing, it would be possible to argue that when a person knows or is taught the value of the knowledges, when he actually values their epistemic work in relation to other values by way of education and experience of good, that knowledge and that valuing merge as one integrative act of the same person. At this stage, the cognitive, volitional and affective become a single pleasant experience of valuing. I think that Zagzebski's virtue theory (1996) could very well support the integrating feature of the valuing experience. If valuing presents itself integrative of different components (cognitive, volitional, affective), we need to at least caution ourselves against oversimplification. I believe, therefore, that the redundancy suggested by this chapter about knowledge of the value of knowledge in general, and more specifically scientific and historical knowledge in relation to values and citizenship, was necessary and therefore merits consideration in a serious discourse about values and/or citizenship in the new century.

References

Adey, P., & Shayer, M. (1997, June). *Teaching thinking through science and the role of context in teaching thinking*. Paper presented at the 7th International Conference on Thinking. Retrieved from http://www.nie.ac.sg:8000/~wwwnie/think/

Agazzi, E. (1979). Analogicità del concetto di scienza. Il problema del rigore e dell'oggettivitá nelle scienze umane. In V. Possenti (Ed.), *Epistemologia e scienze umane* (pp. 57–76). Milan: Massimo Edizione.

Alvira, T., Clavell, L., & Melendo, T. (1991). Metaphysics. (L. Supan, Trans.). Manila, the Philippines: Sinagtala. (Original work published 1982)

Artigas, M. (1989). *Filosofia de la ciencia experimental*. Pamplona, Spain: Eunsa.

Boix-Mansilla, V. (2000). Historical understanding: Beyond the past and into the present. In P. Stearns, P. Seixas, & S. Wineburg (Eds.), *Knowing, teaching & learning history: National and international perspectives* (pp. 390–418). New York & London: New York University Press.

Broudy, H. (1988). *Uses of schooling*. New York & London: Routledge.

Carr, D. (1995). Roughing out the ground rules: reason and experience in practical deliberation. *Journal of Philosophy of Education, 29*(1), 137–147.

Choza, J. (1988). *Manual de antropología filosófica*. Madrid, Spain: Rialp.

Cooper, N. (1994). The intellectual virtues. *The Journal of the Royal Institute of Philosophy, 69*, 459–469.

Dagger, R. (1997). *Civic virtues: Rights, citizenship and republic liberalism*. New York & Oxford, UK: Oxford University Press.

Degenhardt, M. A. B. (1982). *Education and the value of knowledge*. Boston: George Allen and Unwin.

Egan, K. (1997). *The educated mind: How cognitive tools shape our understanding*. Chicago & London: The University of Chicago Press.

Fartos-Martinez, M. (1979). La metodología de las ciencias y algunos de sus problems. *Anuario Filosófico, 12*(3), 31–63.

Garcia-Alonso, L. (1977). Fuentes del subjetivismo. *Anuario Filosófico, 10*(2), 199–209.

Gardner, H. (1999). *The disciplined mind: What all students should understand*. New York: Simon & Schuster.

Hamlyn, D. W. (1972). Objectivity. In D. F. Dearden & R. S. Peters (Eds.), *Education and the Development of Reason* (pp. 246–247). London & Boston: Routledge.

Handal, G., Lauvas, P., & Lycke, K. (1990). The concept of rationality in academic science teaching. *European Journal of Education, 25*(3), 319–332.

Hare, R. M. (1975). The logic of good. In R. Beck (Ed.), *Perspectives in Philosophy* (3rd ed., pp. 402–411). New York: Holt, Rinehart & Winston.

Ikuenobe, P. (1998). Communitarianism, liberalism, and an epistemic view of critical thinking. *Inquiry, 18*(1), 73-94.

Innerarity, D. (1994, March 16). Sobre la dificultad: Las virtudes del tiempo. *Aceprensa 38*, 94.

Mansukhani, R. (1999). The nature of phronetic understanding. *Sophia, 28*(1), 9–19.

Maxwell, N. (1994). Towards a new Enlightenment: What the task of creating civilization has to learn form the success of modern science. In R. Barnett (Ed.), *Academic community: Discourse or discord?* (pp. 86–105). London & Pennsylvania, IN: Jessica Kingley Publishers.

Ng, M. L. (2000, June). *Valuation, evaluation, and value education — On inquiring the ability to value: A philosophical perspective*. Paper presented at the International Conference on Values Education and Citizenship Education in the New Century, Hongkong.

Phenix, P. (1964). *Realms of meaning: A philosophy of the curriculum for general education*. New York: McGraw Hill.

Polo, L. (1997). *Etica: Hacia una version moderna de los temas clasicos* (2nd ed.). Madrid, Spain: Aedos Union Editorial.

Provençal, Y. (1987). Une analyse de la notion d'objetivité. *Philosophiques*, *14*(2), 361–380.

Runes, D. (Ed.). (1976). *Dictionary of Philosophy*. Totowa, NJ: Littlefield, Adams & Co.

Saint Simon, Y. (1992). *Freedom of choice*. New York: Fordham University Press.

Sklar, L. (2000). *Theory and truth: Philosophical critique within foundational science*. Oxford, UK: Oxford University Press.

Southgate, B. (1996). *History: What and why? Ancient, modern, and postmodern perspectives*. London & New York: Routledge.

Stein, E. (1989). *On the problem of empathy*. (W. Strein, Trans.). (3rd ed.). Washington, DC: ICS Publication. (Original work published 1917)

Stone Wiske, M. (Ed.). (1998). *Teaching for understanding: Linking research with practice*. San Francisco: Jossey-Bass Publishers.

Wojtyla, K. (1993). The problem of the will in the analysis of the ethical act. (T. Sandok, Trans.). In A. Woznicki (Ed.), *Person and community: Selected essays* (pp. 3–22). Vienna: Peter Lang. (Original work published 1955)

Zagzebski, L. (1996). *Virtues of the mind: An inquiry into the nature of virtue and the ethical foundations of knowledge*. Cambridge, UK: Cambridge University Press.

CHAPTER 5

Quality Assurance, Language Policy, and Civic Participation: A Paradoxical Argument on the Educational Values of Hong Kong

Ronald W. Y. Tang

Abstract

To argue against the current discourse on the language policy of Hong Kong, which has mainly focused on economic rationalism, a more holistic view with the educational value of language with respect to one's civic duty in light of dialogic constructivism will be suggested. It proposes that the quality of a language as resources has to have something to do with the formation of one's self and life history, the identification of a collectivity where one's identity is appropriated, and the proliferation of a potential dialogic environment where creativity emerges in contrast to the current notion of a technical mentality of language use which leads to a closure of meaning making in our language policy. And it is towards such quality, which is based on the kind of value where identity, community, and the potential of a hermeneutic situation play fair that enhances understanding, this paper is driving.

Introduction

"The mother tongue expressed a nationality's soul or spirit, since it was a collective achievement par excellence, language was also the surest way for individuals to safeguard the authenticity they had inherited from their ancestors as well as to hand it on to generations yet unborn, and, finally, that worldwide diversity in language and in culture was a good and beautiful thing in and of itself, whereas imitation led to corruption and stagnation."

Johann Gottfried Herder

I would like to start with two assumptions that, (1) it is only when one speaks with one's mother tongue that one articulates and thinks simultaneously and spontaneously, and (2) only when the above criterion is fulfilled can the concept of civic participation be realized in a dialogical manner through which the kind of quality that embraces freedom, creativity and democracy can emerge through community activities held in school.

Quality and value-addedness are two of the most popular terms in the current educational reform in Hong Kong. I believe that these terms are equally dominant in most other parts of the world. What makes Hong Kong the unique case is the close connection between the language policy discourse and conception of quality and value, which has clearly been reflected by the community's involvement in the course of its development especially in the past few years. In this paper, I will first of all give a brief sketch of the situation and then discuss the evolution of Hong Kong's language policy in the light of the Education Commission Report 7 (ECR 7) on two levels. The first is the ideological level where the notion of quality and value as conceptualized in relation to language use will be discussed. The second is the practical level where the action of participants concerned will be reported. To argue against the current discourse, which has mainly focused on economic rationalism, a more holistic view of the educational value of language with respect to one's civic duty in light of dialogic constructivism will be suggested. It proposes that the quality of a language as a resource has to have something to do with the formation of one's self and life history, the identification of a collectivity where one's identity is appropriated, and the proliferation of a potential dialogic environment where creativity emerges in contrast to the current notion of a technical mentality of language use, which leads to a closure of meaning making in our language policy. It is towards such quality, based on the kind of values where identity, community, and the potential for a hermeneutic situation of fair play that enhances understanding, that this paper is driving.

The Notion of Quality in Contest

The handover in 1997 marked the end of Hong Kong as a British colony for 150 years. The ideology of eulogizing English as an indispensable medium for communication if not transaction, has indisputably permeated all walks of life in Hong Kong. This is reflected by the keen fight to get permission to use English as the medium of instruction, both by the schools who claim to be eligible to do so and the parents concerned who wanted to exercise their choice even without understanding the outcome.

The Lucky Number

The number 14 for some is a symbol worth memorizing. It is the number of a special kind of schools, out of twenty, which have successfully appealed to have the right to use English as the medium of instruction. By coincidence, this happened on the fourteenth of March, 1998. This was the day when the Appeal Committee announced the result of those schools which had had their applications for deserving the qualification of using English as the medium of instruction reviewed. Pertinent to the controversy of which schools are justified in using English as the medium of instruction are two interesting points, which this paper would like to mention at the outset. The first one concerns the response of the schools, students, and parents. The second is the criteria used by the Committee for deciding which language a school should use.

It was revealed that the criteria for deciding which schools should be qualified to use English as the medium of instruction had been relaxed, which could, as one newspaper commented, quite justifiably lead to "those schools which chose not to appeal may now feel aggrieved at seeing the ground rules changed so late in the day" (South China Morning Post, March 14, 1998). Two implications arise here. Criteria for the decision must be arbitrary though the chairman of the Committee, Cheung Shun-kwong of the City University claimed that they, including Tsui Bik-mei of the Hong Kong University and Yue Yeuk-hoi, a solicitor, had been trying to be objective. But the statement he made after the announcement, which went, "to be able to use English as the medium of instruction is not an award, and it isn't a penalty if schools are told to use Chinese," unintentionally but accurately revealed how the two languages were perceived by the public, those at whom his announcement was aimed. In short, language was perceived as certain kind of cultural capital, something which is used as a stepping stone that may lead one to something else in Peters' words (1977) rather than as Charles Taylor (1995) has conceptualized, as an enlightening channel through which new terrain can be disclosed. Furthermore, behind the scenes was a mechanism which made it difficult to convince the schools, the students, and the parents to believe in the objectivity and reliability of the criteria for it gave the impression that it could be changed at any time. Without a clear point of reference, all parties involved could do nothing but leave the decision to what Weber terms "life chances" or even a state of "luck."

Looking back at the first point reinforces this "luck" notion. All three parties, the schools, the students, and the parents seemed to have been waiting for the result of a lucky draw. Let's first look at how the parents responded. A family moved to the area where their ideal school was located. The reason they did so was to have a better chance and right of access to their ideal school. However, the failure of their application for this ideal school destroyed their dream. Another loser said it wasn't fair. One parent hoped that the school would try its very best to show the Education Department their wishes (Ming Pao, March 14, 1998). Cheung Shun-kwong concluded on the following day in the same newspaper that "it is like a storm … and some of the parents are too emotional" (Ming Pao, March 15, 1998). His further remark went "the only way to be fair in this case is not to make any decision at all" (Ming Pao, March 15, 1998). From the above statements, a very clear picture can easily be drawn. "Storm" provides the nature of the setting. "Emotional" indicates the nature of the behavior of those concerned. The unwillingness to make a "rational" decision, intimated by Cheung's statement, suggests the possibility of an "irrational" outcome.

Educational versus Economic Value

Ruth Hayhoe, former director-designate of the Hong Kong Institute of Education, made the following comment when interviewed by a journalist, "I think what they, the Hong Kong parents, have to understand is that their children may actually be disadvantaged by a poor quality English medium school. But it's difficult for less educated parents to grasp that" (South China Morning Post, July 29, 1997, p. 17). The above comment raises the question of whether the parents have made a rational choice on the issue and rational in what sense. Before we come to a conclusion about this question, it may be helpful to review what sort of a rationale lies behind the controversy. The following extract seems to highlight this point.

Ruth Hayhoe in the newspaper mentioned above had said, "Young people should be able to talk about economics and political studies, geography and history in their own language (Cantonese) first" (South China Morning Post, July 29, 1997, p. 17). This is due to the fact that "It's ridiculous to have these young people on the bus speaking 'Chinglish' (mixed code of Cantonese and English) all the time because they don't know the concepts of geography and political science in Chinese, but they don't feel comfortable conversing in English" (South China Morning Post, July 29, 1997, p. 17). However, Rosanna Lo, a student from Methodist College, offered her own opinion in the same newspaper that she "preferred English to be the medium of instruction, for most of the textbooks and reference books available in bookstores are written in English." For that reason, if these texts are taught in Chinese (Cantonese), students have to "spend half their time looking up the meaning of new words in the dictionary." Nevertheless, she felt caught in a dilemma because on the one hand, "it is not likely that a local student will be speaking English at home all day long" whilst on the other "graduated from a Chinese secondary school is just perceived as less employable in the job market" (South China Morning Post, January 24, 1998).

The two different attitudes above come from two kinds of people, the first is an educator and the second is an "educatee." It seems as though they have a different focus. As Ramirez and Boli in their articles have claimed, education as an institution is closely linked to the sphere of political and economical development (Boli & Ramirez, 1986; Ramirez & Boli, 1982, 1987). The above opinions have grasped the practicality that involves political, economic, socio-cultural, and educational factors. The problem is due to being caught between the dialectic of individual and collective development. The polarity of the above two views where one (the educator) supports mother-tongue teaching and learning out of educational consideration while the other (the educatee) prefers a second language with economic prospect as the priority of her endeavor seems to be the focus of debate. They represent two kinds of value. The former is based on the consideration of the growth of an authentic self (intrinsic) while the latter takes economic value (extrinsic) as its priority.

The above two different sorts of value clearly reflect what was observed by Alasdair MacIntyre almost twenty-five years ago. He explains that there are two purposes in education, which are entrusted to teachers as their mission in contemporary society. However, these purposes cannot coexist within the context of modernity. What are these two purposes? And why can't they coexist? MacIntyre explicates that the first purpose is "to shape the young people so that they may fit into some social role and function that requires recruits." And the second purpose is to teach "young persons how to think for themselves, how to acquire independence of mind, how to be enlightened" (MacIntyre, 1987, p. 16). In MacIntyre's view, we have the difficulty of serving the two satisfactorily at the same time. As it is pointed out by him they "are mutually incompatible" (MacIntyre, 1987, p. 17). Even though MacIntyre in his essay is pretty pessimistic about this, he doesn't forget to remind the teacher that it is their job to "ask themselves how that kind of an (educated) community is to be reinvented" (MacIntyre, 1987, p. 34). The article by Tsui, Shum, Wong, Tse, and Ki (1999) in a way echoes MacIntyre's observation when it concludes after having reviewed the development of the language policy in Hong Kong that "underlying an issue as sensitive as language policy, there are political, social, economic and educational concerns" (p. 197). However, "It had always been social and economic agendas which were presented to the public for refuting sound educational arguments" (Tsui et al., 1999, p. 205).

Redeeming the Notion of "Quality"

According to the report of a meeting of specialists on the use of vernacular languages in education held in Paris in November 1951, it was confirmed that "it is axiomatic that the best medium for teaching a child is his mother tongue" (Tsui et al., 1999, p. 11), which has been supported by a succession of reports in Hong Kong for the past 150 years, namely the Annual Report in 1866, the Burney Report in 1930s, the 1965 White Paper, the 1973 Green Paper, the Llewellyn Report in 1982, the fourth and sixth Education Commission Report in 1990 and 1995–1996 respectively, and the Medium of Instruction Guidance in 1997. However, the consistency of the language policy has clearly reflected that parental preference and economic development are the factors that have driven the government to endorse the initiative of using mother tongue as the medium of instruction with reserve (see Tsui et al., 1999 and Bolton, 2000 for a more detail historical sketch). What captures this paper's attention is Pierson's observation that "Cantonese could have … a symbolic value … Cantonese might … become the symbol of freedom, democracy and independence" (as cited in Tsui et al., 1999, p. 211). If we accept his argument, Hong Kong's parents seem to have "traded in" the value of emancipation when teaching and learning can take place in one's first language for economic gain, the outcome of which they might not be assured. In MacIntyre's words (1987), they have chosen to be socialized to fit into the functionary system. Symbolically, they have sacrificed their right of articulation.

What are the considerations that have caused the introduction of such a "good-for-learning-and-teaching" principle be delayed for so long? Tsui et al.'s conclusion points out the importance of parental preference and the business sector's concern for Hong Kong's economic development. However, they seem to have provided no argument as to whether such a concern makes sense or whether it might: (1) only be out of ignorance of the assumption that using English as the medium of instruction means better learning; or

(2) be due to the narrow-minded view or opinion of the role of language as a whole. Before we go on with our discussion on the above issues, I would like to elaborate on how the above assumptions and the value on which they are based come about. Then, a different notion of quality, which is bred out of a dialogical constructivist conceptualization, will be suggested.

Hidden Agenda

The fact that Hong Kong is part of China predetermines its dependence both historically and geographically. The reality that Hong Kong has been cut off from its motherland necessitates its struggle for independence culturally. And the practicality that Hong Kong is a place where the East and West meet re-engineers itself time after time to accommodate its survival by economic interdependence. The above three limitations have set Hong Kong in a position where the claim for ontological difference becomes a luxury. Positively speaking, these limitations can be a form of vivacious vitalization. Bearing this in mind, it is not difficult to understand why Hong Kong's language policy in education is put in such a way. I don't mean that there is no alternative. On the contrary, there must be and should be from an educational point of view and I would suggest the role of language be conceptualized not merely as a tool for achieving something beyond itself. There will be further discussion of this later.

Albert Memmi (1990) in his book *The Colonizer and the Colonized* gives the following description of the colonized who is depicted as "neither responsible nor guilty nor skeptical, for he is out of the game. He is in no way a subject of history any more … always as an object. He has forgotten how to participate actively in history and no longer even asks to do so" (1990, p. 158). How much of this depiction can still be applied to Hong Kong's present situation deserves attention. However, the last line "no longer even asks to do so" seems to indicate the problem on two levels. "Not knowing" that it is a problem is one. Being "deprived of the ability to articulate" as a result of it, is the other. The former is the result of being governed on the ideological level whereas the latter indicates a situation where the possibility of a hermeneutic community is suppressed on the practical level. This is especially true when the language issue is taken into consideration. Memmi claims that for the colonized to recover his autonomy and separate destiny, he has to go back to his own tongue for he "no longer knew his language except in the form of a lowly dialect" (1990, p. 200). Whether the above description still holds true in the context of Hong Kong deserves further study. However, it has at least provided the psychological aspect underpinning the evolution of its language policy. But the story doesn't stop there, for Hong Kong's internationalization preceded its decolonization process, during which English was regarded as a symbol assuring a smooth transition at least from an economic point of view.

Philip Hughes, Professor Emeritus at the centre for United Nations Educational, Scientific and Cultural Organization (UNESCO) of the Australian National University in Canberra, pointed out in the seminar "Learning: The Treasure Within" held on April 30, 1998 at The Chinese University of Hong Kong that "to know … to do … to live together … and to be" are the four pillars, with which our education has to equip the younger generation especially at this time in our growth. To establish these four pillars, language is essential. However, the choice of language to shoulder such a mission represents the projection of a certain value or frame of reference. It is the purpose of this paper to provide an alternative to the current concept of which language to be used to establish the four pillars. This is where we now turn to examine and argue for the kind of quality that takes civic participation as a constitutive element of being an active citizen in a hermeneutic situation with a dialogical manner where one's own language paves the way.

Redeeming Quality on the Ideological Level

To start with, Peters' conceptualization of the notion of quality perhaps would shed further light on our understanding. Peters (1977) maintains that quality isn't a notion as easy to grasp as most educational administrators think it is. Due to limited space in this paper, what I am going to do is just extract those aspects, which are important for our discussion. First of all, in Peters' description, the notion of quality is closely associated with value. Only when something is taken as valuable would one treat that as something with quality whether it be intrinsically or extrinsically (or instrumentally) thought of. By intrinsic, Peters means something that is "thought to be valuable for what it is rather than for what (it may) lead up to" (Peters, 1977, p. 26), and, it is a matter of attitude that makes the difference. Furthermore, since education is the terrain where power and interest are involved, "politicians and economists may envisage different objectives (or frames of reference) for schools and an educational system." In general, "they may tend to look on a school in a much more instrumental way" (Peters, 1977, p. 25). Educators, however, may have their own criteria to say what an educated man should be like. It is within this dilemma that this paper is trying to argue for a "quality" value, following the same line of thought as stated in ECR7 in using the term "quality" to distinguish from the mediocre where value has been devalued.

Peters' essay provides three characteristics of being an ideal educated man. The first is the commitment to what is regarded as valuable in itself, which requires a general attitude of spontaneous enjoyment. In short, one should engage oneself in things "for what there is in them as distinct from what they may lead on to or bring about" with a non-instrumental attitude. The second is knowledge and understanding, which implies that what is demanded is more than just being skilled, which involves knowing that, not just knowing how. The embodiment of knowing that entails the ability to be discriminating and be aware of problems, the solving of which requires alertness rather than inert understanding. The last is the concept of wholeness, the notion of which rules out the possibility of following narrow specialism, being just trained and narrowly confined to one form of awareness. In sum, it requires such a criterion of all-round understanding (Peters, 1977, p. 28). The above three intrinsic qualities are the criteria that Peters thinks have to be built into the notion of being educated. The notion of quality is even more demanding when Peters quotes Socrates to say "it is not mere life that is worth living but the good life." Just as a good life cannot be conceived uni-dimensionally, so schools should not "be looked at purely in one frame of reference" (Peters, 1977, p. 37). It is within Peters' framework of analysis that we now set to scrutinize the notion of quality and value in ECR7 where the language policy is specified.

The ECR7 is the seventh report advising on the development of education in Hong Kong. Since the early 1980s, the publishing of these seven reports had witnessed so to speak the transition of Hong Kong from a British colony back to a city under the sovereignty of the Mainland. When closely examined, it is not difficult to find that underlying the rhetoric of these reports, identity is pretty much an issue directing the perspective taken in their writing. In other words, they reflect the kind of value(s) that the reports have identified with in determining the kind of quality the educational system wants to pursue. This can be seen in the process through which the kind of language policy that has been negotiated and then put forth. I would say the ECR7 was strategically composed to arouse an awareness of a survival crisis in Hong Kong. The suggestion they make clearly shows the picture.

Let's begin with a quotation from the ECR7, which says:

> Concern about the quality of school education is an international trend. Many developed countries such as Australia, Singapore, the United Kingdom and the United States have been studying ways and carrying out reforms to improve the quality of school education. Like them, Hong Kong faces new challenges and demands. Our education system should adapt to these changes and meet the demands of a dynamic world. We have to rely on quality education to contribute to the personal growth of our students, to build a competent work force to promote social, economic and cultural development and to increase our competitiveness in the international market. (ECR7, 1997, p. 3)

Quality in the above context is interpreted as some sort of cultural capital, by means of which one can increase one's competitive power in the market. Personal growth is seen as a process of accumulating this capital while schools, principals, and teachers are then treated as factories, producers, and labors respectively. This is analogous with the capitalist economic system, the mechanism of which serves as a factory aiming at producing massively, with no difference in quality (the student), processed by the same hand (the teacher), checked by the same machine (examination), ordered by the same client (the market and probably the parents), and referring to the same signs (the indicators). Quality assurance, value-addedness, effectiveness, and efficiency mentioned in other parts of the ECR7 are terms that are also "indicators."

Obviously, the ECR7 has imposed the logic of enhancing and measuring economic growth on to managing the institution of education. Under such a system, the language issue becomes part and perhaps the major policy of the government's strategy to attain such goal. Within this context, language, in our case English, is taken as an instrument through which Hong Kong can have access to the international market. It is not difficult to understand why English Medium Instruction (EMI) has become the parental preference for it is closely linked up with economic development. There is no denying this fact in reality. However, there will be problems with teaching and learning in general when English becomes the medium of instruction rather than a subject for study. The problem can be conceptualized on two levels: Firstly, the above target-oriented strategy only serves the expectations of those in control. They don't seem to understand that once the students are out of the classroom, they are back to reality where their mother tongue is normally used. It is not the purpose of this paper to discuss how English could be learnt better. Our focus will be solely on the educational aspect of language use especially when participation in community inquiry in school is taken as a preparation for assuming one's duty as a citizen in society. Using the mother tongue should be taken as a major step towards getting such an idea fully expressed. This paper will enter more discussion on this later. For the time being, how the ideology of the above mentioned problem comes about is our focus.

For the past decade, the ECR has set a highly competitive state of mind for Hong Kong. This competitiveness is taken as crucial to help sustain both the political and economic interests of the state. Within this context, personal interest becomes subservient. The intensification of time, space and resources represses individuality. In order to make it manageable, everything is reduced to numerical term for mass control. This is substantiated by Ramirez's research of the emergence of mass schooling (Ramirez & Boli, 1987). As a consequence, mass outrivals community in terms of its manageability. The difference between community and mass is that the former implies a unity of diversity with heterogeneous voices where individuality is not erased while the latter bears only a homogeneous and monotonous sign.

If English is considered as the link between the local and the global and/or international, the decline in standards would mean the loss of competitiveness in the current discourse. In this case, the language issue is tied in with success in terms of its capacity for access on the international level. We can see the reason why, though so many reports and educational findings have supported the use of mother tongue as the medium of instruction, Cantonese has been regarded as secondary. Even so, English is only treated as a tool. In short, the thought behind the drive to learn English in Hong Kong doesn't contribute to learning English as a subject in itself but rather takes it as a medium which may lead to something else, and it is the economic value underlying the whole premise. Consequently, Peters' notions (1977) of "commitment," "understanding," and "wholeness," which are regarded as the criteria for determining intrinsic education, will not appear.

Redeeming Quality on the Practical Level

In commenting on the ideology behind the current educational reform in England, Fielding (1999b) concludes that the ethical aspect of education has been taken over by the technical one. He believes that language itself plays a role in shaping beliefs and actions. As such, he suggests redeeming our education by speaking "the nuanced language of education, not the metallic language of the market" (p. 287). He criticizes what he regards as the present pathological condition of education, the cause of which is due to the sheer weight of external expectation, where "dialogue disappears as reciprocity retreats." He emphasizes the importance of the presence of a community through which the education of persons can take place (p. 286). This is what MacIntyre (1987) shares. Fielding's highlight of a dialogical environment entails the shaping power of language. Fielding claims "If we began to talk with each other in a language that is more attuned to the intellectual and emotional realities which we all now face, we would begin to think and feel differently about what we do and why we do it" (Fieldings, 1999a, p. 176).

Ian Frowe (2001a), in trying to theorize Michael Fielding's view, explicates that there are two notions of educational practice, namely the "natural" and "social." The effect of the involvement of language in these practices is to allow participants to be "able to communicate with each other ... [to] facilitate the ability of people to engage" and "a means of formulating and articulating the 'rules, principles and standards' which inform the practice" (p. 91). The latter is characterized by practices that "entail human beings engaging in a complex cooperative activity suitably informed by a set of socially established principles." What distinguishes the language of the latter from the former is its capacity to "enter into" the practice that helps shape, inform, and mould the discourse, which involves the articulation of one's beliefs, values, wishes, and desires. In a way, language of this kind "actively constructs a new reality" and brings "about something which previously did not exist" (Frowe, 2001a, pp. 92–93). In another essay, Frowe continues the elaboration that "language and reality are so closely interwoven that to describe the language is also to describe the reality" (Frowe, 2001b, p. 183). The educational implication here is "it is through the implicit and invisible introduction of a particular language that the audience is encouraged to start viewing its practice from a different perspective" (p. 185). Bearing this in mind, it can be conceptualized that language can be part of the evolutionary process of one's worldview. It is more than a vehicle for transmission. It is not merely a means. In short, it has its own life in a dialogical manner.

With the above conceptualization, Frowe assigns the language that shapes the current educational practice as the language of "performativity," the essence of which according to Frowe, "embraces a radical misconception of the nature of education." He further comments that "The language of performativity sees education as closer to a natural practice than a social practice," the result of which would turn education into a technical process "whose operation is subject to identifiable causal relationships and is controllable and predictable." The metaphor of school as a factory is used by Frowe (2001a) to describe the situation, within which "'inputs' of 'raw material,' which are then subjected to a set of 'standard processes' resulting in (suitably quality controlled) 'outputs'." And it is assumed that all children will learn in the same way, need to learn the same things and that the central pedagogical technique is that children have things 'done to them' in accordance with some pre-specified set of procedures" (pp. 95–96). We can identify some of the above characteristics through examining the educational policymaking process and the conception of citizenship promoted through the school curriculum in Hong Kong.

Morris, Kan, and Morris (2000) observes "the curriculum reforms emerging in Hong Kong are increasingly promoting a nationalist/integrative doctrine which attempts to deny the existence of a local culture beyond that of its lifestyle" (p. 259). The last few words are of immense importance, signifying that it is an alienating form of device. Though Chinese values are emphasized, however, they are only "portrayed in a way that suggests that they are a homogeneous and monolithic entity" where fulfillment of obligations and acceptance of responsibilities are placed higher than pursuit of rights (p. 255). In a way as it is interpreted by I. Scott that "the process of policy making is returning to a more elitist orientation" and "the political system is becoming 'disarticulated'" (as cited in Morris, 2000, p. 253). Firmly stated, this form of "disarticulation" can clearly be identified in the implementation of the language policy in Hong Kong.

I would postulate that the current cry for quality assurance and value-addedness is a systemic pathology. By systemic, I mean the ideological overarching structure being mutually reinforced by stakeholders that are involved in Hong Kong's education. By systemic pathology, I refer to the imbalance, which has lost the equilibrium that concerns the well being of human. In the case of Hong Kong's language policy, the phenomenon of pathology manifests itself in the choice of medium of instruction both by the schools and parents, who disregards that using one's own tongue as a medium of learning helps create a healthier environment for the intellectual and social growth of their children as their voices and identity will not be suppressed.

The above reflection is based on two of my assumptions I would like to reiterate here. Firstly, it is only when one speaks with one's mother tongue that one articulates and thinks simultaneously and spontaneously. And secondly, only when the above criterion is fulfilled can the concept of civic participation be realized in a dialogical manner through which a different sort of quality that embraces freedom, creativity and democracy can emerge through community activities held in school. There is no denying that those schools, which take English as the medium of instruction, can have some other kind of community activities in school. However, when the concept of active citizenship is involved, which entails the possibility of allowing critical or even subversive thinking that helps transform the present structure, the capacity to think and articulate in one's own language is crucial, and it is within a school community that such potential can be nurtured.

Articulation as Participation: The Way to Quality Assurance

One purpose of this paper is to relate the capacity of expressing oneself in one's own tongue to civic participation as a citizen. However, the notion of citizenship changes through time. It is toward the elaboration of that concept we now turn.

After introducing three types of citizenship, namely liberal individualism, communitarian, and republican, Lawson regards that we are now in a time when the concept of citizenship has evolved into a fluid concept beyond the boundaries of nation, region, and even space and time (Lawson, 2001, pp. 164–165). Nevertheless, once we cannot live without getting ourselves involved in a community, the debate on the conditional relationship between rights and responsibilities continues. By studying three schools in her research on students' participation in community work, Lawson arrives at the conclusion that "when community work was seen purely as a way of gaining experience in order to have something positive to include in a CV, it did not seem to have much of an impact on pupils in terms of encouraging active citizenship." She comments that "schools are promoting a form of citizenship education that teaches people what they need to know to cope with life and society as it is, rather than providing opportunities for discussing and challenging issues and questioning the status quo" (p. 176). Does Roberto Alejandro interpret reality hermeneutically by saying "citizenship should not be addressed only as a legal category" (Alejandro, 1993, p. 77)? Does it not remind us of Morris's study of Hong Kong's situation, where citizenship has always been nurtured to enhance passivity? Giving way to allowing schools to use English as the medium of instruction points to this in two ways. Having labeled whether overtly or covertly the Chinese Medium Instruction (CMI) school students as secondary is one, and allowing EMI school students to be deprived of their right to be nurtured to articulate, is the other.

Following this line of thought, the language policy, particularly the permission for 114 schools to use English as the medium of instruction, will be discussed and examined. It is pointed out in Tsui et al. (1999) that parental preference and economic development are the reasons for the resistance to an educational sound theory of language in teaching, due to an assumption that using mother tongue as the medium of instruction would lead to a decline in English standards. This leads to a misleading conception that there is a linkage whether covertly or overtly implied between using English as the medium of instruction and the automatic triggering of the acceleration of learning with quality, the process of which is totally ignored. Although it was proposed and has been implemented that positive discrimination in terms of providing more resources would help improve the English standard of those who opt for mother tongue instruction, this would only widen the gap by having labeled the Chinese medium schools, which in turn discourages parents from sending their children to this type of schools (Tsang, 1997). Such a notion of quality has put language in a place where there is no connection between thinking and speech. We think when we speak. I assume that more than ninety percent of Hong Kong secondary students only imitate when they speak English, which is their second language. I myself had the experience that when I wanted to speak English while I was still in school, most of the time I had to find a suitable word, a phrase or even a sentence in English, the structure of which had to match with that of my mother language, before I had the courage to talk to people in English. I dare say that this is the common experience of most secondary school students in Hong Kong. We imitate but not think when we speak. Furthermore, it has also created in our students and parents the sense that competence in English would seem, automatically, to be able to solve all problems in education at least strategically. However, they have ignored the fact that alienation from one's own language entails a discount of the capacity to think through one's language, which in the author's view is the foundation of learning.

To elaborate on this point, I am going to discuss the difference between "learning a language" and "learning through a language," which can be a totally different thing. By "learning a language," I mean that whether a learner's idea can be fully expressed during the process of using that language in the process of learning is not the first priority for it is taken for granted that this is not possible. In that case, the form and structure of that language becomes the focus rather than the idea or theme of the discussion around which that language to be learnt circulates. On the other hand, if "learning" is given priority, then the language through which we communicate "our ideas in details" in order to learn must be our first language, that is our mother-tongue. The difference is, in the latter case, that we don't have to be conscious of the correctness of the medium we use, that is, consciousness of the correctness of the structure and "designative" function of that language is bypassed, and that it will achieve what Taylor (1995) puts as to disclose new stance and a web of relations or speech community.

Referring to the theories of Halliday and Vygotsky (a linguist and a psychologist), Gordon Wells (1999) explicates how knowledge can be co-constructed in a dialogical manner with the child as the centre and the teacher the director. He emphasizes that the mediating tool, of which language is one of the most important, is crucial in facilitating students' learning through activities. He summarizes Vygostsky's theory by saying it "proposes a collaborative community in which, with the teacher as leader, all participants learn with and from each other as they engage together in a dialogic inquiry." Reflecting on Halliday's theory (1993), which says "the ontogenesis of language is at the same time the ontogenesis of learning" (p. 93), he maintains that "the explanation of language development is to be found in the study of conversational interaction" (Wells, 1999, pp. xii–xiii). In a sense, language itself is an indispensable artifact or "tool of tools" in Vygostsky's words which "mediates the associated mental activities in the internal discourse of inner speech" (as cited in Wells, 1999, p. 7). In educational terms, this is where teaching and learning takes place. One important point that Halliday makes is that "language does not consist of sentences; it consists of text, or discourse" (Halliday, 1978, p. 2), which is both the process and the product. It implies that a community where interaction takes place especially in the form of language is what makes the creation of knowledge possible. It is only when everybody within such community makes an effort to contribute that knowledge is generated. To discover speech, one must think. In the same way, to think, one must not only rely on the synchronic dialogic possibilities, but also the diachronic dialogic one(s), which is the pre-knowledge already nurtured by our mother tongue. One point Wells has noted which is of paramount importance to the choice and implementation of the language policy in the context of Hong Kong is that "it is through participation in informal conversation in the context of everyday events and activities that the child's learning of and through language takes place" (Wells, 1999, p. 22). It goes without saying that there will be no effective alternative to one's mother-tongue.

Perhaps, Vygotsky's differentiation between scientific and everyday concept can be helpful to our understanding. By everyday concept, is meant something that is learnt unsystematically in a spontaneous way whereas by scientific concept, is meant (as mostly happens in school), that which is presented and learnt as part of a system of concepts (Wells, 1999, p. 30). As Hong Kong students only have the chance to use English at school, the concept that is used in the course of teaching is scientific in nature. As such, everyday usage is lacking. During the learning process, the learner has to be consciously aware and volitionally involved. The crucial point is the learner is consciously aware of the systematic language concept and its corresponding representation between one's mother tongue and second language rather than the meaning it entails. Consequently, both the teachers and the learners will not be able to participate in what Wells calls community inquiry through genuine interaction. Rather, it will be a process of systematically looking for correspondence between two languages. If this argument can be accepted, using English, a second language, as the medium of instruction automatically eliminates the potential for participating in an interactive manner. The interaction arranged is mainly and purposefully directed to the learning of that language rather than meaning itself. As school is a place where civic duties have to be nurtured, it is a supposition that through participation in community activities at school, a predilection for action in later life will be gained" (Lawson, 2001, p. 170). Assuming that one's own language is the main artifact through which one immerses in the development of a social text or discourse, the elimination of one's right to speak in one's own tongue entails the eclipse of one's opportunity to get oneself involved.

As we earlier quoted from Alejandro (1993), "citizenship should not be addressed only as a legal category," on the contrary, it "ought to participate in the living process of interpreting the legal texts which define the community while identifying its values and its goals, its judgements and its hopes" (p. 77). To achieve this, one has to conceptualize language as "the reservoir of tradition" and a "medium" where human condition is grounded. In other words, it is through language that one can mediate the past with the present so that a possible future can be projected just as described by David Linge in his Editor's introduction to Gadamer's Philosophical Hermeneutics "the hermeneutical phenomenon encompasses both the alien that we strive to understand and the familiar world that we already understand" (Linge, 1976, p. xii). Alejandro summarizes this concept of a dialogical citizenship by saying "Citizens are citizens to the extent that they are engaged in a fourfold dialogue: dialogue among themselves; dialogue with the past; dialogue with the institutions and traditions, and dialogue with themselves"

(Alejandro, 1993, p. 76). The presence of such a hermeneutic situation entails the weaving of webs of relationship where each individual has to be engaged linguistically in their negotiation with the others. From an educational point of view within the school context and the language policy in particular, every student should be nurtured in a situation that allows them to fully express themselves without any barrier to their articulation among interlocutors. More importantly, there should be channels through which they are encouraged to critically speak out rather than be inhibited from doing so by whatever means. Given that my two earlier mentioned assumptions are correct, students in the EMI schools are suffering from the loss of this sort of primordial hermeneutic situation. The kind of quality that emerges from it must be that under technical control and deprived of the freedom to disclose or unfold itself to possibilities with choice. As I said earlier, they are ideologically governed and practically deprived.

Conclusion

It has been observed by Stephen Ball in the context of education that "efficiency is asserted over ethics. The humanistic commitments of the substantive professional — the service ethic — are replaced by the teleological promiscuity of the technical professional — the manager" (Ball, 1999). As the issue of language is still regarded as the threshold within a qualifying system through which quality and value can be processed, English is relatively in greater demand. However, this paper attempts to provide a different perspective on the role of language. It is the view of this paper that to have quality teachers and students in educational terms, we need teachers to be educated not merely in terms of their being qualified to perform certain skills including teaching English, but rather to cultivate in the mind of our students the confidence to express themselves in the way they feel comfortable with. They should be able to exhibit spontaneity, especially when identity and citizenship are taken into account as one of the criteria of quality, which requires them to articulate in what Alejandro coins a "hermeneutic situation." Within this context, mother tongue as the medium of instruction is the only choice. Only when one is nurtured in such a way can MacIntyre's "educated public" emerge. Without the possibility of freely expressing oneself in one's own tongue, it is really doubtful if it can be achieved.

It is the purpose of this paper to argue that the conception of quality based on economical value will ultimately and ironically betray itself. In the case of Hong Kong, the above postulation is clearly reflected in the course of the development of the language policy. When the notion of quality is conceptualized in relation to the ideological concept of identity and citizenship, it is claimed that only when such ideology is critically studied can the kind of uncorrupted quality mentioned at the beginning of this paper by Herder emerge, and it is only within such milieu can teaching really perform the kind of job it is supposed to do.

References

Alejandro, R. (1993). *Hermeneutics, citizenship, and the public sphere*. Albany, NY: State University of New York Press.

Ball, S. J. (1999). Education, majorism and the 'curriculum of the dead.' *Curriculum Studies*, *1*(2), 195–214.

Boli, J., & Ramirez, F. O. (1986). World culture and the international development of mass education. In J. K. Richardson (Ed.), *Handbook of theory and research for the sociology of education* (pp. 65–90). New York: Greenwood Press.

Bolton, K. (2000). The sociolinguistics of Hong Kong and the space for Hong Kong English. *World Englishes*, *19*(3), 265–285.

Education Commission, Hong Kong. (1997). *Education Commission Report No. 7: Quality School Education*. Hong Kong: Hong Kong Government.

Fielding, M. (1999a). Taking education really seriously: Two years hard labour [Editorial]. *Cambridge Journal of Education*, *29*, 173–181.

Fielding, M. (1999b). Target setting, policy pathology and student perspectives: Learning to labour in new times. *Cambridge Journal of Education*, *29*(2), 277–287.

Frowe, I. (2001a). Language and educational practice. *Cambridge Journal of Education*, *31*(1), 89–101.

Frowe, I. (2001b). Language and educational research. *Cambridge Journal of Education*, *35*(2), 175–186.

Halliday, M. A. K. (1978). *Language as social semiotic: The social interpretation of language and meaning*. London: Arnold.

Halliday, M. A. K. (1993). Towards a language-based theory of learning. *Linguistics and Education*, *5*, 93–116.

Lawson, H. (2001). Active citizenship in schools and the community. *The Curriculum Journal*, *12*(2), 163–178.

Linge, D. E. (1976). Editor's introduction. In H. G. Gadamer, *Philosophical hermeneutics* (David E. Linge, Trans. & Ed.). Berkeley, CA: University of California Press.

MacIntyre, A. (1987). The idea of an educated public. In his *Education and values: The Richard Peters lecture*. London: Institute of Education.

Memmi, A. (1990). *The Colonizer and the Colonized* (H. Greenfeld, Trans.). London: Earthscan Publications.

Ming Pao, March 14, 1998. "The Storm of Mother-tongue Education: Before and After the Verdict" (in Chinese), A4

Ming Pao, March 15, 1998. "My heart is heavy" (in Chinese), A6

Morris, P., Kan, F., & Morris, E. (2000). *Education, civic participation and identity: Continuity and change in Hong Kong. Cambridge Journal of Education, 30*(2), 243–262.

Peters, R. S. (1977). The meaning of quality in education. In his *Education and the education of teachers*. London: Routledge & K. Paul.

Ramirez, F. O., & Boli, J. (1982). Global pattern of educational institutionalization. In Altbach et al. (Eds.). *Comparative Education* (pp. 15–37). New York: Macmillan.

Ramirez, F. O., & Boli, J. (1987). The political construction of mass schooling: European origins and worldwide institutionalization. *Sociology of Education, 60*, 2–17.

South China Morning Post, July 29, 1997. Mother tongue holds the key to English, C. K. Lau, p. 17.

South China Morning Post, January 24, 1998. Letters to Editor: List of 100 schools rekindles language debate, p. 14.

South China Morning Post, March 14, 1998. Teaching issues, p. 14.

Taylor, C. (1995). *Philosophical arguments*. Cambridge, MA: Harvard University Press.

Tsui, A. B.-M., Shum, M. S.-K., Wong, C.-K., Tse, S.-K., & Ki, W.-W. (1999). "Which agenda? Medium of instruction policy in post-1997 Hong Kong. *Language, Culture and Curriculum, 12*(3), 196–214.

Wells, C. G. (1999). *Dialogic inquiry: Towards a sociocultural practice and theory of education*. New York: Cambridge University Press.

Tsang, W.-K. (1997). The development of retrospect and prospect with Hong Kong's medium of instruction policy comments on "Medium of Instruction Guidance for Secondary Schools" (in Chinese). *Ming Pao Monthly, 11*, 18–22.

PART II

Varieties of Values Education for Citizens

CHAPTER 6

The Development of Values Through the School Curriculum

Monica J. Taylor

Abstract

Everywhere governments are concerned about the development of young people as members of society and for their individual academic potential. Schools are the main institutional focus for ensuring that young people develop socially acceptable values. Governments and their agencies find it relatively easy to prescribe the kinds of values they would like young people and citizens generally to demonstrate. But neither governments nor schools are so sure about whether and how values are taught or caught. Whilst the values emphasised may vary across societies and schools, there is currently common interest in education for citizenship in many countries across the world.

This paper examines, by reference to current policy and practice in England, some of the issues and tensions in trying to develop certain values through the curriculum and in teaching and learning practices. By drawing on research evidence, some critical questions are posed for schools and policy makers who wish to meet their objectives, both in making provision in schools for developing values and in actually developing in young people the values required by society. Reflections on the issues from one Western country may have wider application and interest for other countries engaged in similar exercises as the world confronts new opportunities and challenges at the beginning of the 21st century.

Introduction

The very generality of the title of this chapter, like the whole domain of values (in) education itself, poses many challenges. The lack of specificity and concrete statements is daunting for many schools. In my experience, teachers are relatively good at answering particular pragmatic or practical questions like "What day/time is it best *not* to timetable Personal and Social Education?" or "How can you get Simon to stop calling out in class?" Teachers are often less good at facing (or is it only articulating to or discussing with a researcher?) diagnostic, positively oriented, longer-term, or more evaluative questions, such as they might pose to a "values education agony aunt." Questions like:

> "My class is not working very well together, as a social group; what strategies can I use to encourage them to be more kind and helpful to one another, and how can I judge if they are successful?"; or

> "I shall be the form tutor responsible for the Personal and Social Education of this class of pupils for five years through secondary school. How can I ensure that I approach the Personal and Social Education (PSE) curriculum (as specified by the school/government) with appropriate strategies which take account of pupils' learning abilities and developmental stage; what will count as evidence of their evolving values, attitudes and beliefs; and what should be my/the school's response?"

In fact, teachers, even the more reflective of practitioners or curriculum managers, rarely seem to consider such grounded questions, about what are, after all, very common teaching and learning situations in values education. Such a position, at least in an English context, is essentially, at the heart of the topic of this chapter. Why should this be so? Does it matter? And is it the fault of teachers?

In this chapter, I want to explore, with illustrations from evolving policy, practice and research in England, some of the social and educational confusions and tensions surrounding values education and consider what may be needed to enhance the development of values through the school curriculum. These may have wider resonance in other contexts. If governments, schools and citizens claim to value values — or at least socially acceptable values — then how can schools be helped to improve in their role as values educators and in developing young people as contributing members of a society? In this chapter, I shall unravel some of the hidden curriculum background to the development of values through the school curriculum and, in so doing, make some implicit and explicit suggestions for its delivery.

Confusions

Philosophically, I would echo John Wilson (see Halstead & McLaughlin, 2000; *JME* special issue, 29:3, 2000) in emphasising the need to try to be clearer from the beginning, about some of the key terms which have already been loosely used: "development," "values" and "curriculum." At the risk of being somewhat pedestrian, I think it is worthwhile taking a little time to explore some academic and professional issues, to see how these relate to questions of policy and practice, and to try to make some conceptual and empirical distinctions. In so doing, we shall encounter some of the challenges which teachers are expected to resolve in their practices. We must also explicitly acknowledge at the outset that the school is only one values educator, and possibly the least powerful (who knows?), alongside the family, media, peers and other "values communities" (see Halstead & Taylor, 2000, pp. 10–11). Indeed, it is a common arrogance of values education research, perpetuated here, to ignore non-school values educating agencies, though schools in their own endeavours certainly do not.

What is "Development"?

Even in such a meeting point of East and West as Hong Kong, we should not assume cross-cultural comparability in meaning and understanding when thinking and talking about values development. I was interested in the fact that I was originally asked to speak about the "nurturing" of values through the school curriculum and I wondered about the meaning(s) of "nurture" in Chinese culture. In an English values context "nurture" tends to be associated with a faith dimension, typically nurturing into Christian tradition, and there is a pastoral aspect, with the image of the Father feeding his flock. Against this has to be set the key concept in Western education of developing critical thinking and, what is also often valued, an open mind. Yet the concepts of faith or ideological "nurture" and "critical openness" seem antipathetic, if not mutually exclusive. Whilst I am definitely in favour of "critical openness," I also recognise the significance of "nurture" in early childhood values development, in the sense used by the philosopher of education, R. S. Peters, of "entering the palace of reason through the courtyard of habit" (1966). For there is clearly a tension: How do we get started in the development of values and virtues with the young if it is not by encouraging them in certain habits?

In the West "development" seems to be an overused and somewhat sterile word. To a great extent this is due to the predominant influence of Larry

Kohlberg's cognitive-developmental stage theory of moral development and all the complex micro-level research, measurement and theorising to which this has given rise. Psychological accounts of "development" have focused on individual growth towards moral maturity, development which can be coded and categorised by means of reasoning in response to hypothetical dilemmas in the Moral Judgement Interview (Colby & Kohlberg, 1987; Colby et al., 1987), and, in a simplified form, through Jim Rest's Defining Issues Test (1979) or John Gibbs' Socio-moral Reflection Measure (Gibbs, Basinger, & Fuller, 1992). For teachers interested in using available measures for assessing pupil change there are significant difficulties, such as the need for training, understanding the measurement, what is actually being measured, what the results mean and how they can be used in relation to the age group. Such challenges are too demanding for most teachers in the time they have available. Mark Tappan (1998), who favours a socio-cultural approach to moral education, using narrative to mediate and shape experience, has drawn attention to the "zone of proximal development," and guided participation in shared socio-moral activities.

In our recent review of the research literature on *The Development of Values, Attitudes and Personal Qualities*, undertaken for the school inspectorate (Ofsted) in England, Mark Halstead and I defined individual "development" as follows:

> Growth towards maturity, which may be gradual and discontinuous, which may involve passing through a number of stages and which normally occurs as a result of guidance and stimulus from family, school and community, as well as other influences including peer culture and the media. (Halstead & Taylor, 2000, p. 3)

More relevant, I want to argue, in the context of this paper, are the processes of education and the personal and social development of individual young people as an outcome of these learning experiences in school. Thus we are primarily concerned with the enhancement of provision for values education and in this sense the institutional development of the school itself. Here we are in largely uncharted territory. Though there have been evaluations of programme implementations (e.g. Battistich, Watson, D. Solomon, Schags, & J. Solomon, 1989; De Haan, Hanford, Kinlaw, Philler, & Snarey, 1997; Gibbs, Potter, & Goldstein, 1995; Higgins, 1991; Lind & Althof, 1992), apart from snapshots in school inspections every four years, institutional values development has rarely been researched over time (see Jackson, Boostrom, & Hansen, 1993, for a notable exception).

What are "Values"?

In our collection of papers in *Values in Education and Education in Values* (Halstead & Taylor, 1996), Mark Halstead offered a working definition of values:

What are Values?

> *Principles, fundamental convictions, ideals, standards or life stances which act as general guides to behaviour or as reference points in decision-making or the evaluation of beliefs or action.…*
>
> (Halstead, 1996, p. 5)
>
> *For individuals, including teachers, values are 'closely connected to personal identity and integrity' (p. 5). In a school context we are also concerned with the values which the school promotes as a learning community.*
>
> (Taylor, 1998, p. 1)

In our later review we suggested some examples of values: love, fairness, equality, freedom, justice, happiness, security, peace of mind, truth (Halstead & Taylor, 2000, p. 3). Other societies might emphasise these or other values.

Values in Society. Individuals and institutions, such as schools, may have values. Indeed, some schools have statements of the values which they wish to promote (about one-quarter in a nationally representative survey in England in 1997–1998; also see Taylor, 2000a). But can nations or regions have values? And if so, what are they? Would you, for instance, say Hong Kong has clear and distinct values, which most people would recognise and subscribe to? How do you know? And what do you count as evidence? What are the areas of value conflict? My guess is that it might be controversial to ask whether Hong Kong as a Special Autonomous Region can have values, since the values might, because of Hong Kong's history, vary from those officially espoused in mainland China. Indeed, with devolution within the U.K. regional/national issues of this kind are becoming increasingly salient. This may be another reason for England to require schools to focus on citizenship education.

In fact "values" had a high profile in the mid-1990s in England partly because of the National Forum for Values in Education and the Community set up by the erstwhile School Curriculum and Assessment Authority (SCAA, 1996a). The Forum, comprising 150 members — many nominated by national organisations with concerns for young people or education — was constituted to make recommendations on:

- ways in which schools might be supported in making their contribution to pupils' spiritual, moral, social and cultural development; and
- to what extent there is any agreement on the values, attitudes and behaviour that schools should promote on society's behalf' (SCAA, 1996b, p. 1).

Statement of Values from the National Forum for Values in Education and the Community

The Self. We value each person as a unique being of intrinsic worth, with potential for spiritual, moral, intellectual and physical development and change.

Relationships. We value others for themselves, not for what they have or what they can do for us and we value these relationships as fundamental to our development and the good of the community.

Society. We value truth, human rights, the law, justice and collective endeavour for the common good of society. In particular we value families as sources of love and support for all their members, and as the basis of a society in which people care for others.

The Environment. We value the natural world as a source of wonder and inspiration, and accept our duty to maintain a sustainable environment for the future. (SCAA, 1996c, pp. 3–4.)

The Forum agreed that there are some shared values but, importantly, that there is no consensus on the source of these values or how they are applied. It identified a statement of "values" on society, relationships, self and the environment, with implications for attitudes and action. Interestingly, this was widely endorsed by the public in a Mori poll (1996), though the statement on the family was controversial and considered too weak by some. This statement was to have formed the basis of guidance to schools, until, with the election of a new government in 1997, the development of values education took a different direction, thus illustrating its susceptibility to political vicissitudes.

Politically, values statements seem to occur when governments are newly elected or are into their pre-election year; governments want to claim the moral high ground. In Britain the Labour party has been keen to align itself with "decent values" ... "of compassion; of social justice; of the struggle against poverty and inequality; of liberty; of basic human solidarity ..." (Runnymede Bulletin, 1997). Coincidentally, in 2000 a new values debate started between the political parties. The issue was whether the "*British people*" (as though this group were in itself clear and uncontested) are interested in the *status quo*, or, as the then Secretary of State for Trade and Industry described it, in "*values, principles and ideals*" (he seems to imply these categories are different). He even suggested some values which British people should (or do? it was unclear) hold: "*decency ... care, concern, compassion ....*" It is, of course, this distinction and the actual gap between the prescriptive and the descriptive which is so important.

Is consensus about a minimal framework of values enough? It is surely in the playing out and interpretation of values in particular contexts — at the margins and in the pushing of boundaries in personal encounters and national events — that values controversy and conflict occur and we discover our individual beliefs and values and a nation's barometer. Indeed, should governments give a values lead to society? Is it appropriate in a liberal democracy for governments to prescribe values in education? Should schools' values reflect society's values or seek to change them? However such questions are answered, the values of a given society form the context for values education in schools.

Values in Education. Earlier I referred ambivalently to values (in) education. I think it is worth trying to draw some conceptual distinctions, although, in practice values education and values in education are closely linked. (Indeed, colleagues at the Scottish Consultative Council on the Curriculum contest the division (Barr and McGhie, 1995; SCCC, 1991).

Values in education, the values that are interwoven in the life of the school, its practices and relationships, have largely lacked investigation. It is not difficult to see why, since these values may be recondite, unspecified and unclear. We know little, for example, of how teachers' own values or their ideologies of teaching and learning influence their approaches to values education. Yet, in many ways, it is this informal context of formal values education endeavours which can make or break the school's success, both in provision for the development of values and in terms of pupils' developing their own values.

What are "Values in Education"?

> These are the values, which a school adopts.
>
> Values are conveyed in teaching and learning processes.
>
> Values are embedded in school structures, management, policies, language and relationships.
>
> Values can be both explicit and implicit.
>
> They can be 'substantial values' (such as honesty, respect) and 'process values' (such as reflection, caring).
>
> Values in school reflect the values and structure of society, of the education system, the National Curriculum, inspection and assessment.
>
> (Taylor, 1998, p. 1).

The School Curriculum and Values Education. If we can talk about values in society, and in terms of school-based education then we should define what is meant by values education in the curriculum. We're values educators aren't we, so this should be easy. But in some ways, at least in England (but probably elsewhere too) this seems to be at the heart of the problem. We are unsure what the values curriculum comprises, what to call it and how to include it as part of the school day! In England we have had a National Curriculum for over ten years, with a series of reviews and add-ons. The current stress on literacy and numeracy is one such. In the original conceptualisation of the National Curriculum, Religious Education (RE) was made a statutory part of the basic curriculum. The then National Curriculum Council (NCC) suggested that a "broad and balanced curriculum" should include certain cross-curricular themes: careers education and guidance, environmental education, economic and industrial awareness, citizenship, and health education. These all made clear reference to values (e.g. on citizenship see NCC, 1990, p. 4). Since then, careers education and guidance and certain aspects of health education have become statutory, but other themes have struggled to find a place in an already crowded curriculum. There have been constraints on delivery, such as timetabling, resourcing and staff expertise (Saunders, Hewitt, & MacDonald, 1995). Further confusion is engendered in that the schools inspectorate make judgements about school provision for Spiritual, Moral, Social and Cultural (SMSC) Education, another set of categories cutting across the subject-oriented curriculum. Thus the scope of values education is reflected in an empirically based definition, drawn from a nationally representative survey of values education in primary and secondary schools in England in 1997–1998 (Taylor, 1998, p. 1).

What is "Values Education"?

This is a relatively new umbrella term for a range of common curriculum experiences:

- spiritual, moral, social and cultural education;
- personal and social education;
- religious education;
- multicultural/antiracist education;
- cross-curricular themes, especially citizenship, environment and health;
- pastoral care;
- school ethos;
- extra-curricular activities;
- wider community links;
- collective worship/assembly; and
- the life of the school as a learning community.

Only in the last two or three years has renewed interest been shown in young people's personal and social education in England. Values education is one of the most sensitive areas of government policy in education and one which is open to political influence. This is clearly demonstrated by ongoing changes downgrading values education in favour of an emphasis on citizenship. The government appointed advisory groups on citizenship and the teaching of democracy in schools, personal, social and health education, and creative and cultural education, as well as a panel for sustainable development education. At the same time a government agency, the Qualifications and Curriculum Authority, undertook an initiative on values education. Despite keen competition and lobbying from other advisory committees, in the review of the National Curriculum, the then Secretary of State for Education, favoured the advice of his erstwhile university tutor in Politics, Professor Bernard Crick, who chaired the group on citizenship.

In 2002 in secondary schools citizenship education became a statutory entitlement as a foundation subject, in addition to a non-statutory framework for Personal, Social and Health Education. In primary schools PSHE and citizenship are non-statutory. National guidelines, focusing on what pupils may be expected to know, understand and be able to do, were issued prior to implementation in 2002. Decisions about detailed content and delivery are to be left to individual schools, but they are expected to address three strands of citizenship: social and moral responsibility; community involvement and political literacy, whenever possible through active learning approaches. Citizenship is expected to: contribute to pupils' spiritual, moral, social and cultural development; promote key skills; and provide opportunities to promote other aspects of the curriculum.

Schools are beginning to consider how they can demonstrate their provision for citizenship education and are seeking appropriate teaching and learning strategies. Qualitative research on cross-curricular learning in twenty secondary schools in five Local Education Authorities (LEAs) in 1999 indicated that schools were experiencing most difficulty with mapping curricular provision for political literacy. But a certain degree of confusion about implementation was evident in the reactions of senior staff responsible. "Its just another initiative"; "We do it anyway, what does it matter what its called"; "I'll have to get the Head of History to look into it and see where it comes up"; "I suppose we shall need to have a curriculum audit and see how we can demonstrate to Ofsted how it comes in" — were common reactions.

Such responses chimed with those in an earlier nationally representative survey in which both primary and secondary school staff claimed that the main influences on values education were not led by national curriculum reviews, inspection frameworks, LEA initiatives or discussion documents. They were much more likely to be a result of staff-perceived need, whole-school initiatives and pupil-related issues (Taylor, 2000a). But, not surprisingly, given the stress on subject disciplines, secondary staff were twice as likely as primary teachers to claim Ofsted inspections had been influential on developing values in the school. Schools have to account for their SMSC provision and produce a follow-up action plan, especially if it is found wanting in some way.

Further evidence, which will not sit well with government, comes from England's participation in the IEA Civic Education Survey (see Torney-Purta, in this volume). Some 70% of head teachers surveyed (N = 133) disagreed or strongly disagreed that citizenship should be taught as a separate subject. Most (60%) thought it should be integrated into subjects related to human or social sciences, or integrated into all subjects (50%). Such responses may indicate certain practical difficulties, such as finding discrete time for citizenship or appropriately qualified staff to teach it, and/or may demonstrate conceptual confusion or ideological differences about curricular emphases. However, if government is seriously interested in both evidence-based teaching and learning and the statutory introduction of citizenship then it must be concerned about teachers' views and what lies behind them, as well as the level of young people's knowledge and understanding of concepts and issues in citizenship, on which the IEA study has also collected evidence (see Kerr, Lines, Blenkinsop, & Schagen, 2001).

Is the new focus on citizenship education just a matter of curricular redefinition and a reflection of current social and political trends? Over the last 25 years the focus for values education has at one time been on religious education, at another multicultural education, later on cross-curricular approaches, now citizenship. Or is there a more fundamental conceptual change to the curriculum, moving away from individual choice, values, attitudes and personal qualities to an emphasis on group processes, political structures and institutional roles? Pre-implementation it is too soon to tell. But in my view, conceptually values education is wider than citizenship (see definition above) and is delivered through a correspondingly greater range of curricular and educational experiences. A statutory focus on citizenship will make it more problematic for schools to accommodate RE and collective worship in the timetable, especially at the higher age ranges, areas in which traditionally and ideologically schools have claimed to put their values efforts (Taylor, 2000a). And it is not clear how other important values, such as the spiritual, environmental, cultural and aesthetic, will be addressed through the school curriculum (see Halstead and Taylor, 1996). Moreover, those of us who would want to claim that moral values are essential to our concept of the human person and should be at the heart of the educational experience are unlikely to be satisfied with a moral education apparently limited to moral responsibility within citizenship (see Halstead in this volume).

Tensions

So what might lie behind such ambivalent responses to more specific plans for developing values through the school curriculum? Any education system or institution, especially if it feels uncertain of direction — not least because of value pluralism, or because it needs to respond to social change — will experience certain tensions, according to its particular history and situation.

Tensions occur at various levels, three of which will be considered here: government policy; school policy and practice; and teacher experience.

Tensions for Governments

Governments have a major influence on educational policy, no matter how much is left to choice and variation at the local level. Educational policy making has to balance academic and social development, paying due regard to age-related developmental trends and social objectives in the context of a wider social vision.

Goals: Development of Social and Moral Values, Character and/or Key Skills and Individual Achievement. The dichotomy may be expressed as a conflict between the value of money versus values for life or living. The development of individuals' economic potential, necessary to sustain a country or region compared with the development of morally good citizens continues to be a real tension in educational policies, not just in England. Social and moral dispositions and individual attainment are nearly always polarised and only nominally seen as complementary or interdependent. However, there is continuing evidence that employers claim to be interested in personal qualities not just qualifications. Linked to this is the value placed on education as subject knowledge-based and the stress on basic skills, such as literacy and numeracy.

Yet rapid technological changes are making such conceptions obsolete. Adaptability, flexibility, critical thinking and the application of key skills and attributes to problem solving have become by-words for success. Hence the development of moral habits and personal qualities is all the more important if the application is to be humanistic not merely mechanistic. A radical reconceptualisation is needed to see the full developmental potential of an education where the moral dimensions are on an equality with, for example, the technological or scientific. This would change societies and global living. Arguably many of the world's most complex challenges have an ethical component, which require the socio-moral and intellectual skills of individuals in workplace institutions.

Means: Ages and Phases for Implementation of Values Education. An education in values starts at home and habits are formed in the pre-school years. So an emphasis on values at the secondary or tertiary phases, without having made provision for formal education in values at earlier ages is, in my view, misguided. Curriculum content and teaching and learning strategies and experiences need to be appropriate to different ages and conceptual stages. Our knowledge of what works for whom, when and why is improving with ongoing research into learning processes and practices in values education (Emler, 1996). Unfortunately there has been relatively little research into early childhood values acquisition (see Halstead & Taylor, 2000, pp. 18–19). But that is where logically any government would start to plan a coherent developmental values education policy and strategy for research and practice. But usually governments start at the secondary level where an education in values is perceived as most needed.

Visions: International, National and Local Perspectives. It is not surprising that governments everywhere seem to be stressing the need for citizenship education. In an overview of the background to values education in 26 countries in Europe in the early 1990s, several underlying societal concerns were already evident: social crises, pluralism, religious influences and nationalism were prominent (Taylor, 1994). Since then, in the West at least, the perceived fragmentation of societies has increased. Whilst many societies have become more transparently pluralistic, with increasing social, ethnic and cultural diversity, diversity should not be mistaken for social fragmentation. In England social and cultural diversity varies regionally, and in urban, suburban and rural locations. This is reflected in government and school policies and practices. An emphasis on citizenship is intended as a corrective to develop a greater sense of, and loyalty to, the community, the relationship of the individual, not just to other individuals, but through participation in local social institutions, to develop greater awareness of and involvement in social movements and in political processes. It appears to be paradoxical that this occurs as nationalistic forces are growing within the United Kingdom. At the same time, there needs to be concern about the parochialism of some localities, which tends to fit with cultural imperialism, xenophobia and racism. Global communications, the all-embracing influence of multinational corporations, environmental issues, and terrorism beyond national boundaries mean that an education in values has to be multifaceted. Schools have to reflect and filter all these perspectives.

Tensions for Schools

Even if we as academics, government policy makers and teachers are often unsure quite what "developing values" means conceptually or empirically, schools world wide are required to make provision for an education in values of some form. Even if schools accept that they have a role in values education in a pluralistic society, each is faced with contestable choices about the values which it adopts as an educational institution, in its structures and processes, in its policies, and in its strategies and practices for values education through the curriculum.

Principles and Policies

- *Effective Academic and Values Education*: how to balance the academic and the values curricula; should there also be an entitlement to a values education? the ability range of pupils, their ethnicity, social catchment, parental pressure and whether the school is genuinely comprehensive might influence this decision;
- *Response to National Guidance in School Values Structures*: the extent to which to follow national guidance on values education or SMSC development; this has implications for the emphasis the school places on values in the foundation subjects of the curriculum, in extra-curricular activities, in the life of the school and in some form of separate provision, such as PSE;
- *Relationship Between Religious Education and Other Aspects of Values Education*: how to make links between values education, RE, collective worship and citizenship (especially in meeting statutory requirements); clearly the religious foundation of a school and the religious and cultural backgrounds of the pupils will affect decisions about policy and practice;
- *Extending Cultural Development*: how to take account of cultural diversity, or alternatively monoculturalism, in the school, especially in relation to equal opportunities; what attitude to take to youth cultures; how to promote an educational culture in school where being academically successful is good;
- *Whose Values? What Values?*: whether the school (and all schools) should subscribe to certain "substantive values," as advocated in the most recent government policy, and how they should be interpreted in the school; whether the school should produce its own values statement and consider how it fits with national guidance and other related policies; how do the values in such statements fit with parents' values; on whose authority does the school teach which values?
- *Values in the Educational Process*: how values education in school relates to educational and "process values" of inquiry, critical reflection, rational discussion and the intellectual virtues of sincerity and goodwill, commitment to procedure and argument, willingness to negotiate perspectives;

- *Forming a Values Education Partnership*: how inclusive the school can be in conducting its values education and in making and reviewing policy; how can it balance the often diverse views and values of teachers, pupils, parents, communities; and how can partnership with parents and communities contribute to pupils' personal development?

Implementation and Practices

Delivery Structures: The Specialist Values Educator Versus the Form Tutor as Values Educator. All schools where some form of values education is timetabled face the structural decision about who is to deliver it. The school's apparent choice is between the subject specialist's knowledge base, usually with "recent and relevant" training, being part of a "subject department" and greater commitment, as opposed to the more personal knowledge of, and relationship with, the student, which the form tutor usually has from everyday contact. Form tutors may lack confidence and are sometimes reluctant to deal with sensitive issues. The implicit tension here is between professionalism and caring, but decisions are often made on more *ad hoc* practical and pragmatic grounds, such as which teachers happen not to be timetabled to teach. Rarely do schools have a mixed system of both specialist and form tutor delivery. Visitors with special expertise may help augment and update knowledge and experience in particular curriculum areas, such as drugs and sex education.

Curriculum Content. In the area of values, unlike most other subject areas, schools are not given a programme of study, but guidelines as to the kinds of topics and themes that should be covered. It is open to schools to choose curriculum content appropriate to the age and stage of the pupils. Schools generally review their PSE curriculum annually and make modifications in the light of local issues, pupil needs, the level of interest shown and the apparent success of the teaching material. Many commercially published materials are widely available and are usually accessible to teachers, though some schools experience a shortage of materials due to funding restrictions. However, despite official endorsements to SMSC development through all curriculum subjects, not just in PSE, curriculum materials support for this has been lacking. The Charis project has produced classroom materials, developed by teachers for English, Mathematics, French, German and Science, for the upper and lower secondary phase. These materials are distinctive in that they aim to enhance SMSC development from a Christian perspective. They have been generally welcomed by Christian and non-Christian teachers as helpful in raising their awareness of how it is possible to include spiritual and moral perspectives in their subjects (Shortt, 2000; Taylor, 1997, 2001). In the light of renewed emphasis on citizenship, schools will also be seeking appropriate materials, such as those developed by the Citizenship Foundation for socio-moral development in the primary school (Taylor, Hill, & Lines, 1998). Evaluations of these projects provide useful feedback to the producers about take up, usage and pupil response.

Pedagogic Strategies. Teachers who favour a transmission and didactic model of teaching often feel less comfortable with values education and are generally less successful from a pupil perspective. Whilst some teachers employ different teaching styles in their subject teaching as distinct from PSE, there is evidence that some younger teachers, even in science subjects, are now claiming that their pedagogies are similar in both. Discussion is probably the single most widespread technique (Taylor, 1994), and if used diagnostically and strategically it can be effective in improving moral reasoning (Blatt & Kohlberg, 1975). However, many teachers would benefit from training in how to facilitate rather than orchestrate a discussion in which most class members can participate. In view of the growing stress on active learning and emotional literacy, teachers will be seeking new strategies.

Circle Time has become an increasingly popular approach in primary schools for developing a range of socio-moral skills and personal qualities, including enhancing self-esteem, sharing feelings, showing care and consideration for others, and developing an understanding of class rules (see Halstead & Taylor, 2000, pp. 50–51). A qualitative study involving observation of Circle Time and teacher and pupil interviews has, however, revealed that teachers need training in the use of the technique and the various forms which it may take if they are to be sensitive to the level of participation and responses of pupils, who themselves need to learn to take rules of disclosure and privacy seriously (Taylor, 2003).

School Councils are also being widely seen as a strategy contributing to citizenship education, by providing a structure for developing an understanding of democratic practices within the school community and giving pupils a voice (see Halstead & Taylor, 2000). About one-fifth of schools had a school council in 1997 and they are likely to become more common as a means of demonstrating provision for citizenship education. Qualitative research, involving observation and interview, has enabled an in-depth examination of schools' and pupils' expectations of and participation in school councils, and through them a range of personal and social learning outcomes and benefits to the whole school community (Taylor, 2002).

Tensions for Teachers

Being a values educator is something that goes with the territory for every teacher. But not every teacher feels comfortable or confident focusing on values. Often much more support is needed in school and in professional development, both in terms of an up-to-date knowledge base and appropriate pedagogical strategies, so as to build up a professional community of values educators. This would increase the chance of matching the formal curriculum messages with those of the informal curriculum of relationships and behaviour.

The Personal and Private Related to the Professional and Public. In my view teaching is a performative activity. A good performer knows when and how to listen as well as to talk. This is especially true in relation to teaching and learning in values. Those teachers whom I have observed who are most appreciated by their students and who are successful in providing stimulating and meaningful values learning opportunities are often those who are prepared to be a little disclosing about themselves — to put, as it were, something of themselves into the learning experience. Of course it matters how this is done: not in any moralising or high-handed way, nor in a way which is too friendly and attempts to identify too closely with the pupils, but to indicate fellow feeling, or to provide some insight, and best of all to indicate explicitly what the teacher learnt from personal experience. This can have a particularly strong effect with "at risk" students, as an evaluation of a social mentoring intervention showed (Taylor, 2000b). There is no reason why humanising and personal touches have to be confined to PSE lessons — why not throughout the curriculum and learning environment? Indeed, young people are quick to spot if a teacher acts differently in PSE lessons from their other subject teaching (Taylor, 1996). On the other hand, some teachers, often for good personal reasons, which should be respected, do not wish to bring their personal lives into the classroom, and anyway a critical issue in this context is to consciously set limits to what a teacher is prepared to disclose, for students do not always receive or treat personal information with appropriate sensitivity, with respect to adults or peers.

Handling Sensitive Issues. Linked to this concern, but needing to be separated from it, is the reluctance or dislike of some teachers to teach about what, for them may be embarrassing, controversial, or matters of which they are ignorant or lack up-to-date knowledge. Certain aspects of sex education or drug education are usually cited as problematic for teachers.

Sometimes teachers are exempted from such teaching and colleagues cover their lessons, though again students easily notice such changes. So this, in turn, relates back to the question of whether or not a school should have a specialist team of values educators who feel comfortable and moderately confident to address all the issues. Such a group, or individual teachers within it, are also more easily able and more likely to receive ongoing and specialised training thus enabling them to keep abreast of developments and to share information, strategies and support. A values education survey in England discovered that nearly half the teachers claimed to have had some whole-school training on aspects of values education in the previous two years: In secondary schools it was usually about developing a values statement or policy, or on sex education; in primary schools it was more about strategies and methods, such as Circle Time. However, in almost three-quarters of the schools training was only carried out by a member of staff without any input from outside (Taylor, 2000a).

Mind the Gap! Teachers are at the heart of values signals and messages from both the formal and informal curriculum. What they say and how it is said can easily counter any explicit values espoused by the school and in the curriculum under study. Pupils are adept at noticing this, indeed in interviewing young people one finds that they usually have a ready fund of evidence about discrepancies and perceived injustices (Taylor, 1996). On the other hand, they appreciate explanations, listening and apologies. They clearly attend both to the informal values curriculum and to the formal curriculum. Teachers have much influence on young people's lives and how they are treated counts just as much to them as it does to adults, perhaps more so, as they often consider themselves to be under various constraints in the school. So in their general conduct in the school, in relationships and in their explicit teaching, teachers, whilst not needing to set themselves up as exemplars — which in many schools would be extremely challenging to live up to — do need to be self-conscious about the power of positive and negative behaviour.

Towards an Effective Valuing and Values Learning Community: Meeting Developmental Needs

On the basis of research and evaluation into values education over several years, I was commissioned to write a guide to the issues for the Association of Teachers and Lecturers, one of the largest teachers' unions in Britain. In that guide I suggested some key performance indicators for the valuing and values learning school (Taylor, 1998, pp. 18–19), see Table 6.1.

Table 6.1: The Effective Valuing and Values Learning School

Characteristics	Evidence
Headteacher has a vision for values.	• Headteacher has clear goals for values in school and the kind of ethos to be achieved by a central focus or several continuous or successive approaches.
Strong professional leadership.	• Headteacher leads development and communication in values education, with agreement and support of senior management and with common purpose.
Values given high profile in teaching and learning and in life of school.	• Academic and affective development are seen as interrelated and complementary.
School promotes itself as a values learning community.	• All staff agree values and SMSC development essential part of school's purpose and constantly strive to improve practice.
Structures and processes to facilitate values are in place, understood and kept under continuous review.	• School development plan sets out objectives, means and resources for values education over at least 3 years. • Related policies (values statements, SMSC, equal opportunities, curriculum and teaching and learning) exist and are coherent.
Valuing and support for staff.	• Recognition that teachers are the best resource. • There is an SMSC/Values coordinator with senior management support, time and resources. • Whole-school training for all staff and curriculum training. Values dimension in teaching is on the agenda of the Professional Development Interview. • Involvement of "experts" with school in developing professional practice.
Examining and evaluating practice.	• Questioning, observing, reflecting on practices in values. • Examining school ethos, respect, responsibility, relationships, celebrating achievements in SMSC development. • Cross-curricular audits, raising awareness of values across subjects, planning interdepartmental values projects.

Table 6.1: (Cont'd)

Characteristics	Evidence
Empowering pupils: responsibility, self-esteem, self-discipline.	• Actively involving pupils in their values learning in the curriculum and school life, opportunities to develop responsibility. • Having high expectations of pupils — attitudes, personal opportunities and behaviour. Systems of support and sanction well known. Caring, fair and firm discipline.
Promoting and valuing home-school partnerships.	• Recognition of parents' rights and responsibilities for the SMSC development of their child(ren). • Working with parents to develop a genuine values partnership; survey parents' values expectations, discuss and generate clearer understanding of mutual expectations, boundaries and agreed practices.
Working with and valuing the community.	• School sees itself as a resource for the whole community and as benefiting from the community. • Active local involvement, for example, in citizenship, environment, community projects. • Being aware of clear values aims and outcomes and learning from differences and diversity.
Staff commitment and confidence about values (in) education.	• Climate of openness, critical reflection and debate about values issues. • Ethical reasoning about practices and in decision-making. • Professional competencies, consistency and adaptability.

Central to effective provision for the development of values in a school are planning, review and staff development. Taking a critically open perspective and a questioning approach can aid whole-school evaluation of values development. So I also offered a checklist of questions which schools might use on training days for self-evaluation (Taylor, 1998, p. 21), see Table 6.2.

Table 6.2: Evaluating a Whole-School Approach to Values

1. a. What is your understanding of the school's approach to values education?
   b. What are the main ways in which you consider it is taking it forward?
   c. Who do you see as taking a leading role in values education in school? How?
2. a. Is there a clear/ shared understanding by teachers and other staff of the school's approach(es) to values?
   b. How is this reached, articulated? Are all staff, governors, parents involved?
   c. Can you give an example from practice of how you would support your answer to 2a? (e.g. INSET, policy development, a critical incident with a pupil).
3. a. What priority would you say is given to values education in this school?
   b. Is this recent, ongoing or *ad hoc*? What evidence do you have for your judgement?
   c. How are you involved with values in school? If you are involved in teaching values in a subject, does this differ from what you do as a form tutor/teacher?
4. a. What particular values (substantive values, such as honesty, or process values, such as participation) do you think the school tries to promote?
   b. What has influenced these values (SCAA, LEA, Diocesan, community/family issues, school/pupil issues, parent/governor request)?
   c. How does practice relate to policy on this? How do staff interpret these values?
   d. Can you think of a time when you experienced a dilemma or conflict on a values issue in school? How was this resolved?
5. a. Is the school seriously evaluating its own progress in values education?
   b. If so, how? Is evaluation done in a structured way (i.e., through departmental, pastoral reviews with a written outcome)? Is it done through review of the curriculum? Has any progress been made on developing coherence and progression across the curricular experience of pupils? Is it done through school ethos and behaviour?
   c. Can you give examples of pupils' values learning/development from your own teaching, pastoral activities or observation of the life of the school?
6. a. Did you have any initial training related to values education? If so, how useful was it?
   b. Do you feel adequately prepared to deal with pupils' values development? If it were possible, would you like more INSET, time, workschemes, clearer aims, definitions, specified outcomes, curriculum resources?
   c. What specific support do teachers need to be enabled to do values education as role models, in their (subject) teaching, and to promote values in the life of the school?
7. a. What do you see as constraints on the school's values work?
   b. What do you see as particularly promising developments in the school's values work?

Conclusions

There are many confusions, tensions and paradoxes in the theory and practice of developing values through the school curriculum. There are no easy answers or clear ways forward with guaranteed success. This is not surprising, since not only is education a young art and science, but also the development of values is a complex and contested area. Moreover, it is both under-researched and under-resourced in terms of support to teachers and yet continually over-exposed and debated publicly. Everyone has some comment and opinion about values questions because values are central to the nature of the society in which we live and in which we wish to live. This is healthy in a pluralist democracy.

The current trend towards emphasizing citizenship education is an attempt to increase awareness of social and political processes and practices and to stimulate the desire to participate in and contribute to community life. Schools can be communities in which students can be encouraged to think, to feel and act for others and not just out of self-interest, and to have a sense of belonging to and being a part of something beyond themselves. The provision of educational opportunities and experiences that are conducive towards such ends must be central to the development of values needed for the healthy and ethical interaction of individuals and societies in the global world of the 21st century. And we in our professional roles as practitioners, advisers, inspectors, trainers, researchers and policy makers can only continue to strive in partnership for more reflection, insight, evidence, understanding and clarity in this challenging and vital task within the school environment.

To focus on developing particular values as such, in the school curriculum may be to misconceive the school's role. As we go into the 21st century it is becoming clearer that conflicts of values are inherent in being a member of a pluralistic democratic society and, the more so, in living in a global world. Thus the school needs to work actively with young people to empower them to develop the dispositions and skills to cope with values conflicts, to know what they are choosing between in terms of principles and values and to make positive choices, which they are willing to justify.

References

Barr, I., & McGhie, M. (1995). Values in education: The importance of the preposition. *Curriculum, 16*(2), 102–108.

Battistich, V., Watson, M., Solomon, D., Schaps, E., & Solomon, J. (1989). The child development project: A comprehensive programme for the development of prosocial character. In W. M. Kurtines & J. L. Gewirtz (Eds.), *Moral behavior and development: Advances in research, theory and applications*. Hillsdale, NJ: Erlbaum.

Blatt, M., & Kohlberg, L. (1975). The effects of classroom moral discussion upon children's level of moral judgement. *Journal of Moral Education*, *4*(2), 129–161.

Colby, A., & Kohlberg, L. (1987). *The measurement of moral judgement: Vol. 1. Theoretical foundations and research validation*. Cambridge, UK: Cambridge University Press.

Colby, A., Kohlberg, L., Spiecher, B., Hewer, A., Candee, D., Gibbs, J., & Power, C. (1987). *The measurement of moral judgement: Vol. 2. Standard issue scoring manual*. Cambridge, UK: Cambridge University Press.

De Haan, R., Hanford, R., Kinlaw, K., Philler, D., & Snarey, J. (1997). Promoting ethical reasoning, affect and behaviour among high school students: An evaluation of three teaching strategies. *Journal of Moral Education*, *26*(1), 5–20.

Emler, N. (1996). How can we decide whether moral education works? *Journal of Moral Education*, *25*(1), 117–126.

Gibbs, J. C., Basinger, K. S., & Fuller, D. (1992). *Moral maturity: Measuring the development of sociomoral reflection*. Hillsdale, NJ: Lawrence Erlbaum.

Gibbs, J. C., Potter, G. B., & Goldstein, A. P. (1995). *The EQUIP program: Teaching youth to think and act responsibly through a peer-helping approach*. Champaign, IL: Research Press.

Halstead, J. M. (1996). Liberal values and liberal education. In J. M. Halstead & M. J. Taylor (Eds.), *Values in education and education in values*. Lewes, UK: Falmer Press.

Halstead, J. M., & McLaughlin, T. H. (Eds.). (2000). Philosophy and moral education: The contribution of John Wilson [Special Issue]. *Journal of Moral Education*, *29*(3), September.

Halstead, J. M., & Taylor, M. J. (Eds.). (1996). *Values in education and education in values*. Lewes, UK: Falmer Press.

Halstead, J. M., & Taylor, M. J. (Eds.). (2000). *The development of values, attitudes and personal qualities: A review of recent research*. Slough, England: NFER.

Higgins, A. (1991). The just community approach to moral education: Evolution of the idea and recent findings. In W. M. Kurtines & J. L. Gewirtz (Eds.), *Handbook of moral behavior and development* (Vol. 3, pp. 111–141). Hillsdale, NJ: Lawrence Erlbaum Associates.

Jackson, P. W., Boostrom, R. E., & Hansen, D. T. (1993). *The moral life of schools*. San Francisco: Jossey-Bass.

Kerr, D., Lines, A., Blenkinsop, S., & Schagen, I. (2001). Citizenship and education at Age 14: A summary of the international findings and preliminary results for England. Slough, UK: NFER.

Lind, G., & Althof, W. (1992). Does the just community experience make a difference? Measuring and evaluating the effect of the DES project. *Moral Education Forum, 17*(2), 19–28.

Mori. (1996). [Findings of the consultation on values in education and the community]. Unpublished data of a research study conducted for SCAA.

National Curriculum Council. (1990). *Education for citizenship (curriculum guidance 8).* York, UK: NCC.

Peters, R. S. (1966). *Ethics and education*. London: Allen & Unwin.

Rest, J. (1979). *Revised manual for the Defining Issues Test*. Minneapolis, MN: University of Minnesota.

Runnymede Bulletin (1997). A new vision for Britain. *Runnymede Bulletin*, no. 306.

Saunders, L., Hewitt, D., & MacDonald, A. (1995). *Education for life: The cross-curricular themes in primary and secondary schools*. Slough, UK: NFER.

School Curriculum and Assessment Authority. (1996a). *Education for adult life: The spiritual and moral development of young people*. SCAA discussion papers No. 6. London: SCAA.

School Curriculum and Assessment Authority. (1996b). *The national forum for values in education and the community*. Final Report and Recommendations (SCAA 96/43). London: SCAA.

School Curriculum and Assessment Authority. (1996c). *The national forum for values in education and the community*. Consultation on Values in Education and the Community. London: SCAA.

Scottish Consultative Council on the Curriculum. (1991). *Values in education*. Dundee, UK: SCCC.

Shortt, J. (2000). The rationale of the Charis Project. In M. Leicester, C. Modgil, & S. Modgil (Eds.), *Values, culture and education*. London: Falmer Press.

Tappan, M. (1998). Moral education in the zone of proximal development. *Journal of Moral Education, 27*(2) 141–160.

Taylor, M. J. (1994). *Values education in Europe: A comparative overview of a survey of 26 countries in 1993*. Dundee, UK: CIDREE.

Taylor, M. J. (1996). Voicing their values: Pupils' moral and cultural experience. In J. M. Halstead & M. J. Taylor (Eds.), *Values in education and education in values*. Lewes, UK: Falmer Press.

Taylor, M. J. (1997). *Evaluation of the Association of Christian Teachers' Cross-Curricular Christianity Charis Project*. Final report to the trustees of the Jerusalem Trust. London.

Taylor, M. J. (1998). Values education and values in education: A guide to the issues. London: Association of Teachers and Lecturers.

Taylor, M. J. (2000a). Values education: Issues and challenges in policy and practice. In M. Leicester, C. Modgil, & S. Modgil (Eds.), *Values, culture and education. Vol. 2*. [Institutional Issues]. London: Falmer Press.

Taylor, M. J. (2000b). *Research and development support for remotivating young people through social mentoring and values education*. Final evaluation report to values education for life. Birmingham, England.

Taylor, M. J. (2001). *Evaluation of the curriculum resources of the Stapleford Centre (1995–2000)*. Final report to the trustees of the Jerusalem Trust, London.

Taylor, M. J. (2003). *Going round in circles: Implementing and learning from Circle Time*. Slough, UK: NFER.

Taylor, M. J., Hill, C., & Lines, A. (1998). *Evaluation of the Citizenship Foundation's primary school materials, "You, Me, Us!"* Final report to the Citizenship Foundation, London.

Taylor, M. J., & Johnson, R. (2002). School councils: Their role in citizenship and personal and social education. Slough, UK: NFER.

CHAPTER 7

Preservation of Wilderness: The Need to Go Beyond Intrinsic Values and Rights?

Wing-po Lam and John C. K. Lee

Abstract

In Hong Kong the wilderness is facing threats. To protect the low lying coastal areas from the growing pressure of development, convincing environmental ethics subscribed by the general public are needed to mount up social pressure to formulate comprehensive policy on conservation. This study focuses on examining the environmental ethics embedded in the instructional materials and programs of major green groups. How the green groups publicize their environmental philosophies through articles or education programs are influential in convincing the public to support and initiate environmental conservation. There are various environmental positions. Some may go for the intrinsic values in Nature, some may regard that it is immoral to disregard the rights of Nature, while others look for the instrumental values of Nature to help saving the wilderness. A discussion on the intrinsic environmental value, environmental moral and instrumental value follows to compare the pros and cons of justifying the need for environmental conservation through different ethical perspectives.

Dwindling Wilderness Being Encroached

In Hong Kong the wilderness is facing threats. Previously coastal areas left relatively untouched or just facing low environmental impact are now encountering intrusion of large-scale development or are degraded by development in close proximity. Some areas like Mai Po, though currently designated as protected areas, might be degraded by high density development on the periphery of adjacent land parcels, including those in Shenzhen. The relatively hilly terrain of Hong Kong makes land reclamation of the coastal waters a common option for land supply. This is also efficient as the Government need not spend so much time in settling disputes over the acquisition of land from the landowners. However, the natural coastline, together with the wetland ecosystem full of diverse organisms will be gone or severely damaged by large-scale development schemes. It is necessary to make the public be aware of the value of the wilderness.

This short chapter intends to review and discuss the following issues:

- changing perceptions towards the wilderness;
- attitudes of local citizens towards environmental conservation;
- the major approaches to justify environmental conservation;
- ethical positions reflected in selected publications of green organisations.

Changing Perspectives Towards the Wilderness

Wilderness, according to the *American Heritage Dictionary*, is an unsettled, uncultivated region left in its natural condition. The definition given is basically neutral without any inclination towards positive or negative value judgment. Going back in time humans tried to keep themselves away from the wilderness. Both wild animals and plants may be a menace to humans. Wild animals can be legally hunted for meat or for pleasure or killed merely to protect humans from being harmed. Wild plants can also be poisonous to humans. The wilderness is basically given a negative value; it is a place to avoid. A positive value evolves only when it is conquered and under the control of humans, that is, no longer a wilderness.

The unknown and not fully understood wilderness comes to people's mind as a place of uncertainty and risks. The negative feeling often comes about because of people's ignorance of the operation of natural processes there. Wilderness had better be conquered for humans' sake. Thus the wilderness only starts to bear *goodness* when it is tamed, conquered and has become controllable. Before the battle is over, the wilderness is often perceived negatively and is not worth deliberate protection by humans.

Perception does not come out of nowhere. It is shaped by personal experience, culture, technology, etc. Increasing people's knowledge enhances their understanding of the workings of Nature. For example, in the United States the wilderness which became known as Yellowstone was deserted. In the 19th century when settlers headed towards the West Coast and reached Yellowstone, they perceived the place as a hell on Earth. The mud volcanoes sounded threatening and the boiling water, with high sulphur content, from the geysers was unfit for drinking. They just wanted to move away as quickly as possible leaving the place more or less untouched. It was not until 1872, when the U.S. Congress perceived this as a place of unique spectacular beauty, that the land became the first National Park in the United States.

The ability to manipulate nature changes further humans' perception of the wilderness. Transport makes the place accessible, while air conditioning and insect management makes the place comfortable and inhabitable. Thus the wilderness is nothing to fear but can be useful to humankind. The natural beauty, the mineral resources, and so forth, in the wilderness can be assets to humans. The wilderness is no longer a liability.

The perception of instrumental value of wilderness to humans sets the stage for exploitation. Resources, whether they are plants, animals or minerals are stripped off the land for use by humankind. The notion that the wilderness must be untamed to be useful together with this exploitative attitude degrades the quality of the environment. Incomplete knowledge and understanding of the wilderness tends to lead humans to think that they are still far away from going off the edge. Thus, there is not much inclination to conserve the wilderness.

To sum up, an awareness of the overuse of the wilderness only very recently raised, recognizes, the need to conserve this no longer abundant resource. In Hong Kong the wilderness is facing ever increasing degradation due to the rapid growth of the metropolis. The upland areas are quite well protected by the Country Park Ordinance. However, the coastal waters and the wetland areas in the low lying zone convenient for reclamation is dwindling, and very much in need of conservation. The demand for its use from a multitude of users, requires convincing value arguments must be produced to justify policy to conserve this resource.

Attitudes of Local Citizens Towards Environmental Conservation

In Hong Kong, environmental conservation is no stranger to the local population. Currently, air pollution is a major environmental concern. The Chief Executive and policy makers speak about the topic frequently. The three major bus companies all actively research the feasibility of using less polluting fuels for their buses. Some minibuses have also joined pilot schemes for using gas to reduce pollution.

However, all these speeches and occasional attempts to be green do not mean that citizens in general are green practitioners. In a survey conducted by the Environmental Campaign Committee and the University of Hong Kong (Chung, 1993), nearly all respondents felt that they had a responsibility to improve the environment. They also thought that all parties, including the government, the private sector, the district boards, the municipal councils and educational sector were not doing enough for environmental protection. However, the survey also showed that only 13.4% of the respondents had participated in any kind of environmental protection activities and less than half (46.5%) of the respondents said that they were prepared to pay more for environmental products. Lack of effort at environmental protection, and being unwilling to pay more for environmentally sensitive goods, might arise from people being unable to convince themselves that the environment has something that is worth paying for.

On trivial matters, people will act in a "green" way. For instance, using both sides of sheets of paper does not cause too much inconvenience. In fact, it can save money. However, when asked to pay more for waste or sewage treatment, people have to weigh-up if the extra money they are going to spend can justify the extra good they gain from better water quality. Similarly, it is hard to persuade a commuter to give up the convenience of using a private car and to take public transport for the sake of making the air cleaner.

Despite the fact that education for the environment includes statements like "It is concerned with the formation of attitudes that lead to a personal environmental ethic" (Education Department, 1999, p.10), it is quite rare for teachers, whether through the formal or informal curriculum, to place much emphasis on these aspects. Most of the activities organized at the primary level tend to contribute to education about and in the environment, though a more holistic treatment including education for the environment is frequently emphasized in the literature (Lee, 1997).

Learning objectives, like showing concern, developing a sense of responsibilities, and taking action to alleviate environmental problems, are frequently in the sample lessons put forth in *Guidelines on Environmental Education in Schools* (Education Department, 1999). Quite often students are told what they ought and ought not to do, but are seldom led to think deeply about why they ought to act in that way to protect the environment, nature, or the wilderness. When it comes to crucial moments in environmental decision-making, people simply convince themselves that the right thing to do is "business as usual." To help students find out why they ought to and ought not to is important to help them justify their own actions and support policies FOR the environment. Otherwise, when they have to choose between his or her own good and preserving nature, students cannot easily find strong justification to sacrifice his or her own good in exchange for the well being of the environment.

Browsing through the sample instructional materials of the leading green organizations, schools and the Education Department, topics related to the political, social and economic aspects of the environment are not lacking. However, the normative side does not seem to have treatment in comparable depth. Maybe, searching for reasons for doing something good for the environment, whether they are reasonable, rational, or defensible are too removed from concrete environmental problems like ozone depletion or deforestation. Trying to answer questions relating to rationality may not be a solution to environmental problems immediately. However, one may wonder if environmental problems can be solved without discussing them on a more philosophical level. As mentioned by Milbrath (1998, p. 6), "We are the only creatures that can imagine our extinction. That special gift of understanding places a unique moral responsibility on humans. Once we have contemplated the future, every decision that could affect that future becomes a moral decision. Even the decision not to act, or to decide not to decide, becomes a moral judgment."

The Major Approaches to Justifying Environmental Conservation

In these environmentally conscious times, most people agree that there is a need to be responsible for the environment. What is lacking in environmental education programs is the attention given to environmental ethics, which examines the moral basis for environmental responsibility. The public do not need convincing further of the need, as shown by the considerable level of environmental consciousness. Instead, one should focus on the moral foundations of environmental responsibility, and how far this responsibility extends.

Environmental ethics made its formal debut with the publication of Peter Singer's paper "Animal Liberation" in 1973. Other schools of thought have come up one after another in the search for a new ethical basis to deal with environmental problems. Some are more individualistic, like focusing on animal rights and liberation, while others may go for a more holistic approach like the land ethics put forth by Leopold in the 1940s and advocated by Callicott (1984). These new schools of thought, often categorized as a non-anthropocentric/intrinsic values approach, emerge as an alternative to the perspective at the other end of the spectrum, commonly called man-centered, anthropocentric, or instrumental. The latter is quite often criticized as reflecting a technocratic perspective or inadequate to solve environmental problems.

In the following sections, some documents and instructional materials from green organizations in Hong Kong are examined to find out to what extent "environmental ethics" is presented and the ethical positions reflected with reference to the two major approaches, namely, intrinsic and instrumental. It must, however, be emphasised that the following examples cited are for illustrative purposes only rather than necessarily representative of the holistic ethical stance of these green organisations in Hong Kong.

Ethical Positions Reflected in Selected Publications of Green Organisations

There are a few well established green organisations in Hong Kong. Some, like the World Wild Fund For Nature (WWF) are well known internationally. Others, like the Conservancy Association, have a rather long history of development locally, while some, like Green Power, are comparatively more recently established. They constantly promote environmental education on their own or in collaboration with schools.

To arouse public concern about the imminent danger faced by wildlife and the wilderness, green organizations put forth justifications. Referring to the web site of the Conservancy Association, the importance of the Deep Bay wetland is quoted:

1. *Home of the wild animals*	• Various types of animals and plants can be found in the wetland. • The wetland can provide food, water and rest area for the wild animals. • The wetland provides the ground for reproduction of wading birds. • The wetland is the ground where the migratory birds come to rest and refuel.
2. *Environmental Conservation*	• The plants and the bacteria in the wet land can clean up the water through breaking down the pollutants. • Wetland can replenish underground water.

3. A sources of food and raw materials	• Wetland can hold water temporarily and alleviate flooding problems. • The wetland provides rich food resources like fish, shrimp and rice for Man. • The plants on the wetland can be used as building materials, fuel, medicine, etc.

The importance or the benefit of the wetlands looks rather far-reaching as it includes the welfare of animals, water regulation and cleansing function at the ecosystem level and lastly, a resource base for humans. The first two are intrinsic while the last one is obviously instrumental.

Despite the fact that the rationale for protecting the wetland being spelt out explicitly, the underlying argument is not discussed. An ecosystem is made up of a huge number of parts. It is necessary to examine when the conflict of interests between the parts happens, how the moral dilemma in satisfying differing interests is to be prioritised and how the ranking can be justified, including both the living and the non-living. Such discussions also seems to be lacking even in the full instructional package for the Mai Po Wetland published by the WWF.

Animal Rights

Quite a lot of values associated with the wetland, as put forth by the Conservancy Association in the example above, are intrinsic. The major characteristic of intrinsic values are that humans do not have to be there as the valuator (Schonfeld, 1995). It is not a value felt by humans. For example, the fact that the entities have well being of their own makes them morally considerable, in other words, bio-diversity is out there in the ecosystem whether or not humans are there.

Some of the intrinsic values stated tend to be individualistic. The welfare of the wild animals is important such that they should not be robbed of their food resources and habitat. Green Power also seeks wilderness protection through animal rights. Humans have to restrain their activities to leave the wilderness in its existing condition. In a comment by Green Power (1989) in "Heading towards Sustainability" published by the Environmental Protection Department, animal rights is mentioned twice:

- Many major environmental concerns are skimmed over or not mentioned at all, for example, animal welfare is not even discussed.

- No mention of animal rights.

It is the moral responsibility of humans to care for these animals, which are supposed to have the right to access for food and water that justifies the protection of the wilderness to maintain their habitat intact. Apparently, the claim seems to be very appealing, and sound in the sense that it is like extending human rights to animals especially sentient ones. Such rights can hardly be wrong. Nevertheless, in human society where there are still so many human rights problems remaining unsolved, the rights of animals can hardly be put strongly on the agenda. Moreover, the rights may only be comprehensible on the part of the more communicative or higher order "organisms." Besides humans are in no way capable of maximizing the welfare of all the organisms. Thus, subscribing to moral responsibility for the living world can lead to trouble reconciling the degree of moral significance to be assigned to different types of wildlife in the ecosystem.

Animal rights and liberation is limited in its power to tackle environmental concerns at the species level. Endangered species with a high probability of becoming extinct are quite often used to justify the need for preservation. The Conservancy Association (1998) puts forth the justification for wildlife protection at Mai Po as spelt out below:

> In recent years, over 60,000 waterbirds have wintered around Mai Po and Inner Deep Bay, including *endangered species* such as Saunders' Gull and a quarter of the world's population of the Black-faced Spoonbill. During Spring and Autumn migration, some 20,000–30,000 waders regularly use the Mai Po mudflats as a site to rest and feed before they continue their long journey. The highlight at those times, is the chance of seeing *rare* birds such as the Spoon-billed Sandpiper, Spotted Greenshank, Asiatic Dowitcher and Grey-tailed Tatler. (italics mine)

This short paragraph makes use of species rarity as the rationale to justify protecting the habitat. The goodness associated with rarity is that seeing the rare birds is the "highlight of the times." Here one may have to ask the simple question whether just being rare is a convincing enough argument. Being rare or in the endangered state can be something natural and does not necessarily arise from the wrong deeds of humans. One may argue that the fact of these waterbirds becoming extinct may not matter so much as species come and go naturally as part of the evolutionary process. The dying out of the species may not have an adverse impact on the operation of the ecosystem. Holistically, one may also say that the ecosystem can be healthier after removing the less fit species.

To convince the public of the need for the preservation of wildlife, some protagonists turn to "uniqueness" as illustrated in the following information published by Hong Kong Dolphinwatch Limited (2000):

> What kind of dolphins are these? Sousa chinensis, or Chinese White Dolphins, or Indo-Pacific Humpback Dolphins, are one of some 79 cetacean species. They can be found in geographically isolated populations from South Africa to Australia, and up the Chinese coast to the Yangtze River. The populations in Southeast Asia are *unique* in their colouring: born almost black, they quickly change to light grey, then slowly become white or pink as the grey colouration recedes. (italics mine)

One may question if the uniqueness of a life form offers a convincing argument to justify protection. A picture drawn by a child is "unique." Shouldn't uniqueness be equated with worth? There must be something more than "rarity" or "uniqueness" to justify invoking conservation measures. In the rest of the web page, major topics include what is/are killing the dolphins and what one can do to save the dolphins and exhortations to write to the government urging for the dolphin's protection. However, there is no further discussion on how to put up a very convincing justification to support the need for conservation.

In comparison, the panda is not only rare and unique, it is also a national symbol of China whereas to lots of people, the Chinese White Dolphin is just another species of marine animal despite its uniqueness in colouring. Though the species may be comparable on moral grounds, it doesn't possess the symbolism making it significant enough to draw attention to the need for further measures for its protection. In fact, it is often the symbolic value which is more influential in preservation, like the saving of the whooping crane of the United States or the panda of China.

Nature as Work of Art

Just focusing on the moral responsibility for the rights of an individual living thing or a species cannot address the problem that the wilderness, as a holistic entity, is facing. The complexity, integrity, and mystery of nature are often used as a justification. Nature is far too complex for humans to understand thoroughly before being considered morally. As the Conservancy Association (1998) mentions, nature as a work of art, by its very existence, is imbued with an intrinsic moral significance:

> The stand of inter-tidal mangroves fringing Mai Po and Deep Bay is the sixth largest in China, and the reedbed stands are one of the largest in Guangdong Province.

The Conservancy Association justifies the preservation of the grandeur as one of the greatest of that sort of landscape within the national boundary. Confining one's vision to the local area, the argument sounds strong. However, comparing to the other well known scenic areas in the rest of China, the local wetland might be far from spectacular enough to convince the public or government decision makers to provide special care and attention for it. Strictly speaking, such intrinsic value cannot avoid being ranked by humans, in just the same way as degree of moral significance. Thus, areas given a low rank are unlikely to get a significant position on the environmental agenda.

Bird watching is a prominent activity organized by the WWF and the Conservancy Association for the general public in the hope of raising awareness of the beauty of the birds and their habitat. One intended outcome is to justify the efforts at protection. Intrinsic value tied up with the unique and spectacular natural beauty of the wilderness has resulted in many successful cases of successful conservation such as the setting up of country or marine parks to preserve the wilderness.

However, "intrinsic" beauty is very much a subjective thing. The beauty perceived by humans in the wetland may not be beautiful at all in the eyes of the general public. In fact, this part of the wilderness can be perceived by some people as ordinary or even ugly in its natural state, so it may be justifiable to reclaim the land and replace it with man-made environments of elegant resorts surrounded by exotic plants. The dispute over the future utilisation of the Long Yuen wetland in Hong Kong does not come up unexpectedly. Moreover, the wetland is not unique and large patches can still be found somewhere else in China or other parts of the world. Nature as a work of art becomes even less justifiable for the far less spectacular wilderness remaining behind. The variation in the perception of the beauty also does not make it a good justification for the conservation of the wilderness, as consensus is hard to reach for the formulation of environmental policy. Furthermore, the justification may fall short of protecting that part of wilderness needing the most protection.

Quite often the beauty value assigned may seem insignificant relative to the economic value of development unless there are some other values associated with the wild life or their habitats. In China even the very "beautiful" Yangtze Gorges and the wildlife associated with them have had to give way to the hydroelectric power and flood control project. Despite their ecological value, they are far less a national symbol than the panda. This kind of variation in judging beauty makes it hard to reach a consensus which would lead to conserving the wilderness, except for very spectacular sites like the Arches National Park in Utah, the United States or Ayers Rock in Australia. It is only such eye catching, emotive and distinctive landmarks that can convince people to justify conservation stance over development. Such spectacular subjects may be the obvious choice though they are not necessarily the most valuable ones to preserve in terms of ecological integrity or the varieties of life form.

Instrumental Approach

Solely inclining to the intrinsic value approach and focusing on the rights of animals, the respect for other life forms, and nature as a work of art may initially sound compelling reasons why man ought to do something good for the environment. However, it may not be so. Ridley and Low (1993, p. 3) ask if selfishness can save the environment rather than appealing through sacrifice, selflessness and moral shame:

> People are not generally willing to pay for the long term benefit of the planet. To save the environment, we'll have to find some ways to reward individuals. Exhorting them to self sacrifice for the sake of "humanity" or " the earth" will not be enough.

The instrumental approach does not necessarily imply unrestrained exploitation and expansionism. Rewarding individuals may at the same time contribute to saving the environment. Views related to resource conservation and development seem to be quite explicit in the publications of green organizations like the WWF.

For advocates of the intrinsic value approach, endangered species or the extinction of life forms is a common rationale for wilderness preservation. Humans have the moral responsibility to not intimidate the pleasure and welfare of the life forms in nature. In a bio-community, life forms are to be respected so that they can pursue their ways of life (Callicott, 1992). The loss of habitat of the wild organisms violates this moral principle. Such principles might still prevail, but the incorporation of the relevance of species extinction to the welfare of humans is treated more seriously in publications of green organizations like the WWF. Here is a passage, titled "Why

Bother about Species Extinction?", from the WWF (1994b) fact sheet on this issue:

> First of all, every life form in nature has its own irreplaceable role irrespective of human understanding. *Humans*, like all other mammals, are at the top of the food chain and depend on a diverse ecosystem for survival. In the process of civilisation, *humans* utilise all sorts of natural resources for survival and development. Unsustainable exploitation of natural resources causes habitat destruction or alteration, and eventually, extinction of wildlife species. The relations between the organisms found on earth are very complex and are inter-dependent on each other to sustain further generation. Whenever a species declines suddenly, other species, including *humans*, will be affected. After a wide range of wildlife become extinct, it is questionable whether ever *humans* will be able to survive. Extinction is forever. The loss is irreversible and that is why it is urgent that we protect now. (italics mine)

The message starts by stressing the irreplaceable role of wild life in nature irrespective of human understanding. However, the rest of the message focuses on the fact that humans, being at the top of food chain, strongly depend on the well being of organism lower down the food chain. Extinction is not just the concern with the loss of a particular species. Instead, it is the survival of humans that matters in the argument. The justification here is mainly instrumental or anthropocentric. The instrumental value of the species in forming the foundation of a food chain is strongly emphasized to justify avoiding species destruction.

In another location from the web site, WWF (2000) sets forth the importance or the value of the Mai Po/Deep Bay wetlands:

> Apart from birds, the reserve has many other features of importance. The heart of the reserve is made up of 24 traditionally operated shrimp ponds (locally called "*gei wai*"), which are now the only such ponds in Hong Kong, and possibly in this region of China. This unique system of shrimp production is increasingly being seen as an example of the sustainable use of a wetland because shrimp production relies on the natural productivity of Deep Bay. The ponds are stocked by flushing in the naturally occurring young shrimps from Deep Bay, which then feed on detritus and plankton inside the pond.

Again, the WWF extends the value of the Mai Po Reserve beyond being important as the sanctuary of the birds. The unique operation of shrimp ponds as sustainable development benefiting humans' economic activity are included as justifications for conservation.

Summing up, to justify environmental conservation, there are some instances where green organisations incline mainly towards intrinsic or ecocentric values. However, instrumental or anthropocentric views do not seem to be excluded in promoting environmental movement.

Discussion

Enjoyment of Wilderness

To identify the true value of wilderness, tangible values that are comprehended and appreciated and accepted by the general public must be elicited. Just imposing intrinsic values on the wilderness is not adequate. The values must be visualized, heard, or sensed by humans to rationalize the need to preserve the places for human enjoyment.

The perception of beauty is a very subjective judgment. To some people, a desert landscape barely covered with vegetation is hell on Earth. However, in the eyes of others, the orange brown rock outcrops are the most beautifully colored sculptures on Earth; this beauty is valued for its own existence and is not to be compared with any human manufactured artifacts. Some traces of intrinsic value seem to be embedded in the perception. However, it is the utility of the instrumental value derived from the appreciation of the landscape that generates the human motivation to preserve a particular piece of wilderness.

Clearly the degree of natural beauty is the result of human feeling. For example, a distant thundering sound can be fearful, as it is described in the lyrics of the song Circle Game composed by Joni Mitchell in 1965. On the contrary, some people may find it enjoyable to "chase" thunder and lightning. There are tours in the North American desert where thunderstorms are frequent and very spectacular when the lightning strikes across the clear sky over the dry landscape.

Just saying that the intrinsic beauty is out there is vague. It is probably more fruitful to increase human's perception of such beauty for sensually stimulating or psychological enjoyment of the wilderness if one wants to justify its conservation.

Contribution of Instrumental Value Approach

Anthropocentrism has often been blamed for the degradation of the environment as the human-centered value system excludes the wilderness for moral consideration. This seems to be true as quite a lot of wilderness has been abused or over-utilized to satisfy human greed. These days land supply shortage leads to the wilderness being more intensively used, thus accelerating its deterioration. Nevertheless, anthropocentrism is not necessarily so evil as frequently claimed. If instrumental value is embarked upon in a sensible way, the wilderness can probably be sustained.

Humans may adopt an unrestrained, exploitative and expansionist attitude towards the wilderness by extracting the last ounce of use out of it. No wonder this perception of the wilderness merely as a stock-pile or sewer is detrimental and is not going to do any good for humans either. One can hardly deny that this attitude still exists. Humans cannot totally constrain themselves from economic activity just for the sake of letting the wilderness remain out there in its own exclusion. The perception of the sanctity of the wilderness in the broad sense and wilderness as a library to enhance people's quality of life can provide the grounds for promoting the preservation movement (Leiss, 1986). People must realize that, "Ecosystems function splendidly without humans but human society would die without a viable ecosystem. Individuals seeking quality of life require a well functioning society living in a well functioning ecosystem. That logic tells us that we must give top priority to our ecosystem, second priority to our society; only when the viability of those two systems is assured is it permissible to go our own way" (Milbrath, 1998, p. 3).

The feasibility of the justification of any conservation activity to be considered by society is crucial for the success of initiating such a task. The introduction of an instrumental value approach may be more direct and comprehensible. Natural wonder is not entirely intrinsic. Basically, it is the aesthetics as perceived by humans that matters, and creates the need for its protection. The perception of uses is context-sensitive and there can be polarisation of views as illustrated by the pioneers and the U.S. President on Yellowstone. However, it can be kneaded and shaped in a positive way. For example the value of preservation of the wilderness as an occasional retreat for urban dwellers helps to maintain the wild conditions from other competing uses.

No More Opposition

Dualism tends to polarize views that might not be favorable to justification of environmental protection. "Deep ecology takes for granted an economics based "zero-sum" picture of the world and nature, in which humanity can thrive only at the expense of nature" (Bradford, 1993, p. 421). An anthropocentric or instrumental value approach tends to be equated with immoral deeds, whilst a non-anthropocentric or intrinsic value position tends to be perceived and credited as selflessness of man towards the environment. Daly (1995, p. 622) holds that "It is a further mistake to identify intrinsic value with morality and instrumental value with prudence and then set up an opposition between them, as Sagoff does." Recognizing intrinsic value in nature would lead to the obligation to protect and increase that value. The realization comes in the form of paying attention to the instrumental value.

Colewell (1987, p. 109) regards humans as part of nature rather than subscribing to traditional concepts like Human vs Nature or Human vs Environment in the outmoded duality between human and nature.

> All values are instrumental. The important intellectual and moral question is which instrumental value is best suited to promoting the activity of environmental complexes in ways that are responsive to the life requirements of all its members.

Some green organisations try tearing down the wall between the two approaches, the WWF (1994a), in a fact sheet about the rare plants in Hong Kong, justifies why we should protect rare plants:

> Plants provide food, medicines and raw materials for humans and both food and habitat for wild animals. The wild relatives of crop plants are crucial in the breeding programs for resistance to pests and diseases, which make modern agriculture possible. Many plant species have beautiful flowers, fruits or foliage and provide pleasure both in the wild and in cultivation. Future needs for plants and their products are impossible to predict so it would be foolish to label some plants as "useless" just because we do not currently use them. Finally, many people believe that, as the dominant species on the planet, we have a moral responsibility to protect all other species, regardless of their potential value to us.

The passage tries to include both approaches. The anthropocentric approach extending to the future generation comes first, and the intrinsic values approach in the name of moral responsibility offers a justification for protecting those that might not have been included in the former approach. Adopting separate ways in approaching the problem in no way promotes more comprehensive protection of the wilderness.

Instrumental value and intrinsic value should not exclude one another in a pragmatic perspective. One may admit that the intrinsic beauty exists out there as a phenomena, irrespective of whether anyone is appreciating it. However, this value of intrinsic beauty must be subjectively and explicitly treasured by individual humans to be worth preserving. This tight connection should not be broken if the preservation of the wilderness is to be justified. To focus only on the objective intrinsic value and the rights of nature breaks the essential link for putting the issue on the agenda (Salmon, 1996). People can hardly be convinced to refrain from overusing the wilderness just for the sake of preserving wildlife and the natural landscape there. If they are aware of the fact that degradation thus caused will render the resource no longer available for their own enjoyment, they may be motivated to restrain themselves on moral ground from abusing the wilderness. Humans as the ultimate intrinsic value to justify pro-wilderness action seems necessary. The intrinsic values of the wilderness, like natural beauty, bio-diversity, and so forth, must be perceived as being instrumental as well, for them to be a socially convincing justification and to be included as a moral consideration.

To criticise instrumental value and the replacement of it entirely with intrinsic value is not helpful to preserving the wilderness. If humans understand that the wilderness out there is a sanctuary as the source of clean air, potable water and nutritious food and a library providing much of the knowledge to improve their quality of life, they will act rationally to contribute to its preservation. To conclude, justifying the preservation of wilderness from a human-centered viewpoint through making the intrinsic values explicit and enhancing these values further may be the pragmatic direction to follow.

Looking Forward

Quite a lot of effort has been spent on increasing our knowledge about and in the environment through education. Students and the general public are also aware that some of their actions are beneficial for the well being of the environment. However, some issues are far more complicated than the consensus might suggest, like using less water. Issues like whether the wilderness, say, a piece of wetland, should be left intact for the sake of conserving natural resources arouse social unrest. Traditionally, limited time is allocated to have deeper thinking into the rationale for holding stances in environmental issues. There is the tendency to take it for granted that it must be right to protect animal rights, to preserve rare species, to save the Planet for the sake of future generation, and so forth. However, such standpoints are debatable when one questions if human rights are respected too, what good qualities are associated with the rare species and why should one care more for the future than the present generation. Without going into the investigation of such standpoints, people may not be convinced and would ultimately seek for more radical actions like reclaiming the wetland and killing off the rare species to achieve their desired objectives, like transport improvement or financial compensation for land acquisition. Disputes and conflicts amongst various stakeholders over environmental issues cannot be resolved ultimately without deeper understanding of the ethics concerned with the don'ts and do's for the environment.

Environmental ethics is far more difficult to tackle than just providing students with the knowledge and field techniques for investigating environmental problems. Few attempts have been made in the past to expose the students to critically consideration of the ethical aspects. To be "critical" means not subscribing to one particular environmental standpoint only. Maybe, it is time to switch more of our resources in environmental education to the ethical aspects, to discuss the ideas and concepts guiding our way of environmental thinking, notions which influence the way we see it as a problem, a cause, or a solution. Despite the variety of environmental ethics and the difficulty in deciding which one is the more desirable to subscribe to, more discussion and reflection on the ethical aspects would contribute to the build up of more defensible positions for environmental movements. Otherwise, "So long as contemporary society appears to be working reasonably well, and leaders keep reaffirming that society is on the right track, the mass of people will not listen to a message urging change" (Milbrath, 1998, p. 6).

References

Bradford, G. (1993). Towards a deep social ecology. In M. E. Zimmerman (Ed.), *Environmental philosophy: From animal rights to radical ecology* (pp. 418–437). Upper Saddle River, NJ: Prentice Hall.

Callicott, J. B. (1984). Non-anthropocentric values theory and environmental ethics. *American Philosophical Quarterly*, *21*(2), 299–306.

Callicott, J. B. (1992). Animal liberation and environmental ethic: Back together again. In E. C. Hargrove (Ed.), *The animal rights/environmental ethics debate* (pp. 249–261). New York: State University of New York Press.

Chung, R. T. Y. (1993). *Survey on community attitudes to the environment: Final report*. Hong Kong: Environmental Campaign Committee and the University of Hong Kong.

Colewell, T. (1987). The ethics of being part of nature. *Environmental Ethics, 9*, 99–113.

Conservancy Association. (1998). *Ramsar Conservation*. Retrieved May 18, 2000 from the Conservancy Association Web site: http://home.netvigator.com/~cahk/ramsar/index.html.

Daly, H. E. (1995). Reply to Mark Sagoff's "Carrying Capacity and Ecological Economics." *Bioscience, 45*, 621–624.

Education Department. (1999). *Guidelines on environmental education in schools*. Hong Kong: Curriculum Development Council of Education Department.

Green Power. (1989). *Comments on "heading towards sustainability" — the third review of progress on the 1989 White Paper*. Retrieved May 18, 2000 from the Green Power Web site: http://user.hk.linkage.net/greenpow/html/essay/3review2.htm.

Hong Kong Dolphinwatch Limited. (2000). *Hong Kong Dolphinwatch Limited information*. Retrieved May 22, 2000 from the Hong Kong Dolphinwatch Limited Web site: http://www.zianet.com/dolphins/info.htm.

Lee, J. C. K. (1997). Environmental education in schools in Hong Kong. *Environmental Education Research, 3*(3), 359–371.

Leiss, W. (1986). Instrumental rationality, the domination of nature, and why we do not need an environmental ethic. In P. P. Hanson (Ed.), *Environmental ethics: Philosophical and policy perspectives* (pp. 175–179). Burnaby, British Columbia, Canada: Simon Fraser University .

Milbrath, L. W. (1998). Living sustainably. *Electronic Green Journal*, 9. Retrieved July 4, 2000 from the University of Idaho Web site: http://egj.lib.uidaho.edu/egj09/milbrat1.html.

Ridley, M., & Low, B. S. (1993). Can selfishness save the environment? *Atlantic Monthly*. Retrieved September 12, 1997 from the Atlantic Monthly Web site: http://www.theatlantic.com/politics/environ/selfish.htm.

Salmon, E. (1996). Towards an ethic of our environments: A course correction for deep environmental ethics. Retrieved September 8, 1997 from http://www.mosquitonet.com/~esalmon/env/thesis/index.html.

World Wild Fund for Nature Hong Kong (1994a). Rare plants in Hong Kong. *Factsheet No. 10*. Retrieved May 19, 2000 from the World Wild Fund for Nature Hong Kong Web site: http://www.wwf.org.hk/efsheet/fs_10.htm.

World Wild Fund for Nature Hong Kong (1994b). Endangered species I. *Factsheet No. 20*. Retrieved May 19, 2000 from the World Wild Fund for Nature Hong Kong Web site: http://www.wwf.org.hk/efsheet/fs_20.htm.

World Wild Fund for Nature Hong Kong (2000). *Mai Po: An overview*. Retrieved May 19, 2000 from the World Wild Fund for Nature Hong Kong Web site: http://www.wwf.org.hk/eng/maipo/introduction/wildlife.html.

CHAPTER 8

Education That Is Religious Education

Peter T. M. Ng

Abstract

Educators are familiar with John Dewey's sayings that "education is for growth (of life)." Whitehead (1949) has even remarked that "there is only one subject-matter for education, and that is Life in all its manifestations." His more famous saying followed: "The essence of education is that it be religious." Hence, the title of the present paper is "Education That Is Religious Education," which is emerged from Whitehead's illuminating thought.

The present paper attempts to re-evaluate the role and value of religious education in the new century. The author begins by studying the changes the subject has been undergoing in the past forty years, the challenges it is now facing and the possibilities for the development of a new form of religious education in the 21st century. The emerging Religious Education (RE) is found to be more related and concerned about life, with special reference to the search for human spirituality, and the cultivation of integrative values in human life. Two cases, one from Taiwan and one from Hong Kong, are cited as illustrations for more recent attempts in promoting a whole-person education for students by life education integrated with religious dimensions. The Hong Kong case, a Quality Education Funded project, is in particular, a bold attempt to help teachers of Religious Education from schools of different religious traditions to join hands together in the search for the spiritual qualities in human life, hence "Religious Education — in Search of Education for Quality Life."

Can I Be Considered Educated Without Having ...?

Hong Kong society has been debating the directions of reform for our education system in recent years. According to the Education Commission (2000) consultative document, the reformers are premised on the overall aims of education summarized in the following two statements:

> Education holds the key to the all-round development of a person and prepares him/her for work and life. Education nurtures talents for the society and promotes its prosperity and progress (p. 1); and
>
> The role of education should be to help people enhance their quality and potentials. Education should enable everyone to be in charge of their own life and to build a future for themselves. (p. 3)

The following questions which have once been raised by Veronica Williams (1993) and others in England may well be worth considered by our educational reformers too. She writes:

> Although I —
>
> - have studied the knowledge, processes and practical application of Science and Technology, **can I be considered educated** without having considered the ethical ends to which they might be put? (p. 32)
> - have keyboard skills, **can I be considered educated** without having considered the uniqueness of my existence? (p. 32)
> - know all the continents, rivers and capitals, **can I be considered educated** if I have not faced the questions of my share of responsibility for creation? (p. 32)
> - could give a list of all the drugs and their uses and effects, **can I be considered educated** if I have not been given access to any visions of the ultimate value of human life? (p. 32)
> - know all the physiological details of sex, **can I be considered educated** if I have never encountered the idea of sacredness of the human body? (p. 32)
> - know how to earn a living, and to enjoy the status and possessions it brings, **can I be considered educated** if I have never considered the joy and fulfillment to be gained from a walk by the sea, birdsong, true friendship or being creative? (p. 32) (bold faces mine)

At the start this new century, educators are becoming more aware that it will not only be an age for the advancement of information technology, it will also be an age for new forms of knowledge, development of new ideas, new cultures, new beliefs and value systems. Education will not be a mere learning of knowledge, concepts, ideas or skills, there is something more to be demanded of education. As educators, we are familiar with the famous words of John Dewey that "Education is for growth (of pupils' life)." Dewey has also reminded us that our students learn little from experience unless they could "reflect" on them ("reconstruct their experiences, is the more precise term he used"). In his "My Pedagogical Creed," Dewey (1921) wrote:

> I believe, finally, that the teacher is engaged, not simply in the training of individuals, but in the formation of the proper social life. I believe that every teacher should realize the dignity of (his or her) calling; that (he or she) is a social order and the securing of the right social growth. I believe that in this way the teacher always is the prophet of the true God, and the usherer in of the true kingdom of God. (p. 32)

Dewey was merging the social aims of education into the religious grounds for it, though he was often thought to be an agnostic.

Alfred North Whitehead (1861–1947), a British genius mathematician and educator, reminded us also that education should ultimately be "life education." In his presidential address to the Mathematical Association of England, Whitehead (1949) spoke on the aims of education and remarked: "There is only one subject-matter for education, and that is Life in all its manifestations" (p. 18). His most famous saying followed thus: "The essence of education is that it be religious" (p. 25). The title of this paper, "Education That Is Religious Education," indeed emerges from Whitehead's illuminating thought.

"Life" should be at the core of all education but somehow it has been overlooked or misplaced. The problem with our education today is precisely this misplacement of "life" in education. Thomas Moore (1992), in his bestselling book, *Care of the Soul*, commented:

> The great malady of the 20th century, implicated in all of our troubles and affecting us individually and socially, is "loss of soul." When soul is neglected, it doesn't just go away; it appears symptomatically in obsession, addiction, violence, and loss of meaning. (p. xi)

To this, Thomas Groome (1998) echoed, "The most dehumanizing aspects of Western education stems from its neglect of learner's spirits, with dire psychological and social consequences" (p. 326).

Religious Education That Concerns About Life

Religious Education is perhaps one of the few school subjects which puts the concern for life at the core of its curriculum. I may recall a few scholars from England and describe how the emphasis has been kept in the subject throughout the past forty years. Since the 1960s, there has been a drastic change in the aims of Religious Education in England. The movement is best described as a developmental trend from "bible-centred" to "life-centred" approaches. An Oxford educator, Harold Loukes (1961) was among the pioneers who advocated "learning through experience" in the teaching of religious education. According to Loukes, religious education is at root "a conversation between older and younger people on the simple question, 'What is life like?'" (p. 148). For Loukes, the job of a Religious Education teacher is to set students thinking and searching for meanings of life in an atmosphere of sympathetic dialogue (p. 175).

In most school subjects, the cognitive aspect dominates. Theories and ideas are taught for their importance in the abstraction of knowledge. The persons behind the theories and ideas, and their life and struggles as human beings, are put aside as unimportant. Contrary to this, religion is meant to be the search for the deepest and most profound concern of a human being towards life and destiny. According to Einstein, to know an answer to the question of "what is the meaning of human life, or for that matter, of the life of any creature?" means to be religious (quoted from Calaprice, 1996, p. 151). That is why stories and biographical narratives of persons and peoples, their ups and downs, success and failure, laughter and tears, are frequently found in religious education textbooks (Religious Education in Secondary Schools Project Teacher's Handbook, 1977).

Edwin Cox (1983), a notable religious educator of the seventies, once suggested that certain basic awarenesses, which he called "sensitivities," relevant and crucial to religious education. For clarity's sake, he listed six of them:

- a sense of the mystery inherent in life;
- a sense of continual change;
- a sense of our relationship to, and dependence on, the natural order;
- a sense of order in what we experience;
- a realization that there are other persons in the universe; and
- a sense of right and wrong. (pp. 37–48)

According to Cox (1983), the development of these six sensitivities would cultivate awareness of one's surroundings and would lead to a realization of fundamental questions about one's life such as: "Why is life here?" "How do I relate to the people and the world around me?" and "What is my significance as a person?" (p. 136). Such are examples of the sensitivities that underlie a religious response to human experience. Indeed, it should be our task as educators to enable students to move beyond mere facts of life, by raising questions about them and by attempting to interpret life and give it meanings. This is what education is meant to be and is precisely what religious education aims to achieve.

While the phenomenological approach to the study of religion was developed in the late 1970s in England, Michael Grimmitt (1978) worked out his "dual approach," integrating the phenomenological approach (he called it "the dimensional approach") with the life approach (he called it "the existential approach") developed over preceding decades. In his dual approach, Grimmitt suggested that religious education should go beyond the phenomenological approach, which aimed at enabling students' merely "learn about religions." For Grimmitt, religious education should also aim at enabling students' "learning from religions about themselves." He explained (1982):

> Enabling pupils to learn from religion means helping them to transfer insights gained from their study of religion to their own situations ... in coming to terms with questions about their own identities, their own values and life-styles, their own priorities and commitments, and their own frame of reference for viewing life and giving it meaning. What I am proposing is that RE should encourage the evaluation of one's understanding of religion in personal terms and the evaluation of one's understanding of self in religious terms (i.e. in terms of the religions being studied) ... On this view, encouraging development of this dimension of a pupil's experience of self is the distinctive contribution that RE can make to his or her personal development within the curriculum (p. 143)

Grimmitt (1983) defined "education" as "a process by, in and through which pupils may begin to explore what it is and what it means, to be human" (p. 60). He then argued that religious education as a subject in school should be sharing the same concern and contributing to the process of humanization, hence his book, *Religious Education and Humanization* (p. 60).

We normally ask students in class or after our lectures, "What do you think?" We seldom ask them "How do you feel about that?" or "Does it have any impact on your life?" What are the differences? The latter questions require students to look into their feelings about an issue or topic and reflect from their personal experiences. This should be part of what we call "critical thinking" — to be self-reflective and self-critical. As one of the subjects taught in the school curriculum, religious education concerns not merely about human life, it cares for the quality of life. Such questions like "What does it do to your life?" would certainly open up a new way of enquiry that our school education has otherwise neglected.

Veronica Williams confirmed again the significant role of religious education in values education in the 1990s. In the article, "Towards an Education in Beliefs and Values" (1993), she wrote explicitly:

> Religious education is central to the teaching and learning of beliefs and values because religious beliefs underlie many of the value positions which people hold to … In order that a balanced view is given of values and beliefs associated with most issues involving human life, a religious dimension needs to be presented. Religious Education can encourage a reflective approach to life, where thought before action and good judgement become a way of life. (pp. 32–33)

The Problem of Knowledge in Schooling and Curriculum

Transmission and development of knowledge must always be two of the most important tasks of school teaching and learning. However, we must at the same time be alive to some of the pitfalls of knowledge in our schooling and curriculum development.

It seems impossible for modern schools to function without differentiation of knowledge into subjects and disciplines. Nevertheless, Whitehead's words should be taken seriously again as he has confirmed that: "The result of teaching small parts of a large number of subjects is the passive reception of disconnected ideas, not illumined with any spark of vitality" (Whitehead 1949, p. 14). He went on to claim that: "There is a proverb about the difficulty of seeing the wood because of the trees. That difficulty is exactly the point which I am enforcing. The problem of education is to make the pupil see the wood by means of the trees" (p. 18). There are dis-connections of knowledge in our schooling and curriculum among different subjects, and the real life of students. Something has to be done for a curriculum integration that takes life as the centre of gravity.

Another pitfall of knowledge in our schooling and curriculum is the false positioning of knowledge about life and wisdom of life. Donald Walter (1997) has made this point strongly, arguing:

> Because our society equates education and wisdom itself with mere knowledge, and because we see this accumulation of knowledge as the be-all and end-all of education, we fail to recognize life for the opportunity to … [develop] our full potentials as human beings; and the adventure of discovering hitherto unknown facets of our own selves. (pp. 12–13)

Such mis-positioning of knowledge and life education is also evident in the textbooks that claim to be life-oriented. After a content research of textbooks, Robb (1996) complains that:

> In almost all the texts examined, the bulk of the content in each of the [life-oriented subjects] comprised specific technical information. Although some writers do propose some content which encourages responsible behavior, these make up a small part of the proposed content. (p. 6)

Something has to be done to take wisdom of life into our schooling and curriculum so that, in addition to all bits and bytes of knowledge about life, students may know the relevance and meaningfulness of all that they have learnt in their living.

What else students may be afterwards, education in this new century should aim at empowering students with wisdom of life, and the courage to be (oneself), the courage to live and the courage to make responsible choices. These are precisely what modern religious education is seeking to achieve (see Cox, 1982, pp. 53–57; Lee, Ng, & Lee, pp. 199–212). Teachers of religious education or other subjects should constantly be reminded of their primary tasks as educators and of these words of Whitehead (1949): "There is only one subject-matter for education, and that is Life in all its manifestations" (p. 18).

Integrative Religious and Life Education

Religious and life education can indeed be integrated within the school curriculum. I shall now cite a couple of successful attempts as illustrations for the integrative religious and life education, one in Taiwan and one in Hong Kong. I shall start with the case of Taiwan.

The Ministry of Education in Taiwan invited a high school, Stella Matutina Girls High School (SMGHS), to help develop a "Life Education Curriculum" for the Ministry since 1997. SMGHS is a Catholic private high school in Tai Chung. The Life Education Curriculum of SMGHS was originally a curriculum of Religious and Moral Education developed in the school over some years which was then revised under the government guidelines and was taken over as a blueprint for all other schools in Taiwan. In fact, Life Education has already been added to the formal school curriculum in Taiwan in September 1998. The aims of this new "Life Education Curriculum" endorsed by the Ministry of Education are as follows. They are taken from the curriculum of National Changhua Jen-Ai Schooly, Taiwan (2002) (彰化仁愛實驗學校):

- Helping students to grasp the meaning of life so that they may respect and love life, and to enrich their own life;
- Helping students to know themselves, to build up self confidence and beliefs, developing their potentials, and actualizing themselves;
- Helping students to be self-reflective, to strengthen the inner peace and harmony with the outside world, to transcend relations between the outside world and the self; and
- Helping students to build up positive and authentic visions of life, to cultivate health and a well-rounded personality (translation mine).

It is interesting to note that the government has invited a religious, Catholic school (and not a non-religious school) to help with the development of a Life Education Curriculum. In fact, it is not just one Catholic school which has been concerned with life education. Many other religious schools have also been active. For instance, one Buddhist tertiary institution, The Research Institute of Thanatology, Nan Hua Management College (南華管理學院生死學研究所) (1999), organized a big conference on "The Curriculum of Life Education" in 1998 and produced much materials which it published on a web-site for public reference.

For the second example, I report on the project I started in my Department of Religion at the Chinese University of Hong Kong. In the year of 1998, my department, with a grant from the University Grants Committee, started a pilot project called: "The Project for Strengthening the Teaching of Ethical, Civic and Religious Education in Schools" (August 1998–January 2000). We started this project with ethical, civic and religious education because, firstly, they are closely related subjects which are value- and life-oriented, and secondly, most schools with religious backgrounds in Hong Kong are in fact integrating Ethical and Civic Education within the subject Religious Education. Two of our most important tasks were: Firstly, the building up of connections and working relationship with teachers of Religious Education and also ethical and civic education; and secondly, the construction of the web-site of Ethical, Civic and Religious Education (ECRE) (http://home.school.net.hk/~ecre). Our primary aim was to help Hong Kong secondary school teachers to be more alert to issues about life in their religious, ethical and civic education curricula. Being greatly motivated by the intensive need of support and enrichment for school teachers, we determined to further develop our project and seek more financial support.

In 1999, we received another block grant from the Quality Education Fund of the Hong Kong Government. We were entrusted to launch another project: "Religious Education: In Search of Education for Quality Life," affirming our belief that life should be the key concern for education and the ultimate aim of quality education must be quality life. It is precisely one of the mostly asked questions has been: What do we mean by "Quality Life"? If we may repeat the words from Einstein (quoted from Calaprice, 1996, p. 151) which I have quoted before, this question about quality life education points exactly at the religious dimension of education.

Our new project aims to provide religious education teachers with greater vision of the value of Education for Quality Life and to facilitate the use of the ECRE web-site for greater impact on themselves and students. Our primary task was to strengthen the perception of religious education teachers on the value of "Education for Quality Life," and ensure that "Education for Quality Life" was one of the primary aims in their teaching.

Two of the main features of our project are the School Partnership Scheme and the ECRE web site.

In our School Partnership Scheme, we have invited Religious Studies teachers from 20 Hong Kong secondary schools from different religious traditions, namely Buddhist, Catholic, Confucian, Islamic, Protestant, Sek Sek Yuen and Taoist, to come together to work out lesson plans. This allows them to draw as much as possible from the vast resources and great wisdom enshrined in their respective religious traditions. The themes of their lesson plans are under three specific areas:

- Facing Life and Death: A Consideration of Various Religious Viewpoints
- Seeking Values for Quality Life: Insights and Wisdom from Various Religious Traditions
- A Global Village: Getting along with Peoples of Different Religious Beliefs

It is our conviction that there are vast resources and great wisdom in the various religious traditions which can bring insights to the development of value and life education in Hong Kong.

Secondly, we have further developed our ECRE web-site, which is intended to be a meeting place for teachers and educators concerned with Education for Quality Life, and an online resources center for them. Meanwhile, there are more than 40 lesson plans under the three key areas, with a catalog of collections of more than 600 items related to Life Education and Religious Education. There is a forum called "Teachers' Meeting Place," where more than 250 teachers and educators are currently registered. They can download complete lesson plans, contact all other members by e-mail, and join our discussion forum where they can share their visions and ideas, smiles and tears.

We have recently started a discussion on "Education without life is … and education without religion is …" in our Teachers' Meeting Place at this web-site.[1] It is interesting to note that there is another educational site, "Education to Home" (http://bkacademy.eth.net/index.htm) on the internet inviting similar discussions, with such thought-stimulating sentences as: "Education without Vision is a Waste, Education without Values is a Crime, Education without Mission is a Burden." It may be surprising to many, yet we think it is quite natural to find this parallel program, entitled: "Life Values: An Education for Life" (http://livingvalues.net) which was started by Brahma Kumaris World Spiritual Organization in 1997. Brahma Kumaris is an Indian monk and he has borrowed much of his wisdom from the Indian religions. This is another good example of an integration of religious and life education.

The above are just a couple of examples showing how resources from the different religious traditions can be used for the development of value and life education, both in Taiwan and Hong Kong, not to mention other on-line web-sites. Indeed, there are vast resources from most of the religious traditions that educators can explore and borrow insights for ongoing development.

Concluding Remarks

Professor Lu Jie, one of the keynote speakers at the International Conference on Value Education and Citizenship Education in the New Century organized by the Chinese University of Hong Kong in 2000, quoted the following words from Albert Einstein, saying:

> But let us not forget that knowledge and skills alone cannot lead humanity to a happy and dignified life. Humanity has every reason to place the proclaimers of high moral values above the discoverers of objective truth. (Lu, 1996, p. 29)

Who are the discoverers of objective truth? We know that they are the great scientists and mathematicians. But who are the proclaimers of high moral values? If we return to the original text of Einstein from which Professor Lu has quoted, the sentence following reads:

> Humanity has every reason to place the proclaimers of high moral values above the discoverers of objective truth. What humanity owes to personalities like Buddha, Moses, and Jesus ranks for me higher than all the achievements of the enquiring and constructive mind. What these blessed men have given us we must guard and try to keep alive with all our strength if humanity is not to lose its dignity, the security of its existence, and its joy of living. (quoted from Dukas & Hoffmann, 1979, pp. 70–71)

Hence, religious education will have much to contribute to value and life education. I may recall the story of "Cry Wolves!" or "The Wolves are Coming!" (狼來了！), of which a new version was attempted to convey a different set of values about life.[2] The original story was a very simple one, describing a shepherd boy who wanted to play tricks on the other peasants by crying : "The Wolves are Coming!", when there were no wolves around. So the peasants who came to help him were furious at his cheating and time-wasting. The boy did this a second time. Then the time came when the wolves really appeared and attacked the sheep. The shepherd boy started crying : "The Wolves are Coming! The Wolves are Coming!" Nobody listened or bothered to help him because he was labeled "a dishonest boy." The story is meant to carry a moral lesson for children, emphasizing that "honesty" is a very important moral virtue. Yet, I wonder whether the shepherd boy (or our children upon hearing the story) understood the lesson from it, or whether he (or our children) just consider people around them to be cruel and sometimes they did not turn up as they were expected.

The new version of the story I developed turns out somewhat differently. In it, I tried to give more understanding to the shepherd boy's motive and to be more sympathetic to his actions. I discovered that because the shepherd boy was so scared while watching over the sheep in the wild, he wanted to test whether the adults or the peasants were really ready to help him in times of need. So he attempted an experiment once and was assured that the peasants were all ready to help. He did it so successfully that he began to build up his confidence in people. Then he tried the second time and found that the people were so nice to him that he gained much more faith and trust in the loving care he had received from the adults, but he did not know why he was labeled "a dishonest boy." Then came the time when the wolves were coming to attack the sheep, the shepherd boy cried aloud: "The Wolves are Coming! The Wolves are Coming!" Despite his crying, no one would bother to help him this time because no one would trust him anymore. However, there was an old man who pondered a while, thinking: "Even though the shepherd boy was dishonest before, what if the wolves really came this time? Why should we not give him one more chance?" So immediately the old man rushed to the boy and he helped him to chase away the wolves.

What happened then? What then would the shepherd boy learn from this? When I read the old story, I doubted whether the shepherd boy could learn any lesson about honesty. However, in the new story (my new version), the ending was that the shepherd boy was so thankful to the old man who had helped him, so he was reassured by the human love and human kindness which he so needed, the when the old man explained to him why other adults did not turn up to help, the shepherd boy began to realize the truth about honesty and he began to admit that he was wrong and asked for forgiveness. His life was changed and he learnt the moral virtue of honesty too.

To sum up, there are two different sets of values in the above stories. One concerns morality and the importance of honesty as a moral value in human relationships. The other concerns religion and the importance of love and trust and forgiveness. The younger generation of this new century seems to reject the moral values our teachers are imposing on them, but at the same time they are yearning more and more for those spiritual and religious values (e.g., trust, love, and forgiveness) that we have been withholding from them. What should we be after now?

Reference

Calaprice, A. (Ed.). (1996). *The quotable Einstein*. Princeton, NJ: Princeton University Press.

Cox, E. (1982). Educational religious education. In J. Hull (Ed.), *New directions in religious education* (pp. 53–57). Sussex, UK: The Falmers Press.

Cox, E. (1983). *Problems and possibilities for religious education*. London: Hodder & Stoughton.

Dewey, J. (1971). My pedagogic creed. In M. S. Dworkin, *Dewey on education* (p. 32). New York: Teachers College, Columbia University.

Dukas, H., & Hoffmann, B. (Eds.). (1979). *Albert Einstein: The human side, new glimpses from his archives*. Princeton, NJ: Princeton University Press.

Education Commission. (2000). *Review of education system: Reform proposals*. Hong Kong: Hong Kong Government Printer.

Grimmitt, M. (1978). *What can I do in RE (or R. E.)?* (2nd ed.). Great Wakering, UK: Mayhew-McCrimmon.

Grimmitt, M. (1981). When is "commitment" a problem in RE? *British Journal of Educational Studies, 29*(1), 42–53.

Grimmitt, M. (1982). World religions and personal development. In R. Jackson (Ed.), *Approaching world religions* (p. 143). London: John Murray.

Grimmitt, M. (1983). *Religious education and humanization.* Sydney: Australian Association for Religious Education.

Groome, T. (1998). *Education for life: A spiritual vision for every teacher and parent.* Allen, TX: Thomas More Association.

Lee, W. O., Ng, T. M., & Lee, C. C. (1995). Becoming autonomous: The quality of the morally and religiously educated person. In P. K. Siu & T. K Tam (Eds.), *Quality in education: Insights from different perspectives* (pp. 199–212). Hong Kong: The Hong Kong Education Research Association, 1995.

Loukes, H. (1961). *Teenage religion.* London: SCM Press.

Loukes, H. (1965). *New ground in Christian education.* London: SCM Press.

Lu, J. (1996). Moral education: A transcendence — from the 20th century to the 21st century (in Chinese). In Zhang Li (Ed.), *Prospect of education in the 21st century: China and the world* (in Chinese) (p. 29). Nanning, China: Guangxi Jiaoyu chubanshe.

Moore, T. (1992). *Care of the soul: A guide for cultivating depth and sacredness in everyday life.* New York: Harper & Collins.

Niu, Z.-C. (1999). The Future of Life Education among Highschool Students: In Prospect (in Chinese). Retrieved from http://faculty.nhmc.edu.tw/~lifedead/class/leplan.html.

Religious Education in Secondary Schools Project. (1977). *Journeys into religion: Teacher's Handbook A.* Lancaster, UK: Hart-Davis Educational Limited.

Robb, W. M. (1996). *Values education for more effective: Moral education, religious education, citizenship education, health education, sex education, environmental education, alcohol education, multicultural education and personal and social education.* Aberdeen, UK: Centre for Alleviating Social Problems Through Values Education.

Walters, J. D. (1997). *Education for life: Preparing children to meet the challenges.* Nevada City, CA: Crystal Clarity, 1997.

Whitehead, A. N. (1949). *The aims of education.* New York: New American Library of World Literature.

Williams, V. (1993). Towards an education in beliefs and values. In Cyril S. G. Selmes & William M. Robb (Eds.), *Values and the curriculum: Theory and practice* (p. 32). Aberdeen, UK: Center for Alleviating Social Problems through Values Education.

Notes

1. To register at our Teachers' Meeting Place, please go to http://home.school.net.hk/~ecre/teacher_register.htm, and then go to the Meeting Place at http://home.school.net.hk/~ecre/teacherplace/teacherplace.htm
2. I told this story to a group of parents and kindergarten children at the graduation ceremony of the kindergarten (K3) in Hong Kong on July 8, 1999.

CHAPTER 9

Teaching Compassionate Social Studies

Matthew Hirshberg

Abstract

This chapter sets citizenship education goals and advocates a general approach for teaching social studies from a compassionate perspective. First, a general framework for discussing citizenship education goals is constructed. "Capability" goals are defined as those concerned with enhancing individual and collective performance in political, economic and social arenas. "Compassion" goals are defined as those concerned with increasing the role of individual and collective compassion in the political, economic and social spheres. The aim of citizenship education should be to help build citizens and societies that are not just capable, but also compassionate. A compassionate society is inclusive, just and harmonious, while compassionate citizens are empathetic, generous, cooperative and critically tolerant. While the importance of improving capabilities is acknowledged, it is argued that capability must be balanced with a strong dose of compassion to yield citizens who will make the world a better place.

A discussion of global education and its importance in broadening the scope of compassion follows, and the potential conflict between globalism and patriotism is addressed and reconciled. The argument is then made that the approaches of social science disciplines, while vital to the production of social knowledge, are inappropriate as bases for teaching compassionate social studies. In teaching compassionate social studies, educators must distance themselves from the dispassionate, removed, amoral and impersonal perspective that typifies established social science. Teaching compassionate social studies requires a participant's perspective on the social world, passionate attention to human joy and sorrow, and attention to ethics.

The chapter concludes with a number of suggestions on how social studies can be taught with compassionate citizenship education in mind. Students should be encouraged to think critically and to discuss multiple perspectives on contestable issues. There should be attention to honouring human differences, and students should be given the opportunity to see the world through others' eyes and help others. Teachers should model compassionate behavior, use cooperative learning methods, and broaden the scope of compassion through global education. In these ways, educators can help produce young citizens who will help make the world a more humane place.

Introduction

Unuhia te rito o te harakeke kei whea te komako e ko?
Whakataerangitia – rere ki uta, rere ki tai;
Ui mai koe ki ahau he aha te mea nui o te ao,
Maku e ki atu he tangata, he tangata, he tangata!

Take away the heart of the flax bush and where will the komako sing?
Proclaim it to the land, proclaim it to the sea,
Ask me what is the greatest thing in the world,
I will reply
It is people, it is people, it is people.

So begins *Social Studies in the New Zealand Curriculum*, the New Zealand Ministry of Education's (1997, p. 6) booklet stating the guidelines for social studies. The passage reminds us that, ultimately, social studies are not about structures and processes; they are about people, their hopes and fears, successes and failures, joys and sorrows. It also reminds us that if we teach without heart, something profound and beautiful is lost from our lessons. Teaching compassionate social studies means teaching from the heart about people. It also means training the citizens of tomorrow to use the power of their minds to think, their hearts to feel, and their bodies to act. If our students learn how to apply heart, mind and body to the social world in an integrated and compassionate way, then the world of the future will be in good hands.

In this chapter, I set goals for citizenship education and advocate a general approach for teaching social studies from a compassionate perspective. After constructing a general framework within which to discuss citizenship education goals, I consider the more conventional goals of enhancing collective and individual abilities to function effectively in political, economic and social arenas. While the importance of enhancing capabilities is thus acknowledged, I argue that capability must be combined with a strong dose of compassion to yield citizens who will make the world a better place. I then move on to discuss goals concerned with increasing the role of individual and collective compassion in the political, economic and social spheres.

This is followed by a discussion of global education and its importance in broadening the scope of compassion, and the potential conflict between globalism and patriotism is then addressed and reconciled. The argument is then made that the approaches of social science disciplines, while vital to the production of social knowledge, are inappropriate as a base for teaching compassionate social studies. Finally, I make a number of concluding suggestions on how social studies can be taught with compassionate citizenship education in mind.

A Typology of Citizenship Education Goals

Citizenship education is an oft-cited goal of social studies, but what should the goals of citizenship education be? This is a very political question, and theoretical, ethical and ideological preconceptions will unavoidably influence whatever answer is put forward. Still, the clear declaration of goals is necessary before a discussion can begin on how to achieve them.

The question of goals is one that social studies teachers have been asking for a long time, and Barr, Barth, and Shermis (1978) have distinguished three broad historical traditions. The oldest tradition, "citizenship transmission," is concerned with indoctrinating the young into the beliefs and practices that will allow them to conform to the prevailing political culture. According to a number of scholars (Grelle & Metzger, 1996; Leming, 1989; Sears & Parson, 1991), this tradition is alive and well today, at least in the United States. A second tradition is concerned with teaching students to think like social scientists, while the third, "reflective inquiry" tradition concentrates on encouraging students to think rationally and critically for themselves. Although the approach of this paper most resembles the latter tradition, it does not fit neatly into any of the three.

Given the complexities of our present world, Barth and Shermis (1980) write, "The goal of citizenship is reached when individuals are thought to have gained the complex skills that go into knowing and understanding their world, learning how to value and how to make choices and being committed enough to participate in different activities that are supposed to have communal value" (pp. 1–2). Still, they point out, that there are a myriad of ways one could interpret this, and little agreement on which perspective is best. How should the world be understood? On what basis should decisions be made? What activities have communal value? Which values are valuable enough to teach?

In defining citizenship education goals, let me first distinguish between collective and individual goals. While collective goals are concerned with the betterment of society (broadly or narrowly defined), individual goals are concerned with the betterment of the student. Collective goals are concerned with improving the general quality of human life at a community, state or global level. We achieve such goals by educating future citizens to be prone to act in ways that will make the world a better place. Individual goals are concerned with improving the quality of each individual student's life. We achieve these sorts of goals by teaching our children how to achieve virtue and happiness.

Next, let me distinguish between three related but separable realms of the social world: the political realm, the economic realm and the social realm. In the political realm, rules, institutions and processes are set up through which power is exerted and order is maintained. Political goals, then, relate to the exercise of power. In the economic realm, goods, services and wealth are produced, distributed and consumed, and that is what economic goals are about. Finally, the social realm refers, here, to everyday social and personal interactions between members of society, and social goals pertain to such interactions. In educating citizens, we are preparing them to play roles in all three realms.

It is now possible to distinguish between six types of goals (see Table 9.1). Collective political, economic and social goals relate to the general

Table 9.1: Six Types of Goals of Citizenship Education

Realm	Level	
	Collective	*Individual*
Political	Collective Political Goals	Individual Political Goals
Economic	Collective Economic Goals	Individual Economic Goals
Social	Collective Social Goals	Individual Social Goals

quality of political, economic and social life, respectively. Individual political, economic and social goals concern the quality of the future citizen's political, economic and social participation. Phrased in general terms of "quality," these goals still lack substance: By what criteria are we to judge the quality of political, economic and social life?

Our answer depends on what's important to us, what we value. As Case (1993) points out, education "cannot and should not be value-free. Every educational goal is an implied commitment to promote certain values or others ... The issue in education is not whether but which values ought to be promoted" (p. 320).

I suggest two values upon which citizenship education goals are and should be based: capability and compassion. To value capability is to place great importance on an individual's or society's power to achieve: Capability-based educational goals pursue such power. To value compassion is to deem it essential that members of society feel and show concern for others: Compassion-based educational goals emphasize such concern.

Capability goals pertain to the ability of a polity to serve its various functions effectively, to do things like allocate roles, produce resources and maintain public order and social harmony. They also relate to the ability of citizens to achieve personal goals effectively through political participation, work and social interaction. The citizenship transmission tradition is concerned with these sorts of educational goals.

Compassion goals are those based on an empathetic and ethical concern for the health and welfare of all humans. A compassionate society is one in which the needs of all are addressed, one in which distributing joy and minimizing the pain and sorrow of all people are major priorities. A compassionate person is one who truly empathises with and desires to help others.

Before I concentrate on compassion goals and advocate their pursuit in the social studies classroom, I will first discuss the more conventional capability goals. I do this with some ambivalence: Although I recognize the importance of promoting collective and individual capabilities, I remain conscious of some of the ways in which relevant indoctrination is not always consistent with goals of compassion or the encouragement of critical thought. Ultimately, education is a balancing act, and goals of capability and compassion must both be pursued.

Capability Goals

The six capability goals are listed in Table 9.2. At the collective level, political

Table 9.2: Capability Goals of Citizenship Education

Realm	Level	
	Collective	*Individual*
Political	Political Stability	Political Efficacy and Effectiveness
Economic	Economic Productivity	Earning Power, Industry
Social	Social Orderliness	Social Manners

stability is crucial to the polity's ability to ensure that decisions are made, laws are obeyed and interests are protected with a minimum of struggle. Citizenship education is crucial in this regard. If future citizens are taught the necessary patriotic beliefs, then they will view the political order to be legitimate and submit to its authority. Patriots are likely to fit into the political order and to make positive contributions to their country. Patriotism makes for a relatively strong, united country, while lack of patriotism could mean chaos or catastrophe. For example, if students are taught to identify with, love, care for, and even make sacrifices for their country, they will be more likely to support their country's war efforts, or even give their lives for their country. When a country's very survival is at stake, the ability to mobilize in support of a war effort is vital, and citizenship education is one means by which nations acquire such capabilities.

In addition, students may be taught further ideological beliefs that reinforce impressions of legitimacy. Depending on the nature of the polity, such beliefs may range from the divine right of kings to democratic theory, from religious fundamentalism to Marxism. Political stability is greatly enhanced when the appropriate ideologies are firmly lodged in the minds of the masses. This allows government to go about its business, for good or ill. The social studies classroom can be a potent forum for ideological indoctrination.

If students are taught what their proper roles will be as citizens, then they will be more likely to play those roles. Thus, for instance, after learning the importance of voting through years of social studies indoctrination, citizens may dutifully go through voting rituals every few years. Their participation may reinforce, in their minds, myths of democracy upon which their beliefs in the political legitimacy of their rulers rests. Further, this ritualised and relatively ineffectual form of participation allows the sense of political efficacy to coincide with a reality of powerlessness. Voting is often followed by ongoing periods during which the citizen's role in politics is one of spectator and idle commentator. During these periods, citizens who have learned proper political non-participation do not interfere with the running of government. Thus, if students can be taught how to think and act politically through citizenship education (among other forms of socialization), they further political stability by supporting the political order, participating in legitimating rituals and remaining passive and acquiescent when required.

Capability goals can be specified at the individual level as well. Politically, I have in mind the citizen's ability to recognize opportunities to use the political system to his or her advantage, and then to go out and successfully do so. Marker (1980) describes these goals:

> Well, as I see it, the main task of education in a democratic society is to produce citizens who are neither apathetic nor cynical. That is, who feel that problems can be solved, that wrongs can be righted, and, most of all, that they personally can participate and influence the direction of the society. The implication for social studies is that somewhere in the curriculum we have to show them how to participate, convince them that their efforts can really count. (p. 78)

Political efficacy refers to the extent to which citizens feel that their political behaviour brings the desired results. Political efficacy can contribute to legitimation and thus political stability at the collective level, but it also is an important prerequisite for political participation. One is not likely to become active politically if one believes one's actions to be futile, and inaction is guaranteed to be ineffectual. Particularly in a democracy, then, it can be important for both political stability and efficacy that students learn to believe in their abilities to affect their political world through conventional participation. Such lessons often promote ideas that are patently false, such as the notion that one's vote actually makes a difference in a major election. However, unrealistic and outright false beliefs in the power of individual political participation can be powerfully motivating, and are routinely taught in the schools, with these goals in mind.

Political effectiveness is basically what Newmann, Bertocci and Landsness (1996) called "civic competence," or the "ability to exert influence in public affairs" (p. 226). This is the degree to which citizens actually have the skills and habits necessary to affect outcomes successfully. Such skills are fostered by the ability to analyse and understand political situations and events, knowledge of political institutions, rules and processes, familiarity with an array of possible modes of political participation, and practice in political participation.

The social studies classroom is an ideal venue for this sort of learning to take place. Through discussions of current events, understanding is furthered as analytical skills are developed. Lessons and role-playing exercises concerning governmental bodies provide knowledge about such institutions and how they work, as well as practice in participation. Mock elections can provide both important knowledge on electoral processes and practice in political organizing, campaigning, speechmaking and voting. Outside the social studies classroom, school elections and student councils provide similar opportunities. Thus the schools can play an important role, not just by socializing students into the impression that they can make a difference, but also by providing them with powerful skills and habits.

A vital, productive economy is a strong, capable one. Schools play a crucial role in transforming children into obedient, efficient, productive workers (Aronowitz, 1973). Bowles and Gintis (1972/1973) point out that "schools are likely to develop in students traits corresponding to those required on the job," because they are similar to many places of work in terms of "bureaucratic order with hierarchical authority, rule orientation, stratification by 'ability' … and a system of external incentives" (Sullivan, 1980, p. 233). Students may learn punctuality, discipline, respect for authority, work ethics, norms of meritocracy, and how to tolerate boredom and delay gratification. Such lessons come naturally as teachers attempt to maintain order and motivation for learning in the classroom (Damon, 1988). Students also acquire crucial productive skills: reading, writing, arithmetic, computer skills, problem solving skills and others.

The school plays a crucial mediating role between the home and the workplace, easing small children into home-like classrooms and then spitting future workers out of business-like high schools. In this regard, social studies lessons play only a supporting role. By helping to instill the proper beliefs, motivations, habits and skills into the future workforce, educators can help to insure a strong, productive economy.

At the same time, educators also further the goal of providing individual students with economic capabilities. Knowledge of how societies work can be useful in the business world, and skills developed in the social studies classroom may even occasionally be put to lucrative use. In addition, certain beliefs may facilitate more effective participation in the economic system, and those beliefs may be promoted in the classroom. For example, people who believe in individualism and the Protestant work ethic may be more industrious, effective actors in market economies. To put it bluntly, teachers wishing to create effective future business tycoons might consider indoctrinating their students in individualism. As will become evident soon, however, this would be detrimental to the pursuit of parallel compassion goals.

Collective social goals are a bit more difficult to specify clearly, but the term social orderliness comes closest to what I have in mind here. A society in which people tend to interact smoothly, with few unnecessary misunderstandings, delays or conflicts, is capable of providing a relatively happy lifestyle to its members. Being a good citizen, in such a society, includes following norms of public behaviour and social responsibility that facilitate smooth, positive interactions. Knowing and being able to practice socially appropriate manners gives the individual the ability to interact with others smoothly and effectively.

Such norms or manners can be learned at school, both through explicit lessons and their practice in the school environment. For instance, social norms relating to waiting one's turn differ greatly among societies. In some countries, waiting in a crowd of elbowing competitors can be a harrowing experience, while queuing in other countries can be a pleasant opportunity for chatting. Not only can functional queuing behaviour be practiced in school settings, social studies lessons can cover such social norms and their value, perhaps in comparative contexts. The resulting knowledge of and practice in culturally prevalent social manners can also improve students' individual abilities to achieve and maintain positive social interactions and relations, as well as their abilities to get what they want from their interactions.

Balancing Capability With Compassion

Because a capable collectivity is stable, orderly, efficient, productive and powerful, it has tremendous potential for doing good, for filling the lives of its members and others in the world with abundance. It also has the potential for great evil. Nazi Germany was an extremely capable collectivity. Powerful propaganda and iron fisted Fascist rule insured political stability, orderly social interactions were the rule, and productive efficiency even extended to the industry of mass genocide. Capability is clearly not enough. What Nazi Germany lacked, more than anything, was an overriding ethic of compassion for all humans. This deficiency is what allowed ethnic minorities and members of other outgroups to be dehumanised and murdered by the millions, what allowed a country consumed by nationalistic fervour and chauvinism to waste millions of lives attempting to conquer its neighbours. Quite simply, compassionless capability can be dangerous.

Lack of compassion need not lead to extremes of oppression, tyranny and genocide. A less dramatic, but equally tragic, result is the dispassionate neglect that pervades humankind at the global level. As a species, we do not have the will to care for our weakest members, and so they suffer and die of destitution and disease. As we have armed ourselves with awesome capabilities, we have made little progress toward the sort of ethical and empathetic orientations that might motivate action for a less painful world.

We are a tremendously capable species, wizards who have produced miraculous machines for building, flying, thinking and communicating. We have grown, bred, engineered and processed vast quantities of food, enough to feed the world, and yet multitudes starve (George, 1977; Lappe & Collins, 1986; Unger, 1996). We are, as Hunt (1991) calls us, "the compassionate beast," and yet we have not begun to use the potential of our compassion. A world in which hunger, oppression and war are eliminated is achievable, but not without the conscious development of the greatest gift we have as humans: compassion. One important venue for that development is the school.

An economic system will be more productive and efficient if those participating in it hold appropriate values. Thus, for instance, a market system that relies on self-interested acquisitiveness to motivate producers and consumers will operate best with the participation of relatively greedy, selfish, competitive individualists. Although efforts to instill such traits in students may be functional in terms of the goal of economic productivity, efforts to do the opposite are more likely to produce compassionate economic actors. Thus a balance between individualism and collectivism, competitiveness and cooperativeness, acquisitiveness and generosity, concern for self and concern for other, may be optimal.

This is the case at the individual level as well. The confidence and ability to achieve wealth and power is a great gift. Combined with deep and broad compassion, the result is an individual who passes his or her gifts onto others. Devoid of compassion, the result, at best, is a greedy, selfish hoarder of riches, at worst a cruel bully. Wealth and power, not guided by compassion, are often wasted or, worse, used in destructive ways. Further, a developed sense of compassion leads to a deep sense of connection with others, something all humans need. Broad and deep compassion for others feeds back into greater kindness and compassion for the self. Thus greater compassion makes life more meaningful and fulfilling, and is in the interests of both the individual student and those he or she will come into contact with throughout life.

To serve the needs of the less capable, we must look past capability and tip the educational balance toward compassion. Yet compassion alone will not feed the hungry or free the oppressed. At both the collective and individual level, it must be combined with capability if it is to be effective. Thus, by combining and balancing the capability and compassion goals of citizenship education, we can educate for the sort of compassionate capability that both individuals and collectivities thrive on.

Compassion Goals

Proposed compassion goals are shown in Table 9.3. An inclusive political order is one in which all people can expect to have their needs and desires given consideration in the political process. If certain classes, ethnic groups, religions or ideological beliefs are excluded, if only certain interests are taken into account in public policymaking, then those who are disenfranchised and neglected are likely to suffer. Compassion for these people dictates the goal of political inclusion. Social studies teachers can promote a climate of inclusion by teaching about the varieties of different life circumstances, nationalities and belief systems in ways that celebrate and honour difference and encourage inclusive attitudes toward outgroups.

One way of insuring that potential outsiders are treated well is to guarantee certain essential human rights to all. When each individual is granted rights to such things as food, health care, clothing, shelter, non-harmful speech and action, access to the political process and protection from physical harm, the quality of the lives of people who would otherwise be deprived of these things is improved. Teaching children about human rights serves the cause of human rights in two ways. First, it gives students, whose rights will be ignored or trampled upon later in life, the opportunity to identify and claim the rights being denied them. Second, it makes all

Table 9.3: Compassion Goals of Citizenship Education

Realm	Level	
	Collective	*Individual*
Political	Political Inclusiveness, Human Rights	Political Tolerance, Critical Thinking
Economic	Distributive Justice	Generosity, Cooperativeness
Social	Social Harmony, Community	Empathy, Altruism

students sensitive to the basic rights of others and have greater empathy for potentially oppressed minorities. If they some day achieve positions of power, they will be less likely to disregard and more likely to promote the basic human rights of others. The result, hopefully, is a more inclusive society in which the protection of basic human rights is an important responsibility of the political order.

Likewise, compassion can be incorporated into individual students' political predispositions. Political tolerance refers to acknowledging difference and accepting co-existence, rather than insisting that others must either conform to our ways or risk oppression. A society of truly tolerant citizens is likely to be a relatively inclusive one. Still, tolerance is not without its drawbacks, and uncritical tolerance can have the negative effect of motivating the toleration of the intolerable (Marcuse, 1965). Thus it is important to teach, not only the general principle of tolerance, but also its limits.

If critical tolerance is the goal, then critical thinking skills and habits are crucial. While critical thinking is a generally agreed upon goal of social studies educators (Unks, 1985), its importance to a truly tolerant society is less recognized. Intolerance tends to be based on negative stereotypes and prejudices; groups of people, due to their distinctive attributes or activities, are judged worthy of exclusion. Research has shown that more knowledgeable students with more sophisticated thinking styles are less prejudiced, while "individuals who are dogmatic, who think in terms of sharp, dichotomous arguments are more likely to be prejudiced and act in discriminatory ways" (Byrnes, 1988, pp. 269–270). Pate (1988) advocates "cognitive training" to "equip students with the mental skills to avoid thinking in oversimple ways and making overgeneralizations" (p. 288), while Byrnes emphasises teaching students to recognize the stereotypes and overgeneralizations used by themselves and others. Through critical thinking, writes Walsh (1988), students "will increase their awareness of their own biases, heighten their openness to rethinking their positions in the face of conflicting evidence, and take time to reflect rather than merely react" (p. 282). Tolerance of those different from oneself and critical thinking, then, go hand in hand, yielding critical tolerance. In Gabelko's (1988) words:

> By developing cognitive sophistication, students grow in critical thinking skills, learn to question, and learn to develop personal meaning through their own experience or investigation.... Students who think, reason and question are less likely to exhibit stereotyping behavior, to discriminate, or to seek scapegoats to conform to peer pressures. (pp. 276–277)

Critically tolerant students can exercise their skills by grappling with questions concerning what ought to be tolerated and what is intolerable. Interactive discussions of issues, rather than authoritative instruction on the proclamations of experts, encourage deep social inquiry and creative rational thinking. A variety of controversial and fascinating issues of tolerance may be raised for classroom discussions. Should peaceful neo-Nazis marching through predominantly Jewish neighbourhoods be tolerated? Should advocates of racial intolerance or violence be tolerated? Should the hoarding of excessive wealth be tolerated while the less fortunate starve? Such questions, which can be argued from either side, provide the opportunity for students to practice deep social and ethical analysis as they come to terms with both the specific issues and general dilemmas of tolerance.

Soley (1996) argues that, through the study of controversial issues like these, students are able to explore critically their own perspectives and those of others. Martorella (1980) emphasises the importance of the interactive nature of discussions: Students become less egocentric and more conscious of alternative viewpoints through such interactions.

Such discussions also raise moral dilemmas, which enhance the moral development of students (Scott, 1991). Stevens and Allen (1996) suggest presenting students with moral dilemmas as a particularly effective method of teaching ethical principles, since "character, morality, and ethics are typically demonstrated by people faced with problems that are difficult to resolve" (p. 156). In these ways, discussions of contestable issues, particularly moral ones, can influence students in compassionate directions.

Another topic which forces students to think deeply, ethically and emotionally is distributive justice. As Fraenkel (1991) states: "If we wish to remedy injustice, we must teach about its opposite. Getting students to think about, and discuss, the idea of distributive justice is a crucial part of their overall education in general, and their social studies education in particular" (p. 40).

Setting distributive justice as the collective economic goal does not really go far enough, since a multitude of conflicting conceptions of distributive justice exist. As Deutsch (1975) reminds us, it is possible to view the distribution of resources to be just if it is based, alternatively, upon contribution, effort, ability, need or the market, or principles of reciprocity, equal opportunity or equity. Some of these bases of distributive justice are more compassionate than others; the unbridled market, for instance, is a particularly unfeeling and amoral, if efficient distributive tool. In other cases, it may not be so much that certain conceptions of distributive justice are more compassionate than other, but, rather, that they direct compassion at different sorts of social actors. Distribution by contribution is preferred by people who are particularly compassionate toward those who are more productive, while distribution by effort is seen as just based on compassion toward those who work hard. Distribution by need is favoured by those who direct their compassion toward the needy.

A broadly compassionate conception of distributive justice would be similarly empathetic toward the productive, the industrious and the needy, but would be particularly sensitive to suffering. It is, therefore, important for students to contend with a variety of conceptions of distributive justice in the classroom, and be encouraged to synthesise rather than becoming dogmatically attached to one limited notion. In the teaching process, it is important for students to come to understand that different systems for distributing and redistributing wealth can result in vastly different social outcomes, with major ramifications for human joy and suffering.

Fraenkel (1991) advocates teaching the importance of justice, that multiple conceptions of justice exist, that it is possible to assess some as superior to others, and that distributive methods that minimize suffering are to be preferred. To judge modes of distribution compassionately, then, students need to be sensitive to the potential and actual suffering of others. Thus, writes Fraenkel, they must be taught that "all people are worthy of respect and consideration simply because they are human.... what we are trying to develop is a sense of identification with others, and we hope for many, a sense of empathy for others. One way to promote this is to have students 'put themselves in other people's shoes' through such activities as role playing, role reversal, and the like" (p. 40). Likewise, Craig (1993) advocates teaching justice "by encouraging our students to enter imaginatively into the experiences and feelings created by social injustice" (p. 333), both through simulations and relating true experiences. Through such approaches, children develop empathetic sensitivities to justice issues.

Generosity tempers naked self-interest with a concern for others, and leads to economic behaviour that improves lives. Generous workers are forthcoming, rather than stingy with their time and effort. Generous employers provide their workers with decent wages and working conditions without being forced to. To teach about generosity, the legacy of generous heroes may be studied, and students can be given practical opportunities to experience the joy of giving.

Cooperativeness counters the possible excesses of over-competitiveness. Classrooms in which students constantly compete for honours and grades tend to produce competitive citizens. In contrast, classrooms in which the cooperative learning approach is taken, where small groups of students are encouraged to work together, to help and learn from each other, produce children with greater cooperation skills and tendencies (Battistich, Watson, Solomon, Sehaps, & Solomon, 1991; Conard, 1988; Pate 1988).

Cooperative learning allows and motivates students to divide tasks fairly, coordinate activities, help others, resolve conflicts, and take others' perspectives as well as communicate their own (Lickona, 1991). If students learn to work together for common goals rather than compete for limited rewards, they will emerge with greater tendencies to take into account the needs, concerns and perspectives of those around them, and to work with rather than against others. Teachers should be cautious, however, in attempting to use cooperative learning techniques in the context of strongly competitive educational institutions. Conflicting motives are likely to create free rider effects and make cooperative students feel that they are being taken advantage of.

Still, cooperative, rather than competitive, learning, under the right conditions, also has the advantage of allowing students to learn empathy and altruism. Not only have more competitive children been found to be less empathetic and altruistic, writes Barnett (1987), but also, "A competitive goal structure, whether induced in the laboratory ... or assessed in the school ... or home ... has been associated with lower levels of sharing and comforting than a non-competitive or cooperative goal structure" (p. 155). Thus cooperative learning is likely to be more conducive to the training of compassionate citizens.

Scholars do not agree on whether empathy consists of a cognitive understanding of the feelings of others, an affective, vicarious replication of those feelings, or a combination of those and, perhaps, other components (Goldstein & Michaels, 1985; Strayer, 1987). In any case, empathy involves some sort of sensitivity to, appreciation of or concern about the feelings of others, and is crucial to compassionate social interaction. Empathy can be encouraged through various techniques that get students to see the world through others' eyes, such as role-playing or inductive techniques. The social environment of the classroom and behaviour of the teacher are important: children who receive affection, interact with empathetic models, or are allowed to express their own emotions, tend to become more empathetic (Hoffman, 1982).

Compassionate individuals look out for the needs and possible distress calls of others and go out of their way to help one another. The ideal compassionate citizen is the Good Samaritan, who, in the biblical parable, stops to help a stranger in need. If the goal is to encourage empathetic and altruistic social interactions through citizenship education, how is that to be accomplished? A well-known study by Darley and Batson (1973) suggests that telling students stories of Good Samaritans is probably not enough. They found that seminary students, who thought they were late for appointments to speak on the parable of the Good Samaritan, tended to hurry by and not to stop to help a slumped victim along their path. Apparently, even for these ethical individuals with the Good Samaritan on their minds, it was a matter of priorities: Sharing with the needy is a secondary concern, usually overridden by more central and urgent matters. When students learn repeatedly that being on time and speaking cleverly is what is important, they will punctually pontificate with exquisite eloquence on the importance of helping one's neighbour rather than actually do so.

As Lickona (1991) points out, it is important for students to consider why they and others do not always behave how they know they should, and a simplified class discussion of Darley and Batson's study might allow for this at the higher levels. An even more compelling potential teaching tool is the horrific 1964 incident in which New York resident Kitty Genovese was stabbed repeatedly to death over a half-hour period while thirty-eight witnesses did nothing. A discussion of this incident can yield an understanding of the nature and dangers of bystander non-intervention (Latane & Darley, 1970), and that understanding may be a potent antidote to its occurrence.

Cialdini, Kenrick and Baumann (1982) define altruism as "actions taken to benefit another for reasons other than extrinsic reward" (p. 339). Whether altruism even exists among humans is a subject for much debate, and young children who have not yet reached the necessary stage of moral development may not be capable of it. They can, however, learn to behave helpfully through positive reinforcement and the presence of prosocial models in their schools. Teachers can begin to explain the ramifications of helpful behavior or its absence, and present students with stories about helpful behavior for discussion (Bar-Tal & Raviv, 1982). Role playing exercises are useful, as they allow students to practice and experience both giving and receiving help. Such exercises, as well as other methods that allow students to see the world through others' eyes, increase empathy as well as prosocial behavior.

Collective compassion yields social harmony and community. This does not mean that conflicts do not arise in the presence of compassion, but they have a greater tendency to be successfully resolved when all protagonists are willing and able to put themselves in others' shoes. A community of compassionate members can create a priceless family-like bond and sense of belonging. Such a community is not only less likely to ignore or oppress certain of its members, it is also more likely to nurture and support distressed or weakened members.

Broad Compassion Through Global Education

At a very general level, compassion can vary along two dimensions, depth and breadth. One way to look at compassion goals of citizenship education is to think in terms of promoting deep, broad compassion among students. Deep compassion is strongly experienced and profoundly motivating. A deeply compassionate collectivity is one typified by inclusion, sharing, and harmonious community. A deeply compassionate individual is one who feels empathy strongly, understands the points of views of others, is loving and tolerant toward others, and is driven to altruistic behavior. The goal of compassion is furthered through the encouragement of deep compassion in the social studies classroom.

Breadth of compassion refers to whom the compassion is directed toward. Very narrow compassion is directed toward only those closest to one. These may include, for example, family or small group members, friends or romantic partners, or others who are extremely close or similar to the self. Broader compassion may be extended to all members of one's race, ethnicity, religion, social class, political party, community or nation. Broader still is compassion for all humans, regardless of national or other group membership. Even broader compassion includes a variety of animals and may motivate vegetarianism. In general, our compassion for others decreases as they get farther away from us in time, space and form.

Broader compassion includes more people (or animals, but let us, for simplicity, restrict ourselves to people). In a more compassionate society, more people are included and accepted in the community or political process, more are granted human rights, more have access to the goods and services they need, more receive help in times of crisis. More compassionate individuals direct their empathy, understanding, tolerance and altruism toward more people.

Broad compassion does not happen naturally — it must be taught. As the Ad Hoc Committee on Global Education (1987) points out, "tolerance and respect for peoples different from ourselves ... have to be worked at because of our natural proclivity to measure the worth of others by their similarity to ourselves and our customs" (p. 246). Compassion goals can be promoted by encouraging truly broad compassion in the social studies classroom. This can be accomplished through what has been termed global education.

Kniep (1986) articulated four main foci of global education. First, attention is given to the study of values, both universal values that transcend culture and the diverse array of values that are distinct to particular cultures. Second, there is a focus on the processes of global political, economic, ecological and technical systems. Third, there is an emphasis on prevailing global problems and issues such as international conflict, human rights and development. Fourth, global history provides context for understanding the present. To these four, Case (1993), drawing upon Hanvey (1976), adds a fifth focus, the consideration of alternative futures for the world. Thus, as Becker and Anderson (1980) point out, global education integrates past, present and future.

Becker and Anderson elucidate some of the ways in which global education breaks with more traditional social studies. First, rather than framing teaching with own-culture (Western) biases, global educators at least attempt to internationalise their perspective and teach more about the so-called Third World. By utilizing the beliefs and values of other peoples to understand their practices (LeSourd, 1991), global educators allow students the opportunity to walk more effectively in others' shoes, thinking and feeling as others would.

Second, global education transcends the parochial by treating "humankind as a unit of analysis," and, in so doing, "emphasizes commonalities shared by all of humankind and encourages students to tolerate and even applaud cultural differences within the human species" (Becker & Anderson, 1980, p. 86). Broad compassion is furthered through study of the broad spectrum of human commonalities and diversities from a tolerant, yet not uncritical perspective. Combined with the rejection of own-culture biases, this means that a broad slice of humankind is studied in an informed, empathetic and respectful manner. Not only does this allow for broader compassion for others, it also promotes what Banks (1980) calls "cross-cultural competency", which, he argues, "should be a key goal of social studies programs designed to prepare students to be effective world citizens in the 21st Century" (p. 122).

Third, many years ago Erich Fromm (1941) complained that attempts by teachers to fill children's minds with large quantities of unrelated information discouraged original thinking. According to Becker and

Anderson (1980), global educators move past such excessive attention to the memorization of morsels of information, toward an emphasis on "the active utilization of factual information in conceptual, ethical, and policy analysis of global problems being experienced by humankind" (p. 89). Such an approach is conducive to both cognitive and moral development, and thus to the sort of critical tolerance that is crucial to compassionate citizenship.

Fourth, rather than treating global affairs as a spectator sport, global education engages students in the "study of themselves as members of the human species, as inhabitants of planet earth, and as participants in the global social order. It emphasizes relating oneself to the world in active, deliberate, and concrete ways" (p. 91). The participant's perspective makes topics more relevant and compelling for students, and makes students think about the roles they do or ought to play in the world. It also may facilitate empathy, as participants are less removed than spectators.

Hopefully, global education promotes among students "the knowledge, attitudes and skills that are relevant to living responsibly in a multicultural and interdependent world" (Fisher & Hick, 1985, p. 8). According to Fisher and Hicks, important knowledge consists, first, of a sense of their own society and how they fit into it, as well as other societies and how those other societies interact with their own. Second, students should have knowledge and understanding of the vast inequalities of wealth and power that exist within and between nations, and of efforts to alleviate these inequalities. Third, they should know about major domestic and international conflicts and efforts to resolve them. Fourth, they should have a basic sense of geography and ecology, and know about methods of protecting the environment. Fifth, they should think of possible futures and know how to work for a better tomorrow.

The attitudes that Fisher and Hicks choose as objectives of world studies (the term they use rather than global education) are the sort that, if held, would all but guarantee a compassionate individual. Students, they write, should have a clear sense of their own and others' worth and dignity. They should be curious to learn about issues, and ready to learn from other cultures. They should willingly put themselves in others' shoes and readily empathize with those who are different from them, and they should value justice. In a similar vein, Tye (1990) writes, "Global education involves perspective taking — seeing things through the eyes and minds of others — and it means the realization that while individuals and groups may view life differently, they also have common needs and wants" (p. 163).

Such attitudes promote compassion that is not just broad, but also deep.

What Case (1993) calls the "perceptual dimension" of global education consists of "the points of view — the matrix of concepts, orientations, values, sensibilities, and attitudes." "Promoting the perceptual dimension," in his words, "involves nurturing perspectives that are empathetic, free of stereotypes, not predicated on naïve or simplistic assumption, and not colored by prejudicial sentiments" (p. 318). Through modelling, story telling and role-playing exercises, global educators can encourage empathy and discourage barriers to it, thus deepening their students' capacities for compassion.

The skills that Fisher and Hicks list enable students to be effective citizens. Students should learn to gather information from a variety of sources, and to communicate their ideas through a variety of media to a variety of people. They should become able to grasp and use relevant concepts and think critically with an open mind. Finally, students should develop the skills to be active and effective politically at a variety of levels. Such skills enhance students' political capabilities, and enhance the possibilities for compassion that is not just broad and deep, but also active.

It would be presumptuous of me, as a political scientist who has taught only at the tertiary level, to suggest curriculum or specific lesson ideas for achieving such goals through global education. Fortunately there are a number of useful books that do this (Fisher & Hicks, 1985; Oxfam, 1997; Reardon, 1988; Walkington, 1999). The point is that global education, as articulated by a variety of scholars, is a crucial component of compassionate social studies, as it broadens and even deepens compassion.

Globalism and Types of Patriotism

Sometimes important capability goals and compassion goals appear to be in conflict. This creates the need to reconcile the apparent conflict, find a suitable compromise between the two goals, or sacrifice one goal for the other. For instance, globalism may conflict with patriotism. The Ad Hoc Committee on Global Education (1987) expressed the problem this way:

> Basic principles of morality and justice require that the interests of all humanity be taken into account, but these basic principles have to be implemented in a world of nations and communities, constituted of special loyalties and commitments. How our duties to our own are to be adjusted to our duties to humanity remains a persistent problem. (p. 246)

In some ways, this tension between globalism and patriotism is functional. For example, the challenge of negotiating this tension engages young minds and helps develop critical thinking skills. As the Committee goes on to point out:

> The kinds of issues that students confront in global education programs compel the use of higher-order mental processes. This is especially true when the student is confronted with the choice of two competing goods- for example, patriotism vs. internationalism, local community needs vs. food for starving foreigners.... (p. 248)

This does not solve the basic problem, however. In this chapter, I have argued that global education is desirable because it broadens the scope of compassion. Elsewhere (Hirshberg, 1993), I have taken the position that patriotism has both positive and negative results; while it creates mindsets which "function to help foster national unity and stability," patriotic preconceptions "also harden the lines of international intolerance and misunderstanding" (p. 211). While patriotism furthers the capability goal of political stability, then, it may threaten global compassion. Similarly, a concern for promoting political stability brings up the worry that globalist approaches may be destructive to patriotism. Can this apparent contradiction be reconciled?

The answer is yes. A number of scholars have made distinctions between what may be considered the positive aspects of patriotism and the negative. The idea is that there may be different sorts of patriots, only some of whom are uncritical, chauvinistic and dispassionate toward outsiders. Some scholars (Alter, 1989; Feshbach & Sakano, 1997; Kosterman & Feshbach, 1989) distinguish between patriotism, as love of country, and nationalism, as disrespect for other nations. Schatz and Staub (1997) distinguish between "blind" patriotism, which "is characterized by unquestioning acceptance of its policies and practices and unquestioning allegiance," and "constructive" patriotism, which "combines affective attachment with the capacity and willingness to question, criticize, and work for change" (p. 229).

Nathanson (1997) distinguishes between "extreme" and "moderate" patriotism. Extreme Patriotism consists of:

> 1. a belief in the superiority of one's country;
> 2. a desire for dominance over other countries;
> 3. an exclusive concern for one's own country;
> 4. an unconstrained pursuit of one's country's goals; and
> 5. automatic support of one's country's military policies. (p. 316)

Such extreme patriotism can exaggerate differences between countries, and promote selfish ethnocentric attitudes and uncritical us-versus-them chauvinisms that can exacerbate international hostilities, conflicts and wars. Extreme patriotism most definitely is in conflict with goals of global compassion, and extreme patriots have been critical of global education in the United States (Lamy, 1990). Nathanson points out, however, that patriotism need not be extreme. Moderate patriotism, in contrast, consists of the following:

1. a special affection for one's country;
2. a desire that one's country prosper and flourish;
3. a special but not exclusive concern for one's own country;
4. support of morally constrained pursuit of national goals; and
5. conditional support of one's country's policies. (p. 317)

Moderate patriotism, Nathanson argues, can serve the positive functions that more extreme patriotism usually serves without interfering with global compassion. Ethically conscious and critically informed positive feelings of caring for one's own country can easily be combined with similar feelings for others. Thus moderate patriotism can coexist harmoniously with global citizenship. As defined by Oxfam (1997), a global citizen:

- is aware of the wider world and has a sense of their (*sic*) own role as a world citizen;
- respects and values diversity;
- has an understanding of how the world works economically, politically, socially, culturally, technologically and environmentally;
- is outraged by social injustice;
- participates in and contributes to the community at a range of levels from the local to the global; and
- is willing to act to make the world a more equitable and sustainable place
- takes responsibility for their (*sic*) actions (in Walkington, 1999, p. 11).

In Case's (1993) view, global education also, ideally, creates citizens who are open- minded, empathetic and resistant to simple stereotypes, black-and-white thinking and chauvinism, and who understand that the world is a complex place. Global education that encourages critical thinking and broad compassion does not conflict with patriotism, but it does influence that patriotism in a moderate direction. History lessons that parade a succession of wars in which "we" were always right, good, heroic and worthy of compassion and "they" were always the opposite encourage extreme patriotism. I am suggesting that we should encourage moderate patriotism and discourage extreme patriotism through global education. The hope would be to produce the sort of desirable citizens described in an American context by Conard (1988):

> Though not characterized by the old, narrow stereotype of the patriotic love-it-or-leave-it American, they are patriotic. Good citizens are multiculturally astute; they have human relations skills that enable them to interact with a multicultural population, and they have a global perspective. They are citizens of the world. They can collaborate with others and look at issues from a variety of perspectives. They cannot be incumbered with prejudicial attitudes that limit their thinking. (p. 283)

Social Science and Compassionate Social Studies

Thus far, I have argued that conventional capability goals of citizenship education must be balanced with compassion goals, and that global education is valuable in this regard, since it broadens the scope of compassion in the classroom. Harking back to the three traditions of citizenship education put forward by Barr, Barth and Shermis (1978), one might say that I have suggested that traditional "citizenship transmission" goals be balanced by a strong dose of compassionate "reflective inquiry." Left out has been a discussion of the tradition of teaching social studies as lessons in social scientific disciplines. How does such an approach affect the pursuit of the compassion goals described above?

According to Barth and Shermis (1980), the idea that social studies should be taught as separate social science disciplines has definitely had its proponents:

> Social scientists who got into the social studies field in the last few years of the 19th Century and throughout the present century approach the task with a single assumption: the social studies is always reducible to the learning of specialized knowledge, each piece of which is contributed by the various social sciences acting as separate disciplines.... Conceived of as separate social science disciplines, the social studies curriculum rapidly became a piecemeal response to the original problem of coping with 20th Century complexity. (pp. 4–5)

Although we have the social science disciplines to thank for the gifts of knowledge made available in the social studies classroom, that does not mean that those disciplines should structure teaching processes. Arguments in favour of teaching the separate social science disciplines in schools, such as those presented by Rice (1980), are not particularly persuasive. Far more convincing have been the scholars who have pointed out why the disciplines are often inappropriate for the social studies classroom.

According to Schneider (1980), 1960s critics of basing social studies on the disciplines, dubbed by Van Til (1971) as "compassionate critics," argued that social studies should, instead, be structured appropriately to the interests, needs and capabilities of the students. "Traditional instruction," relates Scheider, "stifled curiosity and creativity and along with other aspects of schooling dehumanised children" (p. 14). In his often-cited 1960 paper, Engle (1996) stressed the distinction between the analytic goals of research and the synthetic goals of citizenship education. Although concentrating on one narrow discipline allows for deep analysis, it hinders the sort of broad synthesis that allows citizens to make good decisions:

> In marked contrast to the meticulous research orientation of the social sciences, the social studies are centrally concerned with the education of citizens. The mark of the good citizen is the quality of decisions which he reaches on public and private matters of social concern ... A social problem requires that the citizen put together, from many sources, information and values which the social sciences treat in relative isolation. Thus in the social studies the prevailing motive is synthesis rather than analysis ... Facts and principles which are the ends in view in the social sciences are merely a means to a further end in the social studies. The goal of the social studies lies not merely in information but in the character of people. The goal is the good citizen. (pp. 118–119)

As a political scientist and successful teacher at the university level, I have found that the restrictions of my discipline would greatly hinder my teaching efforts if I were to feel bound by them. The boundaries between history, political science, economics, sociology, anthropology, psychology and philosophy are contrivances that allow scholars the opportunity to go into extreme depth on confined corners of reality. Increasingly, however, scholars are finding such confines restrictive, and are, themselves, taking interdisciplinary approaches. No single discipline, by itself, can provide truly enlightening understandings of the great problems of our world. Only by incorporating the approaches of a variety of disciplines can a problem come to life and show its true nature. To remain tied to traditional disciplinary confines is to be out of touch with modern scholarship, the nature of our social world, and the needs of our students.

Still, the traditional disciplines of the social sciences have each established valuable theories and methods for unravelling the mysteries of human interaction. Within each discipline, sophisticated scholarly discourse continues to further the extent to which we humans have come to know and understand ourselves. Even if we choose to present the social world to our students in a holistic way that transcends the limitations of separated discipline, we need not "throw out the baby with the bathwater." We can, at least, take advantage of useful social scientific approaches and teach our students to think like social scientists — but should we?

The findings of Guimond, Begin, and Palmer (1989) suggest that students trained in the social sciences have a greater sense of the role of social systems in producing poverty and are less likely to blame the poor for their plight than are business or natural science students. But Unks (1985) found that many social studies teachers, particularly those not actually trained in the social sciences, were unable to distinguish fact from opinion. If teachers are unable to think critically, asks Unks, how can they be expected to teach their students to? We might ask, if the social sciences provide relatively good training in sensitive social analysis and critical thinking at the tertiary level, why not use their methods in social studies classrooms?

Unfortunately, there are a number of good reasons why the approaches used by professionals in social inquiry are not entirely suited to teaching compassionate social studies. Social scientists tend to examine limited aspects of human behavior from removed, unemotional and amoral perspectives. Teaching compassionate social studies requires a broader perspective, that of a compassionate and ethical participant who pays close attention to human thoughts, feelings and experiences. These are very different perspectives indeed.

To avoid biases, social scientists tend to take the perspective of objective, non-judgmental outsiders looking in. This perspective has clear scientific utility; if the point of social inquiry is to paint as accurate a picture as possible, it is important that scholarly portrayals are not distorted by personal involvement or wishful thinking. Unfortunately, such an approach can prove deficient when brought into the classroom. In fact, students are not just observers; they are participants in their social world and, as such, part of the phenomena they are studying. The more they understand their own roles in social processes, the more they can consciously play those roles well. A removed approach deprives students of an understanding of their own place in the world, and thus limits their abilities to enquire into what sort of citizen they want to be. An involved, compassionate participant's perspective provides the opportunity for far more reflection on the deep issues of social, political and economic participation.

In addition, cold, detached, unemotional treatments of social realities and issues do not suitably prepare students to make decisions about how to respond. Shaver (1980) argues, along with Janis and Mann (1977), that decision-making is not a wholly cognitive process, but one that includes strong affective elements. If we are to educate future citizens for effective decision-making, we must allow them to practice synthesising rationality, ethics and emotion.

The compassionate approach also makes topics far more interesting and meaningful for students. The social world that is studied by social scientists and social studies students alike is important and compelling precisely because social systems and processes cause great human joy and pain. This is something students can relate to. The cold, unemotional approach strips the social world of its essence and leaves many students wondering why anyone would bother with social inquiry. A consciously compassionate approach, by engaging students' empathy and intuitive senses of justice, brings topics alive.

Since deep, conscious, moral reasoning is a crucial citizenship skill, moral development that allows for ethical decision-making is an important citizenship education goal (Stevens & Allen, 1996). The teaching of amoral social science fails to develop ethical decision-making skills, and it fosters the exclusion of morality from social inquiry. An amoral approach may be useful for gathering social knowledge, but it is insufficient for judging what is important and what ought to be done. Moral discourse in the classroom develops vital skills for moral judgement, and deep engagement with a variety of moral claims can open students up to other perspectives and enhance empathy (Oser, 1986).

Pure ideals of "objectivity" and value neutrality are as unreachable in the social sciences as they are in the classroom. Efforts to appear objective and value neutral serve to hide implicit biases from view and promote covert indoctrination with a myth of objectivity. Open, honest portrayal of compassionate values in a critical environment is to be preferred.

An additional issue is whether teachers should intentionally indoctrinate students with particularly desirable values or merely provide a forum through which students can discover values for themselves (Fraenkel, 1980). Of course, the position one takes on these issues depends on one's values. The position I take is that compassionate, humanistic values ought to be taught, but not as dogma. Instead, such values should be allowed to freely emerge from open discussions and exercises conducted in a compassionate and humanistic environment with appropriate compassionate modeling.

A humane society depends, for its preservation, on a critical, compassionate, ethical and active citizenry. If social studies educators are to succeed in transforming children into sophisticated, caring and involved citizens, they must distance themselves from the dispassionate, removed, amoral and impersonal perspective that typifies established social science.

A participant's perspective on the social world, rather than that of an observer, encourages interest and involvement. Whenever possible, students should be taught to view themselves as part of the phenomena they study, and to consider what their roles are and ought to be. Passionate attention to human joy and sorrow brings social issues alive and triggers students' compassion. Students should be encouraged to imagine themselves in others' situations and feel the emotions that others feel. Explicit coverage of ethical issues trains students in a crucial life and citizenship skill–moral reasoning. Students should be encouraged to make deep, critical judgments that explicitly take moral considerations into account. It is this sort of education that will prepare them to be active, compassionate, moral citizens with whom we would be honored to share our society.

Conclusion

Although social studies educators should not ignore concerns about individual and collective capabilities, particular emphasis should be placed on creating compassionate citizens for a compassionate world. Based on the points made above, I can suggest the following fourteen ways in which compassionate citizenship education can be pursued in social studies classrooms.

1. *Honouring Human Differences*: Interpersonal, interethnic, intercultural and international differences should be the topics of lessons that encourage students to respect critically and honour human variation.
2. *Role Taking*: Students should be given every opportunity to see the world through others' eyes through methods such as role playing exercises, the use of literature and videos, the telling of stories and experiences, and guided discussions.
3. *Engaging Discussions*: Discussions of social problems, contestable issues, and moral dilemmas should be conducted in ways that allow students to develop skills in critical thinking, moral reasoning and empathetic role taking.
4. *Critical Thinking*: Critical thinking should be encouraged through asking good questions rather than supplying authoritative answers.

5. *Multiple Perspectives*: Multiple perspectives on issues should be raised, and students should be encouraged to understand, respect, and critically evaluate them.
6. *Compassionate Modelling*: Whenever possible, teachers should model compassionate, generous and fair behavior.
7. *Opportunities for Altruism*: Students should be given actual opportunities to practice real compassionate, altruistic behavior.
8. *Cooperative Learning*: Cooperative learning techniques should be used to the extent that their coexistence with competitive assessment does not create free riders, resentments and conflicts.
9. *Global Education*: Global education broadens the scope of students' compassion, and therefore should be part of the social studies curriculum.
10. *Rejection of the Disciplines*: Conventional social scientific disciplines and their methods should not dictate the structure or content of social studies lessons.
11. *Participant's Perspective*: Students should be encouraged to view themselves as participants in the social world they are studying, rather than observers.
12. *Ethics and Values*: Ethics and values should be deliberately discussed in an open and compassionate atmosphere.
13. *Feelings and Experience Focus*: Students should study not just what people do, but also what they experience and how they feel.
14. *Emotional Expression*: Students should be encouraged to feel and express emotions in response to the social issues or events they are studying.

These fourteen suggestions create a general picture of the sort of social studies classroom that might further the compassion goals listed in Table 9.3. While all fourteen are potentially consistent with the capability goals specified in Table 9.2, they are not necessarily so, and compassion and capability goals may have to be balanced. Hopefully, by teaching compassionate social studies, educators can help produce young citizens who will help make the world a more humane place.

References

Ad Hoc Committee on Global Education (1987). Global education: In bounds or out? *Social Education*, *51*(April/May), 242–249.

Alter, P. (1989). *Nationalism*. London: Edward Arnold.

Aronowitz, S. (1973). *False promises: The shaping of American working class consciousness*. New York: McGraw-Hill.

Banks, J. (1980). Developing cross-cultural competency in the social studies. *Journal of Research and Development in Education, 13*(2), 113–122.

Bar-Tal, D., & Raviv, A. (1982). A cognitive-learning model of helping behavior development: Possible implications and applications. In N. Eisenberg (Ed.), *The development of prosocial behavior* (pp. 199–217). New York: Academic Press.

Barnett, M. (1987). Empathy and related responses in children. In N. Eisenberg & J. Strayer (Eds.), *Empathy and its development* (pp. 146–162). Cambridge, UK: Cambridge University Press.

Barr, T., Barth, J., & Shermis, S. (1978). *The nature of social studies*. Palm Springs, CA: ETC Publications.

Barth, J., & Shermis, S. (1980). Social studies goals: The historical perspective. *Journal of Research and Development in Education, 13*(2), 1–11.

Battistich, V., Watson, M., Solomon, D., Schaps, E., & Solomon, J. (1991). The child development project: A comprehensive program for the development of prosocial character. In W. Kurtines & J. Gewirtz (Eds.), *Handbook of moral behavior and development* (Vol. 3, pp. 1–34). Hilsdale, NJ: Lawrence Erlbaum Associates.

Becker, J., & Anderson, L. (1980). Global perspectives in the social studies. *Journal of Research and Development in Education, 13*(2), 82–92.

Bowles, S., & Gintis, H. (1972/1973). I.Q. in the U.S. class structure. *Social Policy, 3*(4&5), 65–96.

Byrnes, D. (1988). Children and prejudice. *Social Education, 52*(April/May), 267–271.

Case, R. (1993). Key elements of a global perspective. *Social Education, 57*(6), 318–325.

Cialdini, R., Kenrick, D., & Baumann, D. (1982). Effects of mood on prosocial behavior in children and adults. In N. Eisenberg (Ed.), *The development of prosocial behavior* (pp. 339–359). New York: Academic Press.

Conard, B. (1988). Cooperative learning and prejudice reduction. *Social Education, 52*(April/May), 283–286.

Craig, R. (1993). Social justice and the moral imagination. *Social Education, 57*(6), 333–336.

Damon, W. (1988). *The moral child: Nurturing children's natural moral growth*. New York: The Free Press.

Darley, J., & Batson, C. (1973). From Jerusalem to Jericho: A study of situational and dispositional variables in helping behavior. *Journal of Personality and Social Psychology, 27*(1), 100–108.

Engle, S. (1996). Decision making. In W. Parker (Ed.), *Educating the democratic mind* (pp. 117–125). Albany, NY: State University of New York Press.

Feshbach, S., & Sakano, N. (1997). The structure and correlates of attitudes toward one's nation in samples of United States and Japanese college students. In D. Bar-Tal & E. Staub (Eds.), *Patriotism in the lives of individuals and nations*. Chicago: Nelson-Hall Publishers.

Fisher, S., & Hicks, D. (1985). *World studies 8–13: A teacher's handbook*. Edinburgh, UK: Oliver & Boyd.

Fraenkel, J. (1980). Goals for teaching values and value analysis. *Journal of Research and Development in Education, 13*(2), 93–102.

Fraenkel, J. (1991). Distributive justice and social studies education. *Social Education, 55*(1), 38–40, 66.

Fromm, E. (1941). *Escape from freedom*. New York: Hold, Rinehart and Winston.

Gabelko, N. (1988). Prejudice reduction in secondary schools. *Social Education, 52*(April/May), 276–279.

George, S. (1977). *How the other half dies: The real reasons for world hunger*. Montclair, NJ: Allanheld, Osmun and Co.

Goldstein, A., & Michaels, G. (1985). *Empathy: Development, training, and consequences*. Hillsdale, NJ: Lawrence Erlbaum Associates.

Grelle, B., & Metzger, D. (1996). Beyond socialization and multiculturalism: Rethinking the task of citizenship education in a pluralistic society. *Social Education, 60*(3), 147–151.

Guimond, S., Begin, G., & Palmer, D. (1989). Education and causal attributions: The development of "person-blame" and "system-blame" ideology. *Social Psychology Quarterly, 52*(2), 126–140.

Hanvey, R. (1976). *An attainable global perspective*. New York: Global Perspectives in Education.

Hirshberg, M. (1993). *Perpetuating patriotic perceptions*. Westport, CT: Praeger.

Hoffman, M. (1982). Development of prosocial motivation: Empathy and guilt. In N. Eisenberg (Ed.), *The development of prosocial behavior* (pp. 281–313). New York: Academic Press.

Hunt, M. (1991). *The compassionate beast: The scientific inquiry into human altruism*. New York: Doubleday.

Janis, I., & Mann, L. (1977). *Decision making: A psychological analysis of conflict, choice, and commitment*. New York: The Free Press.

Kniep, W. (1986). Defining a global education by its content. *Social Education, 50* (6), 437–446.

Kosterman, R., & Feshbach, S. (1989). Toward a measure of patriotic and nationalistic attitudes. *Political Psychology, 10*(2), 257–274.

Lamy, S. (1990). Global education: A conflict of images. In K. Tye (Ed.), *Global education: From thought to action* (pp. 49–63). Alexandria, VA: Association for Supervision and Curriculum Development.

Lappe, F., & Collins, J. (1986). *World hunger: Twelve myths*. London: Earthscan.

Latane, B., & Darley, J. (1970). *The unresponsive bystander: Why doesn't he help?* New York: Appleton-Century-Crofts.

Leming, J. (1989). The two cultures of social studies education. *Social Education, 53*(October), 404–408.

LeSourd, S. (1991). Integrating pluralistic values for reconstructing society. *Social Education, 55*(1), 52–54.

Lickona, T. (1991). Moral development in the elementary school classroom. In W. Kurtines & J. Gewirtz (Eds.), *Handbook of moral behavior and development* (Vol. 3, pp. 143–161). Hillsdale, NJ: Lawrence Erlbaum Associates.

Marcuse, H. (1965). Repressive tolerance. In R. Wolff, B. Moore, & H. Marcuse, *A critique of pure tolerance*. Boston: Beacon Press.

Martorella, P. (1980). Social studies goals in the middle grades. *Journal of Research and Development in Education, 13*(2), 47–59.

New Zealand Ministry of Education. (1997). *Social studies in the New Zealand curriculum*. Wellington, New Zealand: Learning Media.

Nathanson, S. (1997). Should patriotism have a future? In D. Bar-Tal & E. Staub (Eds.), *Patriotism in the lives of individuals and nations*. Chicago: Nelson-Hall Publishers.

Newmann, F., Bertocci, T., & Landsness, R. (1996). Skills in citizen action. In W. Parker (Ed.), *Educating the democratic mind* (pp. 223–239). Albany, NY: State University of New York Press.

Oser, F. (1986). Moral education and values education: The discourse perspective. In M. Wittrock (Ed.), *Handbook of research on teaching* (3rd ed., pp. 917–941). New York: Macmillan.

Oxfam. (1997). *A curriculum for global citizenship*. London: Oxfam.

Pate, G. (1988). Research on reducing prejudice. *Social Education, 52*(April/May), 283–286.

Reardon, B. (Ed.). (1988). *Educating for global responsibility*. New York: Teachers College Press.

Rice, M. (1980). Social sciences as school subjects: The case for the disciplines. *Journal of Research and Development in Education, 13*(2), 123–132.

Schneider, D. (1980). Tradition and change in the social studies curriculum. *Journal of Research and Development in Education, 13*(2), 12–23.

Sears, A., & Parsons, J. (1991). Towards critical thinking as an ethic. *Theory and Research in Social Education, 1*(Winter), 45–68.

Schatz, R., & Staub, E. (1997). Manifestations of blind and constructive patriotism: Personality correlates and individual-group relations. In D. Bar-Tal & E. Staub (Eds.), *Patriotism in the lives of individuals and nations*. Chicago: Nelson-Hall Publishers.

Scott, K. (1991). Achieving social studies affective aims: Values, empathy, and moral development. In J. Shaver (Ed.), *Handbook of research on social studies teaching and learning* (pp. 357–369). New York: Macmillan.

Shaver, J. (1980). Toward the twenty-first century: Social studies goals for decision-making and research skills. *Journal of Research and Development in Education, 13*(2), 36–46.

Soley, M. (1996). If it's controversial, why teach it? *Social Education, 60*(1), 9–11.

Stevens, R., & Allen, M. (1996). Teaching public values: Three instructional approaches. *Social Education, 60*(3), 155–158.

Strayer, J. (1987). Affective and cognitive perspectives on empathy. In N. Eisenberg & J. Strayer (Eds.), *Empathy and its development* (pp. 218–244). Cambridge, UK: Cambridge University Press.

Sullivan, E. (1980). Can values be taught? In M. Windmiller, N. Lambert, & E. Turiel (Eds.), *Moral development and socialization*. Boston: Allyn and Bacon.

Tye, K. (1990). Conclusion: A look to the future. In K. Tye (Ed.), *Global education: From thought to action* (pp. 157–178). Alexandria, VA: Association for Supervision and Curriculum Development.

Val Til, W. (Ed.). (1971). *Curriculum: Quest for relevance*. New York: Houghton Mifflin.

Walkington, H. (1999). *Global citizenship education*. Sheffield, UK: The Geographical Association.

Walsh, D. (1988). Critical thinking to reduce prejudice. *Social Education, 52*(April/May), 280–282.

Unger, P. (1996). *Living high and letting die: Our illusion of innocence*. New York: Oxford University Press.

Unks, G. (1985). Critical thinking in the social studies classroom. Do we teach it? *Social Education, 49*(3), 240, 244–246.

CHAPTER 10

Does Citizenship Education Make Moral Education Redundant?

Mark Halstead

Abstract

Citizenship education has recently been introduced as a separate subject on the curriculum in many countries around the world, and various claims are advanced in support of this move. Giddens tells us that "citizenship education can improve the lives and school experiences of young people" (2000, p. 14). Hargreaves suggests that it will provide the cement to hold a pluralist society together (1994, p. 37). Others have suggested that it will reduce crime, tackle young people's boredom with and cynicism about politics, counter their suspicion of institutionalised authority (Advisory Group on Citizenship, 1998, pp. 14–16; Crick, 2000, p. 80), and even change the political culture of the country (Advisory Group on Citizenship, 1998, p. 7). There is also a widespread assumption that Citizenship will provide an important and widely acceptable way of delivering moral education and values education more generally (Crick, 1998; Halstead & Taylor, 2000b, p. 170).

It is with the last of these claims that this chapter is concerned, and with the related suggestion that citizenship education might absorb moral education, making the latter redundant as a separate element in the curriculum. But before we can assess the justifications for making Citizenship the main vehicle for moral education, we need to explore the nature of citizenship education and the intentions that lie behind it. Only then can we begin to examine the relationship between citizenship education and moral education and the extent to which they share the same concepts and goals The present chapter is therefore divided into three sections. The first contains a discussion of some of the philosophical complexities in the notions of citizenship, citizenship education and the "committed citizen." The second looks at three possible models of the relationship between citizenship education and moral education. The third offers a number of lines of argument against tying moral education too closely to citizenship education. Examples are drawn mainly from the British context (where Citizenship was introduced as a full National Curriculum subject in 2002), but it is hoped that since the chapter is primarily concerned with underlying principles rather than with practice, the ideas will have wider application.

Citizenship Education and the "Committed Citizen"

If we are going to educate children to become citizens, we need to know what it is to be a citizen. In this section therefore some of the tensions and complexities are explored that are inherent in the concept of citizenship itself, citizenship education and the "committed citizen."

Citizenship

According to Beck (1998, pp. 102–106) citizenship is an "essentially contested concept," and there are certainly widely differing political understandings of the term. In its minimal sense "citizenship" refers to the political and legal status of individual members of a state or other settled human community. Implicit in this status are certain rights and duties, such as the duty to abide by the law of the state and the right to vote, and citizens are equal with respect to these rights and duties. However, this is a rather narrow understanding of citizenship, and it can be expanded in various ways. T. H. Marshall (1950) took this minimal definition further by identifying three distinct dimensions of citizenship, involving civil, political and social rights, and his discussion has formed the backbone of much recent work on citizenship (see, e.g., Barbalet, 1988; Bulmer & Rees, 1996). However, there are a number of other ways in which the thin concept of citizenship can be enriched. Three such ways will now be discussed, though, as we shall see, there are problems in making any of these expanded senses of citizenship the basis of citizenship education.

First, there is the fact that citizens may belong to a diversity of political entities at the same time. The sovereignty of the nation state, which Miller (2000), like many others, sees as central to citizenship, is being eroded and challenged: externally, by economic, political, military and ecological factors which are global or at least international; and internally, by regional and local nationalisms and the increasing ethnic diversity of most modern states. It is probably going too far to extend the concept of citizenship, as do Engle and Ochoa, to the relationship of individuals to "their families, their religious institutions, the workplace, [and] the school" (1998, p. 17), though it is true that each of these institutions can be organised more or less democratically; but the claims made on a citizen's loyalty by both international and devolved communities may certainly lead to a more multi-layered understanding of political identity, as each adds a further layer of civil, political and social dimensions. At best, such multiple citizenship (as it is now often called; cf. Lister, 1998, p. 264) may provide an enriched understanding of what citizenship is. However, there is also the problem of conflicting loyalties, especially where the different groups to which the citizen is attached have divergent purposes.

Secondly, many people have tried to expand the minimal concept of citizenship by arguing that citizenship necessarily includes a cultural dimension. In the nation-state, citizenship is inevitably tinged with the national culture, whether this finds expression in language, religion, history or tradition (Kymlicka, 1999, pp. 94–97; Miller, 2000, pp. 31–33); however, too strong an emphasis on national culture may lead to something like the "Tebbit cricket test," according to which people only have the right to full citizenship if they conform to cultural preconditions (cf. Andrews, 1991, p. 13). Parekh (1991) argues against this narrow view of citizenship and stresses some of the multicultural dimensions of citizenship in pluralist societies. Other commentators have suggested that citizenship may also involve issues to do with the arts, sports, leisure, the environment and technology (cf. Osler, 1999, p. 28). I have discussed some of the problems associated with tying citizenship too closely to culture more fully elsewhere (Halstead, 1995a, 1995b).

Thirdly, the minimal concept of citizenship may be expanded by introducing the notion of the "active citizen," a term which implies that the citizen is actively involved in "shaping the way his or her community functions" (Miller, 2000, p. 28). McLaughlin discusses maximal citizenship in terms of being conscious that one is "a member of a living community with a shared democratic culture involving obligations and responsibilities as well as rights, a sense of the common good, fraternity and so on" (1992, p. 236). McGhie shares a similar vision when she claims that citizenship is a collaborative, participative process that promotes active engagement; is an inclusive process that promotes a sense of belonging; founds on human rights; values diversity; is "aspirational" and actively seeks the well-being of all the members of the community; founds on dispositions; and is a caring process (1999, p. 33). This sense of citizenship presupposes a framework of liberal values and takes for granted the assumption that citizenship education is democratic education (Callan, 1997; Gutmann, 1987; Tamir, 1995). However, not everyone shares these assumptions, and not everyone wants to be an active citizen in this sense. People can legitimately choose to find their fulfilment in other directions.

Citizenship Education

Like citizenship, citizenship education may be narrowly or broadly conceived. In its narrow sense, citizenship education aims to produce "citizens capable of addressing in the ballot box political arguments posed by democratic debate," whereas in the broader sense its aim is to create "citizens who share in a common social endeavour" (Pearce & Hallgarten, 2000, p. 7). The narrow conception is education about citizenship, which is designed to produce informed or politically literate citizens. The task is a cognitive one, of extending children's knowledge and understanding of political ideas, institutions and issues (Beck, 1998, p. 108), and does not extend to developing values or dispositions. This approach avoids the difficulties mentioned above in connection with the cultural dimension of citizenship and the notion of the active citizen; children can simply be taught about these as controversial issues on which they are free to make up their own minds. The broader conception is education for citizenship, in other words, education which is not an end in itself, but which aims to produce not only informed but committed citizens (cf. Wringe, 1992). Citizenship education on this view includes not only political literacy but also moral and social responsibility and community involvement; it therefore includes the development of values, dispositions, skills and aptitudes, as well as knowledge and concepts (Advisory Group on Citizenship, 1998, pp. 11–13, 44–45). On this view, schools have a responsibility to transmit the public values of society and to encourage pupils to develop a commitment to these (McLaughlin, 1995, pp. 27–30).

The distinction between a narrow and broader conception of citizenship education will be discussed more fully in Section 2 below, but it is worthy of note at this stage that although most proponents of citizenship education support the broader approach of education for citizenship, this approach raises a number of complex issues about the aims of citizenship education. The lack of agreement about the public virtues and shared values which form the basis of education for citizenship raises a number of questions about the loyalties and commitments such citizenship involves (cf. McLaughlin, 1992, pp. 242–243). If the aim is to produce the committed citizen, what does this term imply? How do we define a committed citizen? What virtues would we expect the committed citizen to possess, and can such virtues be taught? We must now turn to these topics.

The Committed Citizen

The broader aim of citizenship education, namely to produce citizens who not only share a common identity but have a strong sense of public responsibility and are committed to a common social endeavour, may be understood in one of two ways. On the one hand, there is the citizen who wishes to live a helpful and neighbourly life without questioning the political status quo; on the other, there is the citizen who wishes to be actively involved in the way his or her community functions, for example by campaigning actively for change. The former is sometimes caricatured as a "good-hearted, property-owning patriot who serves as an unpaid JP if asked" (Ignatieff, 1991, p. 77), the latter as a bicycle-riding anti-foxhunting campaigner or as "a bit of a busybody keeping the neighbours in line" (Phillips, 1991, p. 77). The former are sometimes labelled "passive citizen" (Davies, Gregory, & Riley, 1999, p. 50) because they accept the authority of political leaders and do not question official policy, but this terminology does not do justice to the positive virtues and dispositions such as loyalty and civility which characterise their behaviour; I shall call them simply "good citizens." The latter are more appropriately called "active citizens," because their central concern is active participation in the political, civil and social life of the community and they conform to the expanded sense of citizenship already discussed above under the name active or maximal citizenship.

Though different terminology is sometimes used, the distinction between the good citizen and the active citizen (these terms are also used in Crick, 2000, p. 78) reflects closely the commonly made distinction between a conception of civic education which "stresses commitment to the state and/or a preconceived set of values" and one which "stresses participation in public and social affairs" (Morris, 1997, p. 108). The good citizen is a law-abiding member of the community who has a personal sense of responsibility, a moral grasp of right and wrong and a determination to live justly and help others. The virtues of the good citizen thus include the acceptance of authority, obedience to the law, loyalty, patriotism, civility, honesty, personal responsibility and a concern for the welfare of other individuals. This approach to citizenship education has resonances with *vospitanie* (moral upbringing) in pre-*glasnost* Russia, which included elements such as patriotism, the need for hard work, furthering the interests of the collective, accepting the need for order and discipline, and developing a high level of understanding of socio-political issues and the obligations of citizenship (Halstead, 1994). A similar fusion of moral values and loyalty to the state is found in civic education in China and other East Asian societies (Morris, 1997, pp. 124–125). The active citizen, on the other hand, seeks to be more directly involved in the development of his or her community, through participation in debates and discussions and through direct involvement in broadly political activity (e.g., trying to change unjust laws or to democratise voluntary bodies). The virtues of the active citizen therefore include courage, a willingness to challenge injustice, respect for the rights of others, concern for the welfare of society, public accountability, a respect for personal autonomy, public-spiritedness, a commitment to equality, and the questioning of authority (cf. Kymlicka, 1999, p. 81; White, 1996). The distinction between the good citizen and the active citizen is central to the remainder of this chapter.

Three Models of Citizenship Education

On the basis of the discussion so far, it is now possible to identify three models of citizenship education: The first is a value-free approach aimed at providing information about citizenship; the second, a value-laden approach aimed at producing the good citizen; the third, a value-laden approach aimed at producing the active citizen. It is worth noting that the three models bear a close relationship to the three categories which emerged from the data gathered in a recent research project surveying teachers' views of good citizenship in England:

> (1) knowledge characteristics (knowledge of government, world events, world community, ability to question ideas);
> (2) conservative or subject/obedient role characteristics (acceptance of the authority of those in a supervisory role, patriotism, acceptance of assigned responsibilities); and
> (3) social concern characteristics (concern for the welfare of others, moral and ethical behaviour, and tolerance of diversity within society). (Davies et al., 1999, p. 45)

Each of these models will now be examined in more detail.

Model One: Education About Citizenship

The first model is a value-free approach which stands back from the aim of producing good citizens and interprets Citizenship Education as education about citizenship. Based on this model, citizenship education is a subject, with its own body of knowledge, understanding and skills; for example, students learn about what they are entitled to from public agencies and about the rights which the state guarantees to its citizens (as set out in England in the early 1990s in the Citizens' Charter) and the corresponding obligations which it demands. This model is designed to produce citizens who are well-informed or politically literate citizens (cf. Beck, 1998, p. 108; Davies et al., 1999, p. 17), and on this model, there is little overlap between citizenship education and moral education. This is roughly the stance adopted in the documentation for the National Curriculum for Citizenship, which was introduced in England as a separate subject in September 2002; the progamme of study is defined in terms of knowledge, understanding and skills, with no direct mention of values or attitudes (Department for Education and Employment, 1999).

There is a strong case to be made for adopting this approach to citizenship education. First, it may be more important for children to leave school politically literate than with experience of voluntary activities and other forms of participatory experience in the school context (Davies et al., 1999, p. 21). Indeed, Engle and Ochoa argue that it is a responsibility of citizens to be informed, for "participation in a democracy is irresponsible if it is not informed" (1988, p. 16), and in any case knowledge itself is empowering (Advisory Group on Citizenship, 1998, p. 20). Secondly, an approach based on knowledge and understanding avoids many of the difficulties encountered in a value-laden approach (Beck, 1998, pp. 103–108), including the problem of the lack of agreement over the values which citizenship education should promote and the problem of whether the inculcation of beliefs, attitudes and values has any place in a liberal education anyway. A comparison may be made with Religious Education, which used to aim to produce good Christians but now aims simply to produce people who have knowledge and a sympathetic understanding of religion(s). Thirdly, this model avoids the problems of assessment in values education (Halstead & Taylor, 2000a, pp. 55–57), and makes monitoring and assessment much more straightforward. The knowledge and understanding pupils have gained can be tested easily through the General Certificate of Secondary Education (GCSE) and other forms of testing and examination (Cross, 2000). Fourthly, in view of the fact that many teachers appear to be hesitant about their role in values education, and prefer not to engage in it (Halstead & Taylor, 2000b, p. 170), a value-free approach to citizenship education would probably prove much more acceptable to teachers and may have a better chance of long-term success.

However, if values are not directly taught, they will still be embedded in teachers' taken-for-granted worldviews, and will be part of the hidden curriculum (Halstead, 1996, p. 4). Values lie beneath the surface of everything that teachers do, even when they are unacknowledged (McLaughlin, 1995, pp. 20–23). But it is clear that where there is no systematic discussion of values and values issues in the classroom, children will be more likely to develop values haphazardly, and it is not uncommon for the values which pupils develop in school to be different form those the school intends. In these circumstances it is surely better to bring the values into the open where they can become the subject of reflection and debate.

Model Two: Education for Good Citizenship

The second and third models are value-laden approaches, which interpret citizenship education as education *for* citizenship (see above). What distinguishes them from the first model is the recognition that the transmission of values and the development of commitments lie at the heart of citizenship education, though the precise relationship between citizenship education and moral education is left open. Torney-Purta claims that "both moral education and civic education are sub-categories within the larger category of values education" (1996), whereas Crick describes "PSE, moral education and whatever we call education specifically for values" as "necessary but not sufficient conditions for good citizenship" (1998, p. 19). However, as soon as a link is acknowledged between citizenship education and values education, citizenship education gets caught up in some of the current philosophical debates about the role of schools in developing pupils' values. Are schools primarily agents of socialisation? Should they simply reflect society's current values? Or should schools adopt a more active and critical role in leading social change (cf. Halstead & Taylor, 2000, pp. 15–16)?

The second model responds to these questions with the assumption that schools should reflect society's current values and that the role of schools is to socialise pupils into these values. This model aims at producing the "good citizen" whom we have already defined in terms of commitment to the state and to a preconceived set of values. The qualities, attributes and commitments which children are expected to develop on this model are based on obedience to the laws of the land (as a way of promoting social harmony and avoiding social chaos), a clear moral vision of right and wrong, a recognition of the importance of authority in human affairs, an acceptance of assigned responsibilities and duties, and patriotism. All this is justified in terms of the public interest. A fuller statement of the virtues of the good citizen has already been provided above. This view of citizenship is generally associated with a conservative political agenda (Carr, 1991).

The second model of citizenship education has much in common with character education, one of the major strategies for moral education in the United States (McLaughlin & Halstead, 1999). Character education advocates a "deliberate effort by schools, families and communities to help young people understand, care about and act upon core ethical values (Character Education Partnership, as cited in Lickona, 1996). It is based on the belief that adults have a duty to develop good habits in children, to shape and determine their behaviour and thus form their character. Just as citizenship education is seen as a response to a perception of lawlessness and political apathy among young people, so character education is a response to a perceived crisis in their conduct and values; it is seen as central to the task of building a moral society and developing young people's "moral literacy." Character education makes use of a variety of methods, including the use of stories about virtuous action, teaching by example, direct instruction, the study of heroes, the ethos of the school and habituation in good behaviour (Halstead & Taylor, 2000a, p. 37). In much the same way, the Second Model of citizenship education may involve, at the school level, obedience to school rules, acceptance of the teacher's authority and example, direct instruction, and opportunities to practice the virtues of the good citizen.

However, the second model of citizenship education runs into many of the problems and shortcomings associated with character education (McLaughlin & Halstead, 1999, pp. 142–146). In particular, in relating the perceived moral crisis among young people to the need to change individual attitudes and behaviour, it diverts attention from the societal, economic and political factors which may have contributed to the "moral crisis." Conservative values such as obedience to authority, civility and orderliness may be taught as uncontroversial, and not be balanced by an openness to competing conceptions of the true and the good or an emphasis on tolerance, respect, democratic debate, personal autonomy and human dignity. The need for a more expansive understanding of citizenship education is emphasised in the survey of teacher opinion in England mentioned above, in which only about two per cent rated conservative characteristics (such as patriotism and the acceptance of authority) as more important to good citizenship than the factors to do with "social concern" and relevant political knowledge (Davies et al., 1999, p. 47). A large majority of the teachers surveyed (about 80%) related social concern issues (defined as concern for the welfare of others, moral and ethical behaviour, and tolerance of diversity within society) as most important, and these issues are central to the third model.

Model Three: Education for Active Citizenship

The third model of citizenship education is concerned to prepare children for active participation in the political, civil and social life of the community. The participation may involve any of a wide range of public activities helping to shape the life of the broader community. In addition to a degree of political literacy, such participation presupposes a range of democratic values, including a sense of public responsibility, an ability to see beyond one's own interests and commitments to a wider view and a willingness to identify with the broader political community (Miller, 2000, pp. 28–29). Without common values, ideals and procedures such as these, a democratic society "would lack not only coherence and stability, but also freedom, equality, tolerance and many other features of a moral and civilised life" (McLaughlin & Halstead, 1999, p. 148). White (1996) argues that democracy is distinguished by its values — justice, freedom and respect for personal autonomy — more than by specific institutions and procedures, but that for democracy to work citizens need to be disposed to use their knowledge and skills democratically. If education is to prepare pupils for citizenship, she argues that it must help them to acquire the civic virtues or dispositions that citizens require for democratic institutions to flourish (cf. Callan, 1997; Kymlicka, 1999, p. 79–84; McLaughlin & Halstead, 1999, pp. 146–155).

Values education is thus central to the third model of citizenship education, or, more precisely, education in a framework of public values. McLaughlin offers some insights into the concept of "public values":

> Public values are those which, in virtue of their fundamentality or inescapability, are seen as binding on all persons. Frequently embodied in law, and expressed in terms of rights, they include such matters as basic social morality and, in democratic societies, a range of fundamental democratic principles such as freedom of speech and justice. Public values in [liberal] societies also include

> ideals such as personal autonomy and the maximisation of the freedom of individuals to pursue their fuller conception of the good within a framework of justice through the distribution of 'primary goods' (basic rights, liberties and opportunities). The liberal project is to specify a range of public values, free of significantly controversial assumptions and judgments, which can generate principles for the conduct of relations between people who disagree. (1995, pp. 26–27)

From a liberal perspective, private values are more substantial views of human good that goes beyond the public framework. They may be more or less reasonable, and more or less controversial, but what distinguishes them from public values is that there are no conclusive objective grounds, which everyone will accept as appropriate for selecting one set of private values over another. The liberal state will therefore tolerate a wide range of differing private values and adopt a neutral stance between them, so long as they operate within a framework of justice, and it is respect for difference and diversity of this kind, which makes a liberal state pluralist.

The educational task of preparing children for citizenship of such a state thus has a number of dimensions. First, children should be encouraged to develop a substantive commitment to the public values and to the civic virtues or dispositions which allow the public values to flourish. Second, children should be encouraged to explore, discuss and critically reflect on the diversity of values in the private domain, and to make autonomous choices and commitments in this area. Third, they should be encouraged to develop tolerant and respectful attitudes towards those whose beliefs, values and commitments differ from their own. This is roughly the stance adopted in the Final Report of the Advisory Group on Citizenship (1998), on which the new National Curriculum for Citizenship in England is based. A substantial list of values and dispositions is included as an essential element in the active citizenship which is being promoted. These include concern for the common good, belief in human dignity and equality, a proclivity to act responsibly, the practice of tolerance, courage, openness, civility, respect for the rule of law, commitment to equal opportunities, concern for human rights, and so on (1998, pp. 44–45).

It is clear that the third model of citizenship education overlaps significantly with moral education (Beck, 1998, chap. 4). Indeed, Crick argues that "any teaching of Citizenship not based on moral values and reasoning would either be mechanical and boring, or even dangerous" (1998, p. 19). And in the survey of teachers' attitudes to citizenship education mentioned above, respondents regularly maintained that the moral dimensions of citizenship mattered far more than the legal or political dimensions; the good citizen was described as being conscious of the interests of others and the wider society and acting accordingly, and the language of caring, unselfishness, cooperation, meeting community obligations and demonstrating respect was used repeatedly to give substance to the distinguishing characteristics of the good citizen (Davies et al., 1999, p. 50).

In view of the overlap between citizenship education and moral education, the question arises how the school curriculum should be organised, which Crick (1998) discusses in detail. Should moral education, citizenship education, Personal, Social and Health Education (PSHE) and Religious Education (RE) all have a separate slot within the school curriculum? Crick suggests that with young children all these dimensions can be taught together through interactive and experiential approaches like circle time, and that there is no need for careful conceptual differentiation at this level. However, as children grow older, he claims they will need to distinguish more clearly between issues of personal responsibility (the territory of PSHE) and issues of public (the territory of Citizenship) (1998, pp. 18–19). Haydon (2000a, 2000b) faces up to the challenge of what he sees as a continuing disagreement over what "morality" is and a declining interest in moral education in both official and professional discourse, and questions whether there is any longer any need to talk about morality and moral education in schools. He suggests that if citizenship education includes education in public values and the agreed norms of a society, and if PSHE includes matters of personal morality, this makes the idea of separate moral education redundant. It would follow from this, Haydon claims, that the concept of moral education could be abandoned in the school context, though the norms and expectations involved in living together in society would continue to be the focus of educational attention. Such a move would solve the problem of overlap and the further problem that many teachers feel unsure of their role in moral education.

It is possible to view the matter as simply one of labelling and argue that so long as the issues get covered, it does not really matter under what heading they are taught and learned. This is broadly the line taken by Crick, when he says, "What's in a name?" (1998, p. 19). However, I believe there are dangers in blurring the distinction between moral education and citizenship education. Though they overlap, they have different emphases and different concepts and have different goals. In the final section of this chapter I examine some of the dangers of an approach which tries to merge them.

Arguments Against Linking Citizenship and Moral Education

In this final section, some of the problems with merging citizenship education with moral education will be explored. Central to the argument is the belief that morality is a broad concept, covering much more than matters of citizenship and the civic virtues, and that moral education would therefore be distorted if it were taught only or mainly through citizenship education. A separate form of moral education is needed to provide the principles and procedures necessary for developing a critique of some of the values taught implicitly or explicitly through citizenship education.

First, it is clear that while liberals will criticise the second model for putting forward too determinate a framework of values when there are no conclusive objective grounds that justify imposing those particular values on children, the third model in turn presupposes a liberal framework of values, which is clearly necessary for an understanding of citizenship in a liberal democracy, but is not necessary for an understanding of morality. In the liberal framework, religion is relegated to a matter of individual choice, whereas for many people it is the basis of their moral understanding. Tying moral education too closely to citizenship education has the effect of secularising it for these people and thus undermining the basis of their understanding of morality. However much the third model seeks to avoid narrow forms of nationalism or ethnocentrism, it thus cannot avoid other more subtle forms of inequality or cultural domination. For example, it necessarily involves a rejection of the view, which some citizens may hold, that religious attachments are more important than political ones as a source of identity, or that the Islamic umma is more important than the nation state. The aim of education for active citizenship is to help pupils to take a general perspective as equal citizens, but if this general perspective is expanded to include social, moral and cultural elements, it carries the danger of undermining the social, moral and cultural life of minorities and undervaluing difference (Hall, 2000; Phillips, 1991, 2000; Young, 1989). If moral education is to be worthwhile for all children, it cannot be based on assumptions which undermine the beliefs, values, commitments and identity of some. The Third Model faces the problem that the more substantial the framework of public values is, the more people there will be who do not share the values and who therefore feel excluded; but the thinner the values framework is, the less adequate it is as a means of moral education.

Secondly, the private/public distinction which lies at the heart of the third model, is problematic in a number of ways. McLaughlin discusses the difficulty of distinguishing between public and private values in theoretical terms, and the even greater difficulty of distinguishing them in practice (1995, pp. 28–31). These difficulties arise for many reasons — partly because of the increasing intrusion of the public into the private (Hall, 2000, p. 47), partly because issues which were once considered private (such as homosexuality and disability) are being brought increasingly into the public domain (cf. Young, 1990, pp. 110–121), and partly because more recent approaches to morality and moral education, such as the ethics of care, further blur the private/public distinction (Sevenhuijsen, 1998). In any case, it is clear that the "public" values cover only part of the moral life; pupils will not reach a full understanding of moral issues unless they are addressed from both public and private perspectives. When E. M. Forster famously said that if he had to choose between betraying his friends and betraying his country, he hoped he would have the courage to choose the latter, such a conclusion could not be reached, or even understood, if moral education were restricted to public values and subsumed under citizenship education. And Phillips reminds us (1991, pp. 85–86), that being a good citizen is not the same as being a good mother, a good feminist or a good neighbour — or indeed a good friend. Feminist research has made further inroads into the public/private divide by drawing attention to the gendered nature of citizenship and to the fact that citizenship as currently taught in schools contributes to the modern state's valorisation of male-oriented public life (focusing on the responsibilities of the citizen) and devaluing of female-orientated private life (focusing on the responsibilities of the carer) (Pateman, 1989; Foster, 1997). This raises moral issues and highlights the need for a moral critique of citizenship that can only be developed from an external perspective. Once again, it suggests that if citizenship education is concerned with education *for* citizenship, then children also need to be able in some way to stand outside what they are taught in order to develop a moral critique of it, and hence there is a continuing need for moral education to provide an understanding of moral principles and procedures outside citizenship education.

Thirdly, it is clear that an understanding of and commitment to the law is central to the notion of "education for," but this generates a number of problems if education then becomes the main vehicle for moral learning. One problem is that if moral education and "education" are merged in this way, this might mean that because the law embodies many of society's public values, the law comes to be treated as the authoritative basis by which people decide whether things are right or wrong, rather than, say, religion or a humanist code of ethics (cf. Gilbert, 1997, p. 79). The problem is that the law is inadequate as a sole basis for deciding questions of morality. The fact that something is legal does not necessarily make it moral; apart from anything else, the law is open to frequent redefinition and change, whereas (presumably) ethical values remain more constant. The effect of pinning morality too closely to the law could be to confuse children's moral development just at the age when they need most guidance, and to encourage them to become moral relativists. Education must make clear the differences between law and morality, and this is not best achieved by teaching morality through citizenship education. A further problem is that though education will among other things help young people to develop an attitude of respect for the law, to internalise a commitment to the rule of law and come to accept the authority of the law because they understand appropriate reasons for doing so, those virtues in themselves will not provide them with the competence to distinguish a just from an unjust law. If we want individuals to be able to identify an unjust law, this ability will come not from a study of law, but from an understanding and application of principles outside the law, namely, moral principles. It is difficult to encourage commitment to something and an open-minded, critical attitude to it at the same time (McLaughlin & Halstead, 1999, p. 152). Moral education can provide the critical distance needed to evaluate the commitments required by citizenship education.

Finally, we cannot ignore the insights of postmodernist critics and visionaries. There is danger that if we tie morality too closely to a modernist conception based on loyalty to the nation state and the acceptance of socially endorsed legal rules and rational universal democratic principles, both values and morality may be swept away together on a wave of postmodernist hyper-reality. Contemporary society is increasingly marked out by rapid social and cultural transformations, including the globalisation of information and economic enterprise, the emphasis on consumption, the privatisation of public enterprises, job insecurity, the arrival of the digital age, the decline in state provision of welfare, the dominance of the electronic media, and the breakdown of old certainties, and all of these have an impact on our understanding of citizenship. Postmodern critics such as Baudrillard (1983) go further and argue that societies are being replaced by the hyper-reality of virtual cities and imagined communities and that politics are being reduced to a television spectacle, a set of sound-bites and a series of manipulations by spin doctors (cf. Bauman, 1992a, p. 151). As Poster (1995, p. 112) points out, individuals are no longer citizens of a rationally ordered state, eager to maximise their civil rights, nor yet proletarians anticipating the onset of communism, but merely passive consumers faced with a myriad advertising images and self-referential signs. In such a world, it is easy to see modernist concepts of citizenship and individual moral autonomy being "lost in the face of the media's fragmented rendition of the world" (Gilbert, 1997, p. 71). In my opinion, morality — for all its complexities and ambiguities — is too important a part of our essential humanity to let this happen. Bauman argues persuasively that we can regain truly human forms of moral agency in the postmodern age, not by giving children "the learnable knowledge of rules" (1992b, p. 11) based on rational law-oriented ethics, but by looking for alternative conceptions of moral responsibility based on human spontaneity, ambiguity and wonder. John Wilson argues that both perspectives on morality are equally important — the interpersonal dimension which emphasised social norms and rules which operate for our mutual benefit in society (1990, pp. 47–49), and the personal dimension concerned with "the basic ecology … of human desires, emotions and deeds" and "the state of our soul" (Wilson, 1990, pp. 82–88; also cf. McLaughlin & Halstead, 2000). The distinctiveness of morality as a form of thought lies in the fusion of these two dimensions, and there is a danger that the distinctiveness and richness of the concept will be lost if moral education is merged with (or submerged in, or replaced by) citizenship education.

References

Advisory Group on Citizenship. (1998). *Education for citizenship and the teaching of democracy in schools* (Final Report). London: Quality and Curriculum Authority.

Andrews, G. (1991). Introduction. In G. Andrews (Ed.), *Citizenship*. London: Lawrence and Wishart.

Barbalet, J. M. (1988). *Citizenship*. Milton Keynes, UK: Open University Press.

Baudrillard, J. (1983). *Simulations*. New York: Semiotext(e).

Bauman, Z. (1992a). *Intimations of postmodernity*. London: Routledge.

Bauman, Z. (1992b). *Postmodern ethics*. Oxford, UK: Blackwell.

Beck, J. (1998). *Morality and citizenship in education*. London: Cassell.

Bulmer, M., & Rees, A. M. (Eds.). *Citizenship today: The contemporary relevance of T. H. Marshall*. London: University College London Press.

Callan, E. (1997). *Creating citizens: Political education and liberal democracy*. Oxford, UK: Oxford University Press.

Carr, W. (1991). Education for citizenship. *British Journal of Educational Studies, 39*(4), 373–385.

Crick, B. (1998). Values education for democracy and citizenship. In D. Christie, H. Maitles, & J. Halliday (Eds.), *Values education for democracy and citizenship*. Aberdeen, UK: Gordon Cook Foundation.

Crick, B. (2000). The citizenship order for schools. In N. Pearce & J. Hallgarten (Eds.), *Tomorrow's citizens: Critical debates in citizenship and education*. London: Institute for Public Policy Research.

Cross, M. (2000). Key assessment issues. In N. Pearce & J. Hallgarten (Eds.), *Tomorrow's citizens: critical debates in citizenship and education*. London: Institute for Public Policy Research.

Davies, I., Gregory, I., & Riley, S. C. (1999). *Good citizenship and educational provision*. London: Falmer Press.

Department for Education and Employment. (1999). *Citizenship: The national curriculum for England*. London: DfEE and QCA.

Engle, S. H., & Ochoa, A. S. (1998). *Education for democratic citizenship*. New York: Teachers College Press.

Foster, V. (1997). Feminist theory and the construction of citizenship education. In K. Kennedy (Ed.), *Citizenship education and the modern state*. London: Falmer Press.

Giddens, A. (2000). Citizenship in the global era. In N. Pearce & J. Hallgarten (Eds.), *Tomorrow's citizens: Critical debates in citizenship and education*. London: Institute for Public Policy Research.

Gilbert, R. (1997). Issues for citizenship in a postmodern world. In K. Kennedy (Ed.), *Citizenship education and the modern state*. London: Falmer Press.

Gutmann, A. (1987). *Democratic education*. Princeton: Princeton University Press.

Hall, S. (2000). Multicultural citizens, monocultural citizenship? In N. Pearce & J. Hallgarten (Eds.), *Tomorrow's citizens: Critical debates in citizenship and education*. London: Institute for Public Policy Research.

Halstead, J. M. (1994). Moral and spiritual education in Russia. *Cambridge Journal of Education*, *24*(3), 423–438.

Halstead, J. M. (1995a). Voluntary apartheid? Problems of schooling for religious and other minorities in democratic societies. *Journal of Education*, *29*(2), 257–272.

Halstead, J. M. (1995b). Should schools reinforce children's religious identity? *Religious Education*, *90*(3–4), 360–376.

Halstead, J. M. (1996). Values and values education in schools. In J. M. Halstead & M. J. Taylor (Eds.), *Values in education and education in values*. London: Falmer Press.

Halstead, J. M., & Taylor, M. J. (2000a). *The development of values, attitudes and personal qualities: A review of recent research*. Slough, UK: National Foundation for Educational Research.

Halstead, J. M., & Taylor, M. J. (2000b). Learning and teaching about values: A review of recent research. *Cambridge Journal of Education*, *30*(2), 169–202.

Hargreaves, D. H. (1994). The mosaic of learning: Schools and teachers for the next century. London: Demos.

Haydon, G. (2000a). The moral agenda of citizenship education. In R. Gardner (Ed.), *Citizenship and education*. London: Kogan Page.

Haydon, G. (2000b). John Wilson and the place of morality in education. *Journal of Moral Education*, *29*(3).

Ignatieff, M. (1991). Citizenship and moral narcissism. In G. Andrews (Ed.), *Citizenship*. London: Lawerence and Wishart.

Kymlicka, W. (1999). Education for citizenship. In J. M. Halstead & T. H. McLaughlin (Eds.), *Education in morality*. London: Routledge.

Lickona, T. (1996) Eleven principles of effective character education. *Journal of Moral Education*, *25*(1), 93–100.

Lister, I. (1998). Citizenship and citizenship education in Britain. In O. Ichilov (Ed.), *Citizenship and citizenship education in a changing world*. London: Woburn Press.

McGhie, M. (1999). Education for citizenship in schools. In Gordon Cook Foundation, *Conference report: Education for citizenship*. Aberdeen, UK: Gordon Cook Foundation.

McLaughlin, T. H. (1992). Citizenship, diversity and education: A philosophical perspective. *Journal of Moral Education*, *21*(3), 235–250.

McLaughlin, T. H. (1995). Public values, private values and educational responsibility. In E. Pybus & T. H. McLaughlin, *Values, Education and Responsibility*. St. Andrews, UK: University of St Andrews Centre for Philosophy and Public Affairs.

McLaughlin, T. H. & Halstead, J. M. (1999). Education in character and virtue. In J. M. Halstead & T. H. McLaughlin (Eds.), *Education in morality*. London: Routledge.

McLaughlin, T. H. & Halstead, J. M. (2000). John Wilson on moral education. *Journal of Moral Edcuation*, *29*(3), 247–268.

Marshall, T. H. (1950). *Citizenship and social class and other essays*. Cambridge, UK: Cambridge University Press.

Miller, D. (2000). Citizenship: What does it mean and why is it important? In N. Pearce & J. Hallgarten (Eds.), *Tomorrow's citizens: Critical debates in citizenship and education*. London: Institute for Public Policy Research.

Morris, P. (1997). Civics and citizenship education in Hong Kong. In K. Kennedy (Ed.), *Citizenship education and the modern state*. London: Falmer Press.

Osler, D. (1999). Education for citizenship in the New Scotland. In Gordon Cook Foundation, *Conference Report: Education for citizenship*. Aberdeen, UK: Gordon Cook Foundation.

Parekh, B. (1991). British citizenship and cultural difference. In G. Andrews (Ed.), *Citizenship*. London: Lawrence & Wishart.

Pateman, C. (1989). Feminist critiques of the public/private dichotomy. In C. Pateman

(Ed.), *The disorder of women: Democracy, feminism and political theory*. Cambridge, UK: Polity Press.

Pearce, N., & Hallgarten, J. (2000). Introduction. In N. Pearce & J. Hallgarten (Eds.), *Tomorrow's citizens: Critical debates in citizenship and education*. London: Institute for Public Policy Research.

Phillips, A. (1991). Citizenship and feminist politics. In G. Andrews (Ed.), *Citizenship*. London: Lawrence & Wishart.

Phillips, A. (2000). Second class citizenship. In N. Pearce & J. Hallgarten (Eds.), *Tomorrow's citizens: Critical debates in citizenship and education*. London: Institute for Public Policy Research.

Poster, M. (1995). *The second media age*. Cambridge, UK: Polity Press.

Sevenhuijsen, S. (1998). *Citizenship and the ethics of care: Feminist considerations on justice, morality and politics*. London: Routledge.

Tamir, Y. (Ed.). (1995). *Demoratic education in a multicultural state*. Oxford, UK: Blackwell.

Torney-Purta, J. (1996, July). *The connection of values education and civic education. The IEA civic education study in twenty countries*. Paper presented at Journal of Moral Education Conference, University College of St Martin, Lancaster, England.

White, P. (1996). *Civic virtues and public schooling: Education citizens for a democratic society*. New York: Teachers College Press.

Wilson, J. (1990). *A new introduction to moral education*. London: Cassell.

Wringe, C. (1992). The ambiguities of education for active citizenship. *Journal of Philosophy of Education*, *26*(1), 29–38.

Young, I. M. (1989). Polity and group difference: A critique of the ideal of universal citizenship. *Ethics*, *99*(2), 250–274.

Young, I. M. (1990). *Justice and the politics of difference*. Princeton, NJ: Princeton University Press.

CHAPTER 11

Science Is Not Values-Free — Neither in Research, nor in School

Jean-Luc Patry

Abstract

An analysis of values-ladenness of both research and teaching is provided. For the former, we need to distinguish science as activity ("doing research") and science as system of statements. In science as system of statements, it is argued that value statements are acceptable but need to be labeled as such and justified according to the principles of ethics, that is, one must argue why a particular value is appropriate and why another is not. Science as activity is not values-free since any activity is values-laden. However, one must distinguish two levels (corresponding to the object-theoretical and to the meta-theoretical levels) and several phases (finding a topic, doing the research, interpreting the results, applying the research), in which the values are different — this will be analyzed.

This can be applied to teaching. Values education can be done using Kohlberg's approach: This means that the main focus is on how people argue in favor or against particular values, while the values themselves are not primary. We make the proposition to combine this with teaching science by stating such a values dilemma that the students are forced to get information on the topic (on the scientific subject to be learned) to be able to argue in favor or against particular values, examples and experiences with this approach will be reported, and some general conclusions will be drawn with regard to responsibility (as a particular issue of citizenship).

Everything we do conscientiously involves values decisions. Whenever we take a rational action that has an impact on other people (or when we omit to do something that might have an impact on other people), values are at stake. It seems to be stating the obvious to say that no decision we make and put into action is values-free. But values might be more important in some domains than in others. Since citizenship involves decisions which affect many people, the values loading is particularly significant.

Values-impact first refers to statements. We can distinguish descriptive ("x is the case") and normative statements ("x should be the case" or "x ought to be the case") as well as mixed statements containing both elements; one can add several other types of statement, but for the sake of brevity I will consider only these types since the course of this argument can be applied similarly to the other types of statements. My meta-ethical standpoint is non-naturalistic, which means that there is no way to make any derivative connection from "is" to "ought"; this type of conclusion would be a "naturalistic fallacy." Descriptive statements are based on observations, whereas normative statements need to be justified on ethical grounds, as do mixed statements. Only descriptive statements are values-free.

This chapter deals with actions and not with statements. But we are talking about reasoned or rational actions, which means that the responsible decision maker has weighted arguments in favor and against a particular action — and these arguments are statements, hopefully scientific statements (for scientifically reasoned decisions), but frequently based on subjective theories (Groeben, Wahl, Schlee, & Scheele, 1988). Actions being values-laden means that the arguments on which the decision is based include, necessarily, at least one values statement. There might be several of them, and in addition there may also (and will usually) be descriptive and mixed statements. Performing an action means that one is striving for a goal, which implies that one thinks that the goal should be achieved; the performer then needs to bring forward normative arguments stating that, and why he or she thinks this goal is justified. It might well be that a protagonist is not aware of the underlying values statement(s); the next step towards optimum rational decision making would be that he or she becomes conscious about the values and goals he or she is persuing.

It is desirable that people act responsibly. This is a very general justification for values education. Further, it is desirable that the statements are logical, coherent and well justified because then the decision can best be defended. This requires that clear analyses of the values decisions at stake (and of the underlying values statements) in the different fields are provided. This will be tentatively done below, for two fields: research, and teaching. The values-ladenness of teaching can then be used as a foundation for a specific type of values education in school, which will also be explained below.

Values Ladenness of Science in Research

The debate on whether science is or should be values free has been a long one, and it is not possible here to address the main issues of this discussion. Rather, in agreement with the introduction, it will be argued that research is necessarily values-laden. For the analysis, we need to distinguish, with Weingartner (1971), science as activity and science as a system of statements. As activity — which we call research — science is necessarily values-laden, whereas a system of statements can contain descriptive as well as normative statements. Much of the values debate deals with science as system of statements; research issues will be discussed below, that is, science is seen as an activity. As to science as a system of statements, let me just mention that, in principle, it can contain normative as well as descriptive statements. But with Zecha (1984) it is claimed that each type of statement should be properly identified — that one says clearly what kind of statement it is — and (in agreement with the non-naturalistic meta-ethical standpoint) that the justification of the different types of statements should be appropriate: Descriptive statements are related to observations and normative statements are justified with ethical arguments.

The main topic in this first part, however, is on science as action, that is, on values in research. The main focus will not be on normative sciences, like ethics as prototype and theology and pedagogy as scientific disciplines in whose systems of statements values may play an important role. Rather, we are talking here about empirical research, that is, research that aims at descriptive statements. Typical examples would be the natural sciences in which one tries to describe nature, but psychology or history (description and possibly explanation of what has happened in the past) are also a good examples for this kind of research. As an example, I will take the empirical study of values education with children. Note that this research deals with the description of children's values, hence it is descriptive and not normative.

For the discussion several distinctions must be made (see Table 11.1):

First it is necessary to distinguish the different steps within a research study (rows in Table 11.1):

- Research question, researcher's interest, and researcher's paradigm: Every researcher first decides what his or her research will be about: What question do I want to deal with? In the example, the question is "How can we influence the development of children's moral judgment competency?" And he or she also decides whether to use the principles of critical rationalism (Phillips, 1999) or another set of

Table 11.1: Values Decisions Within a Research Process

Step	Level		Examples
	Researcher's decisions	Theory on which decisions are based	
Research question, researcher's interest, and paradigm	Choice of research question and paradigm: **personal values**	What principles should guide the choice of research questions and paradigms? **values-laden**	Importance, selfishness of researcher; critical rationalism, cognitivism
Procedure	Design and application of the optimal procedure given the principles: **independent of personal values** procedure ethically appropriate? **personal values**	How should the optimal procedure be designed and applied? **values-laden**	Representative sample, valid measures, random assignment, deception, etc.
Conclusion	Application of the principles of drawing conclusions: **independent of personal values**; conclusions about values: **personal values**	How should one draw conclusions? **values-laden**	Answer to initial question, be skeptic about procedure, relevance of the study
Application (optional)	What aim do I want to reach in the practical application? **personal values**	What goals should one aim for in practice? **values-laden**	emancipation; enhancement of individual or collective well-being

principles — in the present case, critical rationalism seems appropriate. And finally, he or she has to decide about the theoretical framework or about the paradigm (in a post-Kuhnian sense, cf. Kuhn, 1962 and the new interpretation in Schurz & Weingartner, 1998); for the research question, it would be the application of the paradigm used in the tradition of Kohlberg (1984) based on disequilibrium, dilemma-discussion and use of normative arguments to enhance the children's moral judgment competency;

- Procedure: The second step is to apply the optimal procedure to answer the question: to do an adequate intervention, to use appropriate assessment tools, to have a proper research design, to apply the correct statistical methods, and the like. For instance, one has to decide whether Kohlberg's Moral Judgment Interview should be used, which design to use (e.g., about the sample, the treatment, experimental and control groups, reliability and validity issues, statistical analysis etc.) and the like;
- Conclusion: The third step is to draw conclusions from the results of the study, that is, to give the answer to the initial question and to discuss the implications of this result. In the example, one might say that, yes, the children's moral judgment competency can be increased through creation of a disequilibrium in the sense of Piaget and by having the students discuss arguments in favor of one or the other moral decision. One might also say that one ought to increase the children's moral competency, and so forth; and
- Application: Based on these results and conclusions, one might go ahead and implement some practical procedures which are aimed at reaching certain goals. In the example, the researcher might help some teachers who want to increase their students' moral judgment competency by telling them how they can reach this goal.

Then two levels of arguments must be distinguished (columns in Table 11.1):

- The first level deals with the decisions of the researcher. The question is: What does the researcher do, or in other words: Which option does the researcher choose among the ones available? For instance, the researcher decides to ask the question of values education, to use a certain design, he or she decides what conclusions can be drawn from the results and whether and how they can be translated into practical interventions, for example, in the schools; and

- The second level deals with the principles underlying the decisions on the first level. On what grounds does someone choose a research question, conceive his or her design, draw his or her conclusions, and apply the results? Critical rationalism and the Kohlberg paradigm are such sets of rules or theoretical backgrounds which govern the actions of scientists.

Based on these distinctions we can now analyze where the decisions and principles are values-laden and where they are not. On the first level (researcher's decision), a decision is judged "value-laden" if the researcher bases his or her decision on his or her personal values system, whereas a decision is estimated to be "independent of personal values" if the decision is taken based on other grounds than his or her personal values system — particularly on principles of the second level. On the second level, a set of principles is considered "values-laden" if it contains normative statements, whereas a set of principles is "value-neutral" if it does not. While the latter distinction is not controversial, the former might well be, so it will be explored some more while applying it to the different steps in the research.

As stated above, a decision is "independent of personal values" if the decision does not depend on the personal values system. As said above, any decision depends on values. However, it is important here to note where these values come from. In the first step, research question, researcher's interest, and choice of paradigm, personal priorities play a determining role, therefore it is called "values-laden": A researcher will choose his or her research question based on his or her personal priorities, such as "How important is the question in my opinion," or "What benefit can there be from this research for mankind?", or "What contribution to my personal career can the work on such a question have?" This decision is necessarily values-laden because the priority for some research questions as opposed to others is a personal decision. The same applies to the choice of the metatheoretical base, the paradigm, and the like. For instance, many researchers in values education have chosen this topic because they think improving values education is a contribution to improving the social situation in the world, which in turn is highly required; they prefer critical rationalism as a metatheoretical framework because they believe that "falsification is an important key to progress" (Phillips, 1999, p. 176); and they take Kohlberg's paradigm because it has been powerful so far and it is in agreement with their conception of humans as constructors of their own reality. The values-ladenness of these decisions, therefore, are quite obvious. One can also say:

Criticizing the choice of the research question, of the metatheoretical approach and of the research paradigm means to criticize the priorities of the researcher; the bases for the critique may be found — at least partly — in the principles on the second level (see below), yet they are mostly in the personal beliefs of the criticizing person.

In the second step, "procedure," two kinds of decisions have to be taken. The first set of decisions deals with the optimal procedure to use: Should the researcher use a representative sample or not, should he or she use an experimental (rather than a quasi-experimental) design (cf. Campbell & Stanley, 1963), what measures should he or she use, what statistical procedures, and the like. These decisions are based on a set of rules that can be found in all methods textbooks or guidelines (see, for instance, Wilkinson & The APA Task Force on Statistical Inference, 1999); they are based on a values system on the second level ("theory on which decisions are based") which depends on the paradigm chosen in the first step. With respect to critical rationalism, one can say "Once it is realized that … falsification is an important key to progress …, the path is clear to a fruitful approach to research design" (Phillips, 1999, p. 176). This means: Once the decisions have been taken to use critical rationalism and Kohlberg's paradigm, there is no personal value choice anymore with respect to the methods to use. This can be seen when one analyzes how the choice of one or the other method is criticized by fellow researchers or, for instance, by members of a doctoral committee: Within critical rationalist methods they may argue, for instance, that the validity of the instruments (e.g., Campbell & Fiske, 1959; Cronbach & Meehl, 1955) or the internal and/or external validities of the design (Campbell & Stanley, 1963; Cook & Campbell, 1979) are questionable, that there are plausible rival hypotheses (Campbell, 1969), and the like. In contrast to the first step, the critiques do not argue that the researcher has the wrong values, but rather, that the means to reach the values (in the case of critical rationalism: truth or validity) are inappropriate.

One must acknowledge that it is never possible to do a research which is valid in all regards; rather one has to balance the different validity requirements in order to get an optimal mix of validities under the given, usually quite restrictive conditions (see, for instance, Gastager & Patry, 2001; Patry & Hager, 2000). Maybe fellow researchers criticize that the priorities of the values in the balancing act of designing a research under restrictive conditions are problematic, for example, that a researcher gave priority to an instrument's validity instead of its reliability, despite the fact that an instrument that is not reliable cannot be valid. But these priorities, once again, do not express a personal value system. One can assume that any researcher who follows critical rationalism approves the necessity of high validities, the importance to rule out plausible rival hypotheses, and the like. So researchers do not base their decision to use one or the other design on their personal value systems — although some researchers may have sentimental priorities for certain instruments — but primarily on issues like feasibility, resources, time constraints, and the like. The experience shows that every researcher would prefer to do more sophisticated research but that the marginal conditions do not permit to do so. So overall, these decisions do not depend on the personal value system, but rather on the paradigm one has decided to apply in the first step and on the particular conditions of the research. That is meant with "independent of personal values."

On the other hand, there are some ethical questions to solve (Patry, 2000). For instance, one has to decide how much can be required from the subjects without them having benefits from it. Or the question is whether I am allowed to do a study in a school over three years, and the students have no advantage whatsoever — this could be the case, for instance, in the control group of a values education intervention program. Other possible questions are, among many: Am I allowed to give a risky treatment to children? Am I allowed to deceive experimental subjects for research reasons? Am I allowed to do an observation study with subjects who do not know that they are being observed? These are ethical issues which depend, at least to some part, on the personal values system of the individual researcher; so for instance the scientific community accepts deception under certain conditions (cf. American Educational Research Association [AERA], n.d.), but an individual researcher may reject it on ethical grounds. For this reason, personal values play also a role in the procedure decision.

The third step is about conclusions. Here, again, there are clear rules about how to proceed: One should answer the initial question, one should stick to the results and hypotheses, one should argue about whether the procedure was adequate or where there are potential flaws, and the like. This set of rules is given by the general conception about drawing conclusions, as one can read in many methods textbooks (e.g., American Psychological Association [APA], 1994, p. 18ff.; Borg & Gall, 1989, p. 872); in Table 11.1, these principles are on level 2, the theory on which the decisions are based. The latter, of course, are values-laden, whereas the particular decisions of the researcher in this regard are independent of his or her personal values. So, for instance, if the researcher says that his or her study has confirmed the hypothesis that dilemma discussions increase the moral competency, this statement can be criticized on general rules, but not by criticizing the researcher's personal values.

However, in an educational research study the researcher usually also draws conclusions about values. He or she could say, for instance, that it would be a good thing to use dilemma discussions in the classroom. Here, clearly, a personal value of the researcher is at stake: He or she thinks that increasing moral competency in the sense of Kohlberg is a good thing, that it should be done. Of course there might be good reasons for this — but still it is a personal decision, which he or she will have to defend using an ethical argument (following some normative meta-ethical rules on the level "theory on which decision is based," such as "descriptive and normative statements need to be distinguished, and normative statements need to be justified using more general normative statements" (Zecha, 1984).

The next step is optional, but very frequent in educational research: It is the practical application of the research results or of the theory developed within a research program. For instance, researchers might think about implementing dilemma discussions to enhance the moral judgment competency in schools. Here again, the personal values of the researcher are at stake: The researcher believes that values education is so important that it is justified to put it into action. Like any practical decision, research based practical decisions are based on personal values. Of course, these personal values, in turn, may depend on ethical theories about, for instances, the goals one should aim for in school (level "theory on which decision is based"). But it is the practitioner's — or in this case the researcher's — choice which values to favor: Some may think that mathematics is more important, others emphasize values education, still others prefer social learning, and the like. Hence, in this step once again we have values decisions.

Let me mention that in educational research, very often, step 2 (procedure) involves some practical work — in our example the implementation of a values education program in a school — to test whether the program is effective. Whenever such practical work is done as a treatment in an experimental or quasi-experimental design, arguments of the type to be used in step 4 must also be used in step 2.

There is nothing bad about making values decisions within a research process. First of all, such decisions cannot be avoided. But researchers have to be aware of the fact that they do so, since only then they can make rational and justified decisions. And further, researchers should receive a specific values education dealing, among others, with the issues discussed above so that they can make responsible decisions.

Values education of children and young people is a particular application of research (fourth step in Table 1); it has been justified by Kohlberg (1981) in his paper on "how to commit the naturalistic fallacy and get away with it in the study of moral development." For this application, basic knowledge is necessary — this can justify the choice of a research question like "moral development" (first step). So the approach discussed above is not a challenge to research in values education, rather it can be seen as its support.

2. Values-ladenness of Science in School

Now let me turn to the practical issue, that is, to the fourth step in the system discussed above (Table 11.1). The question is about values of science in school: Is it possible to teach science (or any discipline) in school without dealing with values? There are at least three reasons why a teacher cannot avoid that his or her teaching involves values:

- First, teaching is always conveying values, whether the teacher acknowledges it or not. This has become particularly clear, for instance, in the discussion of the hidden curriculum (Snyder, 1971);
- Second, the very choice of the subject involves some values decisions which will be recognized by the students — this choice is comparable to the first step in the research process (see Table 11.1); and
- Third, the way to teach, the emphasis put on different issues and the like will also convey values to the students.

So teaching is values-laden in any case. This is true for teaching any subject matter. And since teaching a topic is always related to the scientific background of this topic, one can say that science as taught in school is not values free. This applies to mathematics, physics, chemistry, and biology as well as to history, language and literature and social studies and all other subject matters. In physics, for instance, the choice to deal (or not to deal) with nuclear power plants, and if so, how to discuss them, involves values decisions. In history, teaching (or not) issues of imperialism and its consequences (and the way to teach them) depends on values decisions — even the chosen terminology is not values-free. In literature, how can we deal with a piece of art without addressing its essence or message, which usually involves values. As in the case of research, it is appropriate for teachers and teacher trainers, and so forth, to acknowledge this fact and to be rational when deciding about the values. This implies that teachers, too, need to get some values education including both handling values in teaching and knowing about values and their justification.

My intention now is to introduce you to a way to include explicitly values in teaching. In short, I suggest the use of dilemma discussions not only for the purpose of values education, but also to teach the subject matter itself. According to Kohlberg and particularly Moshe Blatt (Blatt & Kohlberg, 1975) one can increase the moral judgment competency through moral dilemma discussions in the classroom. A dilemma is a story in which at least two values are opposed to each other, and the students are asked what they would do in this particular situation. But more important than the "What" is the "Why"; the students are required to argue in favor of or against particular options, and it is the quality and structure of the argument that is the main issue since this is what counts in Kohlberg's moral stage theory. The concept for value education is that (in terms of Piaget, 1963) such dilemma discussions will create a disequilibrium in the students' cognitive moral structure, which eventually will yield an accommodation, which means a re-structuring on a higher stage. This influence is well established in many studies; the effect will not be recognizable within a few days, rather it will be necessary to use repeatedly such discussions and the effect is likely to be seen within several months.

The experience with such moral dilemma discussions shows that the participants are particularly motivated to discuss. However, when discussing dilemmas which deal with topics of school subject matter, they need the information background to be able to argue; on the other hand, the specific motivation produced by the dilemma discussion may be used to promote the information acquisition: The students have particular content-related questions they need to answer to be able to continue the moral dilemma discussion, and the teaching of subject matter can capitalize on that.

Let us take an example: atomic physics. The steps of the suggested approach are the following (see Table 11.2):

(1) The starting point, as in all dilemma discussions, is a dilemma which must be understood by the students. In the particular case the question is whether the nuclear plant of Mochovce should be stopped or not. The dilemma is especially motivating for people in Austria living close to this nuclear plant in Slovakia which is known to be run with an old and insecure technology and which is highly debated in Austria (Greenpeace, 2000);

(2) In the second step, just according to the classical Kohlbergian

Table 11.2: Steps in a Prototypical Approach to Teach Both Values and Subject Matter

	Step	Example	
1	Introduce dilemma*	Should nuclear plant x be built?	class
2	First decision*	Who is in favor, who against?	group
3	First arguments (dilemma discussion)*	Why are you in favor, why against?	group
4	Exchange experience and missing information	Exchange of arguments and information about nuclear plants, necessary to discuss values issues	class
5	Looking for evidence	Get the information!	group
6	Exchange information	Exchange information	class
7	Second arguments (dilemma discussion)*	Why are you in favor, why against?	group
8	Synthesis of information	Present your conclusions to the whole class	class
9	Repeat 4 through 8 if necessary	Repeat 4 through 8 if necessary	group/ class
10	Generalization	Discussion about other nuclear plants and other means of energy generation	group/ class

* value education elements.

dilemma discussion, there will be a first decision of the students whether they are in favor of stopping Mochovce or against it. This first decision is taken without knowing details of the plant. This means, the students know very little. This is the first opportunity to recognize the need to base their decision on more facts;

(3) The third step, group discussion, is the essence of values education. The students argue why they favor or oppose the nuclear plant. It is not possible here to go into details, except for the fact that in order to be able to argue, one needs to have knowledge about the facts. If the students don't know about Mochovce, they recognize it and have specific questions. That's where knowledge acquisition enters the picture, in the next step;

(4) Next, there is then an exchange in the whole class concerning (a) the results of the argumentation, as is done in the values education concept, although the dilemma discussion is not finished yet. What is more important at this state of the learning is that there is (b) an exchange about what kind of knowledge is necessary to be able to

discuss about the dilemma. So, for instance, it is necessary to have more knowledge about radioactivity, about how a nuclear plant works — which requires knowledge about the structure of the atoms and the like — and about security issues, as well as about some environmental issues like what happens when the cooling water evaporates and the like. This is the starting point of the knowledge acquisition phase;

(5) This knowledge acquisition phase is done in a constructivist approach, mainly by the students organizing themselves how to get the necessary information and to exchange the details they have acquired, while the teacher is the manager and counselor of the whole endeavor and provides documentation and the like if required. This happens again in groups, but it is not required that the same groups are formed as in the previous phase, rather the groups can be quite occasional;

(6) After this phase of information acquisition, there is once again a phase of exchange of information in the whole class so that all students get the same level of knowledge. This can happen through some posters or what is called "class conferences" in constructivist teaching or through other media; for instance, we had a class who wrote a newspaper on the issue. This documentation can be used in the further dilemma discussion;

(7) Now the class turns back to the dilemma discussion itself. The students know much more about atom physics, nuclear plants, radioactivity, environmental issues and the like, and they can discuss the issues in a much more competent manner than in phase 3;

(8) Maybe the knowledge status is not yet sufficient, so the phases 4 through 7 need to be gone through once again, with additional material; and

(9) Finally, it is necessary to do some generalizing, that is, to discuss other nuclear plants like Bohunice, Temelin, Chernobyl, Three Miles Island, and the like, for the students to know about actual hazards and accidents. One can also invite a specialist from a nuclear plant or an environmental activists and let the students discuss with him or her, and the like.

Of course this general framework can be adapted according to the specific needs. We have used this design with classes of every age, from first graders through university, and in every case it has proven to be at least as effective as control classes with regular teaching. We are currently doing a more detailed analysis of two classes with differential measures of different kinds; the results show that this kind of teaching yields the same achievements by the students as semi-constructivist teaching (teaching with several constructivist elements, but no values education) (Weinberger, 2001).

Conclusions

Both domains discussed above, research and teaching, turned out to involve many values decisions. The general conclusion can be summarized in three brief statements:

(1) Science cannot be done without values that are relevant in one way or another, neither in research, nor in teaching — whether researchers and teachers are aware of it or not;
(2) It is appropriate to argue rationally about the values at stake; this requires, first, to be aware of the values, and secondly, to know about the kinds of arguments and about rules of argumentation with values. This necessitates some specific values education for the protagonists. Once again, this applies for research (and researchers) as for teaching (and teachers); and
(3) In teaching, in addition, one can capitalize on value issues to get more student learning in the subject matter.

The neglect of values matters both in research and teaching promotes irrational decision making. A careful analysis of the decisions in research and teaching processes can help more responsible actions, since decisions made in full knowledge of all issues which are involved, including values issues, are a prerequisite of responsibility. It is not sufficient, but it is necessary.

References

American Educational Research Association. (n.d.). *Ethical standards of AERA*. Retrieved May 26, 2000, from http://www.aera.net/about/policy/ethics.htm
Amerian Psychologh Department. (1994). *Publication manual of the American Psychological Association* (4th ed.). Washington, DC: American Psychological Association.
Blatt, M., & Kohlberg, L. (1975). The effects of classroom moral discussion upon children's levels of moral judgement. *Journal of Moral Education*, *4*, 129–161.

Borg, W. R., & Gall, M. D. (1989). *Educational research: An introduction* (5th ed.). New York: Longman.

Campbell, D. T. (1969). Prospective: Artifact and control. In R. Rosenthal & R. Rosnow (Eds.), *Artifact in behavior research* (pp. 351–382). New York: Academic Press.

Campbell, D. T., & Fiske, D. W. (1959). Convergent and discriminant validation by the multi-trait-multimethod matrix. *Psychological Bulletin, 56*, 81–105.

Campbell, D. T., & Stanley, J. C. (1963). Experimental and quasi-experimental designs for research on teaching. In N. L. Gage (Ed.), *Handbook of research on teaching* (pp. 171–246). Chicago: Rand McNally (also published as a separate, *Experimental and quasi-experimental designs for research*, by D. T. Campbell and J. C. Stanley, 1966, Chicago: Rand McNally, 1966).

Cook, T. D., & Campbell, D. T. (1979). *Quasi-experimentation: Design and analysis issues for field settings*. Chicago: Rand McNally.

Cronbach, L., & Meehl, P. (1955). Construct validity in psychological tests. *Psychological Bulletin, 52*(4), 281–302.

Gastager, A., & Patry, J. L. (2001, October). *Antagonisms in evaluation*. Invited paper read at the Conference of the Deutsche Gesellschaft fur Evaluation in Speyer.

Greenpeace. (2000). *Slowakische AKW Bohunice und Mochovce*. Retrieved May 26, 2000, from http://www.greenpeace.at/umweltwissen/atom/bohunice/index.htm

Groeben, N., Wahl, D., Schlee, J., & Scheele, B. (1988). *Forschungsprogramm subjektive Theorien. Eine Einführung in die Psychologie des reflexiven Subjekts*. Tÿbingen: Francke.

Kohlberg, L. (1981). From is to ought: How to commit the naturalistic fallacy and get away with it in the study of moral development, moral stages and the idea of justice. In L. Kohlberg (Ed.), *Essays on moral development: Vol. 1. The philosophy of moral development* (pp. 101–189). San Francisco: Harper & Row.

Kohlberg, L. (1984). The nature and validity of moral stages. In L. Kohlberg (Ed.), *Essays on moral development: Vol. 2. The psychology of moral development*. San Francisco: Harper & Row.

Kuhn, T. (1962). *The structure of scientific revolutions*. Princeton, NJ.: Princeton University Press.

Patry, J. L., & Hager, W. (2000). Abschließende bemerkungen: Dilemmata in der evaluation. In W. Hager, J. L. Patry, & H. Brezing (Eds.), *Evaluation psychologischer Interventionsmaflnahmen*. Standards und Kriterien: Ein Handbuch (pp. 258–275). Bern: Huber.

Patry, P. (2000). *Ethische probleme in der psychologie*. Diplomarbeit: Universität Salzburg.

Phillips, D. C. (1999). How to play the game: A Popperian approach to the conduct of educational research. In G. Zecha (Ed.), *Critical rationalism and educational discourse* (pp. 170–190). Amsterdam: Rodopi.

Piaget, J. (1963). *The origins of intelligence*. New York: Norton.

Schurz, G., & Weingartner, P. (Eds.). (1998). *Koexistenz rivalisierender paradigmen. Eine post-kuhnsche Bestandesaufnahme zur Struktur gegenwärtiger Wissenschaft*. Wiesbaden: Westdeutscher Verlag.

Snyder, B. R. (1971). *The hidden curriculum*. New York: Knopf.

Weinberger, A. (2001). *Verbindung von konstruktivistischer Moralerziehung und Wissensvermittlung*. Unpublished master's dissertation, University of Salzburg, Austria.

Weingartner, P. (1971). *Wissenschaftstheorie 1: Einführung in die Hauptprobleme*. Stuttgart: Frommann-Holzboog.

Wilkinson, L., & The APA Task Force on Statistical Inference. (1999). Statistical methods in psychology journals: Guidelines and explanations. *American Psychologist*, *54*, 594–604. (reprint available at the APA homepage: http://www.apa.org/journals/amp/amp548594.html)

Zecha, G. (1984). *Für und wider die Wertfreiheit der Erziehungswissenschaft*. München: Finck und Paderborn: Schöningh.

PART III

Issues in Values Education for Citizens

CHAPTER 12

The IEA Civic Education Study: Ideal Communities of Practice and Realities of Political Experience Among 14-Year-Olds in 28 Countries

Judith Torney-Purta

Abstract

This chapter begins by discussing a model of learning in civic education based on Phase 1 of the IEA Study and on the theory of Etienne Wenger. The IEA model has the individual at its center influenced by family, school and peers, as well as by the discourse in society regarding political, economic, educational and religious values. Wenger's theory points to learning as it is related to experience in constructing meaning individually and with others. Central in this theory is the role of practice of civic skills and values in a community. Further, learning in civic-related areas is related to the formation of identities, linking experiences in families with experiences with friends and at school. The last part of the chapter reports findings from Phase 2 of the IEA Civic Education Study, in which a test and survey was administered to 90,000 students sampled from the grade in which the majority of 14-year-olds are found in 28 countries (Torney-Purta, Lehmann, Oswald, & Schulz, 2001). Some results from Hong Kong SAR are reported and placed in the perspective of results from the other participating countries.

Hong Kong SAR was among the countries whose students performed above the international mean on the international test of civic knowledge and skills. Within Hong Kong SAR, as well as other countries, the more students reported that they studied voting and elections in school and the more civic knowledge they possessed, the more likely they were to say that they planned to vote as adults. Studying in classrooms where there is an open and respectful climate for discussion of social issues also has a positive impact on both the acquisition of civic knowledge and the likelihood of voting. Teachers surveyed in the study believe that civic education has the potential to be very influential. The current emphasis on transmitting knowledge should, in the opinion of many teachers in Hong Kong SAR and other countries, be replaced by stressing either critical thinking or values. Television news programs and also community and school based organizations have untapped potential in civic education. The learning of citizenship values cannot be limited to rote learning. Rather it should involve meaningful learning of civic concepts, active involvement in communities of practice, and concern for students' identities. Seeking to preserve common core principles while exploring complementary methods relating to these ends is an appropriate direction for educators in civic-related areas.

Learning is a term with many meanings, and in an area such as values education it can be an amorphous concept. This chapter focuses on some relatively recent theoretical constructs to describe the process of learning in values and citizenship education in order to better focus the issues. Then the emphasis becomes narrower — on the IEA Civic Education Study and its contributions. Finally, conclusions from what has been studied in this extensive research and generalizations from its comparative cross-national character (with special attention to position of students from the Hong Kong SAR) are summarized in relation to five concepts.

IEA stands for the International Association for the Evaluation of Educational Achievement, the same non-governmental group in Amsterdam that organized the Third International Study of Mathematics and Science (TIMSS). IEA began a study of civic education in the early nineties in nearly thirty countries. This study examined, in a comparative framework, the values young people acquire to prepare them for citizenship and how they learn to take part in their society and its political arrangements. The topics include knowledge and values related to governmental institutions and those related to civil society and the community.

In many countries civic education goals have been thought of as important, but usually as much less critical than goals in other curriculum areas such as science. Seldom is any civics-related subject part of an important exit or entrance examination, for example. The background necessary to participate in government and civil society is not totally ignored, but neither is it seen as part of the credentials every student needs. However, civic values and the associated education necessary for students to achieve them seems to be poised for a surge of renewed interest in a number of countries around the world. Some of this new interest is the result of factors such as political and regime changes. In other countries there is a growing recognition that many young people want to contribute to their communities and bring about a better and more secure world, even though they may be disillusioned by conventional politics and the organizations which their parents' generation found compelling.

Although programs with civic values at their core have expanded across the world, there has not been much rigorous evaluation or research in this area. Because of a lack of benchmarks in specific subjects, it has remained ubiquitous but elusive in the school curriculum. Schwille and Amadeo (2002) discuss this problem across the IEA countries. To give one concrete example, only in the last year has England taken the steps to make civic education part of the statutory curriculum (accompanied by programs of training for teachers and other concrete steps toward specifying a subject matter and how it should be approached).

The IEA Civic Education Study has taken a substantial step toward filling this gap in research. It has done so in at least three ways — by proposing and elaborating a model through a consensus process in which more than 20 countries participated, by its comparative and within country findings in 28 countries, and by providing a carefully crafted, reliable and valid instrument which has been made widely available. The model is discussed in this chapter and in the book that summarized the case studies produced during the first phase of the study (Torney-Purta, Schwille, & Amadeo, 1999). The comparative and within country findings are referred to at several points in this chapter and in more detail in the book covering the study's second phase (Torney-Purta, Lehmann, Oswald, & Schulz, 2001). The instrument developed over several years in the study may be found at the web site for the study and is open for use by researchers.

The Model for Learning Used in the IEA Study

Let me begin by discussing the model of learning we have developed and some recent extensions of it, a model likely to be useful in values education generally. This model was inspired in part by contemporary psychological theories on the ecological approach to studying development (of Urie Bronfenbrenner) and the situated cognition theories (of Jean Lave and Etienne

Wenger). This model captures the individual and societal levels. It portrays young people living within a web of overlapping relationships, each of them with opportunities for personal growth and responsibilities. In the center is the individual student, surrounded by public discourse or discussion of the goals, values, and practices relevant to civic education. This discussion influences the individual student through face-to-face contact with the family (parents, siblings and extended family), the school (teachers, administrators, the intended curriculum and participation opportunities), peer group (as it functions both in and out of school), and neighbors (including youth organizations). In addition to these face-to-face relationships, there is also the impact of television and other media (including the Internet). Our main (though not exclusive) emphases are on the school and the peer group (especially as it functions in schools, organizations, and classrooms). The outer octagon which circumscribes these processes includes institutions, processes, and values in domains such as politics and economics. It also includes positive feeling about the nation. Laws and formal political and legal institutions are one, but only one facet, of this structure.

As the study went forward it became clear that an enriched understanding of processes of learning in relation to the political community would be useful. Etienne Wenger's theory (1998) relating to communities of practice, was an obvious choice. In Wenger's terms, learning involves the growth of meaning, practice, relation to community, and the formation of identity (Table 12.1). Let us look at these concepts as they apply to civic learning (and at the same time compare and contrast the process with learning in science).

The first point is that learning relates to experience in constructing meaningful concepts. In an ideal world, experience both in school and out of school should make political concepts increasingly meaningful to students and help them to connect new information to what they already know. Students participate actively in this process of constructing meaning. To compare with another subject area, the aim of science classes is to help

Table 12.1: Components of Learning (from Wenger, 1998)

Meaning (learning as experience in constructing meaning individually and collectively)
Practice (learning as doing and as mutual engagement in action)
Community (learning as belonging to social groups which recognize competence)
Identity (learning as becoming and creating personal history in a social context)

students develop an understanding of concepts such as gravity. When teaching does not attend to students' misconceptions about such concepts, meaningful learning is unlikely. The aim of meaningful learning should also be utmost in courses where civic education topics are considered. It appears that civic education classes are often taught in a rote fashion dealing with abstract institutional structures that are disconnected both from each other and from the students' own experience. Meaningful learning that helps students understand concepts such as democracy or equality or nationalism is unlikely to occur in such classes. A recent reanalysis of a study in the United States (Niemi & Junn, 1998) found once again what the first IEA study concluded 30 years ago (Torney, Oppenheim, & Farnen, 1975). Having students memorize factual material in order to score highly on a multiple choice test is not the way to ensure that they will either remember or understand the important basic principles of government.

It is well known that much of the student's everyday knowledge comes from the media. Yet few schools do much to help students make meaningful connections between these sources and concepts learned at school. For example, in Hong Kong SAR although study of the media and its relations to political and civic matters is listed in the curriculum, only about half of the textbooks cover this issue (Lee, 1999). This diagnosis of the situation led the developers of the IEA Civic Education Test to include questions giving students examples of political communication similar to that which would be found in the media and asking them to demonstrate their skills and understanding. Other questions asked students to distinguish between statements of fact and statements of opinion. In some countries the items testing skills were among the most difficult for students, perhaps because of lack of attention to media education or because in civic-related classes opinions may be presented as if they were facts.

A second point is that learning is related to practice. This means mutual engagement in action and the opportunity to try out one's knowledge in interpersonal situations, talking about it as a way to make it more meaningful. In science students need to work in the laboratory to see how chemical compounds react in reality not just in the ideal diagrams of the text. In civic education students also need to learn by doing. They need to discuss areas where action might be taken in their schools or classrooms and in their neighborhoods or to influence local governments, moving beyond simple diagrams about how a proposal for legislation is enacted in the national Congress or Parliament. They need to see how their ideas work out (or fail) when put into practice in order to internalize an interpersonal civic dimension within their personalities. Some of the findings of the IEA study suggest that it is unrealistic to expect students to do this without explicit instruction and assignments. We cannot assume that young people will see the subtle messages that their teachers present in their lessons.

The IEA study included a measure of how confident students feel that they and their friends can join together to take action on school problems. The assumption is that such confidence should result in higher levels of interest and participation in conventional adult political activities outside school. In some countries the students seemed very focused on and highly involved in existing opportunities to participate in the school (and even demand enhanced power), but this did not always carry over to political participation outside the school.

A third point is that when we learn, we relate ourselves to a community that has standards of competence and reinforces us in the belief that certain kinds of learning are worthwhile. It is within this community that most students will learn to negotiate their own lives as adults. The parallel in science is that we want students to take the community of scientists as models. In civic education we want students to relate to a community of citizens and to political and community leaders. They need to meet and talk to other civic-minded persons. Perhaps one could say that they need to "swim in a political sea." At the same time they need to realize that communities are not always havens of happy togetherness, but are often divided in opinions resulting in conflict. We also want them to relate to a national community, a level of affiliation that is experienced by some people only in response to a crisis or galvanizing national or international event. One reason that civic education often has a lower status than science training may be that there is not as much esteem across countries for the skills fostered in the community of citizens negotiating conflicts as there is for the skills of scientists.

Finally, learning creates identities, personal histories or trajectories that link our experiences in families with experiences with friends, in school, and in communities. A quote from a recent study conducted in a Central Asian Republic illustrates this. A student was asked to define a citizen. She said this: "Of course, for parents and their children to be citizens [means] for centuries that he has to know the language spoken in the family, follow the traditions of ancestors, and of the history of humankind, at least the history of one's ancestors" (cited in Kanaev, 2000). Civic education everywhere relates to our sense of national identity and national spirit as it comes from the past. In countries which have recently experienced transitions, this sense of national identity is especially important, and the

IEA study includes many of these countries (see chapters in Torney-Purta et al., 1999, especially Lee, 1999). A sense of national identity also comes to the fore at times of national emergency.

Identity related to the economic system also plays a role. In analyzing the IEA data it was apparent that even 14-year-olds seemed to distinguish between the society-related responsibilities of the government (e.g. providing free basic education or promoting honesty and moral behavior) and the economy-related responsibilities of the government (e.g. keeping prices under control or providing jobs for the unemployed). The differences between responses in countries in belief that the government should fulfill these economic responsibilities largely correspond in many respects to differences in beliefs among adults found in studies such as the World Values Survey, suggesting that 14-year-olds are already members of a political culture (cf. Torney-Purta et al., 2001 with Inglehart, 1997).

To summarize, the view of learning that seems appropriate in civic and values education stresses meaning, practice, relation to the community, and the construction of identity. All of the groups detailed in the IEA model contribute to these processes, sometimes in congruent ways and sometimes in ways that embody conflict.

The Design of the IEA Civic Education Study

A description of the design of the IEA Civic Education Study in a little more detail is appropriate at this point.

The study had two phases. In Phase 1, the more qualitative phase, national research coordinators interviewed experts on civic education inside and outside schools as well as analyzing written documents such as curriculum frameworks and textbooks. These very extensive documentary and interview data were summarized within a framework of 18 "Case Study Framing Questions" concerning expectations for what students of age 14 or 15 should know about topics such as individual rights and obligations, national identity, civil society, elections, the role of the media, and local problems. It is important to note that this data collection was not limited to examining official curricula, but included the interpretations and views of experts about what took place in classrooms. Civic Education Across Countries: Twenty-four National Case Studies from the IEA Civic Education Project (Torney-Purta et al., 1999), summarizes the data about expectations for students and ways of realizing them. Based on this first phase, three content domains were designated for consideration throughout the studies:

"Democracy, Democratic Institutions and Citizenship," "National Identity and International Relations," and "Social Cohesion and Diversity." These domains were developed by an International Steering Committee with the National Reseach Coordinators from the participating countries in an extensive consensus building process that took place both during in-person meetings and through electronic communication.[1]

All of the Phase 1 case study materials contributed specifically to instrument design for Phase 2 of the study, in which 90,000 fourteen-year-old students from nationally representative samples were tested during 1999. Teachers in these schools were also surveyed. These results were released in *Citizenship and Education Across Countries: Civic Knowledge and Engagement at Age Fourteen* (Torney-Purta et al., 2001). Sixteen countries tested an older population in 2000, and those results were released in 2002. The instrument focuses on knowledge, skills in interpreting civic communication, concepts of democracy and citizenship, attitudes toward topics such as women's political rights, trust in political institutions, and anticipated participatory behaviors. Influences of the climate for expressing opinions in the classroom were examined, as well as opportunities for school participation and out-of-school influences. Education of parents as well as the students' own expected education were included in prediction models.

The following countries participated in both Phase 1 and 2 having arranged their participation through their respective IEA General Assembly delegates: Australia, Belgium (French), Bulgaria, Colombia, Cyprus, Czech Republic, England, Finland, Germany, Greece, Hong Kong SAR, Hungary, Israel, Italy, Lithuania, Poland, Portugal, Romania, The Russian Federation, Slovenia, Switzerland, and the United States. In addition, Canada and the Netherlands participated only in Phase 1. The following countries participated only in Phase 2: Chile, Denmark, Estonia, Latvia, Norway, Slovak Republic, and Sweden. Chinese Taipei, Korea, and Thailand participated in part of Phase 1 but were unable to complete the Phase 2 testing.

Many observers believed that it would be difficult to find ideas about democracy common among these countries on which to base the test and survey. The International Steering Committee designed the Phase 1 process to overcome this difficulty. We used a democratic method of consultation to work with all of the country representatives. Quotations from Phase 1 documents guided the instrument development; votes from the national coordinators were taken when we came to important choice points. The items were piloted in more than 20 countries (checking the revisions and

Table 12.2: Topics Covered in the Civic Knowledge Test

Domain IA: Democracy and Its Defining Characteristics
- defining characteristics of democracy
- democratic and non-democratic regimes
- evaluating strengths and weaknesses of democratic systems
- incentives to participate in democracy
- problems in transitions of government from non-democratic to democratic

Domain IB: Institutions and Practices in Democracy:
- characteristics and functions of elections and parties
- qualifications of candidates and making up one's mind during elections
- healthy critical attitudes toward officials and their accountability
- basic characteristics of parliament, judicial systems, law, and police
- provisions of constitutions
- basic economic issues and their political implications

Domain IC: Citizenship: Rights and Duties:
- general rights, qualifications, and obligations of citizens in democracies
- citizens' rights to participate and express criticism
- obligations, civic duties of citizens in democracy
- the role of mass media in democracy
- networks of associations and differences of opinions
- the human rights defined in international documents
- rights in the economic sphere
- tradeoffs involved in political decisions about the environment

Domain IIA: National Identity:
- sense of national identity
- recognition of problematic events in a nation's history

Domain IIB: International Relations:
- organizations dealing with matters of economics or the environment
- the United Nations

Domain IIIA: Social Cohesion and Diversity
- recognizing groups subject to discrimination

translations with outside experts as well as national representatives). The topics covered in the resulting 38-item test are found in Table 12.2.

Concepts Helpful in Integrating the Results of Phase 1 and Phase 2

The next section discusses five concepts under which the study's results can be summarized, drawing on the Phase 1 case studies and on the results from Phase 2:

Centrality;
Commonality;
Reality;
Solidarity; and
Complementarity.

First, Centrality of Content in civic education. In the first phase of the study there was very substantial agreement about what the average 14 year old should know and believe about democracy. The three content domains listed above and in Table 12.2 are a summary of that. In addition statistical evidence showed that our 38 item test of knowledge and skills based on these domains has high reliability and a common structure across countries.

There was an important decision to be made about how much emphasis should be placed on knowledge (and specifically in the IEA study how much time should be devoted to questions with keyed correct answers). While this debate was underway, the case-study author from the Netherlands reported that a test of knowledge of detailed facts about Dutch history and government was given to members of the national legislature and teachers. Both groups had far from a perfect score. This led first to some embarrassment, but later to a wave of indignation. The respondents complained that these were questions about trivialities of government, pieces of information that were not essential to being a citizen, a teacher, or a policy maker.

The IEA committees concluded from this and other feedback that content knowledge and skills should be an important element of the instrument but should not account for more than half of the testing time. Civic engagement is only partly dependent upon factual information. This led to the inclusion in the instrument of five types of items, only two of which could be scored for correct answers. (Other items deal with concepts, attitudes, and civic behavior.) The committee was very successful in developing knowledge and skills questions focused on the fundamental principles of democracy and common features of citizenship across countries. No questions were included about particular features of any one country's government (though some countries added these as national options).

In the results of the testing, the Hong Kong SAR was among the countries whose students performed at a level above the international mean on this international test of civic content knowledge and skills. Other countries with similar high performance were Cyprus, Finland, Greece, Italy, Norway, Poland, the Slovak Republic, and the United States (for further details see

Torney-Purta et al., 2001). In another part of the instrument students were asked about their concept of democracy (in questions without correct or incorrect answers). Students in Hong Kong showed themselves to be part of a general consensus in believing that it is bad for democracy when wealthy people have undue influence on governments, when the courts are influenced by politicians, and when people in government give jobs to members of their families. Although the definition of democracy was derived primarily from European rather than Asian concepts, it is interesting that students in Hong Kong SAR largely agreed with the Western European students in their ratings of these threats to democracy.

Other important information about the importance of content knowledge comes from an analysis of predictors of students' likelihood to vote. A series of regression analyses were conducted. Within countries students' scores on the knowledge test were significant predictors of the students' expressed likelihood of voting (even when a variety of other factors were held constant). Thus the schools' role in transmitting knowledge is important. It promotes a well informed citizenry in general and also contributes to young people's expressed willingness to be a participant in the government by engaging in one of the most basic acts of democratic governance.

Another insight about the transmission of content and beliefs in the schools comes from a question regarding the emphasis students saw in their schools' curricula. What did students believe they had an opportunity to learn in their school? (A similar set of questions was asked of teachers.) Of special interest was the fact that students in Hong Kong SAR agreed with their teachers that learning about the importance of voting and elections should be an emphasis in the curriculum. Of even greater importance is the fact that in Hong Kong SAR, as well as in the other countries, students who say that they have learned explicitly about voting and elections in school are more likely to say they intend to vote than those who report they have not learned this (see Torney-Purta et al., 2001, chap. 8). A point mentioned earlier is reinforced by these findings. Teaching indirectly about voting or elections (e.g., by having students learn the history of elections) may have less impact on students' own willingness to vote than teachers being explicit, direct, and pro-active in making the point that every citizen who is eligible should cast a vote.

A second theme of the study as a whole is Commonality in Pedagogical Processes or methods. The agreement found in the first phase of the IEA Civic Education Study about the content of civic education and the psychometric quality of the test was encouraging. More surprising was the high level of agreement among participating national project representatives about how education for citizenship should be conducted. There was commonality in the belief that it should be participatory, related to life in the school and the community, conducted in a non-authoritarian environment with concern for the meaning students attribute to information, and aware of the challenges of societal diversity.

Many of these themes of the first phase were corroborated by the survey data in the second phase. For example, among the most significant predictors of both high civic knowledge and likelihood of voting was the extent to which the students reported that an open and respectful climate for discussion of student opinion characterized the classroom where civic-related topics were discussed. Students who were encouraged to discuss issues about which there might be differences of opinion and who felt that teachers and students respected their rights had higher knowledge and were more likely to say they would be engaged. This points out the importance of Wenger's ideas of participation in communities of practice. In order to begin to find their political identity adolescents need to be incorporated into a community in which political opinions are expressed and to try out their own opinions while listening to those of others. The United States, Norway, and Greece were among the countries that were characterized by especially open classroom climates according to students. Hong Kong SAR was among the countries where students reported less open classroom climate (Torney-Purta et al., 2001, chap. 7).

A third issue is Reality in everyday experience. There has not been universal success in any country in achieving the ideal experience for all students in preparing them for citizenship. And even if such experience might be achieved within a given classroom, often social and political realities outside the school blunt or even contradict a positive message. Many of those who wrote the case study chapters in the Phase 1 book were positive about the potential of youth and their energy and imagination. But they also confronted these realities, for example, in situations where persons in government did not demonstrate the highest moral integrity, when elections seemed irrelevant to political change, or when increasingly commercialized media had more impact on students' priorities than school experience.

From the Phase 2 survey it was clear that somewhat less than half of the students across these participating countries experience the positive factors that would allow them to achieve meaningful concepts, practice usable political skills and involve themselves deeply in the communities of practice which seem likely to lead to active adult civic engagement (Torney-Purta et al., 2001, chap. 7). Of particular concern is the report by teachers that recitations and worksheets are the predominant forms of instruction in civic-related classes (Losito & Mintrop, 2001).

Teachers are clear about how they see the reality of civic education. They believe that civic education has the potential to be very influential. However, they see their prescribed role as teaching knowledge about government, although they believe this is not the most important part of civic education. In Hong Kong SAR, for example, nearly half the teachers believe that the current emphasis is placed on transmitting knowledge, while less than ten percent believe that this should be the emphasis. Instead they would find it ideal to emphasize critical thinking or values (about forty percent choosing each). A similar pattern of teacher responses is observed in Switzerland, to take one other country as an example (Losito & Mintrop, 2001).

The IEA study shows diversity among countries in how well students recognize the realities of political life. In some countries there is a lack of skill in interpreting political communication (which provides an important way for students to learn about political reality). For example, some students have difficulty in inferring which political party issued an election leaflet containing conflicting claims or in interpreting political cartoons or newspaper articles about topics such as environmental pollution where interest groups take different sides. In general, Hong Kong SAR students performed well on these items, while those in Latin America and many of the post-Communist countries performed poorly.

A fourth important concept is Solidarity, that is, cooperative activity with others in pursuit of common goals, usually goals associated with social justice (and often associated with social movements and protest activities). But let us look first at more conventional types of political participation. In many countries there has been a decline in the proportion of young adults who vote or affiliate themselves with political parties. The IEA results suggest that students believe that voting is only moderately important and that joining political parties is not important for adult citizens.

Hong Kong SAR students responded in a way similar to those in the other participating countries when asked if they were likely to vote. They were also as likely as those in other countries to say that adult citizens should participate in conventional political activities, but they placed less importance on adults' participation in social movement activities than those in other countries. For example, they were less likely to say that adult citizens should join environmental or human rights groups. The pattern in Hong Kong SAR with high belief in conventional activity and relatively low belief in social movement participation contrasts, for example, with the pattern in Australia or Switzerland (where young people believed that neither conventional nor social movement activity was important for adults) or in Cyprus, Greece, or the United States (where young people believed that both types of activity were important for adult citizens).

There is also concern about declining trust in public institutions, at the same time there is hope that young people will be prepared to demonstrate peacefully and speak out when faced with injustice or policies that should be criticized. Students from Hong Kong SAR expressed a level of trust in both government-related institutions and in the media that is very close to the international mean for all the participating countries.

There were also differences in the extent to which students reported participating in organizations both inside and outside school that have potential for civic engagement and the experience of solidarity. For example, in Hong Kong SAR, as well as Greece, Norway, and Sweden, 45% or more of students reported participating in student councils or parliaments. Students in Hong Kong SAR also reported relatively high levels of participation in organizations benefiting the community and in collecting money for charity, and average levels of participation in organizations dealing with environmental or human rights problems. Other countries with relatively similar levels of participation were Australia, Chile, Colombia, and the United States. Many of the post-Communist countries reported low levels of participation in these organizations, perhaps because networks of such organizations are not yet widely available in many of these countries (Torney-Purta et al., 2001, chap. 7).

Participation in projects to benefit the community has been encouraged in some countries as a way of promoting students' civic engagement and sense of solidarity. Some believe that as long as this involvement is taking place, we should be less concerned about poor knowledge, low voting rates, or the ability to think critically about particular policies. Others question whether community service experience alone is sufficient, especially if students focus on the local problem without seeing the political or policy forces which contribute to creating it or noting the different positions taken by elected leaders on these problems.

It appears from the IEA Phase 1 case studies and from the analysis of Phase 2 surveys that student associations within schools and communities can play a positive role in enhancing civic engagement, especially when coupled with a climate for free expression in the classroom. This is one conclusion of both the 1999 IEA study and the 1971 IEA study. However, the expectations that teaching styles will become more open to students' opinions and that power will devolve to students in school councils or parliaments have met with considerable ambivalence among many who are responsible for civic education in developed as well as developing democracies.

The final topic or orienting concept is Complementarity. The case studies pointed to the real differences between countries in the structures being used to implement and improve civic education. In some countries having a separate subject that rigorously teaches civic knowledge appears to succeed in equipping students with knowledge of democratic principles and skills in interpreting political communication. In other countries, studying civics as a designated part of the curriculum may produce more mediocre results than the inclusion of citizenship education among cross-curricular themes produces within another system. In another country classroom work may be supplemented with opportunities for action and practice with much more success in fostering civic engagement than in enhancing knowledge. Crises in the struggle for democracy and security at the national level often mobilize young people. Resistance to adult authority or the status quo may energize some young people's engagement, while others move quietly but effectively through increasing levels of responsibility and leadership in their communities, either guided directly by adults or emulating adult models.

Once again in the 1999 study (as in the first IEA study in the 1970s; Torney et al., 1975) it appears that there is no single solution, no magic potion, to enhance all aspects and outcomes of civic education equally and at the same time. Reforms must fit into the context — the social, economic, and cultural aspects delineated in the IEA model. They must fit into the availability of opportunities for diverse young people and at the same time face the reality of political contexts and transitions. The value of communities of practice in which young people feel welcome and experience increasing involvement is clear. Also clear is the importance of involving teachers — their preparation, their sense of security in elaborating on the curriculum, and their commitment — in processes of change and reform.

With these important items demanding attention on the agenda for action, the next several years promise to be a time when increasing attention is paid to citizenship education. Understanding that learning of citizenship values involves more than rote repetition — that it requires meaningful learning, active practice, connection to community, and concern for identity — will help in formulating more effective programs. Seeking to preserve common core principles while exploring complementary methods is an appropriate course to chart for ourselves, and for the next generation of students and teachers in this field.

References

Inglehart, R. (1997). *Modernization and postmodernization: Cultural, economic, and political changes in 43 societies*. Princeton, NJ: Princeton University Press.

Kanaev, A. (2000). *Civic education in central Asia*. Stockholm: Institute of International Education.

Lee, W. O. (1999). Controversies of civic education in political transition. In J. Torney-Purta, J. Schwille, & J. Amadeo (Eds.), *Civic education across countries: Twenty-four national case studies from the IEA Civic Education Project*. Amsterdam: IEA.

Losito, B., & Mintrop, R. (2001). The teaching of civic education. In J. Torney-Purta, R. Lehmann, H. Oswald, & W. Schulz (Eds.), *Citizenship and education in twenty-eight countries: Civic knowledge and engagement at age fourteen*. Amsterdam: IEA.

Niemi, R., & Junn, J. (1998). *Civic education: What makes students learn*. New Haven, CT: Yale University Press.

Schwille, J., & Amadeo, J. (2002). The paradoxical situation of civic education in schools: Ubiquitous and yet elusive. In G. Steiner-Khamsi, J. Torney-Purta, & J. Schwille (Eds.), *New paradigms and recurring paradoxes in education for citizenship: An international comparison* (pp. 105–136). Oxford, UK: Elsevier Science.

Torney, J., Oppenheim, A. N., & Farnen, R. (1975). *Civic education in ten countries: An empirical study*. Stockholm: Almqvist and Wiksell.

Torney-Purta, J., Lehmann, R., Oswald, H., & Schulz, W. (2001). *Citizenship and education in twenty-eight countries: The civic knowledge and engagement of adolescents*. Amsterdam: IEA.

Torney-Purta, J., Schwille, J., & Amadeo, J. (Eds.). (1999). *Civic education across countries: Twenty-four national case studies from the IEA Civic Education Project*. Amsterdam: IEA. Report of Phase 1.

Wenger, E. (1998). *Communities of practice*. Cambridge, UK: Cambridge University Press.

Note

1. Lee Wing On, of the Hong Kong Institute of Education was the National Research Coordinator for Hong Kong and a member of the International Steering Committee. His thoughtfulness has been a great value to our work. We also had input to the first phase from three other Asian countries who were not able to complete the testing.

CHAPTER 13

Citizenship in Transition and Its Implications to Citizenship Education: The Case of Hong Kong

Wing-kwong Tsang

Abstract

On the first of July 1997, the sovereignty of Hong Kong was handed over from the United Kingdom to the People Republic of China (PRC). Accompanying the transmission of sovereignty, the citizenship of Hong Kong residents also underwent a profound change, that is, from the subject of a British colony to the citizen of the Special Administrative Region (SAR) of the PRC. However, the transition of citizenship had in fact taken place in a much longer timeline than the ceremonial evening in the summer of 1997. It can be traced back to Mrs. Thatcher's visitation to Beijing in September 1982, with which the issue of 1997 handover burst into the political scene of the colony. During this 15 years of transition, Hong Kong as a society had underwent tremendous and fundamental changes, among which are two transformation which this chapter is intended to explore. One is the transformation of the institution and culture of citizenship in Hong Kong political system. The other is the transformation of the conception and practice of citizenship education in Hong Kong

Data presented in this chapter are generated from two research projects funded by the Research Grant Council, with project references 160/94H and 4199/98H. The author of this chapter is the principal investigator of the two projects. Co-investigators of the projects include Kin-shuen Louie, Sai-wing Leung, Kwok-cheung Shum, and Joseph Man Chan. The author would also like to acknowledge the kind assistance of the Registration and Electoral Office, Hong Kong Special Administrative Region Government, the Hong Kong Institute of the Asia-Pacific Studies and the Hong Kong Institute of Educational Research, the Chinese University of Hong Kong.

education system. In this chapter, I set out to try to relate these two transformations from an empirical perspective. Based on the data generated from two electoral studies of the 1995 and 1998 Legislative Council Election, I shall delineate the changes in conceptions of citizenship among registered voters in Hong Kong. I shall then locate the findings within the policy context of citizenship education, which only began to take shape and then proliferate after the emergence of the 1997 handover issue. However, before I dwell into explication of empirical data, I think it is necessary to give a brief delineation of the concepts of citizenship and citizenship education.

Conceptualization of Citizenship

In this chapter, citizenship will be defined as the rights, obligations, and power inherent in the status of full members in a modern polity, such as a nation-state. This definition assigns two meanings to citizenship. First, citizenship is seen as a status, that is, the qualified member of a polity in the modern nation-state's world-system. Bottomore (1992, pp. 66–68) terms this aspect of citizenship as formal citizenship and indicates that it is basically a legal concern (see also Burbater, 1990). Secondly, citizenship is seen as a set of rights and obligations arising from the status of formal citizenship. Bottomore (1992, pp. 70–74) calls this aspect of citizenship substantive citizenship and suggests that it relates to social and political institutions and actions. In relation to citizenship education, it is obvious that the substantive aspect of citizenship is the primary concern of citizenship education. Furthermore, substantive citizenship can also be delineated into at least two dimensions. One is the institutional dimension, which concerns the structure and process of how citizenship rights and obligations are institutionalized within the modern nation-state and its civil society. The other dimension emphasizes the cultural and attitudinal aspect of substantive citizenship. More specifically, it explores the attitudes that citizens of a given polity hold towards their citizenship rights and obligations as well as the related political and social institutions. These two dimensions basically have generated two lines of inquiry in the social and political sciences. The institutional dimension can relate to the lines of inquiry of the building of the modern nation-state and more specifically the citizenship generated from it (Bendix, 1977; Giddens, 1981, 1982, 1985; Held, 1989; Janoski, 1998; Mann, 1987; Marshall, 1977; Morris 1980; Somers, 1993; Tsang, 1998; Turner, 1990). The cultural and attitudinal dimension can pertain to the research tradition of empirical study of political culture, political attitude and political behavior (Abramson, 1983; Almond & Verba, 1963, 1980; Campbell, 1960; Inglehart, 1990, 1997; Milbrath & Goel, 1977; Miller & Shanks, 1996).

In accordance with this conceptualization of citizenship, the analytical theme of this chapter, that is, citizenship in transition can be surveyed in the following three ways: (1) transition in formal citizenship; (2) transition in the institutional dimension of substantive citizenship; and (3) transition in the cultural dimension of substantive citizenship. However, in the following pages, I shall confine my analysis to substantive citizenship, which bears direct implications for citizenship education. More specifically, I shall only deal with the cultural dimension of substantive citizenship. The choice may seem to be arbitrary. However, it may be justified in three ways. First of all, there is, of course, the space constraint in writing a book chapter, in which I cannot squeeze everything in at the expense of substantiality and depth. Second, I have presented the analysis of the changes in the institutional dimension of substantive citizenship in Hong Kong elsewhere (Tsang, 1998). Though that analysis begs some updating, for the time being I think it could only be dealt with elsewhere. Lastly, I have to comply with the nature and features of the data sets in hand. They only reveal the cultural and attitudinal dimension of substantive citizenship of Hong Kong citizens.

The two electoral studies used are based on the same conceptual framework generated from the literature on electoral studies in the United States and United Kingdom (Heath et al., 1985; Heath et al., 1991; Miller & Shanks, 1996; Miller & Traugott, 1989). The original framework, which is structured in the form of a funnel of causality leading to voting behavior, is outlined in the Appendix. However, in this paper, I shall not dwell on the details of the voting behavior analysis but shall simply present some aspects of the political attitudes of Hong Kong voters, which are relevant to citizenship education. Hence in the following exposition, four aspects of the political attitudes and opinions of Hong Kong citizens will be explicated. They are (1) general political attitude; (2) political trust; (3) policy preference; and (4) candidate evaluation.

Hong Kong Citizenship in Transition

My analysis of the changes in political attitude or culture of Hong Kong citizens is based on sets of data collected in the two Legislative Council elections in Hong Kong. They are the 1995 and 1998 Legislative Council election in geographic constituencies. These two elections took place before and after the 1997 transition. The two corresponding studies are post-election studies based on a randomly selected sample of Hong Kong registered voters.

In the 1995 study, a random sample of registered voters in the 20 geographical constituencies in *Final Registered Electors 1995* were selected with the kind assistance of the Registration and Election Office. Out of the 4,017 in-scope names, 2,359 of the registered voters were interviewed, a 58.7% response rate (Tsang, 1998).

In the 1998 study, once again with the kind assistance of the Registration and Election Office, a sample of registered voters in *Final Registered Electors 1998* were randomly selected from the five geographic constituencies. Out of the 4,842 in-scope names, 2,993 of the voters were successfully interviewed. It yielded a 61.8% response rate.

General Political Attitude of Hong Kong Citizens

In the 1995 and 1998 studies, there are 20 common items measuring the general political attitude. These items are mainly generated and localized from three constructs that appeared in the National Election Study (Miller & Traugott, 1989). These three constructs are citizen duty, political efficacy and trust in government.

From the confirmatory factor analyses of the items in the 1995 and 1998 studies, which are presented in Figures 13.1 and 13.2 in the Appendix, they confirm that the measurement models of the general political attitude in the 1995 and 1998 studies are basically identical. Both models generate 5 latent variables. They can be characterized as (1) Faith in Democracy; (2) Sense of Citizenship; (3) Distrust in Government; (4) Political Helplessness; and (5) Political Skepticism. The overall performance of the confirmatory factor analysis is satisfactory. As the goodness-of-fit statistics in Figures 13.1 and 13.2 suggest, the model fits well with the data.

The responses to individual items in the 1995 and 1998 studies are presented in Tables 13.1 and 13.2 respectively. The readings in Table 13.1 suggest, first of all, that in the 1995 election, Hong Kong citizens held a strong sense of political skepticism. It can be evidenced in the responses that most of the voters (ranging from 45.9% to 70.7%) agree and strongly agree with the 4 items subsumed under the latent variable Political Skepticism. Secondly, Hong Kong citizens also have a very strong feeling of political helplessness. Among the 6 items subsumed under the latent variable Political Helplessness, all 5 of them are able to capture over 55%

Table 13.1: Responses to Items of General Political Attitude of Hong Kong Voters in the 1995 Legislative Council Election

	Strongly Disagree	Disagree	Either or	Agree	Strongly Agree	Valid Cases
Faith in Democray						
306 Voting is effect means of expressing my view to the government.	1.5	14.9	19.7	57.3	6.7	2,117
307 Directly-elected councilors enhance government accountability.	0.9	12.9	20.6	60.5	5.4	2,063
326 Political organizations enhance the accountability of the government.	1.0	17.9	21.3	54.4	5.4	2,092
Sense of Citizenship						
308 Election is a wasteful activity.	3.9	51.0	16.3	23.3	5.6	2,145
310 As so many people vote, mine doesn't count much.	6.3	51.8	9.9	28.1	3.8	2,178
311 The current electoral system is too complicated to understand.	4.6	50.3	10.3	29.6	5.2	2,192
312 I shall not vote unless it concerns my vested interest.	7.0	62.6	10.2	17.9	2.3	2,186
Distrust in HK Government						
316 Most of the Hong Kong Government policies are right in recent years.	3.1	40.0	38.7	17.0	1.2	2,110
318 Most senior officials of Hong Kong Government are capable.	2.3	28.7	35.0	31.8	2.1	2,060
320 Hong Kong Government hasn't misused public funds.	9.1	56.1	22.0	10.7	2.1	2,083
Political Helplessness						
321 I can't influence government policies.	1.4	21.3	16.1	53.4	7.8	2,146
324 Hong Kong people is helpless in deciding the future of Hong Kong.	0.3	18.4	18.3	52.4	10.5	2,068
325 Politics is too complicated for me to understand.	0.3	8.6	11.6	65.2	14.2	2,177
328 Most of the Hong Kong people don't express their opinions publicly.	0.6	15.5	20.6	56.1	7.2	2,109
314 No matter how we vote, Hong Kong's future won't be better.	4.7	53.0	16.9	22.4	2.9	2,048
319 Most of Hong Kong Government policies are for the benefit of the rich.	0.4	13.3	22.6	53.5	10.1	2,135
Political Skepticism						
309 Candidates consider voters' interest only during elections.	0.9	17.0	27.9	44.0	10.3	2,112
322 Politicians are for their own interests.	0.7	13.0	37.8	40.7	7.9	2,120
323 Politics are corrupted.	0.7	10.9	17.8	58.1	12.6	2,000
327 Political organizations are for power rather than for public interests.	0.3	15.8	37.9	39.6	6.3	2,083

Table 13.2: Responses to Items of General Political Attitude of Hong Kong Voters in the 1998 Legislative Council election

	Strongly Disagree	Disagree	Either or	Agree	Strongly Agree	Valid Cases
Faith in Democracy						
257 Voting is effect means of expressing my view to the government.	1.1	11.9	17.3	57.7	12.0	2,771
258 Directly-elected councilors enhance government accountability.	0.8	13.1	20.6	56.5	9.0	2,678
322 Political organizations enhance the accountability of the government.	0.5	5.8	17.1	67.4	9.2	2,632
Sense of Citizenship						
259 Election is a wasteful activity.	7.8	57.7	15.1	17.0	3.7	2,747
261 As so many people vote mine doesn't count much.	9.8	54.2	9.3	22.6	4.2	2,808
262 The current electoral system is too complicated to understand.	3.8	37.9	13.8	34.6	9.5	2,809
263 I shall not vote unless it concerns my vested interest.	10.7	64.8	7.9	14.2	2.4	2,813
Distrust in HK Government						
266 Most of the Hong Kong Government policies are right in recent years.	4.7	46.5	31.0	16.5	1.3	2,752
267 Most senior officials of Hong Kong Government are capable.	6.2	38.1	31.1	22.8	1.8	2,711
269 Hong Kong Government hasn't misused public funds.	9.2	49.3	24.3	15.1	2.1	2,513
Political Helplessness						
270 I can't influence government policies.	1.7	19.7	15.6	54.0	9.0	2,767
320 Hong Kong people is helpless in deciding the future of Hong Kong.	1.7	32.4	21.1	38.6	6.4	2,578
321 Politics is too complicated for me to understand.	0.5	8.5	12.0	65.2	13.7	2,773
324 Most of the Hong Kong people don't express their opinions publicly.	0.8	17.1	21.4	52.5	8.2	2,703
265 No matter how we vote, Hong Kong's future won't be better.	9.4	62.0	13.5	13.2	2.0	2,699
268 Most of Hong Kong Government policies are for the benefit of the rich.	1.3	25.9	28.0	36.3	8.5	2,684
Political Skepticism						
260 Candidates consider voters' interest only during election.	1.7	22.8	30.7	36.5	8.3	2,702
318 Politicians are for their own interests.	0.4	11.8	39.0	38.3	10.6	2,696
319 Politics are corrupted.	0.5	10.8	19.9	53.5	15.2	2,553
323 Political organizations are for power rather than for public interests.	0.6	16.6	42.8	32.9	7.1	2,632

of the respondents' response. Third, as for the items subsumed under the latent variable Distrust in Hong Kong Government, the responses reveal that there is a strong sense of distrust in Hong Kong Government among Hong Kong citizens. This can be evidenced first of all in the finding that 65.2% of the respondents have indicated that the Hong Kong Government has misused public funds, while 43.1% of them disagree or strongly disagree with the statement that "most of the Hong Kong Government policies are right in recent years." As for the item "most senior officials in the Hong Kong Government are capable," Hong Kong citizens are split in their opinions. Among the respondents, 32.9% agree that the senior officials are capable, while 31% indicate disagreement. Fourth, the responses to the 3 items subsumed under the latent variable Faith in Democracy reveal that Hong Kong voters have a strong faith in democracy. All 3 items are able to secure endorsement from the majority of the respondents (ranging from 59.8% to 65.9%). Finally, the 4 items subsumed under the latent variable Sense of Citizenship indicate that Hong Kong citizens have a strong sense of citizenship. This can be evidenced in the finding that over 50% of the respondents indicate that they disagree or strongly disagree with all 5 statements which bear negative connotation with a sense of citizenship.

Taking these findings from the 1995 election together, we may dissect the political attitude of Hong Kong citizens into positive and negative sides. On the negative side, Hong Kong citizens can be characterized as skeptical, helpless and distrustful political actors. However, on the positive side, Hong Kong citizens do hold a strong faith in the emerging democratic elements in the political system, such as directly-elected legislators and political organizations. Moreover, they also have a strong sense of citizenship. In fact, we can further our analysis of these two faces of political attitude by looking into the correlation coefficients among the 5 latent variables presented in Figure 13.1. They suggest that the 5 latent variables can be grouped into two clusters. From the readings of the correlation coefficients, we can see that Political Skepticism, Distrust in Government and Political Helplessness are positively and significantly correlated, while Sense of Citizenship and Faith in Democracy are also positively correlated. We can also see that these two clusters of latent variables are negatively and significantly correlated with each other. Hence, they indicate that the general political attitudes of Hong Kong voters are aligned into two opposite dimensions. That is, that those citizens holding strong feelings of political skepticism, helplessness, and distrust in government are less likely to be civic-minded and optimistic about democratic development in Hong Kong.

As for the political attitude of Hong Kong citizens in the 1998 election, the findings in Table 13.2 suggest that the general political attitude of Hong Kong citizens remained basically the same. However, we can further the analysis by comparing the means of the 20 items between the 1995 and 1998 studies and see whether there are any significant differences between the means of the respective items. The result of the mean difference comparison is presented in Table 13.3. The findings reveal some salient changes in Hong Kong citizens' political attitude before and after the 1997 transition.

(1) All three items subsumed under the latent variable Faith in Democracy yield significant mean differences. The mean differences are all in the same direction, that is, the means in the 1998 studies are larger than those in 1995. These indicate that Hong Kong citizens have stronger faith in democracy after the 1997 re-unification;
(2) All 5 items under the latent variable Sense of Citizenship also provide significant mean differences. Four of the items, which bear negative connotations, produce mean differences in the same direction. They suggest that Hong Kong citizens hold a stronger sense of citizenship after the 1997 transition. As for the item "the current electoral system is too complicated to understand," it yields a significant mean difference in the opposite direction. This implies that there are more citizens who think that the electoral system in 1998 is more complicated. These changes can be discerned as the changes in empirical reality rather than changes in Hong Kong citizens' political attitude, because the electoral systems in the 1995 and 1998 Legislative Council elections are totally different. In the 1995 election, the electoral system was a single vote, single seat and simple majority system. While in the 1998 election, the electoral system was a single vote, but multiple seat and proportional representation system, which is a much more complicated system to comprehend;
(3) Two out of three items under the construct Distrust in Government produce significant mean differences. They are also in the same direction. They indicate that Hong Kong citizens have become more distrustful towards the Hong Kong Government. In other words, Hong Kong citizens are of the opinion that the Hong Kong SAR Government is less trustworthy than the British colonial Hong Kong Government. More specifically, more citizens are more likely to

Table 13.3: Mean Difference in General Political Attitude between 1995 and 1998 Voters

	1995 Voters		1998 Voters		
	Mean	S.D.	Mean	S.D.	T-value
Faith in Democracy					
Voting is effect means of expressing my view to the government.	3.53	0.88	3.68	0.87	–5.42053***
Directly-elected councilors enhance government accountability.	3.46	0.87	3.6	0.86	–5.06024***
Political organizations enhance the accountability of the government.	3.57	0.8	3.79	0.71	–8.9028***
Sense of Citizenship					
Election is a wasteful activity.	2.78	1.03	2.52	0.98	8.158556***
As so many people vote, mine doesn't count much.	2.74	1.05	2.57	1.07	5.154205***
The current electoral system is too complicated to understand.	2.8	1.07	3.08	1.12	–8.26823***
I shall not vote unless if it concerns my vested interest.	2.46	0.93	2.33	0.93	4.484446***
Distrust in HK Government					
Most of the Hong Kong Government policies are right in recent years.	2.72	0.82	2.63	0.86	3.402226***
Most senior officials of Hong Kong Government are capable.	3.06	0.87	2.76	0.94	10.46826***
Hong Kong Government hasn't misused public funds.	2.41	0.95	2.52	0.96	–1.33204
Political Helplessness					
I can't influence government policies.	3.45	0.95	3.49	0.96	–1.33204
Hong Kong people is helpless in deciding the future of Hong Kong.	3.68	0.9	3.76	0.93	–2.7913**
Politics is too complicated for me to understand.	3.84	0.78	3.83	0.78	0.405751
Most of the Hong Kong people don't express their opinions publicly.	3.53	0.87	3.5	0.9	1.072112
No matter how we vote, Hong Kong's future won't be better.	2.68	0.98	2.36	0.89	10.51025***
Most of Hong Kong Government policies are for the benefit of the rich.	3.59	0.86	3.25	0.98	11.83701***
Political Skepticism					
Candidates consider voters' interest only during elections.	3.46	0.93	3.27	0.96	6.354246***
Politicians are for their own interests.	3.42	0.84	3.47	0.85	–1.86711
Politics are corrupted.	3.69	0.85	3.72	0.87	–1.0694
Political organizations are for power rather than for public interests.	3.34	0.84	3.29	0.85	1.84828

* Sig. = 0.05; ** Sig. = 0.01; *** Sig. = 0.001

think that the government policies are wrong in 1998, than those in 1995. Moreover, citizens' trust in senior officials' capabilities has decreased significantly from 1995 to 1998. The decrease is more evident if we compare the responses to this item in Tables 13.1 and 13.2. As pointed out above, in the 1995 study Hong Kong citizens were split on the trust in senior officials' capability. However, in the 1998 study, Hong Kong citizens had formed a majority view of senior officials, that is, 44.3% of the respondents disagreed or strongly disagreed that the senior officials were capable. As for the item "Hong Kong Government hasn't misused public funds," which produces no significant mean difference, the two means (2.41 and 2.52) as well as the responses in Tables 13.1 and 13.2 also indicate that the majority of Hong Kong citizens hold that both the SAR and the colonial governments have misused public funds.

(4) As for the constructs of Political Helplessness, the mean differences of the 6 items are unable to produce consensual results. Three of the items are unable to yield significant differences, while of the 3 items, which produced significant mean differences, one of them indicates that Hong Kong citizens felt more helpless in political influence in 1998 than in 1995. The item in point is "Hong Kong people are helpless in deciding the future of Hong Kong." Another, on the contrary, indicates more citizens in the 1998 study indicate their disagreement to the item "no mater how we vote, Hong Kong's future won't be better," while fewer citizens in the 1998 study endorse the statement "most of Hong Kong Government policies are for the benefit of the rich." Taken together, we may say that Hong Kong citizens in general maintain a strong sense of political helplessness before and after the 1997 transition; and

(5) Among the 4 items under the construct of Political Skepticism, only one item produces a significant mean difference, which indicates that citizens in the 1998 study are less skeptical about the candidates. This is evidenced in the finding that less respondents endorse the statement "candidates consider voters' interest only during elections" in 1998 than in 1995. Hence, they indicate, once again, Hong Kong citizens remain politically skeptical as before.

In summary, the findings of the Hong Kong citizens' political attitude as revealed in the 1995 and 1998 electoral studies suggest quite clearly that there is a strong sense of political helplessness, skepticism and distrustfulness permeating Hong Kong citizens. Furthermore, Hong Kong citizens' feeling of distrust in government seems to be on the rise since the 1997 transition. However, on the other hand, Hong Kong citizens seem to hold a strong sense of citizenship and faith in democracy. Furthermore, this sense of citizenship and faith in democracy seems to have increased since the 1997 unification. Taking these finding together, we may say that both the positive and negative sides of Hong Kong citizens' political attitudes still prevail after the 1997 transition. On the positive side, Hong Kong citizens hold a strong faith in democracy and have a strong sense of citizenship, and these positive attitudes seem to be growing stronger since the 1997 transition. On the negative side, Hong Kong citizens have strong feelings of skepticism, helplessness and distrust, and their feeling of distrust seems to be on the rise since the handover. Putting these two sides of political attitude together, we may conclude that Hong Kong citizens are trapped in an ambivalent, and apparently contradictory, political attitude.

Policy Preference of Hong Kong Citizens

Apart from looking into Hong Kong citizens' political attitude, the 1995 and 1998 studies also investigated the political opinion of Hong Kong citizens, two aspects of which are policy preference and candidate evaluation. In this section we shall present the findings on the former. The latter will be explicated in the subsequent section.

In the 1995 and 1998 studies, there are 11 common items indicated a significant policy stances that emerged out of the two election campaigns. Confirmatory factor analyses of these 11 items were performed on the 1995 and 1998 data sets. The results of these two analyses are presented in Figures 13.3 and 13.4 in the Appendix. The results have confirmed that the measurement models generated from the 1995 and 1998 data sets are basically identical. They reveal that there are 3 latent variables in Hong Kong citizens' policy preference. These latent variables are (1) Preference in Opposition to PRC Political-Policy Stance; (2) Preference in Civil Rights Policy; and (3) Preference in Socioeconomic Policy. The overall performances of the two confirmatory factor analysis models are satisfactory. The goodness-of-fit statistics presented in Figures 13.3 and 13.4, indicate that the model fits well with the data.

The responses to the 11 items of policy preference in the 1995 and 1998 studies are presented in Tables 13.4 and 13.5. From the readings of Table 13.4, we notice one salient feature of Hong Kong citizens' policy

Table 13.4: Policy Preference of Hong Kong Citizens in the 1995 Legislative Council Election

	Strongly Disagree	Disagree	Either or	Agree Agree	Strongly Cases	Valid
Preference in opposition to PRC Political-Policy Stance						
336 All legislators should be directly elected.	0.7	10.5	18.5	59.6	10.7	1,887
343 Chief Executive of HKSAR should be directly elected.	0.6	7.0	11.1	67.9	13.4	1,890
344 Bill of Right should not be repealed.	0.3	3.0	7.5	72.7	16.5	1,963
351 Reaffirming June-Fourth movement.	0.8	10.6	19.6	56.3	12.8	1,697
Preference in Civil Right Policy						
337 Hong Kong Government should dissolve HKASPDM.	5.3	57.3	19.9	15.9	1.6	1,520
338 Homosexuality should be criminalized.	2.8	38.4	15.8	37.3	5.7	1,934
339 Death penalty should be reintroduced.	1.5	19.9	13.0	54.1	11.5	
Preference in Socioeconomic Policy						
340 Hong Kong Government should implement unemployment assistance.	0.8	10.4	14.9	59.4	14.4	2,210
341 Stop importation of foreign labour.	0.8	5.1	13.2	56.7	24.2	2,241
342 Increase profit tax.	1.7	23.3	22.2	45.8	6.5	1,922
347 Increase the amount of public assistance.	0.1	2.1	6.7	74.3	16.7	2,224

preference, that is, they hold a dissenting stance towards the Chinese Government and to a less extent the Hong Kong Government. This can be evidenced in the responses to the 4 items subsumed under the latent variable Preference in Opposition to PRC Political-Policy Stance. In all 4 items, the overwhelming majority of the respondents (ranging from 69.1% to 89.2%) indicate their preference in direct opposition to the political policy stances adopted by the PRC Government, especially to policy relating to the political structure of the future SAR Government. As for the 4 socioeconomic policy stances subsumed under the latent variable Preference in Socioeconomic Policy, these responses once again point to the dissenting stance of Hong

Table 13.5: Policy Preference of Hong Kong Citizens in the 1998 Legislative Council Election

	Strongly Disagree	Disagree	Either or	Agree Agree	Strongly Cases	Valid
Preference in Opposition to PRC Political-Policy Stance						
325 All legislators should be directly elected.	1.2	12.1	13.7	59.9	13.1	2,408
332 Chief Executive of HKSAR should be directly elected.	1.0	9.7	11.9	60.4	17.0	2,518
333 Bill of Right should not be repealed.	1.2	10.7	15.8	60.4	11.9	2,101
335 Reaffirming June-Fourth movement.	2.4	18.8	27.0	41.6	10.2	2,197
Preference in Civil Right Policy						
326 Hong Kong Government should dissolve HKASPDM.	8.5	59.2	16.0	14.3	2.0	2,023
327 Homosexuality should be criminalized.	4.6	47.3	16.3	26.1	5.7	2,419
328 Death penalty should be reintroduced.	2.7	25.9	15.4	45.1	10.9	2,671
Preference in Socioeconomic Policy						
329 Hong Kong Government should implement unemployment assistance.	1.4	10.8	18.2	58.1	11.5	2,818
330 Stop importation of foreign labour.	0.5	7.0	13.5	58.1	20.9	2,833
331 Increase profit tax.	2.0	33.2	27.3	33.2	4.4	2,444
334 Increase the amount of public assistance.	2.8	20.4	21.7	45.4	9.7	2,742

Kong citizens towards the policy stances adopted by the Hong Kong Government. Finally, looking at the three policy stances under the Preference in Civil Rights Policy, Hong Kong citizens' preferences are less congruent. The majority of the respondents (62.6%) indicate their opposition to the dissolution of the Hong Kong Alliance in Support of Patriotic and Democratic Movement in China (HKASPDM). However, a majority of respondents (65.6%) endorse the idea of reintroducing the death penalty. While in between, Hong Kong citizens are split in the policy stance of criminalizing homosexuality. Taking these preferences revealed in the 1995 study together, we may say that politically Hong Kong citizens are in dissent to the Chinese Government's policy stances, while socioeconomically they are in defiance of the policy stance of the Hong Kong Government. As for the civil right policy, Hong Kong citizens are liberal towards policy relating to freedom of association and the right of defiance but are conservative towards the death penalty.

The readings in Table 13.8 suggest that in the 1998 election, Hong Kong citizens still held on to their dissent stance against political, social and economic policies. First, a majority of the respondents still held on to their dissenting views on the four political policy stances adopted by the Chinese Government. Second, among the 4 policies on socioeconomic policies, 3 of them can still capture a majority of dissent from respondents. The only exception is on the policy item "increase profit tax," which can only attract 37.6% of the respondent's endorsement. As for the 3 items on civil right policy, the policy statement on "dissolution of the HKASPDM" still obtains a majority of respondents (67.7%) dissenting to the dissolution. On the death penalty issue, Hong Kong citizens still have a majority view on the reintroduction of capital punishment. However, as for the homosexuality issue, there is a clear change in the policy preference among Hong Kong citizens. In the 1998 study, a majority view has emerged in disagreement with the policy stance of "criminalizing homosexuality."

In fact, if we compare the responses to the policy preferences in the 1995 and 1998 studies, we can see that some significant changes in policy preference among Hong Kong citizens have emerged. These changes can be analzed in greater detail by a mean comparison of the responses in the 1995 and 1998 studies, which in the 1995 and 1998 data sets are presented in Table 13.6. Readings in Table 13.6 reveal that there are significant mean differences in 9 of the 11 policy stances, furthermore, all 9 mean differences are in the same direction. These findings suggest that Hong Kong citizens' dissenting stance towards government policy are shrinking. First, in the latent variable Preference in Opposition to PRC Political Policy, there are 2 significant mean differences. One is in the item "Bill of Rights should not be repealed." The other is in "reaffirming June-Fourth." They indicate that fewer Hong Kong citizens agreed to these 2 policy statements in 1998 than in 1995. Second, in the latent variable Preference in Socioeconomic Policy, the mean differences in all 4 policy statements are statistically significant. All of them point to the same direction that fewer respondents agreed with these policy statements, which are in direct opposition to the policy stances of the Hong Kong Government. Finally, in the latent variable Preference in Civil Rights Policy, the mean differences in all 3 policy statements are statistically significant. However, the implications of these differences are

Table 13.6: Mean Difference in Policy Preference Between 1995 and 1998 Voters

	1995 Voters		1998 Voters		
	Mean	S.D.	Mean	S.D.	T-value
Preference in Opposition to PRC Political Policy					
All legislators should be directly elected.	3.69	0.82	3.72	0.88	–1.05874
Chief Executive of HKSAR should be directly elected.	3.87	0.74	3.83	0.86	1.52722
Bill of Right should not be repealed.	4.03	0.6	3.71	0.85	13.14443***
Reaffirming June-Fourth movement.	3.70	0.85	3.38	0.98	10.06177***
Preference in Civil Right Policy					
Hong Kong Government should dissolve HKASPDM.	2.52	0.88	2.42	0.91	3.018273**
Homosexuality should be criminalized.	3.06	1.05	2.81	1.05	7.142473***
Death penalty should be reintroduced.	3.54	0.98	3.36	1.06	5.652003***
Preference in Socioeconomic Policy					
Hong Kong Government should implement unemployment assistance.	3.79	0.83	3.68	0.86	4.214467***
Stop importation of foreign labour.	4.01	0.8	3.92	0.81	3.626273***
Increase profit tax.	3.33	0.95	3.05	0.96	3.626273***
Increase the amount of public assistance.	4.06	0.55	3.39	1.000	8.818272***

* Sig. = 0.05; ** Sig. = 0.01; *** Sig. = 0.001

not exactly the same. For the policy statement "Hong Kong Government should dissolve HKASPDM," the mean difference implies that fewer citizens disagree with the infringement of the freedom of association and freedom of defiance. While the 2 other mean differences imply that more Hong Kong citizens oppose the 2 policies. They suggest that Hong Kong citizens have become less tolerant to freedom of association and right to protest but more liberal towards issues on homosexuality and the death penalty.

To conclude the analysis on Hong Kong citizens' opinions of governmental policy stances, we may characterize Hong Kong citizens as dissenters. The majority of them are in dissent with the Chinese Government's political-policy stances, especially those in relation to the development of the political system of Hong Kong. Furthermore, they are also in defiance of Hong Kong Government's stance in social and economic policies. Though such dissenting stances among Hong Kong citizens have shrunk somewhat since the 1997 transition, the overall defiance still permeates the majority of Hong Kong citizens.

Candidate Evaluation of Hong Kong Citizens

So far we have analyzed two aspects of Hong Kong citizens' political attitude and opinion, in this section we shall look into yet another aspect of Hong Kong citizens' political opinion, that is, their expectations of the candidate's performance. There are eight common items in the 1995 and 1998 studies indicating Hong Kong citizens' criteria in candidate evaluation. Figures 13.5 and 13.6 in the Appendix present the confirmatory factor analyses of these items with the 1995 and 1998 data sets. Once again the analyses reveal that the measurement models generated from the two data sets are identical. The analyses have generated three latent variables. They can be characterized as (1) Moderatist; (2) Dissenters; and (3) Service Deliverers. They basically reflect the three expectations of Hong Kong citizens of their representatives to the legislature. The goodness-of-fit statistics presented in Figures 13.5 and 13.6 also confirm that the two models fit well with the data.

The responses to eight candidates' attributes are presented in Tables 13.7 and 13.8. From the readings in Table 13.7, we can see that a majority view can be found in all these attributes. First, in relation to the 2 attributes subsumed under the factor Moderatist, we can see that the majority of the respondents expect their candidates to be moderate in language (54.9%) and be accepted by the Chinese Government (53.9%). Second, the responses to the 4 items subsumed under the factor Dissenter, we can observe that a more definite majority is formed around these items. For example, 88.2% of the respondents expect their legislator to "stand for Hong Kong interests in any HK-China conflict," while 82% and 77.4% of them expect their representatives to dare to disagree with Hong Kong and Chinese governments respectively. Finally, the majority of Hong Kong citizens also expect their representatives to be service deliverers. More specifically, they expect them to work for their neighborhood (83%) and to fight for employees' interests (83.2%). Taking these findings together, we can see that Hong Kong citizens are holding an ambivalent expectation of their representatives. They expect them to be accepted by the Chinese Government yet disagree with the Chinese Government and stand up for Hong Kong's interest in a Hong Kong-China conflict. In short, they want their candidates to be dissenters but at the same time be moderate and not too confrontational so as to be accepted by the sovereign authority in Beijing.

Table 13.7: Candidate Evaluation of Hong Kong Citizens in the 1995 Legislative Council Election

	Strongly Disagree	Disagree	Either or	Agree	Strongly Agree	Valid Cases
Moderatist						
151 Moderate in Language.	2.3	16.9	25.9	48.3	6.6	1,095
155 Accepted by the Chinese Government.	1.8	21.6	22.7	40.2	13.7	1,052
Dissenter						
152 Independent in one's view.	0.6	7.7	14.2	60.8	16.8	1,066
153 Daring to disagree with the Hong Kong Government.	0.5	6.2	11.3	58.4	23.6	1,054
154 Daring to disagree with the Chinese Government.	1.0	7.7	13.9	53.7	23.7	1,046
156 Stand for Hong Kong interest in Hong Kong-China conflict.	0.2	3.0	8.6	53.8	34.4	1,085
Service Deliverer						
157 Work for the neighbourhood.	0.4	6.1	10.5	56.0	27.0	1,095
158 Fight for employees' interest.	0.5	2.8	13.4	56.2	27.0	1,092

Table 13.8: Candidate Evaluation of Hong Kong Citizens in the 1998 Legislative Council Election

	Strongly Disagree	Disagree	Either or	Agree	Strongly Agree	Valid Cases
Moderatist						
167 Moderate in language.	2.7	22.4	27.7	38.7	8.5	1,950
171 Accepted by the Chinese Government.	3.0	20.3	22.9	38.6	15.2	1,875
Dissenter						
168 Independent in one's view.	3.4	22.7	22.8	40.8	10.3	1,841
169 Daring to disagree with the Hong Kong Government.	1.1	7.8	12.0	51.5	27.6	1,916
170 Daring to disagree with the Chinese Government.	1.6	10.2	16.5	46.8	24.9	1,892
172 Stand for HK interest in Hong Kong-China conflict.	0.7	3.3	9.3	51.5	35.1	1,948
Service Deliverer						
173 Work for the neighbourhood.	1.7	9.3	12.9	51.2	24.9	1,971
174 Fight for employees' interest.	1.0	5.0	12.7	50.6	30.7	1,962

Readings in Table 13.8 reveal that Hong Kong citizens' expectations of their candidates did not change much in the 1998 study. The majority of responses can still be found among all 8 items. To investigate whether there are significant changes in these expectations, mean comparison analysis was conducted between items in the two studies. The results are presented in Table 13.9. Among the 8 expectations, there are only 3 producing significant mean differences. They suggest that fewer Hong Kong citizens expect their candidates to be moderate in language, independent in their viewpoints, and work for the neighborhood. Taken together, we may say that Hong Kong citizens' ambivalent expectations of their candidates still linger after the 1997 transition, that is, they still expect their representatives to dissent from the sovereign power on their behalf yet be moderate and not too confrontational.

In fact, such ambivalent expectations of candidates can further be evidenced in the correlation coefficients among the 3 latent variables recorded in Figures 13.5 and 13.6. These 3 correlation coefficients are positively and significantly correlated. They imply that Hong Kong citizens expect candidates to be dissenters yet simultaneously not offend the Chinese Government with radical words or deeds.

Table 13.9: Mean Difference in Candidate Evaluation Between 1995 and 1998 Voters

	1995 Voters		1998 Voters		
	Mean	S.D.	Mean	S.D.	T-value
Moderatist					
Moderate in language.	3.42	0.91	3.28	0.99	3.590998***
Acceptance by the Chinese Government.	3.44	1.04	3.43	1.07	0.223759
Dissenter					
Independent in one's view.	3.83	0.8	3.32	1.04	13.65684***
Daring to disagree with the Hong Kong Government.	3.96	0.8	3.97	0.9	–0.284375
Daring to disagree with the Chinese Government.	3.88	0.88	3.83	0.97	1.294711
Stand for Hong Kong interest in HK-China conflict.	3.44	1.04	3.43	1.07	0.223759
Service Deliverer					
Work for the neighbourhood.	4.06	0.77	3.88	0.94	5.255352***
Fight for employees' interest.	4.07	0.74	4.05	0.85	0.619883

Skeptical, Helpless, Ambivalent and Dissenting Citizens

To recapitulate, in light of the findings on the three aspects of political attitudes and opinions of Hong Kong citizens, it seems that there are a number of ambivalent elements at work within Hong Kong citizens' political attitudes and opinions. With regard to general political attitude, there are strong senses of political skepticism, helplessness and distrustfulness permeated among Hong Kong citizens. At the same time, Hong Kong citizens hold a strong faith in democracy and have a strong sense of citizenship. In relation to opinions on policy preference and candidate evaluation, among Hong Kong citizens, the same ambivalence can also be found. They hold a clear dissenting view against most of the policy stances adopted by the Hong Kong and Chinese Governments. Hong Kong citizens also expect their representatives to be in line with their dissenting stances. However, Hong Kong citizens also expect their representatives not to be too confrontational toward the governmental authorities and even expect them to be accepted by the Beijing authority.

These seemingly ambivalent, if not contradictory, political attitudes of Hong Kong citizens are in fact discernable if we put them within the political and historical context of Hong Kong during the 1997 transition period. Politically, it is stipulated in the Basic Law that the political structure of the HKSAR Government would not be a full democracy and Hong Kong citizens would not be granted their full political rights in the near future. Hence, Hong Kong citizens' political skepticism and sense of helplessness are not simply psychological dispositions but are empirically well grounded in the political situations in which they found them being tightly contained in the political right. In fact, for more than a decade, Hong Kong citizens helplessly watched the negotiation became a dispute, then turned to open confrontation between the British and Chinese Governments over their future. As a result, they have developed a skeptical and even dissenting attitude towards politics and the government authorities. They have also developed a feeling of helplessness toward their own political situations as well as the future. In response to this political situation, it is natural that Hong Kong citizens should turn to the emerging democratic elements, such as voting and directly elected councilors, for salvation and hold a strong faith in democracy. Furthermore, they also a hold strong sense of citizenship. Yet this strong sense of citizenship should not be taken an face value, since in reality Hong Kong citizens are not that active in carrying out their civic duties, such as participating in voting. Therefore, I would agree with Lau and Kuan's contention (1986) that this strong sense of citizenship should be discerned in a normative sense rather than in a behavioral sense. Furthermore, in view of the helpless political situation and the presence of the authoritarian sovereign state, that is, the PRC, Hong Kong citizens have been cautious in adopting a their dissenting stance. Hence, they expect their representatives to be dissenting but not too radical and confrontational.

Citizenship Education in Transition

In the previous section we have explicated the attitudinal dimension of Hong Kong citizenship and have seen how it evolved during the 1997 transition. In this section, I shall further my investigation into citizenship education in Hong Kong. I shall first explain how the 1997 transition still affects the implementation of citizenship education in schools. Furthermore, I shall analyze, specifically, the effect of citizenship education on the political attitude of Hong Kong citizens.

As the development of citizenship education in Hong Kong has been a well covered topic (Tsang, 1994, 1995, 1998), I shall be brief in this account and shall only outline the background for subsequent analysis. First, it has been well documented that since the early 1960s citizenship education was, to all intents and purposes, neglected in the Hong Kong schooling system. The scattered elements found in various school subjects, such as Economic and Public Affairs and Social Studies, could only constituted a kind of apolitical and 'anational' civic education, the outcome of which is the constitution of a kind of "subject political culture" among Hong Kong citizens (Lau and Kuan, 1986; Tsang, 1998; Tse, 1999). However, as the 1997 issue began to surface in the early 1980s, local politicians and educators started to take an interest in citizenship education. In response to the rising demand for citizenship education, the Hong Kong Government published the *Guideline on Civic Education in Schools* (Curriculum Development Committee, 1985). However, the policy measure was criticized by local educators and scholars as conservative and irresponsible (Morris, 1992; Morris & Sweeting, 1991; Tsang, 1985). It basically preserved the apolitical and anational approach to citizenship education (Tsang, 1998). Then, in 1997, the Hong Kong Government published the second edition of the *Guideline on Civic Education in Schools* (Curriculum Development Committee, 1997). The second edition of the Guideline has been characterized by local educators as a great improvement on the first edition, yet the effect of this second Guideline has to be verified.

In retrospect, though citizenship education has been a prominent topic in education policy discourse and has initiated many pedagogical endeavors in the last decade, the effect of citizenship education in school has never been empirically verified. As an initial verification, I have, therefore, made use of the data generated from the 1998 electoral study to provide some preliminary assessment on the effect of citizenship education in transition.

In the 1998 study, a substantial portion of the respondents were recipients of the supposed educational effects generated by the 1985 Guideline. To take 1985, the year of publication of the first edition of the Guideline as the initiating point of citizenship education in transition, we can divide the respondents into those who passed through school education before and after the implementation of the Guideline on civic education. Accordingly, I have defined those who were aged 28 or younger in 1998 as recipients of the citizenship education in transition. It assumes that those who were at the age of 15 or younger in 1985 would have been affected by the supposed educational effect generated by the Guideline. By comparing this group of respondents, which shall be characterized as the Guideline cohort, with the rest of the sample, we may be able to have some idea of how the Guideline and the citizenship education initiatives it generated have affected the political attitude of their recipients. To this aim, I have conducted a number of mean difference analyses between the two subgroups in the sample in the 1998 study.

General Political Attitude of the Guideline Cohort

Table 13.10 has recorded the result of the mean difference analyses between the Guideline cohort and the non-Guideline cohort on the 20 items indicating the general political attitude of Hong Kong citizens. Among the 20 mean differences, 16 of them are statistically significant.

In respect to the construct of Faith in Democracy, 2 out of the 3 mean differences are statistically significant. They indicate that the Guideline cohort have less faith in democracy. More specifically, young citizens in Hong Kong have less faith in voting and in directly elected legislators. With regards to the latent variable Sense of Citizenship, 4 of the 5 mean differences are statistically significant. They all congruently point in the direction that the sense of citizenship of the Guideline cohort is stronger than their older counterparts. For example, the younger citizens in Hong Kong are more likely to disagree with the ideas that "election is a wasteful activity" and "as so many people vote, mine doesn't count much." As for the construct Trust

Table 13.10: Mean Difference in Political Attitude Between Guideline and Non-Guideline Cohort

	1995 Voters		1998 Voters		
	Mean	S.D.	Mean	S.D.	T-value
Faith in Democracy					
Voting is effect means of expressing my view to the government.	3.53	0.84	3.71	0.87	–16.501***
Directly-elected councilors enhance government accountability.	3.48	0.87	3.63	0.85	–11.959***
Political organizations enhance the accountability of the government.	3.74	0.7	3.8	0.71	–2.764
Sense of Citizenship					
Election is a wasteful activity.	2.34	0.85	2.55	1	–17.845***
As so many people vote, mine doesn't count much.	2.35	0.89	2.61	1.09	–23.536***
The current electoral system is too complicated to understand.	2.88	1.06	3.12	1.13	–18.711***
I shall not vote unless it concerns my vested interest.	2.28	0.88	2.34	0.94	–1.552
No matter how we vote, Hong Kong future won't be better.	2.2	0.81	2.4	0.91	–18.899***
Trust in Hong Kong Government					
Most of the Hong Kong Government policies are right in recent years.	2.49	0.68	2.67	0.96	–15.899***
Most senior officials of Hong Kong Government are capable.	2.6	0.82	2.8	0.96	–17.531***
Hong Kong Government hasn't misused public funds.	3.15	0.87	3.26	1	–4.928
Political Helplessness					
Most of Hong Kong Government policies are for benefit of the rich.	3.15	0.87	3.26	1	–4.928*
I can't influence government policies.	3.31	0.92	3.52	0.97	–19.259***
Hong Kong people is helpless in deciding the future of Hong Kong.	2.88	0.87	3.21	1.01	–40.318***
Politics is too complicated for me to understand.	3.68	0.75	3.86	0.79	–20.517***
Most of the Hong Kong people don't express their opinions publicly.	3.45	0.9	3.51	0.89	–2.175
Political Skepticism					
Candidates consider voters' interest only during election.	3.17	0.86	3.29	0.98	–5.538*
Politicians are for their own interests.	3.34	0.74	3.49	0.87	–12.052***
Politics are corrupted.	3.62	0.85	3.74	0.87	–5.784*
Political organizations are for power rather than for public interests.	3.08	0.76	3.34	0.86	–32.7***

* Sig. = 0.05; ** Sig. = 0.01; *** Sig. = 0.001

in Hong Kong Government, 2 out of 3 mean differences are statistically significant, they point in the direction that the Guideline cohort is more distrustful of the capability of their government. In relation to the construct of Political Helplessness, 4 of the 5 mean differences are statistically significant. All four of them point congruently in the direction that fewer citizens in the Guideline cohort feel that they are politically helpless. For instance, young citizens in Hong Kong are less likely to agree to the ideas that "I can't influence government policies" and "politics is too complicated to understand." Finally, with regard to Political Skepticism, all 4 mean differences are statistically significant. They once again congruently point in the direction that the Guideline cohort is less skeptical in politics than their older counterparts. They indicate that the younger citizens in Hong Kong hold a more positive attitude towards politicians, political organization and politics in general than their older counterparts.

Taking these differences together, the supposed effect of the Guideline on the younger citizens in Hong Kong are mixed. On the one hand, the results suggest that the Guideline cohort citizens feel less helpless and skeptical towards politics. It implies that they have a stronger sense of political efficacy. They also suggest that they possess a stronger sense of citizenship. On the other hand, the results suggest that these younger citizens are more distrustful of the capability of the Hong Kong Government. They also have less faith in the democratic elements in the political system of Hong Kong. Putting this stronger sense of political efficacy and the more distrustful attitude towards government together, I am afraid that there may be a possibility that political action arising from discontent may grow in the younger generation of Hong Kong citizens. However, before we come to this conclusion, we must first of all look at the mean difference results of the other constructs.

Policy Preference of the Guideline Cohort

Apart from the political attitudes explicated above, we can further our investigation by looking at the political opinions of the Guideline cohort. Table 13.11 presents the mean differences of the eleven indicators of the policy preference of Hong Kong citizens. Among the 11 policy indicators, 8 of them have produced statistically significant results. Among the 4 policy stances under the latent variable Preference in Opposition to PRC Political-Policy Stance, only 1 mean difference produced a significant difference, that is, the policy stance "reaffirming June-Fourth movement." It indicates

Table 13.11: Mean Difference in Policy Preference Between Guideline and Non-Guideline Cohorts

	Guideline Cohort		Non-Guideline Cohort		
	Mean	S.D.	Mean	S.D.	T-value
Preference in Opposition to PRC Political-Policy Stance					
All legislators should be directly elected.	3.68	0.84	3.73	0.89	–1.165
Chief Executive of HKSAR should be directly elected.	3.84	0.88	3.82	0.86	0.228
Bill of Right should not be repealed.	3.77	0.78	3.69	0.87	2.721
Reaffirming June-Fourth movement.	3.49	0.91	3.36	0.99	5.6*
Preference in Civil Right Policy					
Hong Kong government should dissolve HKASPDM.	2.26	0.72	2.46	0.94	–12.901***
Homosexuality should be criminalized.	2.46	0.94	2.89	1.06	–59.407***
Death penalty should be reintroduced.	2.73	1.01	3.48	1.03	–197.096***
Preference in Socioeconomic Policy					
Hong Kong Government should implement unemployment assistance.	3.52	0.89	3.71	0.85	–17.667***
Stop importation of foreign labor.	3.8	0.82	3.94	0.81	–11.447***
Increase profit tax.	2.92	0.78	3.08	0.99	–8.813**
Increase the amount of public assistance.	3.56	0.88	3.36	1.02	15.907***

* Sig. = 0.05; ** Sig. = 0.01; *** Sig. = 0.001

that the Guideline cohort citizens are more like to endorse the reaffirmation of the June-Fourth. With regards to the Preference in Civil Right Policy, all 3 policy stances produce significant differences. They congruently point in the direction that the younger citizens in Hong Kong are more liberal in their civil rights stance. For example, they are more likely to disapprove of the dissolution of the HKASPDM and the criminalization of homosexuality. Finally, in relation to the Preference in Socioeconomic Policy, all 4 stances yield significant mean differences. However, these mean differences do not point in the same direction. Three of them point in the direction that the Guideline cohort is less likely to dissent with the government policy stances than the non-Guideline cohort. For example, the Guideline cohort is less likely to agree to the policy of implementing unemployment assistance, stopping importation of foreign labour, and increasing profit tax. However, the younger citizens in Hong Kong are more likely to endorse the idea of increasing the amount of public assistance.

Taking the Guideline cohort's policy preferences together, we may say that the Guideline cohort is less dissenting to the SAR Government stances in civil and socioeconomic policies. However, they are more dissenting to the Chinese Government's stance on the June-Fourth movement and to the SAR Government's stance on the public assistance policy.

Candidate Evaluation of the Guideline Cohort

Finally, Table 13.12 has recorded the mean differences in the two cohorts' opinions on the criteria for Candidate Evaluation. Among the 8 criteria, 5 of them have produced statistically significant mean differences. One salient feature that emerging from these 5 mean differences is that 4 out of 5 of them fall within the same latent variable, namely Dissenter. These signify that the young citizens in Hong Kong are more inclined to expect their legislative representatives to act as dissenters to both the HKSAR and Chinese Governments than their older fellow citizens. Furthermore, the other attribute producing significant mean differences is the expectation for candidates to be moderate in language. Taking these findings together, we may say that

Table 13.12: Mean Differences in Candidate Evaluation Between Guideline and Non-Guideline Cohort

	Guideline Cohort		Non-Guideline Cohort		
	Mean	S.D.	Mean	S.D.	T-value
Moderalist					
Moderate in language.	3.08	0.92	3.32	1.00	–13.838***
Acceptance by Chinese Government.	3.36	1.03	3.44	1.07	1.276
Dissenter					
Independent in one's view.	3.47	0.96	3.29	1.05	6.666**
Daring to disagree with HK Government.	4.14	0.83	3.94	0.91	11.781***
Daring to disagree with the Chinese Government.	4.03	0.89	3.80	0.98	13.341***
Stand for HK interest in HK-China conflict.	4.32	0.74	4.15	0.78	12.486***
Service Deliverer					
Work for the Neighborhood.	3.96	0.87	3.87	0.95	1.994
Fight for employees' interest.	4.12	0.73	4.04	0.86	1.801

* Sig. = 0.05; ** Sig. = 0.01; *** Sig. = 0.001

the young citizens in Hong Kong are of the opinion that their representatives in the legislature should be more dissenting or even confrontational than their older fellow citizens think.

The Guideline Cohort: Efficacious, Distrustful and Dissenting Citizens

In view of the findings of the foregoing analysis, we may conclude that young citizens in Hong Kong, that is, the Guideline cohort, are politically more distrustful and dissenting than their older fellow citizens. Furthermore, they feel less helpless and skeptical about politics. In other words, they feel themselves more politically efficacious than their older counterparts.

However, it is still too early to conclude whether such a political profile of the Guideline cohort is really due to the educational effect triggered by the Guideline or is simply due to youthfulness and the radical outlook it entails. Nevertheless, such a political profile of the young citizens in Hong Kong will provide citizenship educators in Hong Kong with some essential food for thought in designing their citizenship education for the future citizens of the HKSAR. This is especially true if we relate these findings to the policy context of citizenship education in Hong Kong during the transition period. As I have explained in detail elsewhere (Tsang, 1998), the policy context of citizenship education on Hong Kong is in a state of fragmentation. It has been dominated by three contradictory projects, namely patronage, domestication and emancipation.

These three contradictory projects basically reflect the triangle of tensions formed by the Chinese Government, the colonial British–Hong Kong Government and the Hong Kong citizens at work during the 1997 transition. First, confronted by mounting social pressure from the local education profession, the colonial government tried to maintain the subject political culture and its patron status and was unenthusiastic about inculcating participatory citizenship education for the future citizens of Hong Kong. Second, Hong Kong citizens, more specifically, members of the local teaching profession, have been persistent proponents of education for democracy, human rights and citizen empowerment in the debate on citizenship education since 1984. Finally, the Chinese government and its supporters have emphasized nationalism and patriotism in citizenship education, which can be construed as part of the domesticating project of the Chinese government's policy of controlling the growing democratization in Hong Kong, especially after the June-Fourth crackdown in 1989.

In the light the aforementioned findings, I think it is time for local educators to put behind them, all the contentions and antagonisms left over from the triangle of tension during the 1997 transition. They should begin to look hard at the political attitudes and opinions of our young citizens in Hong Kong and to contemplate the citizenship education project for the future citizens of the SAR.

Reference

Abramson, P. R. (1983). *Political attitudes in America: Formation and change*. San Francisco: Freeman.

Almond, G., & Verba, S. (1963). *The civic culture: Political attitudes and democracy in five nations*. Princeton, NJ: Princeton University Press.

Almond, G., & Verba, S. (1980). *The civic culture revisited*. Boston: Little Bown.

Bendeix, R. (1977). *Nation-building and citizenship*. Berkeley, CA: University of California Press.

Bottomore, T., & Marshall, T. H. (1992). *Citizenship and social class*. Concord, MA: Pluto Press.

Burbaker, W. R. (1990). Immigration, citizenship, and the nation-state in France and Germany: A comparative historical analysis. *International Sociology, 3*, 379–407.

Campbell, A., et al. (1960). *The American voter*. New York: John Wiley.

The Curriculum Development Committee. (1985). *Guidelines on civic education in schools*. Hong Kong: The Government Printer.

The Curriculum Development Committee. (1997). *Guidelines on civic education in schools*. Hong Kong: The Government Printer.

Giddens, A. (1981). *A contemporary critique of historical materialism: Vol. 1. Power, property and the state*. London: Macmillan.

Giddens, A. (1982). *Profiles and critiques in social theory*. London: Macmillan.

Giddens, A. (1985). *A contemporary critique of historical materialism: Vol. 2. The nation-state and violence*. Cambridge, UK: Polity Press.

Heath, A., et al. (1985). *How Britain Votes*. Oxford, UK: Pergamon Press.

Heath, A., et al. (1991). *Understanding political change: The British voter 1964–1987*. Oxford, UK: Pergamon Press.

Held, D. (1989). Citizenship and autonomy. In D. Held & J. B. Thompson (Eds.), *Social theory of modern society: Anthony Giddens and his critics* (pp. 162–184). Cambridge, UK: Cambridge University Press.

Inglehart, R. (1990). *Culture shift in advanced industrial society*. Princeton, NJ: Princeton University Press.

Inglehart, R. (1997). *Modernization and postmodernization: Cultural, economic, and political change in 43 societies*. Princeton, NJ: Princeton University Press.

Janowitz, M. (1980) Observations on the sociology of citizenship. *Social Forces, 59*, 1–24.

Janoski, T. (1998). *Citizenship and civil society: A framework of rights and obligations in liberal, traditional and social democratic regimes*. Cambridge, UK: Cambridge University Press.

Lau, S.-K., & Kevan, H.-K. (1986). The changing political culture of the Hong Kong Chinese. In J. Y .S. Cheng (Ed.), *Hong Kong in transition* (pp. 26–51). Hong Kong: Oxford University Press.

Leung, S. W. (1993). The "China factor" in the 1991 Legislative Council election: the June 4th incident and anti-Communist China syndrome. In S. K. Lau & K. S. Louie (Eds.), *Hong Kong tried democracy: The 1991 elections in Hong Kong* (pp. 187–235). Hong Kong: Hong Kong Institute of Asia-Pacific Studies, The Chinese University of Hong Kong.

Milbrath, L. W., & Goel, M. (1977). *Political participation* (2nd ed.). Chicago: Rand McNally.

Marshall, T. H. (1977). Citizenship and social class. In T. H. Marshall, *Class, citizenship and social development*. Chicago: The University of Chicago Press.

Mann, M. (1987). Ruling class strategies and citizenship. *Sociology, 2*(3), 339–354.

Miller, W. E., & Traugott, S. A. (1989). *American national election studies data sourcebook, 1952–1986*. Cambridge, MA: Harvard University Press.

Miller, W .E., & Shanks, J. M. (1996). *The new American voter*. Cambridge, MA: Harvard University Press.

Morris, P. (1992). *Curriculum development in Hong Kong* (2nd ed.). Hong Kong: Faculty of Education, University of Hong Kong.

Morris, P., & Sweeting, A. E. (1991). Education and politics: The case of Hong Kong from a historical perspective. *Oxford Review of Education, 17*, 249–267.

Scott, I. (1989). *Political change and the crisis of legitimacy in Hong Kong*. Hong Kong: Oxford University Press.

Somers, M. R. (1993). Citizenship and the place of the public sphere: Law, community, and political culture in the transition to democracy. *American Sociological Review, 58*(5), 587–620.

Tsang, W. K. (1996, February) *The constitution of a defiant electorate: The case of Hong Kong*. Paper presented at the International Conference on Political Development in Taiwan and Hong Kong, organized by Centre of Asian Studies, The University of Hong Kong and Institute for National Policy Research, Taiwan, on February 8–9, 1996. (There are only materials of 1998 in the main text, pls check)

Tsang, W. K. (1998). Patronage, demestication or empowerment? Citizenship development and citizenship education in Hong Kong. In O. Ichilov (Ed.), *Citizenship and citizenship education in a changing world* (pp. 221–252).

London: Woburn Press.
Tsang, W. K. (1995). Between national and citizenship education: Discourse on citizenship education in the 1997 transition. *Education Journal*, *23*, 1–26.
Tsang, W. K. (1994). Decolonized citizenship education: Citizenship education in Hong Kong school after 1997. *Education Journal*, *22*, 237–248.
Turner, B. S. (1990). Outline of a theory of citizenship. *Sociology*, *24*(1), 189–217.

Appendix: Conceptual Framework of the Study

Demographic & Socio-economic Attitudes	General Political Attributes	Specific Political Opinions	Voting Behaviors
Sex	Identification of Political Parties		
Age	Identification of Political Ideology		
Educational Attainment Levels	Trust in Government	Evaluation of Candidates	Voting Turning
Occupational Statuses	External Political Efficacy		
Employment Statuses	Internal Political Efficacy	Opinions on Policy Issues	Electoral Choice
Income Levels	Sense of Citizen Duty		
Types of Accommodation	Class Consciousness		

Modes of Political Participation

Political and Social Connectedness	Media Exposure	Political Participation	Electoral Participation

Figure 13.1: Completely Standardized Solution of Confirmatory Factor Analysis (T-Value) of General Political Attitude of HK Citizens in the 1995 Legco Election

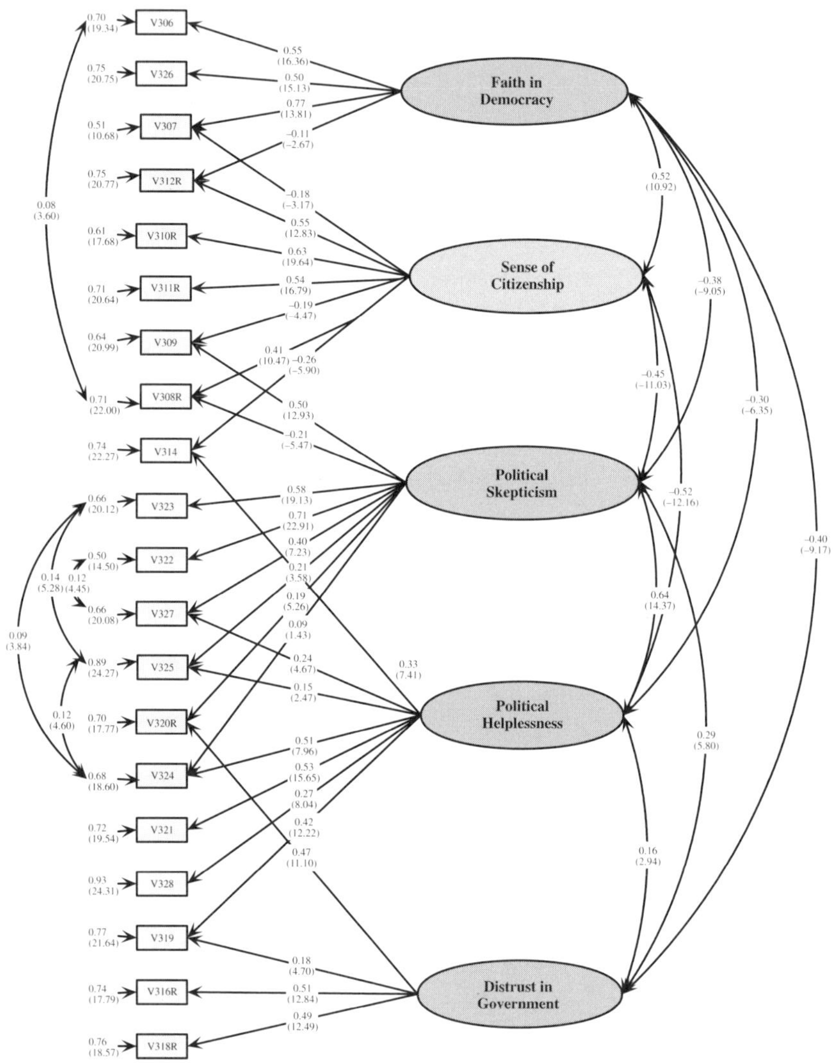

Chi-Square = 332.52, df = 146, p-value = 0.00, RMSEA = 0.03, GFI = 0.98, AGFI = 0.96, NFI = 0.92

Figure 13.2: Completely Standardized Solution of Confirmatory Factor Analysis (T-Value) of General Political Attitude of HK Citizens in the 1998 Legco Election

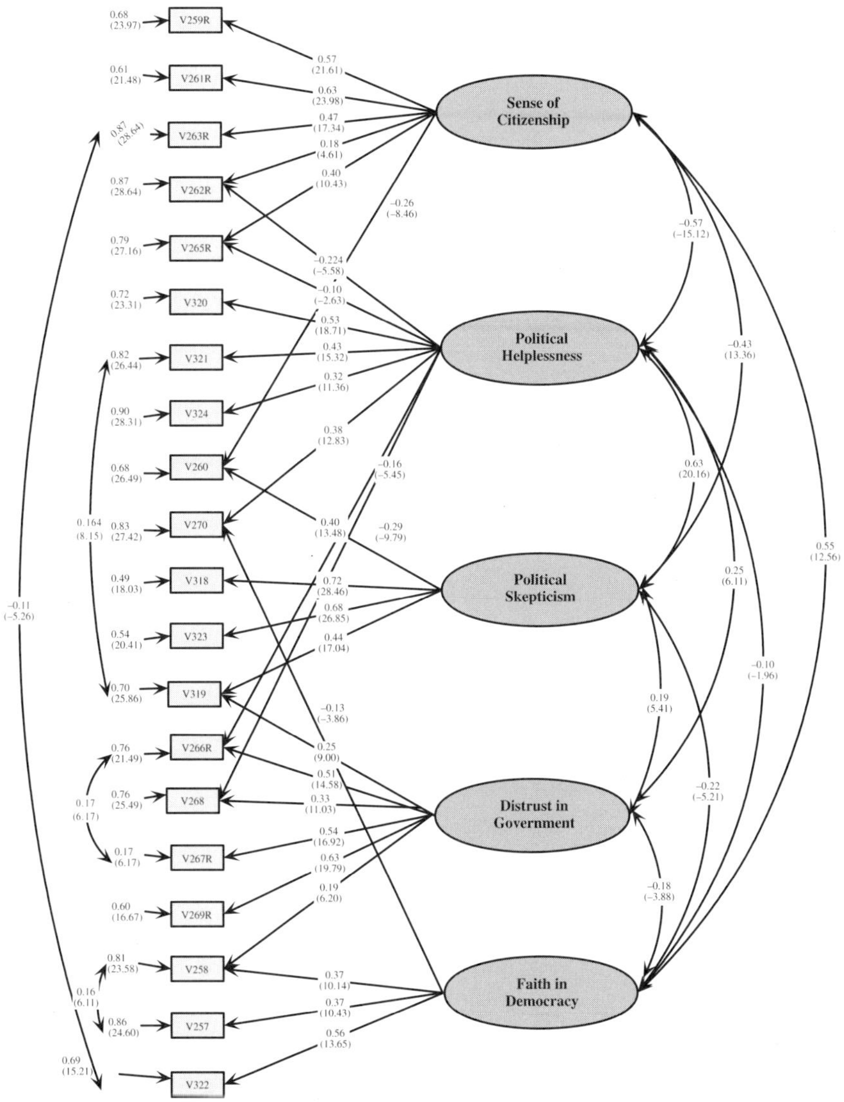

Chi-Square = 405.15, df = 149, p-value = 0.00, RMSEA = 0.03, GFI = 0.98, AGFI = 0.97, NFI = 0.92

Figure 13.3: Completely Standardized Solution of Confirmatory Factor Analysis (T-Value) of Policy Preference of HK Citizens in 1995 Legislative Council Election

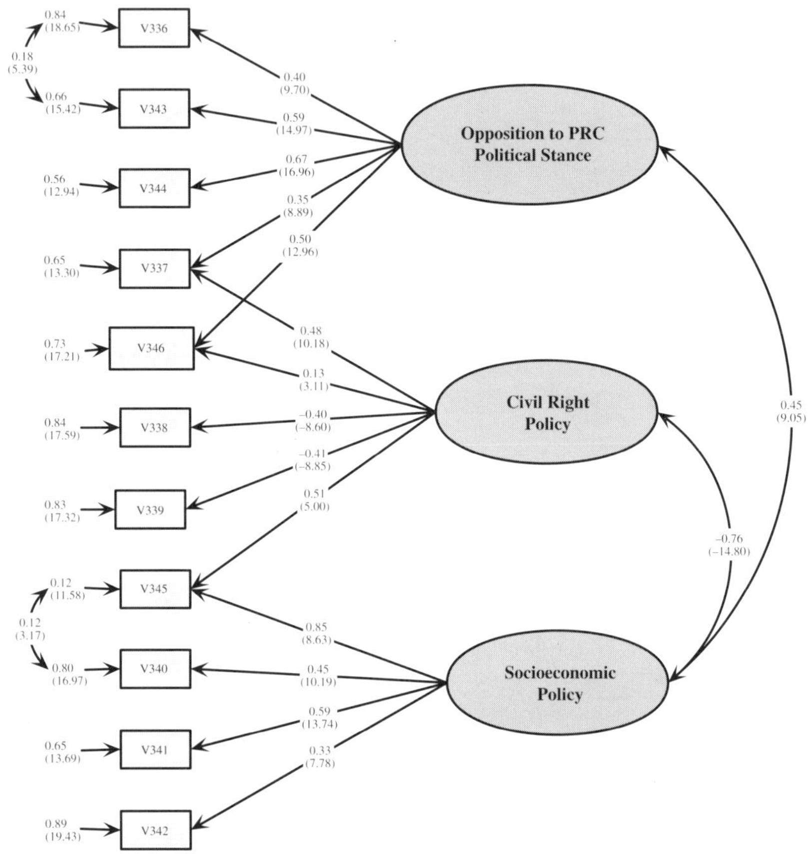

Chi-Square = 60.02, df = 37, p-value = 0.0097, RMSEA = 0.027, RMR = 0.019, GFI = 0.99, AGFI = 0.98, NFI = 0.95

Figure 13.4: Completely Standardized Solution of Confirmatory Factor Analysis (T-Value) of Policy Preference of HK Citizens in 1998 Legislative Council Election

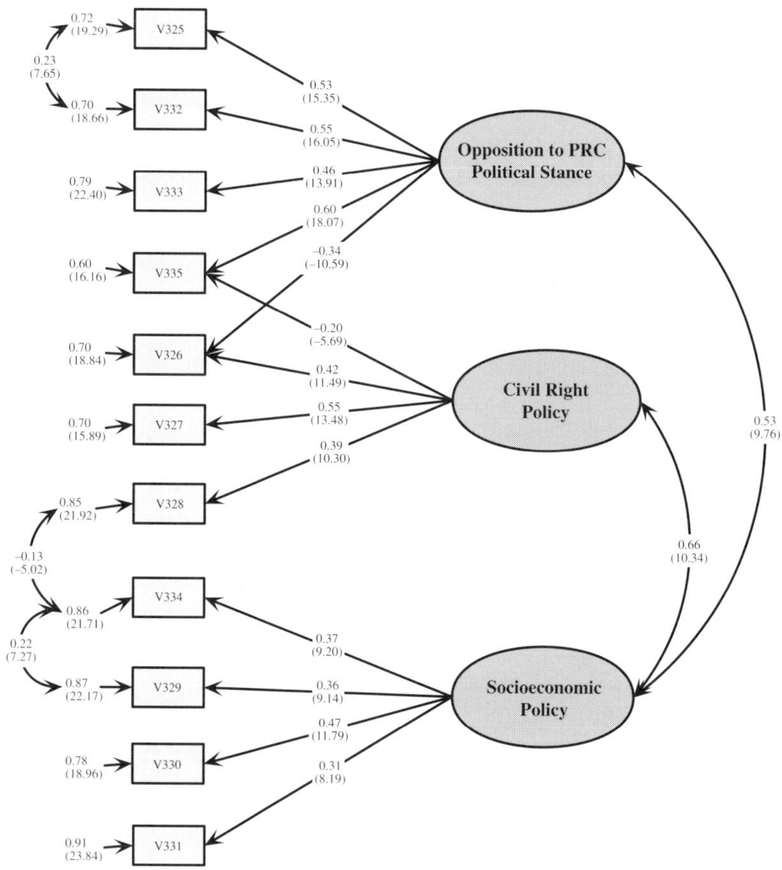

Chi-Square = 92.70, df = 37, p-value = 0.00, RMSEA = 0.033, RMR = 0.026, GFI = 0.99, AGFI = 0.98, NFI = 0.945

Figure 13.5: Completely Standardized Solution of Confirmatory Factor Analysis (T-Value) of Candidate Evaluation of HK Citizens in 1995 Legislative Council Election

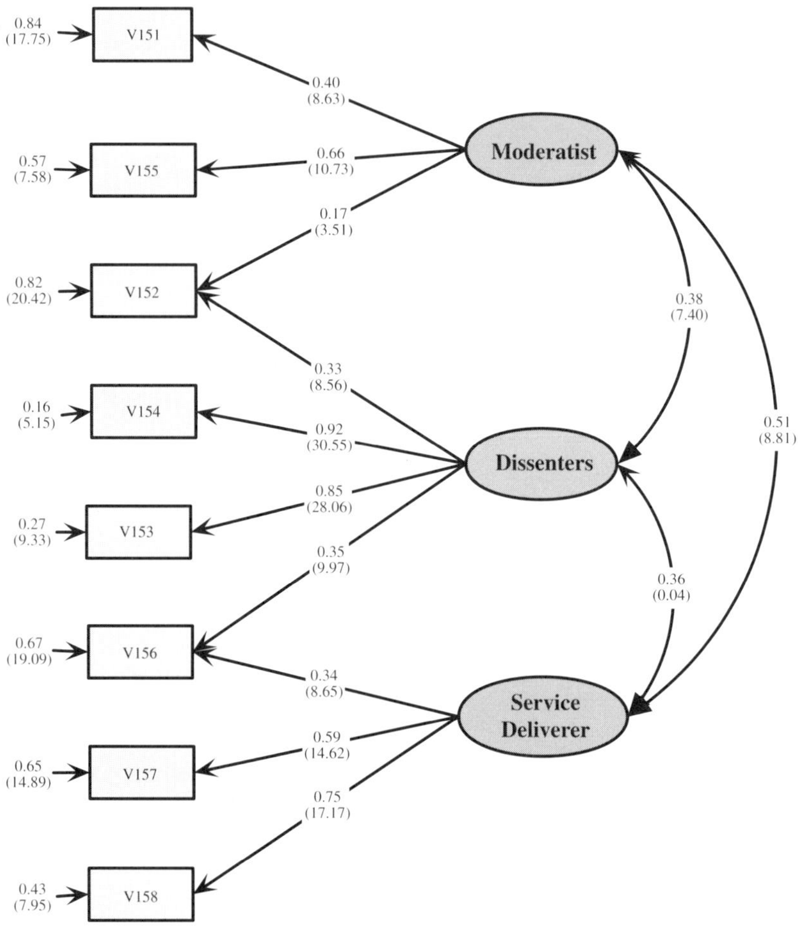

Chi-Square = 38.14, df = 15, p-value = 0.000, RMSEA = 0.0410, RMR = 0.0157, GFI = 0.990, AGFI = 0.975, NFI = 0.978

Figure 13.6: Completely Standardized Solution of Confirmatory Factor Analysis (T-Value) of Candidate Evaluation of HK Citizens in 1998 Legislative Council Election

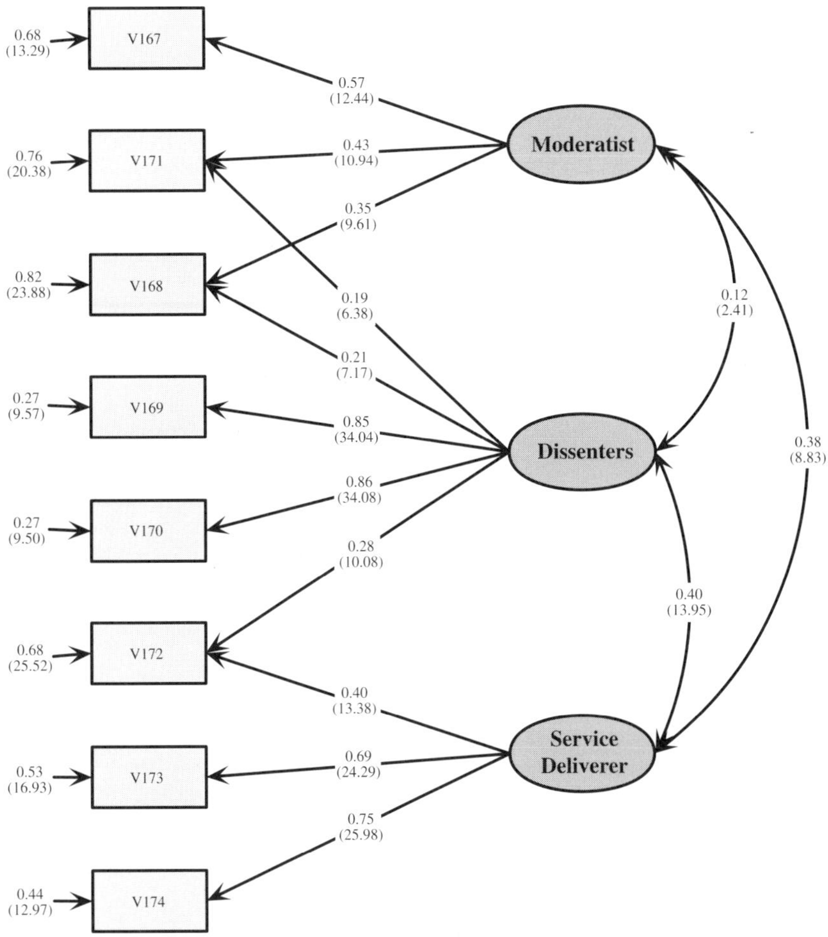

Chi-Square = 63.060, df = 14, p-value = 0.000, RMSEA = 0.0460, RMR = 0.0234, GFI = 0.991, AGFI = 0.976, NFI = 9.79

CHAPTER 14

Representation of Citizenship in the Junior Secondary School Curriculum: The Cases of Hong Kong and Macau

Kwan-choi Tse

Abstract

Citizenship education has aroused much public concern in Hong Kong and Macau since the mid-1980s. Informed by the theoretical discussion of citizenship education, this paper analyses the representation of citizenship in the recent school curriculum in both places. It first gives a brief account of the continuity and change of citizenship education in Hong Kong and Macau in the post-WWII period. Then it contrasts and compares the recent curriculum concerning citizenship education in these places. Finally, it further discusses the implications of these results for future citizenship education programmes in these places. As revealed in recent citizenship education syllabuses at junior secondary levels, both places have defined citizenship education in the broadest sense, and have treated it as a mixture of moral, political and lifeskills education. They juxtaposed both

A paper originally presented at the International Conference on "Values Education and Citizenship Education for the 21st Century" Hong Kong, June 9–11, 2000. The research reported in this article was drawn from the project "The Representation of Citizenship in Chinese Societies: A comparative study of social subjects at primary level in Mainland China, Taiwan, Hong Kong & Macau," which was funded by the Direct Grant for Research of the Chinese University of Hong Kong (1999–2000) as well as "A Study of Civic Education in Hong Kong and Macau," a project funded by the Shaw College student campus work scheme, (2000–01). The author expresses his gratitude to Miss Yeung Yuk-ling, Miss Chok Ching-yee and Miss Koo Wai-sze for their kind assistance in these projects. Of course, any omissions or deficiencies remain the author's responsibility.

nationalistic and democratic education. Also, both pro-establishment and participatory elements were found; and citizenship education in both places stressed international contexts by including elements of global citizenship and/or multi-culturalism. In terms of pedagogy, a more progressive vision of citizenship education is witnessed in both syllabuses. As for evaluation, both syllabuses stress on not only cognitive but also affective achievements and behavioral performances. However, the Macau's syllabus has a smaller and less adequate coverage of national community, international community, and citizenship than its Hong Kong's counterpart. Also, the dominant orientation of Macau's syllabus was more prone to the mode of "citizenship transmission" mainly concerned with developing moral virtues of good citizens and promoting supportive and accommodating relationships with the society, rather than a more reflective and critical approach to citizenship education. However, given that these new syllabi in Hong Kong and Macau are only offered to a handful of schools, their impact on students remains negligible.

School Curriculum and Citizenship Education

The official curriculum document, in the form of a syllabus, covers and defines the objectives, goals and topics for teaching and learning, and underscores the basic orientation of cultural transmission. The syllabus not only states the objectives of the subjects but also delineates the topics and substance of knowledge and information to be learned. Hence, it is important in setting a specification for textbook-production, teaching and instruction time. Also, it serves as an important basis for assessment and examination.

Since the school curriculum (commonly defined as a programme for instruction) is a result of deliberate selection and organization, the treatment of topics and contents in the syllabuses and textbooks is a significant sociological and educational issue (Young, 1971). The development of modern national education systems went hand in hand with the development of nation-states. And citizenship education has become an increasingly significant part of the school curriculum. "Citizenship" basically refers to the rights, obligations, and power inherited in the legal status of full membership of a modern nation-state (Marshall, 1950). Modern states around the world have commonly designed the social subjects like History, Civics and Social Studies, to acquaint the younger generation with a particular political culture and political identity necessary for a political community as well as its members.

Syllabuses and textbooks on social subjects not only provide political knowledge, but also define the normative expectations, appropriate knowledge, attitudes, values and behaviour of an ideal citizen. Thus, the syllabuses and textbooks are the central objects of controversies and they are subject to an ideological critique (Apple, 1990; Giroux, 1983; Whitty, 1985; Whitty & Young, 1976; Young, 1971).

The term "citizenship education" carries descriptive and normative meanings. Complex and multi-dimensional in nature, the content of citizenship education varies in time and space, depending on the nature of a particular political community (Heater, 1990). Since citizenship education is an elusive and contested concept intertwined with different ideologies and normative expectations, it is often used interchangeably with other terms such as political education, civics, political literacy, personal and social education. These terms represent different orientations and traditions concerning the goals, expectations, nature, and practices of citizenship education. Accordingly, scholars also accord and classify different modes of citizenship education (Giroux, 1983; Ichilov, 1994). Civic education or civics is frequently associated with the ideas of liberal democracy. Traditionally civics tends to carry apolitical orientations, focusing upon individuals' relations with the social and civic realms, rather than on their affinity with the political arena. The curriculum mainly relates to the structural, procedural, and legal aspects of political institutions, stressing consensus, harmony, and compliance while avoiding the discussion of controversial issues. Consequently, civics has been accused in come contexts of being associated with conservative politics, aiming to preserve the status quo. On the other hand, political literacy is associated with more radical traditions and particularly with the ideas of participatory democracy. The curriculum tends to be issue-based, confronting controversial issues, and often employing activity-based teaching methods.

Citizenship education has captured much public concern in Hong Kong and Macau during the transitional period from the mid-1980s onwards. Informed by the theoretical discussion of citizenship education, this chapter aims to study citizenship education in Hong Kong and Macau in the following aspects:

(1) To examine the social, historical and institutional contexts for citizenship education in the two places;
(2) To investigate the current objectives, scope, and contents of the citizenship education syllabuses (junior secondary) in each place; and

(3) To compare the similarities and differences in the school syllabuses in terms of the very nature of citizenship revealed.

Before depicting the images of citizenship reflected in the recent formal curriculums in Hong Kong and Macau, this chapter first gives an account of the continuity and change of citizenship education in these two places in the post-war period. Secondly, it contrasts and compares their recent junior secondary "Civic Education" syllabuses with regard to the composite image of citizenship to be transmitted. Finally, their implications for future civic education programmes in these two places are discussed.

Development of Citizenship Education in Hong Kong and Macau from the 1950s to 1990s

Hong Kong and Macau have both experienced significant socio-political changes in the post-World War II era. Accordingly, there has been a change in the educational systems dealing with citizenship education (or commonly called civic education) in the two Chinese societies.

Hong Kong

For much of Hong Kong's colonial era, political power was concentrated in the hands of the Governor, career civil servants and a small group of co-opted élites (Lau, 1982). Hong Kong was basically an administrative-led polity, with the British government's appointed governor and his appointed Executive Council making top-level decisions. Between the 1950s and the late 1960s, in co-existence with a secluded and autocratic bureaucratic polity, a loosely-organised Chinese immigrant society, and a substantial economic growth was a "parochial" and "subject" political culture. Hong Kong Chinese were characterised by an acceptance of the *status quo* and the colonial government, a pervasive sense of political powerlessness and political inefficacy, and a low level of political participation (King, 1981a, 1981b; Lau, 1982; Miners, 1996; Scott, 1989).

As a colony, citizenship rights in Hong Kong have never fully developed, nor have the three elements of citizenship — legal, political and social — developed in equal extent (Tsang, 1998). The colonial government kept a tight control over the development of citizenship rights in Hong Kong. To a large extent, citizenship development in Hong Kong was under the patronage of the colonial government or directly initiated from above. After the serious challenge of riots in 1966 and 1967, the colonial state gradually softened its governance style and played a more active role in regulating economic and social affairs and in providing public services to the community (Scott, 1989).

In congruence with the socio-political circumstances at large, civic education has been marginalized in Hong Kong for several decades. The government was particularly sensitive and suspicious towards political issues in education, and tried to keep them under control. Political education was never officially stated as an explicit educational objective. The colonial government prohibited political activities in schools, and controlled school subjects and curriculum materials via the provision of official circulars and model syllabuses, and officially-approved textbooks and exhortation (Morris, 1992a). Consequently, "civic education" in the period between the 1950s and the mid-1980s was alien and conformist in nature, alienating the students from their indigenous nationality and local politics and fostering the students as "residents" rather than "citizens" (Lee, 1987; Morris, 1992a, 1992b; Morris & Sweeting, 1992; Tsang, 1984, 1994, 1998; Wong, 1981, 1983).

According to Almond and Verba (1963), political culture refers to the norms, beliefs and values within a political system. They make a distinction between "subject", "parochial", and "participatory" political cultures with reference to their orientations towards input, output, system and process. Accordingly, citizenship education in Hong Kong in this period may be characterised as subject-oriented in the sense that the concept of citizenship transmitted, was distorted and one-sided. The curriculum reflected a kind of subject political culture concerned more with administrative output and the political system, rather than political inputs and rights and obligations. It was characterised by a "transmission approach" to political education, carrying supporting beliefs of the pre-existing political institution and a passive image of citizenship. The social subjects chiefly transmitted factual political knowledge and cultivated politically-apathetic citizens. Students' exposures to political topics were mainly restricted to a formalistic description of the structure and functions of the government, and to the government's contributions to solving various social and economic problems. Citizens were defined as passive, obedient, and complacent, and co-operative recipients of governmental services (Morris, 1992b; Tsang, 1998).

Since the early 1980s, the processes of decolonisation and democratisation have initiated significant political changes. With the introduction of representative government from 1982 onwards and the political reform package subsequently introduced by Governor Patten in 1993, the level of democratisation was extended. However, the pace of democratisation was slow and tortuous. Party politics has had an extremely short history in Hong Kong as direct elections for the Legislative Council were not introduced until 1991, and despite the political reform from the 1980s onwards, most power was still in the hands of a few top-level political elites. Though direct elections were introduced to the Legislative Council, two municipal councils and District Boards, their political functions were still limited. So far, there have been no elected representatives into the Executive Council, the highest policy-making body. Thus, against the criterion of western democracy, Hong Kong is not a democratic polity (Miners, 1996; Scott, 1989).

The socio-economic development from the 1970s onwards produced changes in the Hong Kong Chinese ethos, particularly in the way it moved away from a subject political culture to an immature form of participatory political culture (Lau & Kuan, 1988). While there has been a growing normative orientation towards political participation and attentive attitude towards the mass media among the Hong Kong Chinese, people's aloofness and apathy remains strong, and many people stay at the spectator level regarding political participation. Further, the people's sense of political powerlessness has become stronger as a result of the turbulent political environment as well as the rows between Britain and China. Meanwhile, the increasing intervention of the government in social and public affairs gave Hong Kong inhabitants a benevolent, favourable and positive image of the colonial government and increased their expectations of the government (Lau & Kuan, 1988). However, the authority of the Hong Kong government declined during the 1990s. The people became less trustful of and less deferential to public authorities, and showed a less favourable evaluation of governmental performance. Political cynicism and a sense of political inefficacy hence prevailed, with strong feelings of political frustration and alienation.

The long separation between Hong Kong and mainland China and the different rules of governance led to Hong Kong's distinctive socio-economic development and the development of an indigenous culture and "Hongkongese" identity (Choi, 1995; Lau & Kuan, 1988). With the designated return of Hong Kong to China in 1997, change in political membership became a pressing issue as the change of sovereignty meant that Hong Kong people would acquire new national identities as citizens of the People's Republic of China (PRC). Nevertheless, Hong Kong students were often criticised for their lack of civic consciousness and low awareness of their nation and state. The situation invoked worries over the political future of Hong Kong, and elicited public concern for civic education in schools. With the introduction of political reform toward a representative government and the stipulation of China's policy of "One Country, Two Systems," civic education was considered as a major means to promote students' civic consciousness and to prepare for the political change (Bray & Lee, 1993; Sweeting, 1992).

Accordingly, the Hong Kong government adjusted its education policy from a stance of "depoliticisation" to a more active role in promoting civic education, most saliently by the publication of *The Guidelines on Civic Education in Schools* in 1985, and introduction and revision of major social subjects (Bray & Lee, 1993; Morris, 1988, 1997; Morris & Chan, 1997). Also, in 1996, the Education Department published new guidelines on civic education which presented a richer conception of citizenship than the earlier one.

Macau

Portugal established its rule over Macau over four hundred years ago (1557–1999). But as a result of the decline of Portugal on the world stage, together with the rise of a much stronger China and the state of dependency of Macau on mainland China, the Portuguese government in Macau could not maintain its governance without the cooperation and support of the Chinese government. From the end of World War II to the mid-1970s, Macau was a polity under Chinese patronage, together with an insulated bureaucracy and a parochial and subject political culture (Lo, 1995; Yee, Liu, & Ngo, 1993a, 1993b). The PRC established a strong leftist influence in Macau. The 1966 riots further undermined the autonomy and authority of the Macau government. While the Portuguese formally and nominally controlled the top political leadership, China's representatives in Macau and pro-China organizations informally and substantially governed at the grassroots level. Also, the Macau government has been traditionally destabilised by Portuguese politics, and plagued by bureaucratic corruption and administrative incompetence (Lo, 1995).

After the 1970s, Macau experienced rapid industrialisation and urbanisation, as well as a sharp increase in population due to migration from mainland China and southeast Asia. The masses of Macau exhibited a passive political culture (Yee et al., 1993a, 1993b). Politically Macau is a Portuguese colony, but economically and culturally Macau is heavily dependent on mainland China and Hong Kong. From the late 1970s onwards, the Macau government has gradually opened and reformed its political structure and played a more active role in socio-economic affairs (Lo, 1995).

Under the policy of classical colonialism, the Macau government was only concerned with the education of Portuguese children and neglected the education of the Chinese inhabitants. Therefore, educational development in Macau was rather slow and stagnant, particularly prior to the 1980s (Bray, 1992; Chan, 1993, 1995; Koo & Ma, 1994; Wong, 1991, 1992). Partly due to colonial non-interventionist policies, a distinguishing feature of Macau's education system is the phenomenon of self-reliance on the part of civil society, fragmentation of educational provision, and its diversity in terms of the co-existence of multiple-systems. There was no compulsory free education. Macau had no aided sector; and the majority of schools were privately managed, operating with a high degree of autonomy. In the absence of a compulsory unified curriculum and system-wide examinations, individual schools act individually according to their particular preferences and backgrounds. Many schools adopted syllabuses and textbooks from other places, particularly Portugal, PRC, Taiwan, or Hong Kong (Bray & Hui, 1991). As a result, Macau students tend to know more about places other than Macau, their own society.

Civic education was basically invisible in Macau as no official programme was introduced by the government until the 1990s. In general, the civic education being implemented in a majority of private schools was characterised by a permeated approach or solely determined by the form teachers (Wong, 1992). Also, each school varied in background and in the approaches to civic education.

The Sino-Portuguese Declaration in 1987 arranged Macau as a Special Administrative Region of the PRC for at least 50 years after the change of sovereignty in 1999. During the transitional period from 1987 to 1999, the government was preoccupied with a number of major issues such as localisation of the civil service, legalisation of the Chinese language, and translation of Portuguese laws into Chinese. However, political reforms in Macau were implemented much more slowly and narrowly than in Hong Kong. Shortly prior to the handover, the rise in crime and vice, and the deterioration of law and order also evoked much public concern.

With the designated transfer of sovereignty, the Macau government embarked on a series of major education reforms (Koo & Ma, 1994; Wong, 1991). Like their Hong Kong counterparts, Macau adolescents are often accused of a lack of civic consciousness and low awareness of their nation and state. Promotion of civic education and curriculum reform in preparation for the 1999 handover was also put on the public agenda. In 1994, the laws on curriculum organisation for kindergarten, pre-primary and primary schools were made, followed by the provisional teaching syllabuses trialled in some Luso-Chinese schools.

The Civics Curricula in Hong Kong and Macau Contrasted and Compared

In the wave of independence after World War II, education performed the important function of nation-building and national integration for the new born nation-states. For these new nation-states, building up national unity and a new political order were pressing needs. Formal educational institutions were expected to supplement and perhaps replace the role of families to socialise the new generation in a new role of national citizenry and to cultivate a sense of national identity and loyalty. However, unlike other former colonies heading towards independence and building new nation-state, the experience of Hong Kong and Macau is distinctive in being a reintegration with an existing nation-state (China) and, at the same time, maintaining a high degree of autonomy and a different way of life. Since the mid-1980s, Hong Kong and Macau have experienced significant political changes in terms of "de-colonialisation" and change of sovereignty. Accordingly, the shaping of civic education in these two places has been different. The following sections will take the junior secondary civic education syllabuses in Hong Kong and Macau as examples and display their representations of citizenship.

Agent of Change

In Hong Kong, a new curriculum of civic education was issued by the Curriculum Development Council (CDC) in 1998. The CDC, together with its co-ordinating committees and subject committees, has representatives of parents and employers, heads of schools and practising teachers from government and non-government schools, lecturers from tertiary institutions, officers of the Hong Kong Examinations Authority and those of the Curriculum Development Institute, the Advisory Inspectorate and other divisions of the Education Department. Once the syllabus has been implemented, progress is monitored by the Advisory Inspectorate and the Curriculum Development Institute of the Education Department. This enables the individual subject committee of the CDC to review the syllabus from time to time in the light of teaching and learning experiences. The civic education syllabus, recommended for use in secondary one to three, is prepared in accordance with the concepts and curriculum framework proposed in the Guidelines on Civic Education in Schools (Curriculum Development Committee, 1996). The syllabus comprises seven parts: aims and objectives, general introduction, organization of the syllabus, suggested time allocation, syllabus content, suggestions on teaching as well as evaluation. The syllabus content is subdivided into areas, topics, guiding questions, reflection and action. Unlike many former social subject syllabuses, the parts of topics, guiding questions, reflection and action only provide questions, without listing more specific objectives or suggestions on teaching.

In Macau, with the introduction of Laws No.38/94/M and No.39/94/M in 1994 and 1997 respectively, which stated the regulations on curriculum planning and reform for both primary and secondary schools, the development of moral and civic education became an official goal of education. Accordingly, a curriculum reform group was specially formed to initiate the reform. Macau's syllabus was drafted by in-service teachers who were commissioned by the Curriculum Reform Group. From 1995 onwards, the Department of Education & Youth Affairs (DSEJ) published the Moral and Civic Education Syllabuses at both primary and secondary levels. Macau's syllabus comprises seven parts: preface, general aims, contents of subjects, guidelines on teaching, estimated number of lessons, assessment, as well as the teaching-learning organization plan. The teaching-learning organization plan is further divided into content, periods of lessons, specific objectives, and working suggestions.

Mode of Implementation

On the matter of implementation of civic education, the Hong Kong government gives the schools a free hand and proposes a school-based approach to promote civic education without making civic education a compulsory subject. Civic education is one of the electives in the "personal, social and education humanities learning area" at junior secondary level. Also, under the principle of school-based curriculum development, schools may decide whether to implement the syllabus as an independent subject or to incorporate it into other subjects. The syllabus content is designed for the purpose of providing a comprehensive junior secondary civic education curriculum. It is assumed that there are around 30 teaching weeks/cycles in one academic year, and at least 2 consecutive periods (approximately 80 minutes) per week/cycle are recommended for the teaching of the subject. The syllabus is so designed that the topics can be covered within 50 periods, which also allows teachers to select teaching contents flexibly according to the situation of their schools and students. The remaining teaching periods can be employed in wider or in-depth studies of certain topics according to the interests of students and the current development of society.

In Macau, according to the 1999 Moral and Civic Education Syllabus (junior secondary), civic and moral education is taught as a specific academic subject within the core area of moral education. However, the syllabus targets the official Luso-Chinese schools in the first place and serves only as a guide for the private schools. As for time allocation, it is assumed that there are around 36 teaching weeks in one academic year. And one period (usually 45 minutes) per week is recommended to the teaching of the subject. With this arrangement, Macau's teaching time is approximately two thirds of Hong Kong's.

Aims and Objectives

Table 14.1 lists the aims and objectives of the syllabuses in both places. As can be seen, Hong Kong enumerates three aims and fifteen objectives whereas Macau only has nine aims, with more specific objectives given in the individual topics of the teaching-learning organization plan. Both syllabuses are similar in classifying the objectives into knowledge, attitudes and skills, paying special attention to reflection and action. With the syllabus, Hong Kong students are expected to learn and develop the values, attitudes, beliefs and skills which are essential to the well being of individuals and society, so that they will become rational, socially concerned and responsible citizens. In Macau, the syllabus is to cultivate students' positive civic awareness and skills; and to explore the skills both in the acquisition of civic knowledge and in nurturing of a moral sense of mind so as to facilitate students to adapt, learn and grow up when entering the society in future. These syllabuses are common with regard to the specific objectives such as understanding the working conditions of local society and government; cultivating the attitudes of open-mindedness, objectivity, toleration, democracy, and rationality, the spirit of rule of law, and civic values such as concern for others and caring for the community, sense of belonging and identity with regard to the community and the nation, as well as the skills of making judgements, thinking, managing and analyzing information.

As for the differences, Hong Kong's syllabus is more ambitious and

Table 14.1: Aims and Objectives of Syllabuses in Hong Kong and Macau

Hong Kong	Macau
Junior Secondary Civic Education Syllabus (1998)	Junior Secondary Moral and Civic Education Syllabus (1999)
Three Aims: 1. To develop in students positive civic attitudes, values and a sense of belonging to the family, the community and the state so that they are ready to contribute to the betterment of the family, the community, the state and the world; 2. To help students understand the characteristics of Hong Kong society and the importance of the rule of law, democracy, human rights and justice, and to employ these concepts in daily life; and 3. To develop in students critical thinking and problem-solving skills that would allow them to analyze social and political issues objectively and to arrive at a rational appraisal of these issues. Fifteen Objectives: 1–4. To help students understand: a. the local conditions of Hong Kong, the rights and duties of citizens, the functioning of the government and the communication between the government and the people; b, the special features of Chinese culture and the structure of the Chinese government; c. the matters of concern for Hong Kong, the state and the world; and d. the civic values, such as the rule of law, democracy, human rights and justice; 5–8. To develop the following skills: a. collecting, analyzing, synthesizing, evaluating and expressing information; b. critical thinking and creative thinking; c. problem-solving and making independent judgments; and d. effective communication and cooperation to arrive at corporate decisions; and 9–15. To cultivate the following attitudes: a. concern for the people, the community, the state and the world; b. willingness to consider problems from different perspectives; c. courage to express opinions; d. willingness to employ civic values in daily life; e. enthusiasm to participate in public affairs and contribute to the community and the state; f. sense of identity and belonging to the community and the state; and g. open-mindedness and objectivity towards different cultures, values and ways of life.	Nine General Aims Cover the Aspects of Knowledge, Skills, and Attitudes: 1. To understand the stages and features of psychological and moral development; 2. To understand legislative, administrative, and judiciary mechanisms; 3. To understand some political affairs; 4. Be able to attend, understand, judge and respond to daily life independently; 5. Be able to observe, collect, organize and analyze information systematically, to conclude and to write up report; 6. Be able to reconstruct one's personal outlook on life and values system in the light of everyday experience; 7. Ardently love and respect oneself, others, family, society, community, and the world; 8. Respect and abide by the law; and 9. Uphold democratic, open, rational, pragmatic, positive, and tolerant attitudes.

Sources: Education Department of Hong Kong Special Administrative Region (HKSAR) (1998:2) and The Curriculum Reform Group, the Department of Education and Youth Affairs of Macau (1999:4).

inclusive in terms of what it aims to achieve. In accordance with the new guidelines, the syllabus aims to meet the challenges of political transition after 1997 and to prepare the students to become contributing citizens to society, the country and the world. The aims include development of a sense of belonging to Hong Kong and China, understanding the characteristics of Hong Kong society, and the importance of democracy, liberty, equality, human rights and rule of law. Hong Kong's syllabus shows a strong preference for "communitarianism," hence placing a great emphasis on cultivating a sense of belonging and making contributions to the community. It also encourages active and participatory citizenship. The view of citizenship as revealed encompasses communitarianism, liberalism, participatory and critical elements of a citizen. The general orientation of Hong Kong's syllabus brings together the elements of communitarianism and liberalism. Communitarianism is a social-political philosophy which has emerged in reaction to liberalism and utilitarianism. It accords primacy and the intrinsic values to community and the importance of communal life to individuals, reconciling self-interests and public interests, highlighting the sense of belonging and identity on the part of individual members of a community and participation in public life. This tradition emphasizes obligations, duties, shared values, norms and common good, empathy, cooperation, sharing, mutuality, participation, as well as the cultural and traditional attachments. Communitarianism cherishes the virtues like voluntary work and services and views them as the way to nurture community spirits. In the tradition of Hong Kong consultative and administrative-led politics, the syllabus also underlines the significance of communication between the people and the government.

Meanwhile, Hong Kong's syllabus inherits the tradition of liberalism by highlighting the notions of the rule of law, democracy, human rights, and social justice. It also highlights critical thinking and problem-solving skills as the aims of citizenship education. An emphasis was put on the teaching of controversial issues as well as developing students' critical thinking. As such, the syllabus has exhibited a more reflective and critical orientation than former syllabuses of social subjects and the guidelines.

In an earlier article, Morris and Morris (2000) point out that the Hong Kong syllabus extends the scope of civic education in a broader context, including national, regional and global settings, and a more explicit promotion of patriotism and cultural nationalism, as well as a greater concern for ethnic and cultural diversity. The recent syllabus put a greater emphasis on values such as national pride and national identity, a recognition of ethnic and cultural diversity, the promotion of critical thinking, creativity and active citizenship. There is also an emphasis on interpersonal and moral values, providing students with instruction on the moral responsibilities of the individual to support the interests of the community. The syllabus emphasizes the citizen's responsibilities to the collective good, rather than their rights as individuals. It is also noteworthy that students are encouraged to evaluate critically the government's performance with reference to their trust-worthiness, effectiveness and honesty, but not with reference to their representativeness. It elevates the rule of law as the most important values to be transmitted. Although democracy is highlighted, it avoids any attempt to define the term democracy, leaving it subject to different interpretations and decontextualizing the discussion of democracy from any specific political context.

Macau's syllabus combines moral education and civic education, hence it has a stronger orientation to moral education and education for living. Accordingly, there are aims to understand the stages and features of psychological and moral development, and to be able to reconstruct one's personal outlook on life and values system in the light of everyday experience. In addition, the orientation of Macau's syllabus is more conservative with regard to its emphasis on preparing the students to "adapt" to their social life and the society at large, instead of initiating change. As far as political ideas are concerned, Macau's syllabus underscores the teaching of democracy and rule of law. In the syllabus, students are expected to be law-abiding citizens.

Cultivation of values, attitudes, beliefs and competence, not only knowledge, is a common emphasis in both syllabuses. Hong Kong's syllabus places a great emphasis on the development of values, attitudes, beliefs and competence as well as the acquisition of knowledge (Education Department, 1998, p. 2). And these elements permeate all the teaching content and are included at the end of the table of "syllabus content" for each grade level (Education Department, 1998, pp. 5, 21). The purpose of "reflection" and "action" in different areas is also to help students develop respective values, attitudes, beliefs and competence. The universal core and sustained individual values involved include sanctity of life, truth, aesthetic capacity, honesty, human dignity, rationality, creativity, courage, liberty, affectivity, individuality, self-reflection, self-regulation, self-cultivation, principled morality, self determination, open-mindedness. The universal core and sustained social values include equality, benevolence, kindness, freedom, common good, mutuality, justice, betterment of humankind, plurality, due process, democracy, rationality, tolerance, common will, equal opportunities, human rights and responsibilities, culture and civilization heritage. The attitudes mentioned in the syllabus are optimistic, participatory, critical enculturation, creative disposition, appreciation, commitment, civic and social concern, empathetic, positive, respect. The prominent beliefs are that either individuals, group effort, action, values, or education can make a difference, and result in the betterment of human societies. The syllabus also enumerates a number of competences to be cultivated: self-reflection and cultivation, self-determination and regulation, empathy, critical thinking, creative thinking, acquiring and using information, assessing involvement, corporate decision making, making judgments, communication, cooperating, promoting interest, civic and social awareness, upholding principles. Obviously the syllabus intends to strike a balance between individual-centred and community-centred values.

Another characteristic of Hong Kong's syllabus is its emphasis on actions in the process of civic education (Education Department, 1998, p. 3). Students are encouraged to apply what they have learnt in their daily life. The questions of the part "action" are designed to help students make independent judgments on the action to be taken (or not to be taken) according to their abilities and willingness so that students may become "autonomous citizens."

Organization and Content

Closely allied with the objectives contained in the syllabus are the coverage and organization of the topics. Tables 14.2 and 14.3 respectively show the organization and content of both syllabuses. In Hong Kong, the syllabus content of each level covers six areas which include "family," "neighbouring community," "regional community," "national community," "international community" and "citizenship and civil society," with 41 topics in total. The coverage is wider than that of Macau. Also, Hong Kong's syllabus is more even in terms of distribution, with 1 to 4 topics in each area at each grade level. Among the six areas, "citizenship and civil society" (with 11 topics) is the biggest, followed by "regional community" (10), "national community" (6), "neighbouring community" (6) "international community" (5), and "family" (3).

In Macau, the syllabus is structured around 10 major themes: "personal growth," "human relationships," "value systems and outlook on life," "ways of thinking," "research methods," "individuals and groups," "relationships among China, Portugal and Macau," "United Nations," "law," and "mass

Table 14.2: Framework of Hong Kong's Syllabus

Levels / Areas	S1	S2	S3	Subtotal
Family	1.1 Relationship among family members	2.1 The functions of family in civic education	3.1 Family problems and support services	3
Neighbouring Community	1.2 My neighbour and I 1.3 Neighbourhood organizations	2.2 District organizations 2.3 My district and I	3.2 A study of issues within district(s) 3.3 Voluntary organizations and voluntary work	6
Regional Community	1.4 The political and economic development of Hong Kong 1.5 The characteristics of the Basic Law 1.6 Residents of the HK Special Administrative Region	2.4 Political structure 2.5 Supervision of powers 2.6 A study of current issues	3.4 Political participation 3.5 Communication between the government and the people 3.6 Elections 3.7 Reporting and commentary on current issues	10
National Community	1.7 Our land and our people 1.8 A study of current issues	2.7. The founding and development of the People's Republic of China (a) The background of establishment (b) The symbols of the state (c) Important events and figures (d) Current development 2.8 A study of current issues	3.8 The citizens and the government of the PRC (a) The Constitution (b) Citizens (c) Political participation (d) The structure of the state 3.9 A study of current issues	6
International Community	1.9 A world of diversity 1.10 Global citizenship	2.9 Heritage of human civilizations 2.10 Historical events of worldwide significance	3.10 Major global issues	5
Citizenship and Civil Society	1.11 Life and dignity 1.12 Equality 1.13 Freedom	2.11 Rights and duties 2.12 Cooperation 2.13 Love and concern for the country and society 2.14 Fellowship among human beings	3.11 The rule of law 3.12 Democracy 3.13 Fairness and justice 3.14 Critical thinking	11
Subtotal	13	14	14	41 (Total)

Note: Education Department of HKSAR(1998:5–6). The numbers prior to the titles of individual topics indicate the time order of learning.

media" (see Table 14.3). Altogether there are 30 topics, and each topic is further divided into three units. The Macau's syllabus accords primary importance to the theme of "individuals and groups" (8 topics), while "ways of thinking," "research methods" are the least. Other themes commonly contain 2 to 3 topics. Also, there are some blank areas at certain grade levels.

The differences in areas or themes across the syllabuses reveal their different emphases on civic education. While Hong Kong's syllabus separates the areas of "family" and "neighbouring community," Macau's is divided into the themes of "human relationships" and "individual and groups." Hong Kong's syllabus makes regional community and national community independent areas, but Macau's integrates them as a single theme — "Relationships among China, Portugal and Macau." In addition, Hong Kong's syllabus has a wider coverage of "international community," whereas Macau's has only two topics in the same area. With more lessons and teaching time, Hong Kong's syllabus could have a more adequate and in-depth treatment than its Macau counterpart, particularly on areas such as family and neighbourhood. Also, the Hong Kong syllabus could provide more details about the areas concerning local community, China, international community, and citizenship. On the other hand, Macau's syllabus has less space for discussion.

Hong Kong's syllabus also advocates a more balanced and reflective approach to the issues. For the area of "citizenship and civil society," there are topics like life and dignity, equality, freedom, rights and duties, cooperation, love and concern for the country and society, fellowship among human beings, the rule of law, democracy, fairness and justice, and critical thinking. The syllabus highlights the advantages and weaknesses of Hong Kong, supervision of powers, a study of current issues, political participation, communication between the government and the people, elections, reporting and commentary on current issues.

By comparison, Macau's syllabus highlights personal growth, human relationships, value systems, law and human rights, social problems, and the training in research and thinking abilities. Hence, there are special independent areas about "ways of thinking," "research methods" and "mass media" and there are nine special topics concerning social problems such as smoking, drinking, theft, corruption, suicide, discrimination, gambling, drugs and pornography. Macau's syllabus makes "thinking methods," "research methods" and "mass media" independent themes, while Hong Kong's permeates them into other individual topics.

Comparing Table 14.2 and Table 14.3, there are some overlapping topics

Table 14.3: Framework of Macau's Syllabus

Levels / Themes		S1		S2		S3	Subtotal
Personal Growth	1.4	Self-understanding (a) Self-esteem; (b) Emotion management; and (c) Balanced development	2.4	Successful Persons (a) Steps to be successful persons; (b) To realize one's potential, on the way to success; and (c) Achieving the ideals.	3.4	Planning for Future (a) Aptitude tests; (b) Further studies and taking a job; and (c) Achieving the ideals.	3
Human Relationship	1.5	Human Relationships (a) Friends; (b) Parents; and (c) Teachers	2.5	Gender Relations (a) True love & infatuation; (b) Gender and roles; and (c) Heterosexuality and homosexuality.	3.5	Marriage and Family (a) Meanings of marriage; (b) Happy marriage; and (c) Divorce and extra-marital affairs.	3
Value Systems and Outlook on Life	1.7	The Quest for Truth, Good, and Beauty (a) Truth; (b) Good; and (c) Beauty.	2.6	Discovery and Reconstruction of Values System (a) Discovery of values system; (b) Reconstruction of values system; and (c) Different value systems.	3.7	Ethical Development (a) Psychological tests; (b) Introduction to ethical development; and (c) Clues to ethical development.	3
Ways of Thinking	1.8	Thinking Methods (a) Paying attention and understanding; (b) Judging; (c) Making responses.					1
Research Methods			2.7	Research Methods (a) Data-collection methods; (b) Data management & analysis; and (c) Report compilation and release.	3.8	Evaluation of Research Report (a) Survey; (b) Analysis; and (c) Language.	2
Individuals and Groups	1.1	Freedom and Limits (a) Born to be free; (b) Mutual respect; (c) The boundary of people, place, and event	2.1	Groups and Individuals (a) Human dignity; (b) Group for individual; and (c) Government of the people.	3.6	Stability and Prosperity (a) Gap between the rich and the poor; (b) Welfare and charities; and (c) Economic assistance.	8
	1.6	Groups (a) Nature of conformity; (b) Group pressure; and (c) Popular culture.	2.6	Crowds (a) The forces of crowds and follow like sheep; (b) Group thinking; and (c) Rational crowd.	3.9	Social Problems (a) Corruption; (b) Suicide; and (c) Discrimination.	

Individuals and Groups (cont'd)	1.9	Social Problems (a) Smoking (b) Drink (c) Theft	2.9	Social Problems (a) Gambling (b) Drug (c) Pornography			
Relationships among China. Portugal and Macau	1.2	Macau (a) Macau & the relationships between China & Portugal; (b) Administrative structure of Macau; and (c) Features of Macau community.	2.2 2.3	China Macau (a) Capitalism; (b) Socialism; (c) One Country, Two Systems. Basic Laws (a) China's constitution; (b) SAR; (c) Basic Laws of Macau.			3
United Nations	1.3	United Nations (a) Its history; (b) Its composition and functions; and (c) Universal Declaration of Human Rights.			3.1	Worldwide Harmony (a) Environmental protection; (b) Sharing of resources; and (c) Independence and co-existence.	2
Law					3.2 3.3	Law (a) Introduction to Law; (b) Legislature; and (c) Spirit of rule of law. Law and Human Rights (a) Protecting Human Rights; (b) Understanding of human rights from different perspectives; and (c) From consensus to consensus	2
Mass Media	1.10	Audio-visual Media (a) Advertising on TV (b) Movies (c) Popular music	2.10	Printed Media (a) Printed media across time and space; (b) Between lines and words; (c) Comics in focus.	3.10	Media of News and Current Affairs (a) News report, truth and facts; (b) News report and leadership; and (c) Freedom of the press and self-discipline.	3
Subtotal	10		10		10		30 (Total)

Note: the numbers prior to the titles of individual topics indicate the time order of learning.

(as indicated by the shadowed areas): family relationship and family problems, neighbourhood organizations and voluntary organizations, government and local political framework, Basic Law, "One Country, Two systems," China, freedom, law and rule of law, democracy, equality and fairness (discrimination), human rights, rights and duties, cooperation, love and concern for others and society, fellowship among human beings, rational and critical thinking (ways of thinking), global citizenship (worldwide harmony), global issues, and so forth.

As mentioned above, in the past there has been an omission of nationalistic education in Hong Kong's formal curriculum. With the integration with China (PRC) rather than to independence, Hong Kong and Macau have changed their formal curricula to reflect the new political circumstances: a new emphasis on relations with China rather than an identity as a newly-emergent nation-state as found in many other post-colonial states. Compared with the past, the most salient feature in Hong Kong and Macau is an emphasis on national identity. A trend due to the impact of transfer of sovereignty on the school curriculum was an increase in the topics allocated to the study of China, the relationships between Hong Kong (Macau) and China, political transition, and a specific reference made to the *Joint Declaration and the Basic Law*. For the area of "national community" in Hong Kong's syllabus, the topics such as our land and our people, the founding and development of the PRC, the symbols of the state, important events and figures, current development, the constitution, citizens, political participation, the structure of the state were included. In Macau's syllabus, for the area of "relationships among China, Portugal and Macau," there are topics dealing with Macau and the relationships between China and Portugal, China Macau (Capitalism, socialism, One Country, Two Systems); Basic Laws (China's constitution, SAR, Basic Laws of Macau). However, the Hong Kong authorities downplayed the British influence and the British colonial legacy, whereas the Macau government took pride in Portuguese culture and still inserted the Portuguese influence into the curriculum. Hence special topics were devoted to Portugal, Portuguese culture and the lives of the Portuguese in the syllabus.

Civic education in both places stresses international contexts by including elements of global citizenship and/or multi-culturalism. In Hong Kong, for the area of "international community," there are topics like "a world of diversity," "global citizenship," "heritage of human civilizations," "historical events of worldwide significance," and "major global issues." Multicultural education is a central tenet of Macau education, and it is partially reflected in Macau's syllabus. Therefore, there are topics dealing with the relationships among China, Portugal and Macau, gender relations, homosexuality and heterosexuality, discrimination, mutual respect, different value systems, human dignity, human rights, economic assistance at international level, United Nations, and worldwide issues like environmental protection, sharing of resources, independence and co-existence.

Compared with Hong Kong's syllabus, Macau's syllabus is more fragmented as it lacks a clear notion of citizenship that links the individual topics together. The syllabus presents a bulk of topics about personal, moral and social education rather than a package of systematic citizenship education. With the dominance of topics about personal growth, human relationships, value systems, and ethical development, the syllabus is more like a kind of personal, social and moral education, rather than a more critical and participatory version of citizenship. Among the political topics in Macau's syllabus, far more items are about "political system" and "political output," rather than "political input" and "self as a political actor." They are mainly concerned with transmission of factual political knowledge. Students' exposure to political topics is restricted to a formalistic description of the structure and functions of the Government and the government's roles in providing social services to Macau's community, for example, social welfare, educational protection, anti-corruption, and so forth. More importantly, most of the political topics included are very simple and superficial, concerned with formal political institutions, whereas little space is devoted to informal politics and socio-political skills. Except for human rights, democracy, and rule of law, many essential political concepts or ideas are either superficially covered or excluded completely.

Suggestions for Teaching

In terms of pedagogy, a more progressive vision of citizenship education is witnessed in both syllabuses. In Hong Kong, each section of the "syllabus content" is divided into three parts, namely, "guiding questions," "reflection" and "action." The topics at different levels are arranged from the learner's perspective, beginning with the easy and proceeding gradually to the difficult, and from the immediate environment to the distant. Under this principle, all the topics in every learning area have been arranged in the same way from secondary one to secondary three (see Table 14.2). A salient feature of the contents of the syllabus is that they are presented in the form of guiding questions for teachers' reference. This is to indicate that civic education is an exploration of issues together with the students rather than a one-way transmission of knowledge and values. The aim of such an approach is to enhance students' abilities to discuss, reason, make decisions and think critically; so that they can approach an issue from different perspectives, analyze different viewpoints, reflect on their own values and beliefs, before making constructive suggestions (Education Department, 1998, p. 3). Also, teachers are encouraged to design learning activities which allow students to be actively involved in collecting, analyzing, synthesizing, and evaluating information in response to the guiding questions. In addition, there are special topics for the study of issues.

As for the suggestions on teaching, "participation" is highlighted as another important element in civic education in Hong Kong's syllabus (Education Department, 1998, p. 49). Although classroom teaching cannot allow students to participate directly in social or political affairs, "participatory learning activities" can provide students with some personal experiences. The so-called "participatory learning activities" usually include viewing video programmes, films or slides and discussion thereafter; designing posters or slogans; preparing newspaper cuttings; holding exhibitions; analysis of current affairs; conducting interviews, role plays, group discussions, simulation games, quizzes, debates and case studies. As different activities have different learning focuses and outcomes, teachers are advised to select appropriate teaching activities in accordance with the nature of topics, teaching objectives and ability of their students.

Though "participatory learning activities" can provide opportunities for acquiring knowledge, skills, attitudes and values, they are futile if students have not undergone deep reflection during the learning process. "Reflection" is an important means to make learning meaningful to oneself and to enhance comprehension and synthesis in learning. It also encourages students to become active learners who will respond to what has just been learnt. In conducting learning activities, teachers are encouraged to facilitate students' reflection on what has been learnt as well as their own values and beliefs. Following students' reflection and internalization in the learning process, students are encouraged to choose appropriate actions to apply what they have learnt, in accordance with their abilities and willingness. Teachers are also encouraged to keep students' progress in these actions under regular review in order to evaluate their performances.

The classroom environment is supposed to provide direct experiences of civic education and constantly affects the implementation and effectiveness of civic education. Hence, teachers are advised to build up an open a supportive atmosphere of mutual respect and a suitable environment for conducting different learning activities during lessons. Ground rules and regulations could be agreed upon by both parties so that discussion can be objective and there is respect for everyone's opinions. Following the civic education guidelines, when teaching a controversial issue, teachers should have good mastery of the topic and be "affirmative-neutral" (Education Department, 1998, p. 49). It is in this way that students' civic attitudes can be developed.

Finally, extra-curricular activities are also viewed as a significant complement to classroom teaching for civic education. Under suitable circumstances, teachers could arrange for students to participate in social services and affairs to enhance civic learning (Education Department, 1998, p. 50).

In Macau, in line with Piagetian theory, there is an emphasis on internalization of moral values with regard to moral education. The syllabus emphasizes reconciling the development of pupils and the social reality, balancing the needs of adolescents and the guidance of adults. The syllabus recommends multiple and lively methods of teaching, including visits to government departments. As for individual topics, there are numerous detailed working suggestions on teaching. Similar to the case of Hong Kong, Macau's syllabus suggests more than 30 forms of participatory learning activities and worksheets, including story-telling, viewing video programmes, class discussion, designing posters or slogans, collecting newspaper cuttings, analysis of current affairs, case studies, role plays, games, quizzes, and volunteering.

Suggestions on Evaluation

As for evaluation, both syllabuses stress not only cognitive but also the affective achievements and behavioral performance. According to Hong Kong's syllabus (Education Department, 1998, p. 52), as the main objective of school civic education is not just to inculcate knowledge but also to help students attain the development of the whole person, evaluation of their performance in citizenship education should go beyond the knowledge domain. Evaluation should thus take into account students' mastery of attitudes, values and competence in civic learning, as well as their application in situations as demonstrated by their participation in citizenship education activities. The syllabus includes several basic principles about evaluation of students' learning outcomes in citizenship education: 1. Since the purpose of evaluation is not just to find out how much knowledge students have acquired, standard test formats to determine students' grading cannot be relied on to assess students' learning. The assessment of students' learning outcomes may be conducted through profiling students' performances in the process of reflection and action. Meanwhile, it is necessary to establish some standards which can reflect the objectives and the framework of the syllabus; 2. Evaluation should reflect the learning process of students, with a view to improving the syllabus, the teaching methodology and the learning methods. Thus, the strategies for evaluation should aim at helping students to extend their learning experiences; 3. Evaluation of students' learning outcomes should be a continuing process; 4. Evaluation should be reliable-information-based, well-planned and supported with a variety of effective and valid evaluation and assessment instruments; and 5. Evaluation should be an interactive process, taking place in an environment of trust and support. And the parties involved should know clearly the objectives of evaluation and all be given opportunities to provide feedback during the process.

Because a range of objective tests could be used to assess students' learning outcomes in knowledge acquired, far few instruments have been developed to measure objectively students' mastery of skills and changes in attitudes and values. A number of evaluation instruments aiming at assessing students' attitudes and skills are thus suggested in the syllabus for teachers' reference (Education Department, 1998, pp. 53–54). To evaluate students' skills in communication, data collection, problem-solving and evaluating events, teachers may consider assigning projects, debates, group discussions, simulations and essay writing. Evaluation of attitudes and competence usually requires a longer time. Apart from the teacher conducting evaluation, students may be encouraged to develop self-evaluation skills by keeping a personal portfolio and collecting their work such as homework assignments, letters, drawings, essays, activity reports and other records.

In Macau, there are only very brief guidelines on the principles of assessment. The syllabus ascertains the importance and functions of assessment, but emphasizes that moral education is basically a cultivation of intrinsic affection and attitudes, which are not suitable for using external behaviourist methods for assessment. But assessment is recommended in the form of observing students' performance in schools, in addition to tests of knowledge. Again, details about assessment are provided in individual topics of the teaching-learning organization plan, with a number of evaluation forms and worksheets, for example, students' emotional performance, their views on parents, human relationships, and so forth. Finally, the final outcome of assessment is recommended to be recorded in crude grades only.

Preparing Students for Citizenship? The Possibilities and Limits of the School Curriculum

So far, this paper has reviewed the socio-political situations and the development of civic education in Hong Kong and Macau over the recent decades. These socio-political changes have significantly influenced the shaping of civic education in both places. Unlike the cases of mainland China and Taiwan in which citizenship education was highly politicised, citizenship education in Hong Kong and Macau from the 1950s to early 1980s was generally characterised by "depoliticization" and "denationalization" (Tse, 1999a, 1999b). For the sake of self-defence (British government), or due to incompetence (Portuguese government), citizenship education was in a state of poverty and barely visible. The colonial government in Hong Kong exercised tight control over the educational system and marginalised political education. In contrast, Macau was characterised by a fragmentation of educational provision and a lack of formal civic education until the 1990s. In Macau, the state's sluggish orientation resulted in slow progress of development in education in general and civic education in particular. Civic education has been less developed in Macau than in Hong Kong. Indeed, while the Hong Kong government took an initiative in commencing civic education in the early 1980s, the Macau government only initiated its civic education programme after the running of civic education programmes by other educational bodies.

With the changes in the socio-political milieu after the mid-1980s and the issue of new syllabuses, there has been a break away from the former depoliticised legacies in education. Table 14.4 displays the distinctive features concerning Hong Kong's and Macau's syllabuses. As revealed in Table 14.4, both governments have defined civic education in the broadest sense, and have treated civic education as a mixture of moral, political and lifeskills education. In Hong Kong, the composition of the civic education committee in 1996 required accommodation of different opinions while reserving differences to win wide recognition and acceptance from all groups in the community. In Macau, civic education was treated as a branch of moral education, based on moral and legal norms to cultivate good citizens.

The recent syllabuses in both places combined liberal and critical modes of orientation. They juxtaposed both nationalistic and democratic education, so that patriotic education went hand in hand with an affirmation of the values of human rights and democracy. Also, both pro-establishment and participatory elements were found; and civic education in both places stressed

Table 14.4: A Comparative Analysis of the Citizenship Education Curriculum in Hong Kong and Macau

Distinctiveness	Hong Kong	Macau
Socio-political Change	Decolonalisation and reintegration with China, Partial democratisation and representative government	Decolonalisation and reintegration with China, partial democratisation
Syllabus	Civic Education Syllabus (Junior Secondary) (1998)	Moral and Civic Education Syllabus (Junior Secondary) (1999)
Agent of Reform	Curriculum Development Council	Group of curriculum reform, the Department of Education and Youth Services
Reference of Documents	1996 Guidelines on Civic Education as blueprint	In accordance with the 91 Law on Educational System, Laws 38/94/M and 39/94/M, and Laws on Secondary Curriculum Organization (1994)
Implementation Strategies	An optional subject under the scope of humanities and social subjects	A compulsory subject under the scope of moral education in government schools
Time Allocation	Three years, approximately 120 hours for the whole syllabus	Three years, approximately 81 hours for the whole syllabus
Major Aims and Objectives	• Cultivate positive value systems and civic attitudes, a sense of belonging to family, community and state, so that to contribute to family, community, state and the world; • Understand the features of Hong Kong society, apprehend the significance of rule of law, democracy, human rights and justice and put them in practice; and • Cultivate students with critical thinking and problem-solving skills, to analyze social and political problems with objective attitudes, and to make sensible judgements.	• Prepare students to become good citizens with reference to certain moral and legal principles; • Ensure a solid foundation for adapting a more complex socio-political environment; and • Cultivate students' positive civic awareness and skills, exploring skills in the acquisition of civic knowledge and in nurturing of a moral sense of mind so as to facilitate students with sufficient abilities to adapt, to learn and to grow up when entering the society in future.
Key Topics and Coverage of Curriculum	Six major areas: family, neighbourhood, community, nation-state, global society, citizenship and civil society	Ten major themes: personal growth, human relationships, value systems and outlook on life, ways of thinking, research methods, individuals and groups, relationships among China, Portugal and Macau, United Nations, law and mass media

Pedagogy	Emphasis on participatory learning activities, reflection, building up an open and mutual-respect classroom climate, adopting affirmative neutral strategies in teaching controversial issues, provision of suitable extra-curricula activities for students' participation in social services and affairs	Emphasis on internalization with regard to moral education, recommending multiple and lively methods of teaching, including visits to government departments
Assessment and Evaluation	Evaluation encompasses knowledge, attitudes, values and competence in civic learning, as well as their application in situations. Apart from standard test formats, assessment is conducted through profiling students' performances in the process of reflection and action. Evaluation as a continuing and interactive process and reflect the learning progress of students	Assessment is recommended in the form of observing students' performance, instead of examination, plus the use of conduct assessment
Highlights of Citizenship Education	• Preparation for 1997 handover, salience of topics about China and political ideas, politicisation of the curriculum; • Seven domains of knowledge, values, attitudes, beliefs, competence, reflection, and action (participation); • Learner's perspective and learning process of students; • Autonomous, rational individual, socially concerned and responsible; • Regular and systematic school-based evaluations of pupil learning outcomes & of school programme; and • With a special focus on teaching and handling controversial issues, developing critical thinking, wise decision-making, creative thinking, independent judgement, self-reflective abilities and upholds principles.	• Preparation for 99 handover; multi-cultural education; • Skills-learning, especially ways of thinking and research methods, critical understanding of mass media; • Self-examination; • Personal and social education; • Ascertain freedom, democracy, and rule of law; and • Balancing individuals and community.

international contexts by including elements of multi-culturalism and/or global citizenship.

Despite the similarities in terms of socio-political context, and reintegration with mainland China, civic education in Hong Kong and Macau remains slightly different. The primary causes lie in the differences in colonial rule and the priorities of government policies, as well as the perceptions of curriculum planners in the two places. As can be seen from the objectives and topics contained in the syllabus, the conception of citizenship in Macau's syllabus was an incomplete and fragmentary one. Macau's syllabus is also less nationalistic than that of Hong Kong as there are fewer topics about China.

When compared with the past, there has been a marked increase in the attention to national community and qualities of a citizen in the recent syllabuses. However, whether a more reflective and critical approach to citizenship education can take effect remains doubtful, given that there is often a gap between intended curriculum on the part of the curriculum planners and experienced curriculum on the part of teachers and students. As discussed in the section "Mode of Implementation," due to the curricular design, these new syllabi are not widely implemented at school levels. With their limited delivery only to a small proportion of students, their impact on students should also be qualified. In Hong Kong, despite the calling for implementing citizenship education through social subjects, making use of the junior secondary curriculum for citizenship education is undermined by the distorted, biased, formalistic, and non-critical presentation in textbooks (Tse, 2000). Also, previous experiences show that the issue of the official curriculum documents would not naturally bring radical, fundamental, and swift changes in implementation of civic education at school level. Political education in Hong Kong secondary schools still exhibits problems of "depoliticisation" and "moralisation" of political education, and under-implementation of political education (Leung, 1997; Tse, 1997a). Furthermore, some recent studies show that most school teachers still conform to a conventional approach to citizenship education and showed a striking continuity with the past (Tse, 1997b).

In the case of Macau, the barriers are even greater, as a salient feature of Macau education is its cultural and educational dependence. Macau relies on experts and resources from outside (particularly Hong Kong) in preparing civic education programmes, producing textbooks and teaching materials, and training of teachers. Also, the official control over education in recent years has provoked resistance from the private educational sector, and many reform measures were deferred if not shelved.

Finally, although the new syllabuses in Hong Kong and Macau have been prepared to reflect changes in sovereignty, the prospect of citizenship education has been limited by the conservative constitutional framework imposed on both places. Given the above factors, the possibilities of citizenship education are called into question. Besides curriculum reform, there must be a number of complementary measures in political reforms, in addition to an improvement in instruction and teacher training.

References

Almond, G. A., & Verba, S. (1963). *The civic culture.* Princeton, NJ: Princeton University Press.

Apple, M. (1990). *Ideology and the curriculum* (2nd ed.). London: Routledge.

Bray, M. (1992). Colonialism, scale and politics: Divergence and convergence of educational development in Hong Kong and Macau. *Comparative Education Review*, *36*(3), 322–342.

Bray, M., & Hui, P. K. F. (1991). Curriculum development in Macau. In C. Marsh & P. Morris (Eds.), *Curriculum development in East Asia* (pp. 181–201). London: Falmer.

Bray, M., & Lee, W. O. (1993). Education, democracy and colonial transition: The case of Hong Kong. *International Review of Education*, *39*(6), 541–560.

Chan, Y. Y. (Ed.). (1993). *The present state of development in Macau.* Hong Kong: Wide Angle. (In Chinese)

Chan, Y. Y. (1995). *Social problems in Macau.* Hong Kong: Wide Angle. (In Chinese)

Chan, Y. Y. (1997). *Four places across the straits.* Hong Kong: Wide Angle. (In Chinese)

Choi, P. (1995). 1997 and decolonization. In S. Romaniuk & D. K. W. Tong (Eds.), *Uncertain times: Hong Kong women facing 1997* (pp. 27–33). Hong Kong: Hong Kong Women Christian Council.

Curriculum Development Committee. (1996). *Guidelines on civic education in schools.* Hong Kong: Curriculum Development Committee.

Curriculum Development Committee. (1998). *Junior secondary civic education syllabus.* Hong Kong: Curriculum Development Committee.

The Curriculum Reform Group, the Department of Education and Youth Affairs of Macau. (1999). *Moral and civic education syllabus (Junior secondary education).* Macau: The Curriculum Reform Group, the Department of Education and Youth Affairs of Macau.

Education Department. (1998). *Syllabuses for secondary schools — civic education (secondary 1–3).* Hong Kong: Government Printer.

Giroux, H. (1983). *Theory and resistance in education: A pedagogy for the politics of the opposition.* New York: Bergin & Garvey.

Heater, D. (1990). *Citizenship: The civic ideal in world history, politics and education*. London: Longman.

Ichilov, O. (1994). Political education. In T. Husen & T. N. Postlethwaite (Eds.), *International encyclopedia of education* (2nd ed., pp. 4568–4571). New York: Pergamon.

King, A. (1981a). Administrative absorption of politics in Hong Kong: Emphasis on the grass roots level. In A. Y. C. King & R. P. L. Lee (Eds.), *Social life and development in Hong Kong* (pp. 127–146). Hong Kong: The Chinese University Press.

King, A. (1981b). The political culture in Kwun Tong: A Chinese community in Hong Kong. In A. Y. C. King & R. P. L. Lee (Eds.), *Social life and development in Hong Kong* (pp. 147–168). Hong Kong: The Chinese University Press.

Koo, R., & Ma, H. T. (Eds.). (1994). *Macau education: Continuity and change*. Macau: Macau Foundation. (In Chinese).

Lau, S. K. (1982). *Society and politics in Hong Kong*. Hong Kong: The Chinese University Press.

Lau, S. K., & Kuan, H. C. (1988). *The ethos of the Hong Kong Chinese*. Hong Kong: The Chinese University Press.

Lee, S. M. (1987). Political education and civic education: The British perspective and Hong Kong perspective. *International Journal of Educational Development*, *7*(4), 251–263.

Leung, S. W. (1997). *The making of an alienated generation: The political socialization of secondary school students in transitional Hong Kong*. Aldershot, UK: Ashgate.

Lo, S. H. (1995). *Political development in Macau*. Hong Kong: The Chinese University Press.

Marshall, T. H. (1950). *Citizenship and social class and other essays*. Cambridge, UK: Cambridge University Press.

Miners, N. J. (1996). *The government and politics of Hong Kong* (5th ed.). Hong Kong: Oxford University Press.

Morris, P. (1988). The effect on the school curriculum of Hong Kong's return to Chinese sovereignty in 1997. *Journal of Curriculum Studies*, *20*(6), 509–520.

Morris, P. (1992a). The context of curriculum development in Hong Kong: Problems and possibilities (Occastional Paper No. 7). In *Curriculum development in Hong Kong* (2nd ed., pp. 4–22). Hong Kong: Faculty of Education, University of Hong Kong.

Morris, P. (1992b). Preparing pupils as citizens of the special administrative region: Curriculum change and control during the transitional period. In *Curriculum development in Hong Kong* (2nd ed., pp. 120–143). Hong Kong: Faculty of Education, University of Hong Kong.

Morris, P. (1997). Civics and citizenship education in Hong Kong. In K. J. Kennedy (Ed.), *Citizenship education and the modern state* (pp. 107–125). London: Falmer.

Morris, P., & Chan, K. K. (1997). The Hong Kong school curriculum and the political transition: Politicisation, contextualisation and symbolic action. In M. Bray & W. O. Lee (Eds.), *Education and political transitions: Implications of Hong Kong's change of sovereignty* (pp. 101–118). Hong Kong: Comparative Education Research Centre, The University of Hong Kong.

Morris, P., & Morris, E. (2000). Constructing the good citizen in Hong Kong: Values promoted in the school curriculum. *Asia Pacific Journal of Education, 20*(1), 36–52.

Morris, P., & Sweeting, A. (1992). Education and politics: The case of Hong Kong from an historical perspective. In *Curriculum development in Hong Kong* (2nd ed., pp. 144–183). Hong Kong: Faculty of Education, University of Hong Kong.

Scott, I. (1989). *Political change and the crisis of legitimacy in Hong Kong*. London: Hurst.

Sweeting, A. E. (1992). Hong Kong education within historical processes. In G. A. Postiglions (Ed.), *Education and society in Hong Kong: Approaching 1997*. Hong Kong: Hong Kong University Press.

Tsang, W. K. (1984). Review and prospect of the political education in Hong Kong. *Hong Kong Economic Journal*, *8*(5), 34–40. (In Chinese).

Tsang, W. K. (1994). Decolonized citizenship education: A framework of post 1997 Hong Kong school's civic education. *Journal of Education*, *22*(2), 237–248. (In Chinese).

Tsang, W. K. (1998). Patronage, domestification, or empowerment? Citizenship development and citizenship education in Hong Kong. In O. Ichilov (Ed.), *Citizenship and education in a changing world*. London: Woburn Press.

Tse, K. C. (1997a). *The poverty of political education in Hong Kong secondary schools* (occasional paper). Hong Kong: Hong Kong Institute of Asian-Pacific Studies, The Chinese University of Hong Kong.

Tse, K. C. (1997b). *Preparing students for citizenship? Civic education in Hong Kong secondary schools*. Unpublished doctoral dissertation, Department of Sociology, The University of Warwick, England.

Tse, K. C. (1997c). Social subjects and civic education in secondary schools. *New Horizons in Education*, *38*, 10–14. (In Chinese).

Tse, K. C. (1999a). A comparative study of civic education in four Chinese societies: Chinese Mainland, Taiwan, Hong Kong and Macau. *Educational Journal*, *26* (2), *27*(1), 179–200. Hong Kong: Hong Kong Institute of Educational Research, The Chinese University of Hong Kong. (In Chinese).

Tse, K. C. (1999b). Civic and political education. In M. Bray & R. Koo (Eds.), *Education and society in Hong Kong and Macau: Comparative perspectives on continuity and change* (pp. 151–169). Hong Kong: Comparative Education Research Centre, The University of Hong Kong.

Tse, K. C. (2000). Deformed citizenship: A critique of the junior secondary economic and public affairs syllabus and textbooks in Hong Kong. *Pedagogy, Culture and Society* (formerly *Curriculum Studies*), *8*(1), 93–110.

Whitty, G. (1985). *Sociology and school knowledge: Curriculum theory, research and politics*. London: Methuen.

Whitty, G., & Young, M. (Eds.). (1976). *Explorations in the politics of school knowledge*. Driffield, UK: Nafferton Books.

Wong, H. K. (Ed.). (1991). *Education reform in Macau*. Macau: Centre of Macau studies, University of East Asia.

Wong, H. K. (1992). *Civic education in Macau*. Macau: Centre of Macau studies, University of Macau.

Wong, P. M. (1981). *The Civic education and the curriculum of the subject 'Economics and Public Affairs' in Hong Kong after World War II: A comparative perspective*. Unpublished master's thesis, Faculty of Education, The Chinese University of Hong Kong. (In Chinese).

Wong, P. M. (1983). What kind of 'Hong Kong citizen' does the EPA curriculum produce? *Ming Pao Monthly*, *18*(12), 56–59. (In Chinese).

Yee, H., Liu, B. L., & Ngo, T. W. (1993a). *The Political culture of the Macau Chinese*. Macau: Macau Foundation. (In Chinese).

Yee, H., Liu, B. L., & Ngo, T. W. (1993b). Macau's mass political culture. *Asian Journal of Public Administration*, *15*(2), 177–200.

Young, M. F. D. (Ed.). (1971). *Knowledge and control: New directions for the sociology of education*. London: Collier-Macmillan.

CHAPTER 15

Values Education in Thailand: Preparation for Globalization

Kriengsak Chareonwongsak

Abstract

In the push for globalization, especially in developing countries, national development planners have paid insufficient attention to one area, namely, values development. Many countries, including Thailand, have failed to establish clear policy and strategies for the development of the values necessary for success in globalization. To have an ongoing program of developing human resources, the education system is the best channel for inculcating the appropriate values in students and general citizens alike. This paper argues that values education must become the cornerstone of all education in Thailand. That is, values education must become compulsory for every student at all levels, thereby securing Thailand's future as a nation.

The first section of this paper defines the phrase "values education" in light of traditional and current literature. Rokeach's system of classifying values (1973) is used as the foundation for proposing changes to Thailand's values education system. Then, the author gives a brief history of values education in Thailand from a sociopolitical/cultural perspective. The section outlining Thailand's current values education programs includes an analysis of its most relevant problems. The next section outlines the effects of globalization on values education in Thailand. In the future, Thai values education will be required to meet the following needs: (1) to produce personnel who can meet the demands of the new labour market; (2) to create a higher awareness of other cultures and values; (3) to bring balanced development between knowledge and values; (4) to become more contemporary; (5) to combat the dissemination of improper foreign values; and (6) to select and teach positive Thai values. The fourth section of this paper delineates necessary changes in Thailand's values education system. Changes include: (1) deciding which values are preferred; (2) encoding these values within a curriculum; (3) developing a methodology for values teaching; (4) developing values education teachers; (5) developing an evaluation system, and; (6) distributing the responsibility for developing values to various institutions within society. Finally, the author recommends various changes in policy including: (1) creating strong policy that would ensure the nurturing of preferred values in students and; (2) engaging in values education research.

Introduction

Many countries are preparing themselves for the inevitable onslaught of globalization. A quick survey of the development plans of many nations, Thailand included, reveals an emphasis on economic liberalisation and national economic development strategies, steps that would enable these countries to tap into the benefits of globalization. In other cases, education has been stressed as a key factor in developing the knowledge, abilities and professional skills required for sustainable human development in the global labour marketplace. Political agendas are being directed towards co-operation, preserving human liberties and reducing global conflict. In the social sphere, development aims at building quality people and civil societies. The development of information systems is being emphasised for its role in enhancing global interconnectedness. Even environmental concern has evolved into a global endeavour.

However, national development planners have paid insufficient attention to one area, namely, values development. Many countries, notwithstanding Thailand, have failed to establish clear policy and strategies to develop the values necessary for successful integration into a globalized world. As a result, development efforts are unbalanced; emphasis is placed on developing other sectors while ignoring what could be considered the foundation of all other development. Without strong values, economic, political and other forms of development will flounder.

Thailand is one of the many nations that do not give enough attention to values development. Even though the country has extensive policies aimed at boosting the nation's ability to compete in a global context, yet these plans will never be realised without wholesome values. Thailand faces a plethora of problems caused on the one hand by the inability of its people to adapt sufficiently to extensive changes wrought by globalization while on the other hand, many Thais are forsaking traditional values and assimilating globally disseminated Western values, some of which are inappropriate, too quickly. Attacks from both of these directions reflect the immense impact globalization will have on Thailand. The nation is facing a most formidable challenge as her people lack strong foundational values that will equip them to withstand or adapt to changes appropriately.

Anthropologists and sociologists believe that the progress of every nation is correlated with the quality of its culture and values (Komin, 1983). Values are a catalyst for human behaviour and will eventually determine the direction of a society. Thus, if a country adopts inappropriate values, the quality of its people will decline and the stability of the nation will be jeopardised. Thus, it is necessary to develop appropriate values that will help Thailand to develop the human resources it needs to face the challenges of globalization.

To create an ongoing program of developing human resources, education is the best channel for inculcating the appropriate values in students and general citizens alike. The task of nurturing proper moral values must not be left to families or to social mechanisms alone. These two sectors cannot cover the full range of new experiences Thais will encounter within the global context; thus, both formal and non-formal education must be used to instil more than knowledge, abilities and professional skills in students. The ability to face every situation — even the unexpected, abnormal and perhaps even threatening, brought by globalization — with strong, appropriate and right responses can only be taught by values education. Values education will eventually determine the success of an individual, society and nation in managing the transition to a global world. Thus, this paper argues that values education must become the cornerstone of all education in Thailand, that is, values education must become compulsory for every student at all levels. In this way, as Thai teachers shape the character of their students through values education, they will enhance Thailand's ability to succeed in the future.

If values education is to be effective in engineering change within Thai society, it must extend throughout the entire schooling process. It must begin at the point of the child's earliest educational experience and continue until the latest possible opportunity for formalised input, usually at the point of graduation from secondary school. Values are shaped during the primary levels and are seasoned during the secondary school adolescent years, from 13 to 18. The primary years are when the decisions, goals and ideals that will govern the rest of people's lives are incubated. It is also the stage when ethical reasoning skills are developed and lifetime moral paradigms are established (Kohlberg, 1969). Thus, the most important time to impart correct values that will determine the quality of the citizens in society and eventually the success of the nation is during the whole duration of a child's formal education process. Thus, the future of Thailand will be determined by the values nurtured in the lives of its primary and secondary students.

Definition

Values education may be understood from a number of different perspectives. Smith and Montgomery (1996) define it as "… an explicit attempt to teach about values and/or valuing." Huitt (1997) states values education is generally understood to be an individual element of school life or the curriculum, involving examination and communication of an explicit set of values. For this paper, values education is defined as an explicit attempt to teach about values to the students through the educational system in both formal and non-formal education settings using various channels of the educational system. School policies for the development of values must include provision for a curriculum, books, pedagogy, facilitating teachers to become good role models, a positive school atmosphere and examinations. This paper does not include a discussion of concepts such as character training or moral education, although moral, character and ethical training can be subsumed within the framework of values education.

Classification

Currently, values have been classified by academics from different schools in many ways. This paper applies Rokeach's classification (Rokeach, 1973) as a study framework of and for analysis and strategic planning for Thai values education. This tries to make this research insightful and speedy. Rokeach developed a system to classify values as either instrumental or terminal, as follows:

1. Instrumental values are preferred personal behaviours that can be described in the following two ways:
   1.1 A moral value is a behavioural norm or common sense. It helps determine whether something is right or wrong, proper or improper. It is a value that involves consideration of other people. Examples of moral values are faithfulness, responsibility, mercy (compassion), and so forth.
   1.2 Competence or self-actualisation is a value that enables an

individual to have the ability to succeed at something by him/herself, a value that is not necessarily related to ethics.

2. Terminal values refer to the goals, end-points or target values towards which human beings strive. Terminal values are of two types:
   2.1 Personal values — these are the moral goals towards which individuals strive, for example, religious experience, wisdom, and so forth.
   2.2 Social values — the moral end-points towards which societies aim, for example equality, national security, and so forth.

The author will use Rokeach's framework, but not his lists of values, to develop a set of preferred values for Thailand.

History of Values Education in Thailand

Factors That Influenced the Development of Thai Values Education in the Past

Buddhism

Thailand is an intensely religious nation. Most Thais adhere to Buddhism and about 95% of all Thai citizens experience a Buddhist upbringing. In the earliest years of their life, children are taught Buddhist values in their homes, in temples and at schools. Even history is taught from the perspective of the development of the Buddhist religion. Thus, since the "Tai" people migrated south from China along the Mekong River in the 12th century, Buddhism has been the major determiner of norms within Thai society. As a result, values education, in both formalised and informal education settings, from antiquity to the present has been derived mainly from Buddhist principles having a heavy focus on ethical values, including faithfulness, unity, mercy, kindness, helpfulness and gratefulness.

Feudalism

Historical records and archaeological finds indicate that, shortly after inception, Thai society was feudal in nature. Even though Thai culture is over 800 years old, feudalism still plays an important role in determining many values within the modern Thai context. These values include the practice of glorifying those who are powerful or have high social status, the acceptance of governments that impose rather than grant people freedom to express their opinions, the preference to be under the leadership of a government and to rely on leaders instead of being self-initiating, and so on.

These socially accepted values have heavily influenced Thailand's education system and, because they are derived from feudal values, many of them have hindered the development of a modern values education program in Thailand. For instance, one obsolete value that hinders development is the practice of teacher-centred teaching. Students are taught to suppress their opinions and to accept teacher assertions without question. Thus, the Thai education system emphasizes rote learning and complete acquiescence with teachers rather than rational analysis and individual creativity.

This strongly affects the development of values education as students are given no basis for understanding and, thus, have no opportunity to acquire the strong values necessary to manage the day-to-day pressures associated with increasing globalization. Moreover, the education system has seen the mutation and perversion of some traditional values to the point that they are worse than the original feudal concepts from which there were derived. Such is the case of authoritarianism, which in its modern derivation permits the promotion of inequality and favouritism within society. Values education is required to help Thai students distinguish between helpful and harmful traditional values.

Agricultural System

Thai society is rooted in its farms and agrarian traditions. This is why Thai people feel a close bond with nature. Work schedules are arranged according to seasonal cycles, nature is treated as a close relative or family member, and thus agriculture is conducted so as to create no conflicts with this earthy sibling. Various values have evolved from such cultural conceptions, for example moral dictums that encourage people to be helpful and kind to others. Time is conceptualised as part of the natural cycles that cannot be controlled; thus the Thai culture places a lower emphasis on punctuality than Western practice does. The atmosphere in Thai workplaces is expected to be congenial and family-like. In general, most Thais carry a sense of sufficiency about their own lives, no matter how little they may have, but at the same time they are willing to work to resolve critical problems.

In Thailand's education system, some values — such as being helpful and preserving the spirit of brotherhood — are derived from social values of past societies. Yet, other values — such as the value for punctuality, which was introduced to the elementary school curriculum in 1978 revised in 1990

(Department of Curriculum and Instruction Development, 1981, rev. ed., 1990) — have been implemented in an effort to embrace modernity.

Superstition

A strong adherence to the superstitious has inculcated the fear of sicknesses, natural disasters, ghosts and so on into the public mindset. Thais believe they must appease the spirits of ancestors and nature in order to receive protection from disasters. As a result, superstition takes a surprisingly conspicuous role in society, even in prominent political, business and social functions.

To change superstitious beliefs, King Rama V (reigning from 1868 to 1910) instituted a values education that emphasised self-reliance, social progress and self-determination. Even with a history such as this, Thailand still has far to go before values education can be used as a positive force to change harmful social values and to replace them with wholesome ones.

Assimilation of Foreign Culture

With highly developed links in communication, transportation and international trade systems brought about by modernisation of the country, Thai society has assimilated many foreign cultural values, especially those from western nations. Some of these values, such as the value of free thought and expression, the value of seeking knowledge and so on, would be appropriate for Thai values education.

At the same time, others of these so-called "international" values — such as free sexual expression, indulgence in material goods and consumerism produce confusion and damage society. Just as traditional Thai values shaped past and present societies, new incoming values will have an equal power to determine present and future conditions within Thai society. This realisation will be a fundamental element in setting the direction of values education in the current period.

The Development of Thai Values Education in the Past

Thai values education may be divided into four main periods, each distinguished by prominent characteristics, as follows:

The Pre-1870 Period

It occurred at the beginning of King Rama V's reign. At that time, Thai values education placed a heavy emphasis on morals, mostly because education in the Thai society of that time occurred in the temples where monks played a role similar to that of teachers. The curriculum concentrated heavily on studies of Buddhist scriptures and moral precepts. Education occurred in homes, in the palace and in a small number of private schools. During this time, values education stressed values such as loving the king, honouring the religion and defending the nation. These values were important in an age when the threat of foreign invasion and war were real. Politics and government administration were taught to male students. This value remains prominent within the psyche of the average Thai. Recent surveys of Thai values conducted in 1981 and 1987 rank national security as the top public concern (Komin, 1990).

The 1870–1931 Period

It encompasses the mid and latter portions of King Rama V's reign until just before Thailand's reformation when the absolute reign of the king was peaceably replaced by a constitutional monarchy. During this period, the education system continued to affirm values education as a foundation stone of society. However, the teaching of values within the education system became more formalised as a result of King Rama V's important education reforms. He structured Thailand's education system, sent top students abroad to further their education, allowed missionaries to open schools and abolished slavery. At this point values education, or what would be more accurately understood as moral education, was implemented as a formal part of the curriculum.

At the same time, imperial forces were invading the surrounding nations. In 1893, when British forces directly invaded Thailand (Mulasilp, 1973), the values emphasised in the education system began to place more weight on the aspect of seeking of knowledge. However, the change was not very significant.

An Overlap Period Between 1905 and 1977

Significant political changes were introduced in Thailand during this period. Thailand officially became a constitutional monarchy in 1932 and the country embraced modernisation. According to the first National Economic and Social Development Plan (NESDP) created during that period, moral education still held precedence within the education system. However, added components stressed good citizenship, good family relations, communication, country, religion, the king and the law.

Political rather than educational changes helped to shift the focus of values education during this time. The push to give ruling power to the citizens brought democracy as a value into the classroom. Intensive efforts were extended to help people understand how to participate in governing their country. Values education was used to nurture the belief in individual freedoms and rights and help people to see the importance of equality of the individual. Values development during that time helped to advance the people's understanding and acceptance of democracy. Despite the significance and intensity of the shift, values education was not able to transfer the principles and practices of true democracy to the average Thai citizen (Pongpeaw & Sukatipant, 1983). Very little occurred during this period in terms of values education development.

From 1978 to the Present

The Thai government introduced a new curriculum, one that is still being used at present. During the last period, from 1978 to the present values education courses have been formally offered at both the primary and secondary school levels. Modest improvements were made to the values education curriculum in 1990, and, as a result, people became more aware of the issues involved in values education. With increasing globalization, Thais began to realise how modernisation and the information age could destroy their culture and society. However, the youth and the population in general, naively embraced Western values that were, in many cases, radically different and even dangerous. For example, Thai youth began to adopt improper sexual values, to hold imported famous brand name commodities in esteem, to overspend and to glorify inter-gang aggression. As well, during this period, the government began to name the specifics it wished to nurture in its youth. Thailand's 6th NESDP 1986–1990 placed significant stress on teaching children good values and conduct. In addition, the government proclaimed five basic values as being national values. Thus, values education experienced significant development in Thailand during this period.

An awareness of values education spread through society. The Department of Curriculum and Instruction Development as well as various other governmental agencies began to conduct values-based research on Thai children. Experts from overseas were invited to help develop values education courses (Department of Curriculum and Instruction Development, 1978, rev. ed., 1984). Yet, despite the high level of activity and public awareness, there were no significant changes in the values education offered in primary and secondary school courses. After Thailand's economy crashed in 1997, values education was only spasmodically mentioned in national development plans.

Thai Values Education at Present

Curriculum

In Thailand values are taught at the primary school level in what are called "character development classes" which include instruction in the Thai language. In these classes, values are a clearly emphasised component of the curriculum. At the secondary level, values are taught as a part of "social education classes," which include training in religion and citizenship. Values education is encouraged in other subject areas; however, the study of values at the secondary level is not delineated as clearly as it is at the primary level.

To gain a clear perspective of values education in Thailand, it is possible to focus on three key policy documents that outline values education at the primary level (Department of Curriculum and Instruction Development, 1978, rev. ed., 1990), at the lower secondary level (Department of Curriculum and Instruction Development, 1981a, rev. ed., 1990) and at upper secondary level (Department of Curriculum and Instruction Development, 1981c, rev. ed., 1990). These documents will form the main framework for this discussion of the processes, the procedures and the trends in values education within Thailand's present education system. Evaluation of the goals and structure of these documents will highlight trends in course structure, aims and definitions of topics within values education. After studying these documents, the researcher made the following observations.

Values education at the primary level. The goal of values education is clearly defined as the practice of developing the attitudes and practices of seeking knowledge and being diligent, persistent, frugal, faithful, disciplined, loyal, compassionate and caring. In addition, the values of obeying parents, being punctual, seeking unity, being just, adhering to cultural practices, loving work and being committed to national security are listed. Specific values are highlighted for each grade level.

Values education at the secondary level. Contrary to values education at the primary level, the researcher found there was no specification as to the type and scope of values that would be developed in students at each level of their secondary school experience. However, the curriculum planners tried to integrate values education into the various subject syllabi (but did not clearly state the details about which or what values in each subject). Specified values included religious-devotion, commitment to national security, the love of working, devotion to society, sense of belongingness to the same home town, pride in being a Thai, reasonableness, creativity, esteem for national resources and preference for democratic values. If we compare this list of values with Rokeach's classification of values, we will see that these are mostly what he would identify as terminal values. However, values education at the secondary level stresses the development and enhancement of a greater awareness of other people and of the society. For example, in trying to develop pride in being a Thai citizen, students are encouraged to be devoted to their society and to treat all other people equally.

Because the values education curriculum at the secondary level is vague, values education instructors are unclear as to their roles and goals in teaching values education. Thus, many view values education as merely a transfer of knowledge. As a result, students misunderstand or misinterpret the goals of values education and remain uncertain as to how wholesome values can contribute towards nation building. An unclear values education curriculum also makes it difficult for teachers to find appropriate course textbooks, to plan lessons, to assign extra readings, to create classroom activities and to assign homework assignments, and so forth.

In conclusion, using Rokeach's categorisations of values, Thai values education at the primary level would be assessed as having a heavy focus on the development of instrumental rather than terminal values. In instrumental values, there is an emphasis on moral focus at the expense of competence or self-actualisation. At the secondary level, Thai values education does not have the same clarity, with a heavy focus on the development of terminal rather than instrumental values.

Teaching and Learning Styles

Rote memorisation. In Thailand, values education still relies heavily on rote memorisation and dictated class notes. Values education instructor manuals and textbooks fail to give teachers enough information to help students exercise their analytical abilities. Ethics classes are traditionally a test of how well a student can memorise difficult words and difficult texts (Kohlberg, 1964). Thai values education does not promote the exercise of student reasoning abilities to a high enough degree. Thailand's Education Research and Planning Division (1982) determined that students lacked the ability to reason analytically. Thus, traditional Thai study methods do not support the development of complex cognitive abilities in students. Yet, to understand and succeed in an increasingly globalized world, it is vital that Thai young people be able to make correct choices and to discern correctly the difference between right and wrong. Kohlberg states that values education is most effective when combined with ethics education. Anunthavorasakul's research (1996) on the conditions and problems of Buddhism classes in secondary schools, shows that learners reported and found that a sometimes weak or repetitive curriculum caused boredom and a lack of analytical thinking exercises in these courses. So, teaching of Thai values in the described way does not try to cultivate learners who use rationality in making decisions — till they understand, realize the real value and apply it in practice. In this way, current Thai values education in Thailand does little more than transfer knowledge about values rather than ensure that the students have themselves adopted the values.

Little integration into other subject areas. Touinpak (1978, rev. ed., 1990, 1996) found that values education at the primary level occurred most often in character development classes because these classes focus directly on ethical issues. Values education was sometimes inserted into another class called "life-experience class" or into Thai language classes. But English, mathematics or science classes are hardly ever concerned with values education at all. The same pattern occurs in teaching at the secondary school level. Here, values education occurred most often in social studies classes and Thai language classes, but English, mathematics or science classes ignored values education issues altogether.

Tools and media are inadequate or unavailable. Tools and media usage are an important factor governing the success of values education as they help students to understand abstract concepts in concrete terms. However, because schools lack sufficient media (Education Research and Planning Division, 1982), teachers of other subjects — especially those considered "core" — are given a higher priority for the use of media resources. Also, some teachers are not trained in the use of the more modern teaching technologies and require "media-tech" training. Because of this, teachers will often fit values education into any place in their teaching plan, meaning values education does not receive a regular time period in which to be taught. As a result, few students are given consistent values education training.

Teachers

A slant attention to realize the importance of values education. This problem does not exist at the primary level as clear objectives and standards are set describing the expected role of teachers. The content of character development classes, including clearly identifiable values education, is explicitly described in the curriculum. But at the secondary level, there are no specific objectives or suggested methodologies established for values education teachers. At the upper secondary levels, students also focus on the subjects required for university entrance examinations. As a consequence, teachers tend to focus only on ensuring their students will have the knowledge and information required to pass their examinations. This is evidence that many upper secondary teachers fail to realise the importance of values education, resulting in values education being neglected or given a lower priority in Thai secondary schools.

Inadequate knowledge and understanding in teaching values education. When teaching values education, teachers must understand the concepts, curricula and even more importantly, the nature of the students in their classes. However, many Thai values education teachers lack an intimate understanding of the psychological make-up of their students (Charoenying, Pantumanawin, & Prachonpajjanuek, 1979). Values education teachers do not know how to transfer upright ethics and morals to the lives of their students (Amornwiwat, 1987) who must increasingly deal with global issues. To compound the problem, many values education teachers do not know how to evaluate the students involved in values education classes (Silpanilmalaya, n.d.) and, as a result, very little evaluation occurs in values education classrooms (Department of Curriculum and Instruction Department, 1990).

Inadequate critical teaching techniques and skills in teaching values education. Even in the larger city schools, few teachers have been properly trained to teach values education. In primary schools, values education class often consists of long explanations by the teacher and few opportunities for students to ask questions or to express their opinions (Anunthavorasakul, 1996). In some cases, absenteeism of teachers is a chronic problem. Research conducted by Thailand's Department of Curriculum and Instruction Development (1995) found that the reason why students do not want to study values education was because the teachers lacked a proper pedagogical foundation for values education and thus lacked the ability to create interesting lessons (Teachers Council of Thailand, 1990). Because few pre-service teachers specialised in values education, the report noted that many schools lack a consistent and quality values education system. Even if teachers did have the proper training and background in values education, often they are overloaded with other classes and do not have the time to develop quality values education classes, especially at the secondary level. As a result, few teachers can develop values education to the point that it can be used to facilitate sustained national development.

At present, values education does not fulfill its potential of helping students gain the knowledge and wisdom they require for strong and wholesome lives in a constantly mutating global context.

Values Education Materials

Inconsistency of values education materials. Because values education is a foundation for the nurture not only of wholesome students but also of a stable nation, the policies, curricula, teaching manuals, books and all other values education documents must be methodologically organised, not just within each grade level, but also within the whole system. A methodologically ordered system of values education must be created that would begin at the first grade and extend to the twelfth. However, in reality, values education curricula, teaching manuals, textbooks and student workbooks do not flow in a concordant direction. Upon examining values education documents, a lack of unified objectives was observed. For example, Touinpak (1978, rev. ed., 1990, 1996) found widely diverse values education content in the curricular materials, textbooks, and other materials used at the primary level. For example, textbooks contained a strong emphasis on ethical issues but a weaker emphasis was found in the curriculum. Much emphasis was placed on a limited range of issues that could be covered in values education such as "sacrificing" for others, being kind, grateful, merciful and supporting the group, while ignoring other equally important values education issues. As a result, teachers given the responsibility for teaching values education lacked a clear understanding of values education objectives. Curricular manuals did not emphasise a full scope of values or lacked sufficient pedagogical description required to teach values education soundly. In other cases, because of this lack, some values education teachers created their own values education materials and manuals, but ignored whatever values education curricula and instructions were given in prescribed materials from the Ministry of Education. As a result, teachers do not follow the objectives established in the curriculum or may skip one portion of the curriculum because it does not match the media they want to use in their values education classes.

Contents for Values Education Courses

Repetition in course contents. In order to propose changes to the instruction of Buddhism and to make it an important means of values education in Thailand, UarFuah (1991) conducted a thorough evaluation of Thailand's values education system. His survey of teachers and secondary students in Bangkok found that there was much repetition in the content of Buddhism classes — a finding which coincides with Anunthavorasakul's findings (1996) who studied the conditions and problems of Buddhism classes in secondary schools and found that the curriculum must be improved and repetition eliminated as it can cause boredom to the students.

Students

A study was conducted to evaluate the quality of secondary students in 1995 (Office of Education Assessment and Testing Services, Department of Curriculum and Institution Development, 1995). The researchers polled a sample group of 97,000 secondary students and 95,394 primary students to determine the morals and the values of these students in 1996. Students were assessed as to their willingness to sacrifice for others, their social development, their responsibility, discipline and willingness to demonstrate unity. Each value was assigned four levels according to the intensity of feelings displayed by each student. The four levels were: (1) perceive the value; (2) willingness to accept the value; (3) see the advantages of this value; and (4) believe strongly in this value. The study measured the percentage of students who displayed each value at each level of intensity. It was discovered that the majority of students fell in the third level of intensity for all the values. The researchers concluded that the present values education system in Thailand would not produce students who had fourth level moral development.

Thus, despite Thailand's long history of values education, it remains weak, being characterised by an incomplete and incoherent values education program, especially at the upper levels.

The Effects of Globalization on Values Education in Thailand

Rapidly encroaching global values have caused considerable change within Thai society. Yet, despite the attractiveness of modern education technology and possibilities offered by sophisticated distance media, education policy makers must acknowledge the value of values education above that of modern communications, transportation and trade systems. All will eventually be affected by the presence or absence of quality values education in Thailand.

Globalization will affect values education in Thailand in the following ways:

1. Thai values education will be required to produce personnel who can meet the demands of the new labour market

Even though many companies in Thailand, especially those owned by foreign interests, will lack workers who are sufficiently fluent in the technology skills and global know-how, yet the work environment in these companies will demand more than skills alone. Globally-oriented companies will demand workers who have the personal values that will enable them to facilitate peaceful working relationships in intensive workplace conditions. Thai workers will need to adopt values that are more consistent with those held by foreign co-workers. Thus, greater instrumental values (competence or self actualization) — such as open-mindedness, high proficiency, creativity and leadership skills — are needed, not only values with a moral focus, which are already strong in Thai values education. As a result, education institutes should be more active and pay more attention to producing personnel with appropriate values who can meet the demands of competitive global workplaces.

2. Thai values education will be required to create a higher awareness of other cultures and values

The network of the world-wide web has resulted in the widespread distribution of information and cultural values. As a result, Thais must expose themselves to other cultures in order to communicate, to do business or to co-operate intelligibly in a way that will bring mutual gain.

As Thais become more cross-culturally competent, the scope of Thai values education will change. Thais must first learn how to relate to those in different regions within their own nation and then to master the ability to form congenial relationships with people in neighbouring and distant countries. Because of this, the Thai education system must train students to think of themselves as global learners and to view the world as their classroom. In this sense, values education must equip Thais to interact wisely in the global context.

3. Thai values education will be required to bring balanced development between knowledge and values

In order to handle the demands of globalization, Thai leaders are pushing for an education system that can help the nation develop advanced knowledge and technologies. To do this, policy makers are emphasising Thailand's need to become a nation of learners. Furthermore, because of the glamour associated with high technology as well as the Thai penchant for embracing technology without considering its long-term impact on the culture, any additional educational development funds are unlikely to be invested in values education.

Globalization sometimes produces an "overboard" effect, where, if values education does exist, the new values of globalization are emphasised while traditional Thai values, even desirable ones, are ignored. For example, individualism, post-modernism and rationalism are stressed at the expense of traditional Thai values that esteem communitarianism, truth and religious belief. So, even when modern innovations are imported from the West, Thais are unable to use them wisely to bring long-term sustainable advantage to the nation. Thus, meeting the challenges of democracy cannot be equated with embracing high technology alone. The development of strong and wholesome values must run concurrent with every technological advance.

4. Thai values education will be required to become more contemporary

Developments in the fields of economics, society, politics and the environment have accelerated changes in the world. At the same time, current values education in Thailand continues its short-sighted focus on the issues, traditions and methodology of the past. For example, values education courses do not deal with current issues such as the modern lifestyles depicted in music, videos and movies, how to adapt to the pressures of megalopolis living nor how to find a personal identity in an increasingly alienated society (Chareonwongsak, 1998). Values education classes that focus only on developing inner moral attributes and do not deal with real world issues confronting Thai youth, seem to be irrelevant and thus not worthy of attention. Many students are "bored with the old style of values teaching, making them perceive their values classes as boring." Thai values education must address contemporary issues or it will hold no value in preparing a people who can relate to the world around them.

5. Thai values education will be required to combat the dissemination of improper foreign values

The influx of culture and values from foreigners, especially those from the West, is a current difficult to resist because it flows via the information network, which is increasingly effortless and cheap enough to access.

Changing social structures and values have meant that family units are divided. Because living alone is now an accepted practice, young people are separated from the positive influence of other family members. Many experiment with and embrace unfamiliar mores they observe in the popular culture. Parents have no time to take care of their children and to teach them proper values. As such, students are increasingly conditioned to accept improper sexual values, homosexual lifestyles, pre-nuptial co-habitation, the use of dangerous drugs — all practices that do not exist within the traditional Thai cultural framework. In the past, strong homogenous social values helped determine values formation and resultant behaviour choices in Thai society. Now, even some Thai teachers have incorporated improper Western values in their teaching. These mentioned items are disputed widely in every domain of Thai education, and an endeavour to find solutions has been made.

6. Thai values education will be required to select and teach positive Thai values

To enable Thais to understand and judge correctly the global culture into which Thailand is quickly stepping, values education must select the best global values and then teach students how to integrate them with the strongest Thai values. In this way, Thai citizens can be equipped to face the challenges of globalization while, at the same time, not lose the strength of their cultural roots. With this type of mandate, education institutions not only have to ensure that students hold to wholesome traditional values, they must discern which values from both the Thai and the global contexts are best able to help students face the challenges of the future. Unprofitable Thai values should not be advocated in values education classes. Also, instead of seeing globalization and western culture as threats, Thai values education must take the best values and use them to train the future generation of Thais to lead in the global context. In this sense, values education is neither fully traditional nor fully modern.

Globalization will re-shape the essence and expressions of Thai culture to a significant degree. If Thai students are left to their own devices to resolve the bewildering array of issues thrown at them in the mass media, the whole Thai society and the future of the nation could be seriously compromised. Thus educators in Thailand must remedy the lack of sufficient values education as soon as possible. Instead of allowing globalization to control the destiny of Thailand, values education must be employed to "inoculate" Thai youth against harmful foreign values. If strengthened, Thailand's values education could eventually stand as a model for other societies who want to mould a body of strong citizens able to direct the flow of globalization instead of being swamped by it.

Reforming Values Education in Thailand

The following are steps required to reform values education in Thailand.

1. Decide Which Values Are Preferred

1.1. Evaluate the values

The following criteria may be used to evaluate values and determine which ones will give Thailand the optimum advantage from a long-term, macro point of view:

Values that encompass every dimension of both domestic and global existence: A complete set of values should be identified that would allow people to manage every situation and circumstance: their personal as well as their social affairs as well as circumstances involving complex moral issues.

Values that reap mutual advantage for oneself, others, society and the world: "Equality" and "fairness" are not defined as everyone sharing all advantages equally, but instead individual members of society receiving enough so that, on the whole, optimum benefits are achieved for the entire society.

Values that are contemporary: These are values that are appropriate to as many people, at as many times and in as many places as possible.

Values appropriate to the local context: Values education must be adapted to the geographical, economic, social and cultural contexts of the local people groups.

After preferable values are identified, they can be ranked as to how well they will contribute towards the end goal of producing sustained human development in Thailand.

1.2. Select the most appropriate values

Using Rokeach's classification system (see "Definition and Classification"), lists of the most preferred values were created. These values had been highlighted in key literature as necessary for Thailand's long-term viability within the global context.

The eight moral values from Rokeach's list of instrumental values most necessary for Thailand's future viability include gratefulness (Laykarpan, 1988; Ministry of Education, 1986; Sunyawiwat, 1984), courage (Huitt, 1992; Laykarpan, 1988; Whetzel, 1992), honesty/sincerity (Sunyawiwat, 1984; Whetzel, 1992), responsiblility (Council for Global Education, 1997; Huitt, 1992; Jarolimek, 1971; The Office of National Culture Commission, Research and Planning Division, 1987; Whetzel, 1992), humor (Thepsitha, 1990), kindness/helpfulness (Ministry of Education; Smith & Montgomery, 1996; Thepsitha, 1990), justice (Council for Global Education, 1997; Kohlberg, 1969) and self-discipline (King Bhumiphol Adulyadej, 1982; Ministry of Education, 1978, rev. ed., 1984, 1989; The Office of National Culture Commission, Research and Planning Division, 1987).

The instrumental values identified as best leading towards competence and self-actualisation included the values of independence (Ministry of Education, 1989; The Office of National Culture Commission, Research and Planning Division, 1987; Smith & Montgomery, 2000), responsiveness to new situations (Meesook, 1990; Rossiter, 1999; Sungkrit & Noi-suwan, 1992), proficiency (Thepsitha, 1990), ambition/industriousness (Ministry of Education, 1989), creativity (Department of Curriculum and Instruction Development, 1981; Jarolimek, 1971; Laykarpan, 1988), and open-mindedness (Leming, 1997; Ministry of Education, 1986; Sunyawiwat, 1984).

Terminal values with a personal focus deemed necessary for Thailand's future strength as a nation included enthusiasm (Laykarpan, 1988), having a religious orientation (Laykarpan, 1988; The Office of National Culture Commission, Research and Planning Division, 1987) and esteem for wisdom/knowledge (Department of General Education, 1986). Terminal values with a social focus that were identified as a commitment to national security (Laykarpan, 1988; The Office of National Culture Commission, Research and Planning Division, 1987), a commitment to equal opportunity within society (The Council for Global Education, 1997) and a commitment to world peace (Majmudar, 1998; Mourine & Moureen, 1985–1986; Sungkrit & Noi-suwan, 1992).

2. Encode These Values Within a Curriculum

The ideal values education curriculum would: (1) establish values education as a separate entity within the curriculum; (2) integrate values education in every subject area; and (3) teach values at every level. Because the psychological, social, moral and other needs of children are different at each age, values education must adapt to the specific characteristics of children at each age level. This curriculum must also integrate values particularly suited to the particular needs of each locality.

3. Develop Appropriate Methodologies

Because values are expressed in terms of the abstract, the methodologies employed in values education are necessarily different from those used in other subject areas. Requisite methodologies for values education in Thailand include the following:

3.1. The ability to use reason to determine upright morals

Developmental psychologists such as Piaget (1932/1962) and Loevinger (1970) were pioneers in the field of moral and rational development. Their methods helped people come to their own conclusions about the ethical values required in various situations. Students must be taught how to test their opinions against others and to refine them until they are wholesome. Students must be taught how to debate issues in small groups, to share their opinions freely and to voice disagreement (Gailbraith & Jones, 1975).

3.2. The ability to analyse

Thai students must be taught how to filter incoming information, to use scientific procedures to make decisions and to develop correct values on their own. In particular, students must be able to determine whether or not a value will reap positive or negative results for Thai society over the long term.

Students can be taught how to: (1) identify conflicting values; (2) analyse all related information in such cases; (3) identify logical fallacies and argue persuasively; (4) make comparisons between arguments; (5) select the values that pass pre-established criteria; and (6) diagnose which values would be best for a given situation.

4. Develop Teachers

The goals of developing values education teachers are to: (1) train teachers how to teach values education; (2) develop information bases required by values education teachers (including course content, teaching tips on how to teach values education to different levels and student types, and methods of assessment); (3) drill teachers in the skills of transmitting positive values to students (e.g. how to use modern media to teach values education, how to be a confidant to students and how to incorporate values education in other types of classes); (4) develop appropriate values in teachers so they can be wholesome role models for students; and (5) rank values into a system of incrementally arranged values. This would help teachers to emphasise appropriate values to students at different levels (Smith & Montgomery, 1996).

5. Develop an Evaluation System

5.1. Values education indicators must be created

An effective values education program requires effective tools to make the process of acquiring strong values a tangible, logical process. Effective values education indicators must: (1) measure all aspects of values education (the students, teachers, curriculum and the school environment); (2) accurately reflect what is being measured; (3) be easily applied; and (4) be flexible in their application to accommodate regional differences in the way values education is taught.

Experts can be invited to participate in the creation and periodic re-evaluation of indicators.

5.2. Produce a values education curriculum, books and other necessary learning tools

The Department of Curriculum and Instruction Development must produce values education manuals and materials for teachers, students and other involved parties.

6. Distribute Responsibilities for Values Education to Various Institutions Within Society

Values education will become more effective when other, outside-of-school channels for learning values are opened.

6.1. Involve families

Give parents advice on how they can become more supportive in their child's process of forming wholesome values.

6.2. Use many different media formats

In modern society, the media are often the most powerful determiners of the ideas, values, attitudes and behaviour of students.

6.3. Take values education into the communities

Communities are the contexts in which students live and are thus also powerful determiners of value.

6.4. Make use of religious organisations

Thailand has many religious organisations for youth. Because most Thais maintain a deep respect for religious values, these institutions can be useful in teaching moral values.

6.5. Benefit from the resources offered by Non-Governmental Organisations (NGOs)

NGOs have the means and the desire to benefit the societies in which they are located. This step would involve: (1) selecting the NGOs offering the strongest benefit in terms of instilling positive values and initiating action in the community; (2) matching each NGO to the most appropriate group of children, for example zoos for younger children and media groups for teenagers; (3) creating co-operative links between NGOs and education institutions; and (4) creating ways for schools to support values development in social institutions, such as sending newsletters to parents or finding ways that schools can help the underprivileged.

Policy Recommendations

1. Create Strong Policy That Would Ensure the Nurturing of Preferred Values in Students

To develop strong values in all students enrolled in Thailand's education system, the government must take a key role in supporting and enforcing values education by establishing policies that will ensure that students are properly prepared for globalization. National values education policies, agendas and goals as well as a clear standard for values education management must be established.

2. Engage in Values Education Research

Research on appropriate values for Thailand is needed to act as a foundation for analysing existing values education and implementing correct directions with the least amount of mistakes. Examples of required values education include the following: future driving forces that will affect values held by Thai society; an analysis of which values would best equip Thailand for globalization; how should each value be taught at each level in such a way that students internalise and adopt the value as their own; indicators for values education; the role of social institutions in terms of their responsibility to aid values development in students, and so forth.

Summary

Within its multitudinous inanimate forms and functions, globalization has untapped powers to reshape permanently and powerfully even the most minute detail of Thai society. The potential impact of globalization upon even the mostly deeply entrenched values within Thai society could severely destabilise or even derail the nation in the future. Thus, investing the utmost effort in preparing appropriate values development for people and society is necessary in order to support the welfare of the citizens and development of the nation. Values education can be compared to a fortress that will protect the Thai culture and people from the negative influences of other cultures and inappropriate or destructive values. Moreover, values development will ensure that all citizens of our world are able to live together peacefully.

Thus, education institutions, the most suitable instruments for developing people, should take the leadership role in building a strong values education program for Thai students. In this way, the true nature of values education can be realised: as a tool to transform quickly a nation and to prepare it for the changes inherent in globalization.

References

Amornwiwat, S. (1987). Karn pattana laksoot prathom suksa: Tahtee thee thong tobtuan [Development in the primary school curriculum: This must be revised]. *Annual Publication of Faculty of Education, 15* (April–June), 13–14.

Anunthavorasakul, A. (1996). *State and problems of Buddhism subject instruction in secondary schools under the jurisdiction of the Department of General Education*. Bangkok, Thailand: Chulalongkorn University.

Charoenying, B., Pantumanawin, D., & Prachonpajjanuek, P. (1979). *Koomue kruu chareeya suksa* [The manual for ethics teachers]. Bangkok, Thailand: Dumrong.

Chareonwongsak, K. (1998, August 9). Strengthening the community. *Bangkok Post*, p. 4 [Perspectives section].

Council for Global Education. (1997). *Moral education: A parent's questionnaire*. Washington, DC: Council for Global Education.

Department of Curriculum and Instruction Development. (1978, Rev. ed., 1990). *Primary School Courses*. Bangkok, Thailand: Ministry of Education.

Department of Curriculum and Instruction Development. (1981a, Rev. ed., 1990). *Lower Secondary School Courses*. Bangkok, Thailand: Ministry of Education.

Department of Curriculum and Instruction Development. (1981b, Rev. ed., 1990). *Higher Secondary School Courses*. Bangkok, Thailand: Ministry of Education.

Department of Curriculum and Instruction Development. (1981c, Rev. ed., 1990). *Upper Secondary School Curriculum*. Bangkok: Ministry of Education.

Department of General Education. (1986). *Khoomue sangserm prachatippatai nai satarn suksa samansuksa* [Democracy supportive manual for education institutions of general education]. Bangkok, Thailand: Supplies and Educational Materials Division.

Education Research and Planning Division. (1982). *Kan suksa ha gain pokkatit kong radap pattanagan tang jariyatam lae ongprakob ti me pon tho pattanagan tang jariyatam* [Studies on normal measure for morality development levels and effects toward morality development]. Department of Curriculum and Instruction Development. Bangkok: Ministry of Education.

Gailbraith, R., & Jones, T. (1975). Teaching strategies for moral dilemmas: An application of Kohlberg's theory of moral development to the social studies classroom. *Social Education*, *39*, 18.

Huitt, W. G. (1997). *Values: Educational psychology interactive*. Retrieved April, 2000, from http://chiron.valdosta.edu/whuitt/ ol/affsys/values.html.

Huitt, W. G. (1992). Problem solving and decision making: Consideration of individual differences using the Myers-Briggs Type Indicator. *Journal of Psychological Type*, *24*, 33–44.

Jarolimek, J. (1971). *Social studies in elementary education*. New York: Macmillan.

King Bhumiphol Adulyadej. (1982). *Ekkasarn karnwichai rueng kahniyom pue sheewit lae sungkom* [Research paper: Values for life and society]. Bangkok, Thailand: Research and Planning Division, The Office of National Culture Commission, Research and Planning Division.

Kohlberg, L. (1969). Stage and sequence: The cognitive-developmental approach to socialization. In D. A. Goslin (Ed.), *Handbook of socialization theory and research*. Chicago: Rand McNally.

Kohlberg, L. (1964). Development of moral character and moral ideology. In M. L. Hoffman & L. W. Hoffman (Eds.), *Review of child development research: Vol. 1* (pp. 381–431). New York: Russell Sage Foundation.

Komin, S. (1983). *Kan pattana sangkom gap kaniyom* [Social development and the values]. Bangkok, Thailand: Ministry of Education.

Komin, S. (1990). *Psychology of the Thai people: Values and behavioural patterns*. Bangkok, Thailand: National Institute of Development Administration.

Laykarpan, T. (1988). *The relationship between students' ethics according to the perception of the mathematics teachers, parents and the succession in studying mathematics of students in their 1st year in upper secondary school.* Unpublished master's thesis, Chulalongkorn University, Bangkok, Thailand.

Leming, J. S. (1997). *Values and character education in public schools: Should the schools teach moral and civic virtue?* Retrieved April, 2000, from http://www.usae.k12.ut.us/curr/chared/fedproj/his/values.htm

Loevinger, J., & Wessler, R. (1970). *Measuring ego development* (Vols. I, II). San Francisco: Jossey-Bass.

Majmudar, M. (1998, September). *Developing values education for the new millennium through a cross-cultural approach: Sathya Sai Education in human values (SSEHV): Theory and practice.* Paper presented at the Scottish Educational Research Association Annual Conference, Dundee, Scotland. Retrieved April, 2000, from http://www.sathyasaiehv.org.uk.

Meesook, U. (1990). *Trends and new directions in social development in the 13th meeting of the national social welfare.* Bangkok, Thailand.

Mourine, G., & Moureen, N. (1985–1986). Creating a curriculum for global future. *Educational Leadership, 43*(4), 72, 74–75.

Ministry of Education. (1978, Rev. eds., 1984, 1989). *Nungsue thee sor.tor.0801/17153* [Curriculum for primary Schools, book # number 0801/17153]. Bangkok, Thailand: Ministry of Education.

Mulasilp, W. (1973). *Kan pattirup kan suksa nai rathchagan ti ha* [Education reform during King Rama V]. Bangkok, Thailand: The Social Institution of Thailand.

The Office of National Culture Commission, Research and Planning Division. (1987). *Ekkasarn karnwichai rueng kahniyom pue sheewit lae sungkom* [Values for life and society]. Bangkok, Thailand: Research and Planning Division, The Office of National Culture Commission.

Office of Education Assessment and Testing Services, Department of Curriculum and Institution Development. (1995). *Phon karn pramern koonnaparb tang karnsuksa radab mattayom suksa tornthon lae mattayom suksa tornplai pee karnsuksa* [Results of an evaluation of the quality of education in lower and upper secondary schools]. Bangkok, Thailand: Department of Curriculum and Instruction Development.

Piaget, J. (1962). The moral judgment of the child. New York: Collier. (Original work published 1932)

Pongpeaw, P., & Sukatipant, S. (1983). *Gan mueng kong yaowachon* [Youth politics]. Bangkok, Thailand: Chaopraya Publishing House.

Rokeach, M. (1973). *The nature of human values.* New York: The Free Press.

Rossiter, G. (1999). *The values dimension to citizenship education.* Retrieved April, 2000, from http://www.acu.edu.au/ren/citzed01.htm

Silpanilmalaya, A. (n.d.). *Development of criteria for evaluation moral education curriculum at the elementary education level*. Bangkok, Thailand: Chulalongkorn University.

Smith, A., & Montgomery, A. (1996). *Values in education in Northern Ireland, CAIN Project*. Retrieved April, 2000, from http://chiron.valdosta.edu/whuitt/col/affisys/values.html.

Sungkrit, M., & Noi-suwan, W. (1992). *Tittang karnsuksa nai anakot nai roi pee* [The direction of education in the next 100 years]. Bangkok, Thailand: Ministry of Education.

Sunyawiwat, S. (1984). *Koonnapab lae koonnatam nai karn pattana pratet* [Quality and morality in country's development]. Bangkok, Thailand: Chaopraya Publishers.

Teachers Council of Thailand. (1990). *Rai ngan rueng phon karnjud karnrian karnsorn wicha prapootha sartsana radab mattayom suksa tornton lae tornplai tarm laksood mattayom suksa chabab prubproong* [A report: The results of Buddhism teaching and studying management in lower and upper secondary school according to the revised curriculum in 1990]. Bangkok, Thailand: Department of Curriculum and Instruction Department.

Thepsitha, S. (1990). *Naewtang lae kwamkid mai kong karnsungkomsong kroah* [Concepts and new directions for social welfare]. Bangkok, Thailand: Somchai Publishing Company.

Touinpak, S. A. (1978, Rev. eds., 1990, 1996). *Content analysis of morality aspect in elementary school curriculum*. Bangkok, Thailand: Chulalongkorn University.

Uarfuah, P. (1991, October). *Karn suksa priebtiab karnrian karnsorn rueng prapootha sartsana tarm kwarm kidhen khong acharn lae nuckrian radab mattayom suksa tornthon nai rongrian sathit nai krungthep* [The comparative study in the problem in teaching Buddhism according to the opinion of the teacher and the students in the lower secondary school in demonstration schools located within Bangkok]. *Research Periodical*, *2*(133), 33–37.

Whetzel, D. (1992). The Secretary of Labor's Commission on achieving necessary skills. *ERIC Digest*, no. ED 339749. Retrieved from www.ericdigests.org/1992-5/skills.htm

CHAPTER 16

Girls' Status as Learner-Citizens: Issues for Values Education and Citizenship Education

Victoria Foster

Abstract

This chapter examines the implications of the relationship between two contemporary international trends in education for women's equality as citizens. The first trend is that in most western countries, girls are now achieving statistically slightly better average school-leaving results than boys, in turn occasioning a hostile populist "backlash" against this success (Foster, 2001; Martino & Meyenn, 2001). For example, a recent international collection (Mackinnon, Elgqvist-Saltzman, & Prentice, 1998) argues that education in the 21st century will be "dangerous terrain" for women. The second trend is the revival of interest in participatory democratic theory which is reflected in the strong current focus on civics and citizenship education in education systems.

I address the specific question of what happens to the social and educational order when girls begin to gain access to the traditional masculine public spheres of male-dominated curriculum areas. A further question concerns the implications for both girls and boys as learner-citizens, of this greater access. The chapter develops the argument that in the present international climate, it is impossible for girls to be equal with boys as learner-citizens. Girls remain adjuncts to the male learner-citizen, a problem which is not addressed in current models of citizenship education. The two trends under discussion are contradictory, positioning girls within a dialectic of desire and threat in their quests for citizenship (see Foster, 1996b, 1998, 2000).

The chapter begins with a brief overview of the theoretical literature on the gendered nature of citizenship, and its relevance to gender and citizenship education as a field of study. I then describe what has developed into an international backlash against girls' alleged success in education, and go on to analyse the exact nature of this success. I argue that the backlash is fuelled by two rhetorical shifts in the discourses of disadvantage relating to both boys and girls. The final section discussesthe public taboos and private imperatives which operate to circumscribe girls' desires to be equal learner-citizens with boys.

Intimations of Equality: The Theoretical Literature on the Gendered Nature of Citizenship in the Modern State

There is a vast literature (e.g. Benhabib, 1992; Cass, 1994; Leech, 1994; Pateman, 1988, 1989, 1992; Young, 1987) on the gendered nature of citizenship, and "the problem of women's standing in a political order in which citizenship has been made in the male image" (Pateman, 1989, p. 14). Much of this literature focuses on women's exclusion from the ideal of the civic public realm of citizenship which is both normatively masculine, and relies on an opposition between the public and private dimensions of human life. This broad ranging literature has demonstrated that women are in fact outside the frame of patriarchal citizenship and that there is an enormous gulf between the apparent guarantee of full citizenship for women and women's actual lived experience of that guarantee (Leech, 1994, p. 81); and that women's status as citizens is underwritten by a sexual contract (Pateman, 1988) denying them free and equal status with men. Feminist legal theory in particular (e.g. Charlesworth, 1992; Gavison, 1992; Graycar, 1992, 1994) shows that the burden of women's responsibility for work associated with the private sphere has implications for their legal status as citizens.

The substance of the feminist critique of citizenship is that equality for women is not, and will not, be delivered merely by attempting to include women in the normative conception of man as citizen by "laundering some of its ideals" (Young, 1987, p. 58). Furthermore, Pateman (1989) argues convincingly that women, as women, cannot meet the criteria for citizenship (p. 14).

Pateman's (1988) observation that "women are incorporated into a sphere that both is and is not in civil society" underlines women's ambiguous relationship with citizenship (p. 11). It is this contradiction and ambiguity which pose the dilemma for inserting women into conceptions of citizenship. Although this contradiction is addressed in detail by the feminist critique, it is largely ignored in curriculum development in the field of citizenship education.

Gender and Citizenship Education as a Field of Study

In earlier work (Foster, 1997), using examples from Australia, the Netherlands and Scandinavia, I explored some of the ways in which a school curriculum mirrors the modern state's valorisation of public life and devaluing of the private. The citizen-as-male has his counterpart in the learner-as-male. For example, in Australia, curriculum development in citizenship education has not yet adequately addressed the public-private dialectic in social life. This trend in Australia dates back to 1992 when the Mayer Committee developing a national curriculum in work-related Key Competencies decided not to include "Family and Household Management" as a key area of skills and knowledge necessary for all students. This curriculum hierarchy continues unchanged to the present with mathematics and the sciences far more highly valued than areas concerned with life management and so-called private life. Consequently, Australia has not succeeded in incorporating private life into the curriculum. Thus, despite the current revival of interest in Australia and other countries in citizenship education, education continues to perpetuate women's and girls' lack of citizenship status.

There are two further problems which need to be addressed in the development of the citizenship curriculum. The first problem is the low curriculum status which is accorded the knowledge and skills related to the private, domestic sphere of life. For example, Australian curriculum documents have tended to marginalise women as a group with special needs (Foster, 1997), in effect attempting merely to add women to the normative conception of the citizen-as-male in an "add women but don't stir" approach (Foster, 1996a). In the Netherlands, a curriculum reappraisal involving the introduction of the compulsory subject "care" saw the status of these same skills and knowledge fiercely contested (ten Dam & Volman, 1995; Volman, 1997).

The second problem concerns the lack of a theoretical framework for citizenship education (Arnot & Dillabough, 1999, p. 2; Foster, 1997). This second problem is exacerbated by the fact that some of the key theoretical literature is already out of print. When ordering texts for a 1999 graduate course "Gender and Citizenship," I found that Carole Pateman's important book, *The Disorder of Women: Democracy, Feminism and Political Theory* published by Polity Press in 1989 is out of print. The same was true of *Gender, Politics and Citizenship* in the 1990s edited by Barbara Sullivan and Gillian Whitehouse and published in 1996 by the University of New South Wales Press. How many other such fundamental texts are no longer available for students of citizenship education?

In relation to the problem of a lack of a theoretical framework for citizenship education, Arnot and Dillabough (2000) note, "important links between feminist political theory and feminist educational theory have not always been made explicit. As a consequence, education feminism has not had sufficient impact on the restructuring of citizenship and the formation of citizenship education" (p. 21). Furthermore, Halstead (2000, p. 9) argues that the lack of a cogent theoretical framework for addressing the gendered nature of citizenship education as it is currently taught highlights the need for a moral critique of citizenship and citizenship education. Such a critique could profitably begin with Pateman's (1988) notion of the "sexual contract" referred to earlier, and its implications for both boys and girls as learner-citizens.

An International Backlash: Girls' Status as Learner-Citizens

Over the past few years, in most western countries we have witnessed what Weiner, Arnot, and David (1997, p. 620) refer to as a "moral panic" over claims, largely promulgated through the media, that boys are suffering from new forms of educational disadvantage. Common representations are "girls are outperforming boys"; "girls are succeeding at the expense of boys"; "boys are struggling"; "boys are in deep trouble." However, as Mahony and Smedley (1998) point out, these kinds of claims are not new, and have a long history.

Media reporting of the 1998 New South Wales Higher School Certificate results frequently referred to girls' apparent success as "dangerous." Such comments bring to mind Rousseau's claim that "never has a people perished from an excess of wine; all perish from the disorder of women" (Pateman, 1989, p. 17). As Pateman further points out, Rousseau is not the only social or political theorist to regard women as a permanently subversive force within the political order. She elaborates, "although women have now been granted citizenship in the liberal democracies, it is still widely believed that they are unfitted for political life and that it would be dangerous if the state were in their hands. This belief is very complex" (p. 17).

Women are not only believed to be unfit for political life, a fact that is demonstrated by women's low representation (13%) in Australian parliaments. Women are also deemed to be unfit to share equally in the decision-making and higher status positions in civil and social life, that is, public life. In Australia, women are seriously under-represented in a range of occupations as diverse as corporation boards, literature and the arts, chefs, engineers and academics. In New South Wales, while women are 75% of primary school teachers, they are 25% of principals and senior executive staff in schools (New South Wales Department of Education and Training, 1999).

The Nature of Girls' Educational "Success"

To date, girls have experienced only the appearance of success in schooling outcomes since this success is yet to have any impact on post-school employment patterns. Australian research (Foster, 1999; New South Wales Board of Studies, 1996; Teese, Davies, Charlton, & Polesel, 1995; Yates & Leder, 1996) shows that the school-leaving credential has quite a different value for boys and girls, and that while boys design their curriculum choices around the "male career trajectory," girls remain "over-represented in subjects with poor vocational linkages" (Teese et al., 1995). It is paradoxical that while girls demonstrate a stronger attachment to, and dependence on, school credentials, this is not paying off for them as it does for boys. In Australia currently, one-third of male early school-leavers go directly into apprenticeships (Lamb & McKenzie, 1999) while 28% of female early leavers go to no form of employment, education or training (Foster, 1999) or else are pregnant (Milne-Home, 1996).

However, despite the lack of post-school rewards, the strong reaction to girls' improved performance at school suggests that this success is challenging deeply held assumptions about girls' and women's status as learner-citizens, and their proper relationship with education. If equal participation in education and its outcomes is fundamental to one's status as a future citizen, then the construction of girls' success as dangerous and threatening poses serious consequences for their relationship with citizenship and civil society. This point is elaborated later in the chapter.

It is significant that in Australia, the most contested curriculum areas are the high prestige male-dominated areas of Mathematics and Science. It was only in 1997 that in New South Wales for the first time a girl topped 4 Unit Mathematics, the most difficult level of study. Nevertheless, this was widely misconstrued in the media as girls collectively beating boys at Maths and Science, and over a longer period of time. Certainly a significant factor in the recent politicization of girls' school performance is the nature of the contested areas themselves and the casting of girls as interlopers and "space invaders" (Foster, 1996a, 1996b, 1998) in high status educational terrain assumed to be the natural preserve of males. One wonders about the news value of girls beating boys in Life Management or Child and Family Studies or Care, for example!

In fact, while a small, highly select group of Australian girls is achieving equally with, or better than, boys in male-identified subject areas, girls' participation in these subjects remains very low, and in some cases, is diminishing. Girls continue to have low participation rates in higher level Mathematics, Physics where in some states their participation has declined, and in Technology and Engineering Science subjects where they are a tiny fraction of students (New South Wales Board of Studies, 1999, unpublished data).

Of particular concern is the dramatic decline in girls' participation in Information Technology and Computer Studies, particularly in New South Wales where the backlash has been the strongest. In 1991 there were many more girls in Computer Studies than there were in 1998, and in 1998 boys outnumbered girls by more than 2:1 in 2-unit, and by 5:1 in the highest level, 3-unit (New South Wales Board of Studies, 1999, unpublished data). These low participation rates have clear implications for women's entry into technology-related growth areas of the labour market, as well as their influence on the increasing globalisation and construction of knowledge via technology. Women are virtually absent from this important aspect of citizenship.

A Rhetorical Shift in the Discourses of Disadvantage

In Australia at least, there have been two interrelated shifts in the discourses of disadvantage relating to gender. The first is in the construction of girls themselves and the second is in the rhetoric alleging that boys are the new disadvantaged. It is interesting that much of the recently emerging academic literature on boys' education tends to decontextualise boys and men from their asymmetrical power relations with girls and women in society, and in education. For instance, in an entire 1998 issue of the journal, *Change: Transformations in Education* which was devoted to boys' education and published by the University of Sydney, discussion of girls' continuing inferior post-school outcomes was virtually non-existent, as was a consideration of the unchanging nature of the sexual division of labour in private domestic life (Bittman & Pixley, 1997; Dempsey, 1997; Wolcott & Glezer, 1995). These are serious issues for citizenship education.

Just as serious is the general lack of challenge of the rhetoric of "presumptive equality" (Foster, 1995, 2001) on which the concept of male disadvantage is founded. Related to this is the general lack of a critique of the enormous resources currently being poured into compensatory programs for boys (New South Wales Department of School Education, 1994), and of the gendered hierarchy of teaching itself (New South Wales Department of Education and Training, 1999). An exception, however, is the critique of Mahony and Smedley (1998). Current issues of boys and their education are entirely political and are intimately bound up with assumptions about boys and girls as learners.

In Australia, initial attempts to achieve greater educational equality for girls centred on positioning girls within a deficit framework, in which they were seen as lacking in relation to male norms of the educated person. Equity policies encouraged girls to measure up to those norms (Foster, 1992). The following Education and Training Strategy for Women of the New South Wales Ministry of Education and Youth Affairs (1989) is an example of this deficit framework formulated as policy:

In schools, girls:

- have a low level of participation in technical and key science subjects and in highest level mathematics and science courses;
- consider a narrow range of options in making career choices; and
- have lower levels of self-esteem.

It is clearly a major discursive shift from this earlier deficit framework to the current depiction of girls as actively succeeding, and even beating boys, in male educational terrain. The hostility on the part of some to ideals of equality in schooling for girls has taken the form of a refrain around What about the boys! in an attempt to re-assert the primacy of male educational interests (Foster, 1995). This refrain is echoing internationally (Mackinnon, Elgqvist-Saltzman, & Prentice 1998; Martino & Meyenn, 2001).

It is interesting that this refrain is endemic in countries which have experienced quite different policy contexts. For instance, Mahony and Smedley (1998, p. 49) note significant differences between the British "particularly hard version of economic rationalism" and the Australian policy framework which is to some degree underpinned by social justice and equity principles. The subtext of the refrain is that notions of educational equality for girls entail taking something very crucial away from boys: their supremacy as learners, as well as the caretaking resources of women and girls, to which boys are assumed to be entitled. By contrast, male educational interests had earlier been strongly supported by a construction which emphasised girls as lacking, rather than viewing boys themselves as being advantaged (Eveline, 1995).

The construction of boys' continuing advantage in education, particularly in relation to curriculum participation, use of a range of school resources and post-school outcomes (Teese et al., 1995) as "disadvantage," is a rhetorical twist which has been used to great effect both in Australia and Britain in simplistic and emotive accounts (Connell, 1994; Foster, 1999). These accounts have been stated and restated by a handful of very vocal individuals, who have been content to argue their case through the media, rather than in academic or other professional forums. Gilbert (1998) describes this as "a conservative and potentially divisive men's movement, which rejected feminism and wanted boys' work to be seen as separate from the broader project of the democratic reform of schooling." The result is a climate in which the notion of male disadvantage can be stretched to extremes. For example, Michael Brown (1994, p. 9) who teaches at a prestigious Sydney boys' independent school, argues that we are creating a new "underclass": gifted males! He urges that advocacy is needed for the white, male, Caucasian, non-migrant child.

Connell (1994) describes this process in the following way:

> In places where feminist work has created women's studies programs or affirmative action programs (e.g. encouraging girls into science and mathematics), the idea that it is 'boys' turn' for attention and resources is easily spread. This can be reinforced by calling attention to ways in which boys are less successful in schooling than girls: for instance in regard to reading and in higher dropout rates. Combined with statistics about men's earlier death, men's greater rates of injury by violence etc., this can be worked up into a claim that men are the truly disadvantaged group (p. 2; author's emphasis).

Further, Connell (1995) persuasively argues that this process which he calls "masculinity therapy" relies on "a redefinition of power by shifting from the public world to the inner world of emotion" (p. 208) and "a preoccupation with emotional relationships, a speculative method and a satisfaction with snippets of evidence" (p. 210).

The notion of male disadvantage is further bolstered by the rhetoric of "presumptive equality" (Foster, 1995, 2001) which includes the widely popular beliefs that women have achieved equality with men in society, and that women and men are equivalent and symmetrical populations. The asymmetry of men's and women's social relations, for example in relation to employment, is quickly dispensed with, and the conclusion is easily reached that it is men and boys who are now suffering inequality, reflected in catchy media grabs such as men are the future second sex.

Desire and Threat as Dialectical Experiences in Girls' Schooling

Two quite different philosophical approaches to the question of desire can be drawn on to explain the rhetorical shift which has occurred in the construction of girls as learners. Grosz (1989) distinguishes the first tradition, which conceives of desire as a "fundamental lack in being, an incompletion or absence within the subject" (p. xvi), from the second tradition in which desire is conceived not as a lack but as a positive force of production and self-actualisation. In this second sense, at the level of the subject, desire functions insofar as the subject "desires the expansion or maximisation of its power ... it is not an unactualised or latent potential; it is always active and real" (Grosz, 1989, p. xvi).

Policy discourse concerning the desirable educational achievements of girls has at different times philosophically encompassed both the senses of desire which Grosz has delineated. Earlier, girls were constructed as lacking the necessary masculine learner subjectivity as well as the necessary male-defined knowledge. The very meaning of "girl" included a negativity or lack (Jones, 1993, p. 12). In this construction, the lack was to be removed by increasing girls' access to masculine knowledge areas, but not, it transpired, by enhancing their achievement relative to boys in those areas. This first sense of desire as filling a lack resonates with the philosophical and social construction of femininity as "other" to the masculine.

The second sense of desire referred to by Grosz is, however, much more problematic for girls, because it invokes a more normatively masculine orientation to desire, that of actively seeking and pursuing achievement, and to an extent, power. To date, even more problematically for girls, their achievement has centred specifically on predominantly masculine curriculum areas and subject domains. Although the discourse of reform is couched philosophically in Grosz's first sense, the implications for girls of following that discourse, as well as the outcomes, relate directly to Grosz's second sense of self-actualisation. In concrete terms, this has resulted in the perception that girls are interlopers or "space invaders" (Foster, 1996b) in male educational terrain, depriving boys of their prior rights as learners. The crucial point here then is that for girls to desire in this second sense places them not only in a contradictory position as "educated women" (Martin, 1991), but also in a position of threat, which is both actual in school, and potential in relation to post-school life. It is significant that the "What about the Boys!" movement in Australia emerged at the precise moment (and not a moment earlier) that girls were perceived to be outstripping boys in the areas of male power and privilege. This point is obvious if one asks whether there would have been such concern about boys and their schooling if the contested areas had been different.

The first sense of desire as lacking, in which girls are seen as disadvantaged, is relatively safe for girls, posing no threat to hegemonic masculinity and possibly reinforcing it. It is the second self-actualising sense of desire in the educational setting which, by challenging male educational privilege, becomes threatening for girls and women. This is the sense which comes into play when women cease to be constructed as lacking as in the first sense of desire and instead are constructed as actively pursuing their own educational and occupational goals.

This discussion of desire and threat in girls' schooling raises several questions. For instance, what might happen if girls move outside the frame of their construction as lacking in relation to boys? How could girls be the caretakers of boys if they are equal (or better?) achievers? Such a prospect could be very threatening for girls and their education. For example, the current reaction to girls' perceived advances in Maths and Science may well make it very difficult for girls to pursue excellence in those subjects, if they are seen as depriving boys of their rights as the high achievers in those areas. In fact, girls' performance in those subjects actually declined from 1993 to 1994 (New South Wales Board of Studies, 1996), when the backlash period was beginning to gain momentum. The interesting question is also raised of whether, and to what extent, girls and women use caretaking as an accommodative strategy to control the threat against them which is posed by greater equality? Finally, given that the value-added dimensions (to use an economic rationalist concept) of care and caretaking are vastly different according to whether they are done by men or women, where does this leave care as a curriculum issue? This question is very pertinent in Australia where care-related matters have been relegated to the bottom of the curriculum hierarchy, with serious implications for the education of both boys and girls as future citizens (Noddings, 1992).

Public Taboos: Space Invaders in the Space-Between

This section argues that girls cannot be equal as learner-citizens when they are constructed as "space invaders" in male educational terrain (Foster, 1996, 1998). The notion of the space-between is a heuristic device to analyse and explain girls' experiences of contemporary events in education. In particular, it explains the lack of change in post-school outcomes for girls, the insignificant degree of change in girls' participation in male-dominated curriculum areas, despite their successes in those areas, the endemic nature of sexual harassment and the inequitable use of school resources by girls (Australian Education Council, 1992; Collins, Batten, Ainley, & Getty, 1996; Foster, 1999; Teese et al., 1995).

For women and girls, pursuing equal educational and citizenship rights, entails entering a particular space — social, psychological and existential — between and beyond that which is prescribed for women, that is, women's "place," and that which is proscribed to women (Foster, 1994, 1996b). This is a space of lived experience, mediating between private and public spheres, where women and girls attempt to negotiate the conflicting, contradictory (at best), or violent and destructive (at worst) demands of a neo-liberal framework of equality, a framework which retains a masculinist subject at its centre (Leck, 1987; Martin, 1991). Both the individual learner-subject and the epistemological foundations of the curriculum are male-defined (Martin, 1981). Girls are to be given equal opportunity to achieve parity in an education system which is normatively masculine (Foster, 1992).

The patriarchal power relations of schooling and their connection with the public-private dialectic in society make the lived curriculum of schools a complex site of both desire and threat for girls. Equality-directed curriculum reforms require girls to transpose themselves from private realm status to a relatively different position as the equals of males in the public realm of the school. In this process, girls' status is defined and redefined as the "other" in relation to males, in various ways which frequently define girls physically or sexually in terms of their bodies, and constitute reminders of difference.

Both the idea and the concrete reality of public woman violates public-private norms, requiring women to give up the (dubious) protection of the private sphere, and expose themselves to the threat of violence in the public sphere. Similarly, for girls to take up the promises of reforms towards equality in education, in their present form, entails the threat of violence in one form or another.

Education for women is both contradictory (Martin, 1991) and inasmuch as it entails movement into male terrain, potentially threatening and dangerous. Noting that it is not uncommon for women to experience male violence in connection with educational participation, Rockhill (1987) observes that "we know little about how it is lived in women's lives" (p. 316). The mass murder in 1989 of 14 female engineering students at the University of Montreal is a stark example of this violence (Malette & Chalouh, 1991).

Private Imperatives: Caretaking in the Classroom and *What About the Boys!*

This final section discusses one of the most profound aspects of the space-between: that both girls' and boys' schooling experiences are situated in what Griffith and Smith (1987) refer to as a "mothering discourse" (p. 96). This discourse, they suggest, operates according to a "paradigm of the ideal mother," which can be traced back to Rousseau's prescriptions for Sophie's primary function as Emile's helpmate and nurturer in Emile. For example, in contemporary educational discourse, the "social benefits" and "reality" often attributed to the co-educational school setting are, in fact, conflated with the injunction on women and girls to take care of and nurture the interests of others. Brady (1998) provides a detailed historical analysis of the role of women teachers as mother-nurturers and carers.

The phenomenon of girls as caretakers of boys in the classroom, has not received any extended, formal discussion in Australian education policy, although Lewis (1990) discusses this dynamic in relation to the university classroom setting. It is, however, one of the most powerful, albeit subtle, determinants of girls' day-to-day schooling experiences. It is powerful because of its location in the public-private nexus and specifically, as part of the unspoken sexual contract whereby the patriarchal meaning of femininity entails the provision of service, sexual and otherwise, to men (Pateman, 1988, p. 126). Within the sexual contract, the functions of caring, nurturance and emotional support are seen as women's functions. Women are seen as the keepers and cultivators of the nation state and its development (Yuval-Davis, 1997, p. 5). Women, as Benhabib (1987) puts it, are the "housekeepers of the emotions" (p. 95). Men may carry out these functions but they are valued differentially according to whether they are done by men or women. The ways in which both female and male students live the curriculum reinforces this sexual contract. In general, boys eschew any association with the feminine or curriculum areas related to the private, domestic sphere, where girls conversely predominate (Collins et al., 1996). Conversely, in coeducational classrooms, girls are routinely expected to moderate boys' disruptive influence by softening the learning environment and being models of good behaviour, often to their own detriment as learners in a context where boys' needs have primacy.

Education can be seen to be concerned primarily with the initiation of young men as citizens into the "productive" processes of society and its culture (Foster, 1992). Conversely, through its devaluing of the private sphere, education underwrites the natural "non-citizenship of women" (Castles & Davidson, 1999, p. 142) and women's consequent "deviant" status (Yuval-Davis, 1997, p. 5). A clear example of the latter point is the case of pregnant schoolgirls whose rights as learner-citizens are withdrawn when they are routinely labelled by society as deviant and unfit for school life (Milne-Home, 1996).

Conclusion: Moral and Ethical Issues in Values Education and Citizenship Education for Boys and Girls

There is a great deal of evidence that in Australia, as in other countries, boys' curricular and life choices are severely circumscribed by dominant notions of masculinity, and the desire of many boys to eschew any association with the feminine or curriculum areas related to the private, domestic sphere (see Collins et al., 1996). Indeed, education can be seen to be concerned primarily with the initiation of young men as citizens into the "productive" processes of society and its culture (Foster, 1992, p. 58). In this context, women and girls are often cast in the role of caretakers of the learning environment (Foster, 2000) and of boys' needs, according to what Pateman (1988, p. 126) calls an unspoken "sexual contract" whereby the functions of caring, nurturance and emotional support are seen as belonging to women. The ways in which both boys and girls live the curriculum, in its broadest sense, reinforce this sexual contract.

On the other hand, the tenor of the current debates about boys and their schooling is having serious consequences for girls' equal standing with boys as learner-citizens (Arnot & Dillabough, 2000; Foster, 1997, 2000). In this chapter I have raised questions about the ways in which girls may experience and resolve for themselves the simultaneous desire to be "somebody" which education for citizenship implies, and the potential threat to them from those who in turn feel threatened by girls' living out of this desire. The very processes in schooling which aim to empower boys place girls in a contradictory and paradoxical relationship with the rhetoric of equal and democratic participation which characterises much contemporary education discourse. An unspoken question is, what would happen to boys if girls do become boys' equals as learners and stop being their caretakers? Interestingly, during the current backlash period in Australia, there has been no acknowledgment that girls' equal or better achievement in male-dominated subjects would actually be beneficial for boys in that it would give them an opportunity to see girls in a new, healthier light as respected peers and equals. Even more profoundly, how would both boys' and girls' development as learner-citizens be enhanced by a citizenship education curriculum which foregrounded the values of caring in both public and private life?

The answers to these questions have important implications for boys' moral, intellectual and spiritual development, and for their futures as citizens able to participate in equal social and personal relations with women. This educational problem can only be addressed by school programs which encourage boys to broaden their curricular and life choices, and their hopes and dreams for fulfilling human relationships.

References

Arnot, M., & Dillabough, J. (1999). *Constructing a feminist framework on the nature of citizenship in education.* Paper presented at the American Educational Research Association Annual Conference, Montreal, Canada.

Arnot, M., & Dillabough, J. (Eds.). (2000). *Challenging democracy: Feminist perspectives on the education of citizens.* London: Routledge.

Australian Education Council. (1992). *Listening to girls.* Melbourne, Australia: Australian Education Council.

Benhabib, S. (1987). The generalized and the concrete other: The Kohlberg-Gilligan controversy and feminist theory. In S. Benhabib & D. Cornell (Eds.), *Feminism as critique: Essays on the politics of gender in late-capitalist societies* (pp. 77–95). Cambridge, UK: Polity Press.

Benhabib, S. (1992). *Situating the self: Gender, community and postmodernism in contemporary ethics.* Cambridge, UK: Polity Press.

Bittman, M., & Pixley, J. (1997). *The double life of the family: Myth, hope and experience.* Sydney, Australia: Allen and Unwin.

Brady, K. (1998). Teaching as women's work. *Teaching and Teachers' Work: A Publication on Professional and Pedagogical Issues, 6*(4), 1–12.

Brown, M. (1994). Educational opportunities for gifted and talented boys. *Gifted,* October, 9–10.

Cass, B. (1994). Citizenship, work, and welfare: The dilemma for Australian women, *Social Politics, 1,* 106–124.

Castles, S., & Davidson, A. (1999). *Citizenship and migration: Globalisation and the politics of belonging*. London: Macmillan.

Change: Transformations in Education (1998, November), *1*(2).

Charlesworth, H. (1992). *Has the United Nations forgotten the rights of women?* Canberra, Australia: Australian Council for Overseas Aid.

Collins, C., Batten, M., Ainley, J., & Getty, C. (1996). *Gender and school education*. Canberra, Australia: Australian Council for Educational Research.

Connell, R. W. (1994). *Knowing about masculinity, teaching boys and men: Education implications of the new sociology of masculinity and the old sociology of schools*. Paper for Pacific Sociological Association conference, San Diego, CA.

Connell, R. W. (1995). *Masculinities*. Sydney, Australia: Allen and Unwin.

Dempsey, K. (1997). *Inequalities in marriage: Australia and beyond*. Melbourne, Australia: Oxford University Press.

Eveline, J. (1995). The (im)possible reversal: Advantage, education and the process of feminist theorising. *Lararutbildning och forskning i Umea* (Teacher education and research in Umea), *2*(3–4), 29–46.

Foster, V. (1992). Different but equal? Dilemmas in the reform of girls' education. *Australian Journal of Education, 36*(1), 53–67.

Foster, V. (1994). *Making women the subject of educational change: An interdisciplinary and comparative study*. Unpublished doctoral dissertation, Macquarie University.

Foster, V. (1995). "What about the boys!" Presumptive equality in the education of girls and boys. *Proceedings of the National Social Policy Conference, "Social Policy and the Challenges of Social Change," University of New South Wales, Australia, 1*, 81–97.

Foster, V. (1996a). *Whereas the People* and civics education: Another case of "add women and stir?" *Curriculum Perspectives* [special issue], "Reconstructing Civics Education: *Whereas the People* as a prescription for the new civics," *16* (1), 52–56.

Foster, V. (1996b). Space invaders: Desire and threat in the schooling of girls. *Discourse: Studies in the Cultural Politics of Education, 17*(1), 43–63.

Foster, V. (1997). Feminist theory and the construction of citizenship education in the modern state. In K. Kennedy (Ed.), *Citizenship education and the modern state*. London: Falmer Press.

Foster, V. (1998). Education: A site of desire and threat for Australian girls. In A. Mackinnon, I. Elgqvist-Saltzman, & A. Prentice (Eds.), *Education into the twenty-first century: Dangerous terrain for women?* London: Falmer Press.

Foster, V. (1999). Gender, schooling achievement and post-school pathways: Beyond statistics and populist discourse. In S. Dinham & C. Scott (Eds.), *Teaching in context*. Canberra, Australia: Australian Council for Educational Research

Foster, V. (2000). Is female educational "success" destabilising the male learner-citizen? In M. Arnot & J. Dillabough (Eds.), *Challenging democracy: Feminist perspectives on the education of citizens*. London: Routledge

Foster, V. (2001). What about the boys! An overview of the debates. In W. Martino & B. Meyenn (Eds.), *What about the boys? Issues of Masculinity in Schools*. London: Open University Press.

Gavison, R. (1992). Feminism and the public/private distinction. *Stanford Law Review*, *45*(1), 1–45.

Gilbert, P. (1998). Gender and schooling in New Times: The challenge of boys and literacy. *The Australian Educational Researcher*, *25*(1), 15–37.

Graycar, R. (1992). Before the high court: Women's work, Who cares? *14 Sydney Law Review*, *86*, 86–105.

Graycar, R. (1994). Legal categories and women's work: Explorations for a cross-doctrinal feminist jurisprudence. *Canadian Journal of Women and the Law*, *7* (1), 34–58.

Griffith, A. I., & Smith, D. E. (1987). Constructing cultural knowledge: Mothering as discourse. In J. S. Gaskell & A. T. McLaren (Eds.), *Women and education: A Canadian perspective* (pp. 87–103). Calgary, Canada: Detselig Enterprises Limited.

Grosz, E. (1989). *Sexual subversions: Three French feminists*. Sydney, Australia: Allen & Unwin.

Halstead, M. (2000, June). Does citizenship education make moral education redundant? Paper presented at the International Conference on Values Education and Citizenship Education in the New Century, the Chinese University of Hong Kong.

Jones, A. (1993, August). Discourses of disadvantage: The construction of girls at school. Keynote address for National Transition Conference, Christchurch, New Zealand.

Leck, G. M. (1987). Feminist pedagogy, liberation theory and the traditional schooling paradigm [Review article]. *Educational theory*, *37*(3), 343–354.

Lamb, S., & McKenzie, P. (1999). *Patterns of success and failure in the transition from school to work in Australia*. Canberra, Australia: Australian Council for Educational Research.

Leech, M. (1994). Women, the state and citizenship: 'Are women in the building or in a separate annex?' *Australian Feminist Studies*, *9*(19), 79–91.

Lewis, M. (1990). Interrupting patriarchy: Politics, resistance and transformation in the feminist classroom. *Harvard Educational Review*, *60*(4), 467–488.

Mackinnon, A., Elgqvist-Saltzman, I., & Prentice, A. (Eds.) (1998). *Education into the 21st century: Dangerous terrain for women?* London: Falmer Press.

Mahony, P., & Smedley, S. (1998). New times old panics: The underachievement of boys. *Change: Transformations in Education*, *1*(2), 41–50.

Malette, L., & Chalouh, M. (Eds.). (1991). The Montreal massacre. Charlotte Town, Canada: Gynergy Books.

Martin, J. R. (1981). The ideal of the educated person. *Educational Theory*, *31*(2), 97–109.

Martin, J. R. (1991). The contradiction and the challenge of the educated woman. *Women's Studies Quarterly*, *XIX* (1–2), 6–27.

Martino, W., & Meyenn, B. (2001). What about the boys? Issues of masculinity in schools. London: Open University Press.

Milne-Home, J. (1996). Pregnant futures: Barriers to employment, education and training amongst pregnant and parenting adolescents. Canberra, Australia: Australian Government Publishing Service.

Noddings, N. (1992). *The challenge to care in schools: An alternative approach to education*. New York: Teachers College Press.

New South Wales Board of Studies. (1996). *The report of the gender project steering committee*. Sydney, Australia: New South Wales Board of Studies.

New South Wales Board of Studies. (1999). Unpublished data. Sydney, Australia: New South Wales Board of Studies.

New South Wales Department of School Education. (1994). *Evaluation of educational outcomes for girls in New South Wales government secondary schools*.

New South Wales Department of Education and Training. (1999). *10th annual equal employment opportunity report*. Sydney, Australia: New South Wales Department of Education and Training.

New South Wales Ministry of Education and Youth Affairs. (1989). *Education and training strategy for women*. Sydney, Australia: New South Wales Ministry of Education and Youth Affairs.

Pateman, C. (1988). *The sexual contract*. Cambridge, UK: Polity Press.

Pateman, C. (1989). *The disorder of women: Democracy, feminism and political theory*. Cambridge, UK: Polity Press.

Pateman, C. (1992). Citizen male. *Australian Left Review*, *137*, 30–33.

Rockhill, K. (1987). Literacy as threat/desire: Longing to be somebody. In J. S. Gaskell & A. T. McLaren (Eds.), *Women and education: A Canadian perspective* (pp. 315–331). Calgary, Canada: Detselig Enterprises Limited.

Sullivan, B., & Whitehouse, G. (1996). *Gender, politics and citizenship in the 1990s*. Sydney, Australia: University of New South Wales Press.

Teese, R., Davies, M., Charlton, M., & Polesel, J. (1995). *Who wins at school? Boys and girls in Australian secondary education*. Melbourne, Australia: University of Melbourne.

ten Dam, G., & Volman, M. (1996). Women's history and the subject "care." *The High School Journal*, *79*(3), 262–270.

Volman, M. (1997). Care, computers and the playground: Gender and identity in education. *Discourse: Studies in the cultural politics of education*, *18*(2), 229–241.

Weiner, G., Arnot, M., & David, M. (1997). Is the future female? Female success, male disadvantage and changing gender patterns in education. In A. H. Halsey, P. Brown, & H. Lauder (Eds.), *Education, economy, culture and society*. Oxford, UK: Oxford University Press.

Wolcott, I., & Glezer, H. (1995). *Work and family life: Achieving integration*. Melbourne, Australia: Australian Institute of Family Studies.

Yates, L., & Leder, G. (1996). *The student pathways project: A review and overview of national databases*. Report to the Gender Equity Task Force of the Ministerial Council on Education, Employment, Training and Youth Affairs. Melbourne, Australia, La Trobe University.

Young, I. M. (1987). Impartiality and the civic public: Some implications of feminist critiques of moral and political theory. In S. Benhabib & D. Cornell (Eds.), *Feminism as critique: Essays on the politics of gender in late-capitalist societies* (pp. 56–76). Cambridge, UK: Polity Press.

Yuval-Davis, N. (1997). *Gender and nation*. London: Sage Books.

CHAPTER 17

Understanding Professional Communities: Positive Teacher Professional Development Outcomes in Values and Citizenship Education

Libby Tudball

Abstract

As we enter the new millennium, Civics and Citizenship Education (CCE) is high on the formal education agenda in Australia. CCE is defined as one of the core Common and Agreed Goals for Schooling in Australia in the 21st century, and values education is implicit in these goals. Classroom teachers also argue that values and CCE are core work for schools, so their students may be empowered to be active, thinking and responsible citizens in the local, national and international contexts. The Australian government is currently funding a range of programs nationwide, including the development of teacher and student resources and the provision of teacher professional development, with the goal of improving the quality and quantity of CCE in schools.

This chapter firstly explores how the concepts of "quality" values and CCE are being interpreted and developed by policy makers and Victorian teachers, and why CCE is being promoted. Case studies are discussed of schools which can be defined as exemplary "professional communities," where positive outcomes have been achieved in the improvement of teacher and student learning in values and CCE. Research has shown that in schools where professional community is strong, teacher learning is a regular feature. The paper analyses the range of factors leading to the operation of professional communities, along with the implications of these findings for the development of effective professional development models which will in turn lead to improved student learning in CCE in the future.

Introduction

Various forms of Civics and Citizenship Education (CCE) have been evident in Australian schools in the past. However, recent federal and state government initiatives have put these educational concerns clearly back on the Australian education agenda for the new millennium (Board of Studies, 2000; Curriculum Corporation, 1998; Keating, 1995; Kemp, 1997). Teachers and policy makers are recognizing and articulating the need to promote core values in our young people. In a recent in-service course, teachers expressed the view that values and citizenship education should be strongly linked, and they listed the promotion of these values as fundamental: tolerance, respect, cooperation, open-mindedness, compassion, fairness, responsibility. They argued that all students need learning opportunities to empower them to understand democratic practices and to be active and informed citizens in local, national and international contexts. They said that schools can have powerful influences on the lives of young people and provide them with learning experiences to clarify values and model good citizenship. Clearly, a key issue is that effective teacher professional development in this field needs to be developed.

In the past decade, research in Australia has shown that many young people are leaving school with limited awareness of their nation's origins and heritage, democratic processes and government. The findings show students have insufficient knowledge of rights and responsibilities to enable them to function and participate effectively as citizens in an increasingly globalised community (Senate Standing Committee on Employment Education and Training, 1989, 1991; AGPS, 1994). In response to this research, new national policy initiatives have aimed to reform curriculum and increase the quality and quantity of values education and CCE. Between 1998 and 2000, in response to the new CCE push, over 7,000 teachers in the state of Victoria alone have been involved in professional development activities in CCE (England, 2000). Never before has there been such an intensive range of carefully planned professional development (PD) opportunities, based on clearly defined theories and rationales for positive teacher PD.

However, many of these activities have only been able to reach "the stage of raising teacher awareness of new policies and resources" (Elmore and Burney, 1999, p. 267). They are mainly one day or afternoon workshops, held outside the school environment, which are aimed primarily at providing teachers with examples of new ideas and resources. These models of PD often fail to have a sustained cumulative impact on teacher development and student learning. We know that real changes and the pedagogical content renewal required cannot be achieved quickly, but require continued PD over time (Fullan, 1999). As a regular facilitator for many CCE PD activities, I began to observe that some teams of teachers from particular schools were demonstrating the qualities of "professional communities," and seizing many opportunities for professional development in CCE. Clearly, their leaders are acting on the knowledge that school teams working together and connecting the PD to their own situations, are far more effective vehicles for change. The leaders have encouraged collaboration, and provided the organisational support necessary for teacher learning to occur.

Louis, Kruse, and Marks (1996) define "professional communities" as those characterised by shared norms and values, a collective focus on student learning, collaboration, observation and feedback, deprivatised practice and reflective dialogue. Sykes (1999) argues further that professional communities include a "socially constructed web of mutual obligations among colleagues." The teams I observed have been involved in regional network activities, enrolled in extended professional development programs, attended one day workshops and applied for grants to stimulate and fund developments in values and CCE in their own schools. The teachers have developed "quality" programs for CCE, with interesting and diverse teaching and learning approaches, based on well-defined goals for improved student learning. They reflect actively and critically on how and what their students are learning. They have also been willing to share their learning with the wider profession. The groups have been rewarded for their efforts with government awards for exemplary CCE programs. A number of educational reformers have argued that for teachers to be successful in constructing new roles, they need opportunities to participate in active professional communities (Little & McLaughlin, 1993; Louis, Kruse, & Marks, 1996). McLaughlin (1994) argues that,

> ... teachers' professional development takes place not in a workshop or in discrete, bounded convocations but in the context of professional communities — discourse communities, learning communities.... teachers can and typically do belong to multiple professional communities, each of which functions somewhat differently as a strategic site for professional growth. Thus the argument is made that enabling professional growth is, at root, about enabling professional community. (p. 31)

In this chapter, two case studies of Victorian schools drawn from a larger study currently being completed are explored, to develop understanding of how professional communities operate and how they have achieved positive teacher PD and improved student learning in values and CCE. First, the definition of quality values and CCE in the Australian context is discussed briefly, drawing on policy documents and views of teachers from focus group research. Then the range of factors leading to positive professional development and the successful functioning of professional communities are discussed. Finally, I consider the implications of these findings for the development of effective professional development models for values and CCE in the future.

Values and Civics and Citizenship Education in the Australian Context

Australia's Common and Agreed Goals for Schooling in the 21st Century developed by Ministers of Education from all states and territories includes the challenge for schools to

> develop in their students the knowledge, skills, attitudes and values, to enable them to participate as active and informed citizens in our democratic Australian society, within an international context. (Ministerial Council for Employment, Education, Training and Youth Affairs, 1999)

The achievement of this goal necessitates teaching and learning activities and teacher professional development which goes far beyond narrow political education consistent with an old fashioned view of "civics education," to include broader understandings of local, national and international issues in the past, present and future. Further, the goals emphasise that,

> Australians in the 21st century will be active and informed citizens of complex and rapidly changing local and global communities. They will be enterprising, adaptable and socially responsible contributors to our democratic, cohesive, culturally rich and diverse Australian society. (Ministerial Council for Employment, Education, Training and Youth Affairs, 1999)

These goals have strong implications for teachers and schools and require the development of creative and action oriented CCE programs with a great deal of new and changing knowledge. They include the challenge for schools to include dimensions such as Values Education, Cultural Studies, Global Education, Politics, History, Economics and Enterprise Education in their CCE curriculum. They assume that it is important to include key perspectives defined in the nationally developed *Statement for Studies of Society and Environment* (Curriculum Corporation, 1994): Aboriginal and Torres Strait Islander perspectives, social justice, democratic values, ecological sustainability, and tolerance. These are substantial challenges, as they also require the development of a range of skills that are connected to "active" and "enterprising" participatory behaviours.

Teachers and professional development providers are still debating the definition and scope of the concept of CCE, and clarifying what knowledge and skills are required. There is a need also to determine effective teaching and learning strategies and how values and CCE will fit into the existing curriculum and whole school programs. Students' sense of genuine involvement in school governance and real life issues in the community are defined as critical factors in the development of positive feelings about the community (Prior & Stevens, 1998), so this dimension needs to be addressed by teachers and professional development providers. The challenges are considerable given that the formal civics curriculum alone is unlikely to have an impact on students' values, their ability to be "good citizens" and their desire to participate (Prior & Stevens, 1998).

Over $17 million in Australian dollars (approximately $76.5 million in Hong Kong dollars) was spent by the Federal government in 1997–2000 on the publication of new classroom resources for CCE including teacher units, videos, CD-ROMs and readers, and on teacher professional development. In the year 2000 Federal government budget, a further $13 million in Australian dollars (approximately $58.5 million in Hong Kong dollars) was committed to continue professional development for the next three years. But many teachers are unsure about this new CCE "push." "How can it be defined?" "Where does CCE fit in the already crowded curriculum?" and "How can I teach it when I know so little about CCE?" These are questions teachers commonly ask. The 1998 research study on CCE Practice in Australian Schools (Print & Craven, 1998), painted a bleak picture of the state of CCE across the nation. The majority of teachers were identified as having poorly developed conceptual understandings of CCE, and limited relevant training to provide them with the knowledge and pedagogy for effective teaching in this field. The study found teachers "knew little about civics and less about *Discovering Democracy*" (the Federal government funded resources). They felt inadequately prepared to teach the subject matter of "civics" and had poorly developed views of values education. The survey results are not surprising, given that previously published research has documented similar inadequacies in CCE. Other studies have raised concerns about the teaching of CCE and young Australians' inadequate knowledge and preparedness to be active citizens (Civics Expert Group, 1994; Mellor, 1997; Prior & Stevens, 1998; Senate Inquiry into Active Citizenship, 1989, 1991).

However, since 1998, teachers have been involved in extensive professional development. In Victorian schools, there is tangible evidence of the successful development of a range of innovative and engaging teaching and learning programs in schools linked directly to the PD programs. The opportunities created by the substantial funds available to promote CCE has led to the initiation of a wide range of new developments in CCE nationwide. Departments of Education in each state, relevant teachers' subject associations, commercial publishers and professional development providers including Universities and system providers, have responded to the increased interest in CCE. In this paper, the case studies presented demonstrate how teachers have become involved in these multiple opportunities to achieve improved student learning.

What is "Quality" CCE?

Victorian focus group research discussions with teachers to map current practice in CCE (Tudball, 1998) showed that teachers had a clear view of what constitutes "quality" CCE. They believe that CCE must include "the development of a body of knowledge, skills and understandings of the workings of society, including Australia's political and social heritage, democratic processes, public administration and the nation's place in the international community." But teachers echoed the view that:

> Civics education programs focusing on knowledge transmission alone have limited effect ... a school's ethos, its structures and the role models it provides also speak to students about what is important and valued. (Pascoe & Ferguson, 1999)

Teachers commented that the "civics approach" emphasising the formal processes of government is only part of CCE and argued that "... broader understandings including values clarification should be developed, and participation in real life issues is essential." A decade ago, the Senate Inquiry into Active Citizenship concluded that:

> An active citizen is not someone who has simply accumulated a store of facts about the workings of the political system — someone who is able to perform well in a political quiz. An understanding of how the social and political systems work is an essential element, but equally important is the motivation and the

> capacity to put that knowledge to good use ... An active citizen is willing and able to translate that belief into action. (Australian Government Publishing Services, 1991)

Teachers stress that young people must learn how to live and work with each other and act out values including respect, compassion, and acceptance in authentic learning situations. Students should understand how participation and decision-making operate in contemporary Australia and how the nation's civic life might change in the future. In Victoria, the recently published *Studies of Society and Environment Curriculum and Standards Framework II* states that students should develop the ability to:

> Participate as confident, responsible and active citizens in a democratic society which functions in a global context. (Board of Studies, 2000, p. 5)

Teachers believe that students should learn democratic values and attitudes "through engagement in school-based democratic practices." School buddy systems which encourage older children to support younger children, "decision making which takes account of students' opinions," and "genuinely democratic SRC's where students achieve tangible outcomes," were all mentioned as key strategies. Not surprisingly, primary teachers supported a model where young people "learn first to understand the values in their own families and rights and responsibilities at the local level." As they progress into the upper grades of primary, they begin to tackle more complex "civic understandings." The practices prioritised in primary school are active learning: role plays, simulations, excursions and short projects, as well as other teacher directed learning experiences.

All groups of teachers emphasised the values dimension in CCE, which is also a key aim of *Discovering Democracy* materials. The aim states that students should:

> develop personal character traits, such as respecting individual worth and human dignity, empathy, respect for the law, being informed about public issues, critical mindedness and willingness to express points of view, listen, negotiate and compromise. (Curriculum Corporation, 1997, p. 7)

Secondary teachers demonstrated that both "minimalist" and "maximalist" models (Evans, 1995) of CCE are common in schools. Some teachers were clearly more focused on ensuring that their students developed "minimal" knowledge of civil and legal status, the constitution and politics, rather than

> … [a] contextualised maximal model, looking particularly at consciousness of self as a citizen, a self with rights and with the responsibilities to gain civic virtues and capacities to use that in relationship with others. (Dalley, 1999)

Implicit in both curriculum documents and the views of teacher focus groups is the strong belief that quality learning in CCE must be "authentic." Students should be engaged in real experiences both within the school environment and in the wider community. The scope of CCE envisaged to achieve quality outcomes for student learning, does pose real challenges for teachers. It requires PD to engage teachers in varied models and strategies for CCE teaching and learning within their classrooms. There is also a need to develop whole school activities which model democracy and provide links with the wider community. It assumes that CCE is core work for schools and not just the preserve of the Studies of Society and environment staff, rather an area requiring whole staff commitment.

Conditions for Positive Teacher Professional Development Outcomes

In recent research there is a growing consensus that there are key characteristics of effective teacher PD. It should be based on:

> … analyses of the differences between actual student performance and goals and standards for student learning. (PD) should involve teachers in the identification of what they need to learn and in the development of the learning experiences in which they will be involved. (PD) should be primarily school-based and built into the day-to-day work of teaching. (It) should be organized around collaborative problem solving. (It) … should be continuous and on-going, involving follow-up and support for further learning-including support from sources external to the school that can provide necessary resources and new perspectives. It should incorporate evaluation of multiple sources of information on outcomes for students.… It should provide opportunities to gain an understanding of the theory underlying the knowledge and skills being learned. It should be connected to a comprehensive change process focused on improving student learning. (National Partnership for Excellence and Accountability in Teaching, 2000)

There has been recognition of the fact that if teachers are provided with opportunities to develop connections, and share expertise with colleagues who have common interests, this can have a powerful influence on specific education reforms (Halse, 1994; McLauglin & Talbert, 1993). If the teamwork in schools and wider network opportunities continue over time, they avoid what Michael Huberman (1995) has defined as the "lone wolf scenario," and which Little (1999, p. 234) describes as,

> … one in which teachers labor on their own to decide what instruction works, what standard of work is good enough, and what additional knowledge, skills or insights would best serve them and their students…

The Grants to Schools initiative (1998–2000) has been a key element of the Victorian CCE Teacher Professional Development strategy. It was developed to encompass key conditions for positive teacher professional development and to stimulate professional community in schools. Applications were only accepted from teams of teachers, and the PD is primarily situated in the schools. The program has been developed over two years and aimed to encourage implementation of new approaches to CCE and school-based research in CCE. The program recognizes and values existing teacher expertise, but also provides opportunities for subject discipline and pedagogical renewal.

The program supports 25 selected schools in developing their knowledge and understanding of CCE and to implement school-based CCE programs. Each teacher team reflects on their experiences at all stages of the projects through case writing. The teachers were trained to write cases at a Grants schools professional development in-service day. They were then encouraged to become their own researchers, share ideas with each other and other teachers via the Grants schools web site, and at conferences and network activities which have been part of the overall PD strategy. The teachers have also been supported by external staff who acted as critical friends and visited the schools once per term, maintained phone and email contact, developed a newsletter and prepared and delivered professional development for the schools. The support staff responded to the cases regularly. Participating teachers have found that other members of staff in their own school have been willing to write commentaries for them on their cases, which have in turn extended their thinking and provided new perspectives. Many of the teachers have shared their knowledge willingly, and in 2000 they have all been expected to share their practice with other teachers and schools.

The Grants School Program is a model of PD that has not been commonly used in Victorian schools in the past. The CCE Grants have been allocated to schools that are either beginning work on CCE in their schools, developing and improving existing programs, or documenting and publishing exemplary practice in CCE with the intention of informing the wider community. The model encourages teachers to do what Ball and Cohen (1999, p. 10) see as critical in learning in and from practice, that is, for teachers to stand back and analyse their own teaching, and answer such questions as: what is working and what is not working to improve student learning? Where professional community already existed in schools, the Grants model of PD enhanced the collaboration. Teachers in the two following case studies of professional communities all agreed that the PD model encouraged their efforts to work collegially to improve student learning in CCE.

Methodology

The case studies of one primary and one secondary school have been selected for discussion to allow comparison of professional communities in the two sectors. Each school was awarded a CCE grant, after competitive selection in 1998, to work to improve the teaching and learning of CCE in their schools in the period 1998–2000. I held discussions with the teacher teams during their four full-day formal PD days, visited them at school during 1999 and 2000, interviewed individual school leaders and three staff members in each school and observed classes. This research is continuing, and will include further teacher interviews, interviews with school leaders, and classroom and whole school observation.

Case Study 1: Empowering Young Citizens at the Primary Level

School A is a five-year old school located in a developing outer Melbourne suburb on the fringes of farmland. It is a co-educational government primary school with a current enrolment of 510 students. The current principal has been the school leader since its beginnings, and there has been a stable core of staff, which is growing with the school. The team of teachers have used their CCE grant to work together collaboratively to generate innovative whole school and classroom approaches to CCE and to act as their own agents of professional development in conjunction with external support and wider influences. Being involved in the CCE Grants program has supported the structural conditions for the existing professional community to grow and develop (Kruse, Louis, & Bryk, 1996). It has provided funds to allow staff time release to plan, develop and then reflect on their progress and to attend further external PD activities. But other critical elements of a professional community have been important in the positive teacher PD outcomes in the school. After spending time with school leaders, teachers and in classrooms, it was obvious that the teachers have a "collective focus on student learning" (Kruse, Louis, & Bryk, 1996) and are keen to take risks and try new strategies. They assume that the school community affords a rich context for learning where teachers can build on their collective expertise in the course of critical reflection (Little, 1999). It was clear that they work together to:

> ... mobilize and focus teachers' energies on a collective and improved vision of students' education and, along with it, a situated vision of and support for their own learning. (Darling-Hammond & McLaughlin, 1999, p. 389)

As part of their Grants school project, the team developed an integrated unit for students in grades 5 and 6, based around a series of clearly defined goals for CCE that are consistent with the earlier descriptions of "quality CCE." The unit began with the formation of a Junior School Council and the election of office bearers using procedures supervised by qualified electoral officers so the students could experience the processes of voting and democratic procedures. The teachers then used resources for CCE in the new *Discovering Democracy* kits (Curriculum Corporation, 1999) and drew on their existing knowledge of strategies and resources to develop shared goals for a six-week unit on CCE. They decided that all their young citizens needed to develop core values so that they would know how to work together and generate a harmonious environment. They aimed to develop students' understanding of citizens' rights and responsibilities, the process of law and the judiciary, and the functioning of a community. The establishment of a simulated community that operated for more than a month in the classroom, provided students with real experiences of citizens' roles in business, community service, and government institutions. This involved collapsing the classroom walls to create a larger learning space, joining classes together to increase the size of the "community" and team planning and teaching to achieve the many learning goals. First, the students needed to develop their civic knowledge about the functioning of a community and the various roles of citizens. Teacher directed lessons played a part in developing students' understandings of jobs, businesses and services and the government process. The students were invited to apply for jobs. Student skill development was ensured through co-operative group work, individual and shared decision making as they set up shops, a law court, a police station, a parliament, council offices, beauty parlors, secondhand car dealers and many other businesses and services. The social interaction amongst the students was real even though the community was simulated. Students drew on each others' skills and seemed to gravitate naturally to roles which suited individual abilities. For instance, students with good maths skills ran the town bank, keen artists illustrated the newspaper, others became leaders. All students had multiple roles and varied learning experiences. Each business had to buy their land (in the classroom) and was charged according to the position they wanted. Business managers could advertise in the local newspaper or through the local radio station. Students were given $500 in Australian dollars (approximately $2,250 in Hong Kong dollars) per week, but had to pay tax. Children were paid extra for positions of responsibility. They could apply for loans and all learned to use credit cards, and cheque books. The police arrested offending citizens and either fined them or took them to court. Lawyers then represented them and the student jury handed down the sentence. Parliamentary sessions were held twice weekly and there were many laws passed using the Westminster system. Each fortnight, local real police officers came in to extend the students' knowledge of police activities.

Behind the scenes of the simulated community was a professional community of teachers, meeting daily in and out of the classroom, sharing ideas, planning teaching activities to develop students' knowledge and working in a climate of co-operation. Their success was encouraged by the principal and the wider community. The teachers comment that it is development of their students' knowledge of the role of citizens that has been the greatest reward. They believe that innovative strategies like the simulated community could not have been developed easily by individual classroom teachers. It was the combination of social and human resources which led to the success of the project. The teachers at school A are not only collegial within their school community. They are also connected to their wider profession. One of the key teachers has been a CCE regional network leader, and has been involved in the PD of other teachers in statewide forums. He is a member of the Victorian Association of Social Studies Teachers. Other staff in his school commented that his developing knowledge and experience was a vital ingredient in their ongoing PD. Liebermann and Grolnick (1999) argue that,

> ... the effects of collaboration extend in many directions. Working actively with others strengthens the investment that participants have in the network;

> the work becomes quite literally their own. Connecting with other members across schools, institutions, roles, and geography enables participants to develop more complex views of the issues they are concerned about and encourage them to take different perspectives and different ways of knowing into account.

School A had regular visits from an external support person with extensive experience in student leadership and student participation activities, which is now a key goal for development in their CCE program. The requirements of the Grant also applied gentle pressure for the staff to keep reflecting through case writing and to articulate what worked and what didn't. But the CCE initiatives have not stopped as the Grants period draws to an end. The team is now looking at new CCE curriculum development for other student groups in the school and the continuation of the development of a whole school policy for CCE. As Little (1999) says,

> ... teacher learning arises out of close involvement with students and their work, shared responsibility for student progress, sensibly organised time and space, access to the expertise of colleagues inside and outside the school, focused feedback on one's own work, and an overall ethos in which teacher learning is valued.

Case Study 2: Developing Students' Civic Knowledge Through Information Technology

Recent research has begun to demonstrate that the kinds of professional communities vary greatly among schools, and that the type of community may be critical to the effects of restructuring on student learning (Louis, Marks, & Kruse, 1996). School B is a very different professional community to school A. Firstly, school B is an independent co-educational school established by the Anglican church over 100 years ago as a girls school. Today there are more than 1,200 students from kindergarten to senior school. Secondly, the case study focuses on a CCE program based in the specific context of the humanities department, rather than the whole school, and draws only on staff interviews and classroom observations in the secondary section of the school, where students are aged from 12 to 18. The approach to CCE is also very different to school A in its goals, strategies and the manner in which the PD is situated in the school. The school is in a transition period between the leadership of an established, authoritarian principal, who retired last year, and a new leader who is demonstrating an openness to change and curriculum reform. The previous leader had no involvement with the Grants program. Key leadership was provided by the department head and support was provided by the assistant-principal.

The key aim of the school B team was to improve student learning in CCE through the use of *Inspiration* software to enhance conceptual understanding of the government process. This program was connected to the middle school History program, so the goals for CCE were far more centered on civic knowledge and Information Technology (IT) skills than the broader understandings of the rights and responsibilities of citizens and the functioning of communities that were central to the curriculum planning goals in school A. The development of IT skills is high on the education agenda and the staff are looking for ways to integrate IT into strategies for improved student learning.

The school B CCE teachers demonstrate many of the characteristics of professional communities. They engage in constant reflective dialogue about what happens in their teaching and how to develop their students' civic knowledge. While they do not spend time in each other's classrooms, they continually share their ideas and strategies, problems and successes. The school has had a policy for some time that resource booklets for units of work should be developed by staff members in departments to share with colleagues and these become the focus of discussion about teacher practice.

As with school A, the CCE grant provided time release for members of the team to plan and talk and the incentive for collaboration as the team members attended PD days together and commented on each others cases. There is an expectation in school B that all teachers will complete forty hours of IT PD within the school, so that they continually develop their ability to use laptop computers in the classroom to enhance student learning in a range of ways. Much of their professional development is situated within their school where they have learned complex skills from IT staff. Staff in the humanities department have drawn on each other's expertise to apply IT strategies to the CCE content.

There are positive and negative factors impacting on the structural conditions affecting the operation of the professional community within school B. The department shares staff room space, so staff meet together very easily. However, this can also operate as a negative force since the department can act as a boundary in the school. The department is also the primary site for social interaction, and for professional identity and community (Siskin, 1994, p. 5), where "people have concrete things to tell one another and concrete instructional help to provide one another" (Huberman, 1995, p. 32). The department leader (teacher 1) always used "we" when talking about the groups who worked together collaboratively on the *Inspiration* project. Teacher 1 is a highly experienced member of staff who connects with multiple professional communities: her own school and department, the IT department, her statewide subject association, the independent schools association and the university where she is pursuing further studies. She demonstrates the human resources that are vital in professional communities; an openness to improvement, trust and respect for others, knowledge and skills that she wishes to share, and a desire to lead. Teacher 2 is a beginning teacher who has been mentored by the department head. His skills have developed through modeling the strategies of more experienced staff. Involvement in the grants program gave both teachers access to other teachers outside their school who are approaching CCE in a range of ways.

The existing assistant principal in school B felt that the students were developing excellent CCE content knowledge and IT skills through the grants school project use of the *Inspiration* software program. But he expressed a strong view that more integrated approaches to CCE in the middle years should be considered in the future. He believes that quality CCE programs should encompass global perspectives, strong connections with contemporary issues and more links to the local community. His views will challenge the existing curriculum and departmental structure where history and politics as disciplines have been the host to CCE programs. But he believes that the way forward is for CCE to be developed as a whole school policy that includes classroom activities, staff modelling of democratic principles and broader links to the local and wider community. He believes that it is fundamentally through the shared work of the school staff that this will happen.

Conclusion

It seems clear that encouraging the conditions for professional community in schools can in turn encourage positive outcomes for teacher professional development and improvements in student learning. Models of PD should support and encourage teacher reflection, "deprivatisation" of practice, a collective focus on student learning and the other structural and human conditions for professional community. In the United States, the work of the passionate New York District Superintendent, Anthony Alvarado, in developing exemplary and successful professional development which achieves improved student learning outcomes, has been well documented (Elmore & Burney, 1999, pp. 263–291). Alvarado says:

> Our vision of instructional improvement depends heavily on people willing to take the initiative, to take risks, and to take responsibility for themselves, for students, and for each other. You get this kind of respect only when people cultivate a deep personal and professional respect and caring for each other ... without collegiality on this level you can't generate the level of enthusiasm, energy, and commitment we have. (in Elmore & Burney, 1999, p. 270)

Clearly, achieving positive teacher PD outcomes for CCE is a complex process requiring adequate long-term commitment and funding. The teachers in the case studies presented here have responded to the renewed interest in CCE because they believe it challenges young people to think critically about what kind of society they live in, how it functions and how that society should develop in the future, with themselves as active and informed participants. Values education is as important as, and closely linked to, the acquisition of civic knowledge. The teachers would, I believe, agree with the view of McLaughlin and Talbert (1993) that

> Professional community provides the context for sustained learning and developing the profession ... Effecting and enabling the teacher learning required by systemic reform cannot be accomplished through traditional staff development models — episodic, decontextualised injections of "knowledge" and technique. The path to change in the classroom lies within and through teachers' professional communities. (p. 18)

In the case studies discussed, teacher learning is connected to student learning, and the ultimate aim of the teacher PD is improved student learning. When these dedicated professionals see their young students empowered by civic knowledge, able to articulate new views, clarify values and use new skills, it is the incentive they need to sustain and continue their efforts. Teaching in a professional community can be compared with good citizenship. Good citizenship implies an idea or ethic of desirable behaviour, and active participation and membership in both the formal and informal institutions of that society.

References

Ball, D. L., & Cohen, D. K. (1999). Developing practice, developing practitioners, toward a practice-based theory of professional education. In L. Darling-Hammond & G. Sykes (Eds.), *Teaching as the learning profession: Handbook of policy and practice*. San Francisco: Jossey-Bass.

Board of Studies. (2000). *Studies of society and environment, curriculum and standards framework II*. Melbourne, Australia: Board of Studies.

Civics Expert Group. (1994). *Whereas the people: Civics and citizenship education*. Canberra, Australia: Australian Government Publishing Service.

Curriculum Corporation. (1994). *A statement on studies of society and environment for Australian school*. Melbourne, Australia: Curriculum Corporation.

Curriculum Corporation. (1997). *Introducing discovering democracy: School materials project*. Melbourne, Australia: New South Wales Department of Education and Training.

Curriculum Corporation. (1999). *Discovering democracy*. Melbourne, Australia: Curriculum Corporation.

Dalley, S. (1999). Civics and citizenship education: Making connections for everyday and state occasions. In Department of Education, Training and Employment, Australia, *Reflections on practice*. Department of Education, Training and Employment, Australia.

Darling-Hammond, L., & McLaughlin, M. (1999). Investing in teaching as the learning profession, policy problems and prospects. In L. Darling-Hammond & G. Sykes (Eds.), *Teaching as the learning profession: Handbook of policy and practice*. San Francisco: Jossey-Bass.

Elmore, R. F., & Burney, D. (1999). Investing in teacher learning, staff development and instructional improvement. In L. Darling-Hammond & G. Sykes (Eds.), *Teaching as the learning profession: Handbook of policy and practice*. San Francisco: Jossey-Bass.

England, G. (2000). *Report to DETYA, CCEPD strategy*. Canberra, Australia: Department of Education, Training and Youth Affairs.

Fullan, M. G. (1991). *The new meaning of educational change*. New York: Teachers' College Press.

Fullan, M. G. (1999). The limits and the potential of professional development: In investing in teacher learning, staff development and instructional improvement. In L. Darling-Hammond & G. Sykes (Eds.), *Teaching as the learning profession: Handbook of policy and practice*. San Francisco: Jossey-Bass.

Hargreaves, A. (1997). Rethinking educational change. In M. Fullan (Ed.), *The challenge of school change*. Hawker, Australia: Brownlow Education.

Huberman, M. (1995). The model of the independent artisan in teachers' professional relations. Paper presented at the annual conference of the American Educational Research Association, Boston, MA.

Keating, P. (1995). *Government's response to the report of the Civics Expert Group*. Canberra, Australia: Office of the Prime Minister.

Kemp, D. (1997, May 8). *Discovering democracy — Civics and citizenship education* [A ministerial statement in Australia].

Kennedy, K. J. (1998). Preparing teachers for the new civics education. *Asia-Pacific Journal of Teacher education & Development*, *1*(2), 33–40.

Little, J. W. (1994). Teachers' professional development in a climate of educational reform. In *Educational Evaluation and Policy Analysis, 15*, 129–151.

Little, J. W., & McLaughlin, M. (Eds.). (1993). *Teachers' work: Individuals, colleagues and context*. New York: Teachers' College Press.

Louis, K. S., Kruse, S., & Marks, H. (1996). Schoolwide professional community. In F. M. Newman and Associates, *Authentic achievement: Restructuring schools for intellectual quality* (pp. 179–203). San Francisco: Jossey-Bass.

Louis, K. S., Marks, H., & Kruse, S. (1996). Teachers' professional community in restructuring schools. *American Educational Research Journal, 33*(4), 757–798.

Ministerial Council for Employment, Education, Training and Youth Affairs. (1999). *Australia's common and agreed goals for schooling in the twenty-first century*. Canberra, Australia: Department of Education, Training and Youth Affairs.

McLaughlin, M., & Talbert, J. (1993). *Contexts that matter for teaching and learning: Strategic opportunities for meeting the nations' educational goals*. Stanford, CA: Centre for Research on the Context of Secondary School Teaching, Stanford University.

McLaughlin, M. (1994). Strategic sites for teachers' professional development. In P. Grimmet & J. Neufeld (Eds.), *Teacher development and the struggle for authenticity: Professional growth and restructuring in the context of change* (pp. 31–51). New York: Teachers College Press.

National Partnership for Excellence and Accountability in Teaching (1999). Message posted to http://www.npeat.org/dialogue.htm

Print, M., & Craven, R. (1998). *Civics education for the 21st century: Academics consortium project in civics education* (Final Report of the Research Study on CCE Practice in Australian Schools). Sydney, Australia: University of Sydney.

Prior, W., & Stevens, S. (1998). *Civics and citizenship education in victorian schools*. Melbourne, Australia: Deakin University.

Senate Standing Committee on Employment, Education and Training. (1989). *Education for active citizenship in Australian schools and youth organisations: A report by the Senate Standing Committee on Employment, Education and Training*. Canberra, Australia: Australian Government Publishing Service.

Senate Standing Committee on Employment, Education and Training. (1991). *Active citizenship revisited: A report by the Senate Standing Committee on Employment, Education and Training*.

Siskin, L. S. (1994). *Realms of knowledge: Academic departments in secondary schools*. Washington, DC: The Falmer Press.

Sykes, G. (1999). Teacher and student learning, strengthening their connection. In L. Darling-Hammond & G. Sykes (Eds.), *Teaching as the learning profession: Handbook of policy and practice* (p. 157). San Francisco: Jossey-Bass.

Tudball, L. (1998). *Report to the Centre for Civics and Citizenship Education*. Sydney, Australia: University of Sydney.